Ibrahim Tabet

The Powder keg of the Middle East

Ibrahim Tabet

The Powder keg of the Middle East

From its manufacture to the war in Syria

ScienciaScripts

Imprint

Cover image: www.ingimage.com

This book is a translation from the original published under ISBN 978-620-2-28812-5.

Publisher:
Sciencia Scripts
is a trademark of
Dodo Books Indian Ocean Ltd. and OmniScriptum S.R.L publishing group

120 High Road, East Finchley, London, N2 9ED, United Kingdom
Str. Armeneasca 28/1, office 1, Chisinau MD-2012, Republic of Moldova, Europe
Printed at: see last page
ISBN: 978-620-5-94249-9

Table of contents

From the same author:

Empires et Empereurs Européens, éditions Darnétalaises, Darnétal, 2004

History of Turkey from Altai to Europe, Editions de l'Archipel, Paris, 2007

La France au Liban et au Proche-Orient, published by Revue Phénicienne, Beirut, 2012, ("Renaissance Française" award 2012)

La vie à plein temps", a biography by Bernard Fattal, Revue Phénicienne, Beirut, 2014

Le Monothéisme le Pouvoir et la Guerre, éditions l'Harmattan, Paris, 2015 (2015 France-Lebanon prize of the ADELF - Association des Ecrivains de Langue Française)

A Brief History of God, l'Harmattan Editions, Paris, 2017

Introduction

This book covers the turbulent history of the Middle Eastern states from their creation at the end of the First World War to the present day. The frequently used term "Middle East powder keg" refers to the "Balkan powder keg". The explosion of the latter is presented as having triggered the "Great War", especially caused by the game of alliances and rivalries of the great European powers instrumentalizing the nationalisms of small Balkan nations. Another expression borrowed from this period is that of "balkanization" to designate the risk of fragmentation of the Arab East into ethnic and/or confessional entities caused by the conflicts raging there since the American invasion of Iraq in 2003. Even if the scenario of a repeat of a world war is to be ruled out, there are similarities between the two contexts: the same destabilizing interventions by the great powers, the same political instrumentalization of religious and identity-based tensions, and the existence of states that are both in conflict with each other and in the grip of internal contradictions. Few regions in the world today present as many geostrategic stakes and provoke as much interference from international powers. Henry Kissinger's shuttling between the three belligerents in the 1973 Arab-Israeli war and the involvement of American diplomacy in favour of a settlement of the Arab-Israeli conflict illustrate this interest, which is disproportionate to its weight on the world stage.

I aim to show that while the creation of Israel and the coveted oil resources of the region are among the causes of the instability and violence that it has continued to experience, these are also due to endogenous factors, such as the failure of authoritarian and repressive Arab regimes, the general crisis of Islam, or the religious or ethnic heterogeneity of countries such as Iraq, Lebanon or Syria. No region has been and potentially remains the epicenter of so many explosive conflicts: occupation and colonization of the West Bank, hegemonic ambitions of the Iranian Islamic Republic, resurgence of the age-old antagonism between Sunnis and Shiites, rise of radical Islamism, emergence of jihadist organizations such as Al Qaeda and Daech, terrorist threat extending far beyond the region, war in Yemen, wars in Iraq and Syria involving regional and international powers, risk of a new war breaking out between Israel and Hezbollah, military intervention by Turkey to prevent the creation of a Kurdish entity in Syria.

The creation of the "powder keg of the Middle East" is traditionally traced back to the Sykes-Picot Agreement and the Balfour Declaration of the First World War. If the way in which France and Great Britain divided up the region is condemnable, especially according to today's criteria, the drawing of its borders turned out to be less artificial than the advocates of pan-Arabism claim. In the meantime, Iraqi, Syrian, Lebanese, Palestinian and Jordanian nationalisms have developed and all attempts at Arab unification have failed. The responsibility for the fragmentation and divisions of the Arab East cannot yet be attributed to the divisions practiced by the former colonial powers. The same cannot be said of the creation of Israel, which was not only the cause of four major Arab-Israeli wars (1948, 1956, 1967 and 1973), but also of three invasions of Lebanon (1982, 1996 and 2006), and is undoubtedly the main cause of the destabilization of the region.

However, these wars, as well as the so-called "civil" war in Lebanon (1975-1989), did not spill over from the region or threaten world peace, despite the rivalry between the USSR and the United States during the Cold War. Nor did they have as much impact on Europe through terrorism and the influx of migrants as those tearing Syria and Libya apart. One might even have hoped that the Oslo process would have led to an Arab-Israeli peace, but it was only a decoy that allowed the State of Israel to gain time to extend the colonization in Palestine; neither the Israeli left nor the right having the intention of ever returning the annexed Palestinian territories. However, the blockage of this process is far from being the only cause of the explosion of the Middle East powder keg. Wahhabi proselytizing and American support for the Afghan mujahideen against the USSR have largely contributed to the rise of radical Islamism. But the spark that lit the fuse was the attacks of September 11, 2001, followed by the invasion of Iraq in 2003 by the United States and Great Britain. In addition to the disintegration of Iraq, this opened a boulevard for Iran, exacerbated Shiite-Sunni antagonism and led to the birth of Daech. Then came the Western military intervention with catastrophic effects in Libya. Then, in 2012, the war in Syria broke out: undoubtedly one of the most complex conflicts in history due to the number of regional and international protagonists and the geostrategic and oil issues at stake; the country being at the outlet of hydrocarbons from the Gulf to the Mediterranean and Russia's main anchorage point in the region.

Today, the future of the Arab countries does not give much cause for optimism. The 75-year-old Israeli-Palestinian conflict is on the way to equaling the duration of the Hundred Years' War. And the thousand-year-old antagonism between Shiites and Sunnis rekindled by the outbreak of the Iranian Islamic revolution in 1979 is not about to die out. [e]A historical parallel can also be drawn between the Thirty Years' War in Europe in the 17th century and the war in Syria, both in terms of its confessional dimension and the number of local, regional and international protagonists who took part. The recapture of the territory of the Islamic State organization in Iraq and Syria risks being a Pyrrhic victory that will not eliminate the terrorist danger and will further alienate the Sunnis. Lebanon faces an existential threat to its communal balance from the presence of more than one million Syrian refugees on its soil. The number of Christians in the East is shrinking. The demographic, economic and security problems of Egypt, under a military dictatorship, are inextricable. The unity of the Arab countries of the Gulf has been shattered. And Saudi Arabia's stability is in danger of being undermined by the fall in oil prices and the interventionism of the new crown prince, in contrast to the kingdom's cautious foreign policy.

The big winners in the disintegration of the Arab countries are Israel and Iran.

Spanning a century of history, this essay covers the region between Libya and Iran. It is based in part on my previous books, including those on the history of Turkey and of relations between France and the Middle East, as well as on the relationship between politics and religion, which is of particular importance in the tumultuous history of the region. I have also, of course, drawn inspiration from the reference works of authors such as Henry Laurens, Georges Corm and many others, to whom I am indebted and whom I quote frequently. I have also taken up the articles and analyses related to political developments and regional conflicts that I have written over the last dozen years. I am aware of the risk of obsolescence inherent in the section devoted to immediate history. I have therefore eliminated some articles, some because they were too circumstantial, others because subsequent events had deprived them of their raison d'être. In the same way, I have deleted or modified certain passages and added others to take into account these events. Beyond an event-driven history, the book aims to explain the political, social and military developments whose stakes seemed important to me. It tries to make the share of the respective responsibility of the internal and external factors in the manufacture and the bursting of the powder keg of the Middle East and the misfortunes of the Arab world.

The first chapter is devoted to the Franco-British division of the spoils of the Ottoman Empire and the contradictory promises made by the British to the Jews and the Arabs. The next three chapters deal successively with the history of the Arab countries of the region until their independence at the end of the Second World War, the creation of Israel and the birth of modern Turkey and Iran. Chapters five through eight address the failure of attempts at Arab unity and the Arab-Israeli conflict. This is followed by chapters on the fate of Lebanon since the fifteen-year war (1975-1990). The first two Gulf Wars (Chapter 10). Post-Kemalist Turkey and the Iranian revolution (chapter 11 and 12). Political Islamism (chapter 13). The explosion of the powder keg caused by the attacks of September 11, 2001 (chapter 14). The failure of the Arab Spring (chapter 15) and the war in Syria (chapter 16). Chapter 17 analyzes the game of powers since 2011 and the scope of the resounding return of Russia on the regional scene. As for the conclusion, it questions the probable future of the region between balkanization and establishment of zones of influence.

Chapter 1. The manufacture of the powder magazine

In the XIX[e] century, the accelerated decomposition of the Ottoman Empire encouraged Europe's imperialist aims. Its Balkan and Arab provinces are the scene of a bitter rivalry of powers around the famous "Question of the East. This played an important role in the creation of the Balkan powder keg which was to trigger the First World War, and then in the powder keg of the Near East which was set up during the conflict. Three main factors contributed to this: the ambitions of the two great European colonial powers, Great Britain and France, determined to share the spoils of the Ottoman Empire, promised to a final dismemberment; the repression of the aspirations for independence of its Arab provinces, embodied by the movement of the "Nahda"; and the decision to create a "Jewish national home" in Palestine. These events, which are more than a century old, would not continue to explain the current chaos, however, if other crisis factors had not since contributed to the creation of the "new question of the East" .[1]

The "Nahda" movement

[e]In the 19th century, the Arabs of the Ottoman Empire gradually became self-aware through the Nahda. This Arab Renaissance, the equivalent of the European Enlightenment, was a multi-faceted enterprise of intellectual emancipation, nationalist affirmation, Islamic aggiornamento, administrative rationalization and institutional advances. The Nahda expressed both the renewal of Arab culture and the advent of proto-national identities that could be regional, as in Syria, or pan-Arab. "The Egyptian Tahtawi introduced into the Arab political vocabulary the notions of homeland and citizenship based on the primacy of the individual and the equality of all within the national framework, as opposed to the notions of community of believers (*ummah)* and differentiated status between Muslims and non-Muslims[2] . And the Christian Boutros al-Boustani in 1860 for the first time put forward the idea that religious belonging and national belonging are two different things. Until then, the idea of nationality, in the European sense of the term, was rare. The political identity of the non-Muslim subjects of the Sultan was Ottoman, but their "national" allegiance, if such a word could be applied, was the religious "millet" to which they belonged. As for the Arab Muslims, their identity was at once Ottoman, Muslim and Arab, without any contradiction between them. But while Muslim solidarity took precedence over ethnic consciousness, and their political allegiance was to the Sultan-Caliph and the Ottoman state, which seemed to them the only way to defend Islam against European penetration, the coming to power of the Young Turks and their decision to opt for Turkish nationalism contributed to the emergence of an Arab consciousness among some Egyptian and Syrian-Lebanese intellectuals. They were also sensitive to the principle of nationalities advocated by Europe. The period preceding the First World War thus saw the emergence of demands for autonomy within the Ottoman Empire.

The Arab nationalist ideology was formulated in linguistic terms (an Arab is one who speaks Arabic) and in historical terms (it was a question of restoring to the Arabs the glory and prestige of their ancestors). Christians and Muslims participated together in the organizations that emerged during this period. An Arab Congress held in June 1913 in Paris, on the initiative of Syrian and Egyptian nationalists, declared itself in favor of the autonomy of the Arab provinces of the Ottoman Empire. Only more radical secret societies demanded their independence. This is the case of the Young Arabs (al Fatat), an organization created in Paris in 1911. Another current appeared among Muslims, the Pan-Islamic, whose demands were oriented towards the restoration of an Arab caliphate. While many Christians remained very suspicious of Islam, fearing that its power of attraction would eventually engulf Arabism. Finally, some authors foresaw the Zionist danger. Thus Negib Azouri is the author of a book entitled "*The Universal Jewish Peril*", in which he writes in a premonitory manner (it is 1910): "two important phenomena, of the same nature and yet opposed, which have not yet attracted the attention of anyone, are manifesting themselves at this moment in the Turkey of Asia: they are the awakening of the Arab nation and the latent effort of the Jews to reconstitute, on a very large scale, the ancient monarchy of Israel. These two movements are destined to fight each other continuously .[3]

The Nahda was both an intellectual and a political movement, and it did not simply promote the renewal of Arab culture and national sentiment. Jamal el-Din al-Afghani (1838-1897) and his disciple, Mohamed Abdo (1849-1905), who served as Mufti of Egypt, attempted to reconcile Islam and modernity. The latter married what he called the "tradition of the ancestors" (*salafiya*) with a liberal patriotism, opposed both to the maintenance of the political absolutism of Islam and to European domination. For these reformers, it was more a question of Islamization of modernity than of modernization of Islam. Another current is represented by the Syrian Abdel Rahman Kawakibi (1855-1902) whose work, in which he advocated a separation of politics and religion, had a profound influence on Arab nationalist movements. While these "nationalists" embraced the concept of a nation speaking a language on a territory, the "Islamists" considered that a return to the sources of Islam was imperative in order to halt the Arab decadence. Mohamed Abdo is the central figure of this Arab "Islamism". For this current, Muslim countries owed their failures to the fact that they had embraced foreign conceptions and practices. By deviating from the ways of authentic Islam, they had lost their former greatness. In contrast, the proponents of reform blamed not the abandonment of the old ways, but the clinging to them. The latter were in turn divided between two movements. Those who, like Atatürk, thought that there could be no modernization without westernization. And those who advocated a modernization without Westernization. The reform program of the latter, essentially political and cultural, did not concern the Muslim religion itself. The ideology of the necessary confusion of the temporal and the spiritual in Islam was nevertheless gradually replaced by new intellectual currents calling for a reinterpretation of the Koran and an evolution of jurisprudence to take account of the evolution of societies. And several Muslim states adopted European codes that restricted the scope of application of sharia. It cannot be overemphasized," writes Georges Corm, "that modern Islam has long been a reformist Islam. [e]Throughout the nineteenth century and for most of the twentieth century,[e] we witnessed a modernization of the Muslim legal corpus (sharia) in the Ottoman Empire, in Egypt, in Tunisia and in Iran. It is without complex that the governments import entire sections of European law[4] ". And it is advisable, according to him, to distinguish this first pan-Islamism from that which will appear in the last quarter of the XXth century. "The first was a modernizing ideology [...] The second pan-Islamism, on the contrary, [...] was born of the instrumentalization of religion [...] and relies on religious radicalisms of Wahhabi and Pakistani origin that aim to create an "Islamic exceptionalism", outside of any political and social modernity, blocking any democratic possibility[5] ".

The birth of the Zionist movement

[e]At the same time that the idea of an Arab nation was beginning to emerge, the resurgence of European anti-Semitism in the late 19th century provided the basis for modern Zionism. Born in Viennese intellectual circles, this profoundly secular, secular and religiously legitimate ideology is a product of the era of European nationalisms. The regrouping of Jews of various European cultures and nationalities in a nation-state was seen by the founders of the movement as the only possible remedy to renewed European anti-Semitism. Different from Christian anti-Judaism, the latter exploded at this time in Europe, particularly in Central Europe, under the influence of racist theories which saw the Jews as "Semites": a body alien to the European peoples known as "Aryans". The idea of a Jewish or Judeo-Masonic plot to undermine the Christian foundations of Western civilization also spread. "Just as the horror of the Nazi genocide against the Jews during World War II transformed European anti-Semitism into support for the Jewish state, the pogroms in Russia in the 1880s had launched modern Zionism. [e]Advocating the creation of a Jewish home in Palestine, "it had its origins in both the millenarian traditions of the Jewish religion and the nationalist ideologies that flourished in Europe in the 19th century. The return to Zion was seen as a social and political act to remedy the existence of the Jews as an oppressed minority in the Diaspora[6] . However, since their exile, the Jewish idea of this return had always been linked to the cosmic and messianic theme of redemption and collective salvation. "The religious energy generated by this idea over the centuries is converted, in the course of the realization of the Zionist project, into political power... One can only understand Zionist behavior in Palestine or the development of the Arab-Zionist conflict in the light of the messianic roots of the emergence of Zionism and the European context that underlies it[7] . The identification between religion and nationalism, however, aroused the reticence of many Jews attached to assimilation in their adopted homeland, for whom it risked creating a double allegiance and, in so doing,

encouraging anti-Semitism. Zionism was also opposed by the ultra-Orthodox religious who saw it as a heresy.

In 1891, a handful of Jews from Central and Eastern Europe, whose community was the victim of pogroms, and who had created an organization called the "Lovers of Zion", emigrated to Palestine. They founded the first settlements there: *Petah Tikva* (Gate of Hope) and *Rishon Le Zion*, financed by Baron Edmond de Rothschild. This first *aliyah* (ascent to the Holy Land) was a relative failure. The Jewish settlements depended for their survival on subsidies sent to them by Jewish philanthropists who considered their action more humanitarian than political. The real promoter of Zionism was Theodore Herzl. In 1884, this Hungarian journalist witnessed the degradation of Captain Dreyfus in Paris with cries of "death to the Jews". He concluded that it was illusory for the Jews to seek their salvation in assimilation, and that they should have their own state, a refuge for all persecuted Jews. In February 1896, he published *The State of the Jews*, a book in which he called for the creation of a state for the Jews. He wrote that this state would be the "rampart of Europe against Asia, an outpost of civilization as opposed to barbarism", and would therefore enjoy the support of the West. In 1897, he organized the first World Jewish Congress in Basel, which led to the creation of the World Zionist Organization to coordinate political action at the world level. Theodore Herzl was appointed its first president. Further congresses were held in Basel, and in 1901 a Jewish National Fund was established which, with the support of Jewish philanthropists, financed the purchase of land from Arabs and the establishment of Jewish settlements in Palestine. The objective of the Zionist Organization was to get a colonial power to agree to establish a Jewish settlement in Palestine. At the time, the idea of a settlement was a perfectly acceptable aspect of colonial discourse and practice. A new wave of pogroms in Russia at the turn of the 20th century[e] prompted a growing number of Jews to emigrate to Palestine. Tel Aviv was founded in 1909 to accommodate these immigrants. The same year, the first kibbutzim were established; these were cooperative villages operating according to communal and egalitarian rules inspired by the socialist ideology permeating the Zionist movement. Thanks to a skilful lobbying campaign led by Haïm Weizmann, Zionism was to receive, during the First World War, the crucial support of the British government which, through the Balfour Declaration (1917), declared itself in favor of a return of the Jews to Palestine. This support was motivated not only by political but also by religious considerations. Many Anglo-Saxon Protestants shared the eschatological belief that the return of the Jews to Palestine would prefigure the return of Christ in glory at the end of time, according to the Scriptures.

The division of the spoils of the Ottoman Empire

At the same time, France and Britain secretly agreed to divide the Arab provinces of the Ottoman Empire promised to a final dismemberment. And the British government concluded an agreement with the Arabs in order to incite them to rise up against the Sultan. The Sykes-Picot Agreement, the name given to the Franco-British agreement, and the contradictory commitments made by the British to the Zionist movement and the Arabs, are one of the main causes of the creation of the Middle East powder keg. These commitments were not limited to the Arabs and the Jews. It was during the First World War," writes Georges Corm, "that irredentism reached its peak, degenerating into massacres. The Powers made the wildest promises to the communities of the Empire, promising in turn, without the slightest concern for the practical possibilities of realization, the territorial constitution of an Armenian nation, a Kurdish nation, an Assyrian nation....] The most ardent supporters of the Allies were undoubtedly the Christian minorities, who enlisted all the more easily since religious affinities were exploited to the maximum by the

Powers as liberators of the long Muslim domination. After the war, he continues: the unforeseen event was the revolution of Atatürk in Turkey. France and England had to abandon their protégés. This was followed, of course, by new bloody disturbances in which the Turks carried out violent reprisals against the Nestorian, Armenian and Greek populations .[8]

The Sykes-Picot agreements

Concluded in January 1916, the Sykes-Picot agreements owe their name to their two negotiators: Marc Sykes on the British side and François Georges-Picot on the French side. The two powers did not have the same objectives. France had its sights set on Syria (and the future Lebanon) where its economic interests were considerable and where it traditionally enjoyed a great cultural influence. In its negotiations, it sought to obtain a vast area for geographic Syria and invoked particularly its educational role and the protection of Eastern Christians to assert its rights. The British were more aware of the emergence of an Arab consciousness and intended to use it to detach the Arab provinces from the Ottoman Empire and to impose British tutelage on the new states. The agreements, which were kept secret, stipulated that the two colonial powers, which were now committed to the idea of the definitive dismemberment of the Ottoman Empire, would be prepared to recognize and support "independent" Arab states in two zones: zone A, which included interior Syria and the Mosul region, which France alone would be able to "advise", and zone B, which extended from present-day Jordan to Kirkuk, where Great Britain would enjoy the same exclusive influence. In addition, Great Britain would be authorized to directly administer a red zone made up of Mesopotamia and France a blue zone comprising Mount Lebanon, the Syrian coastline and Cilicia. As for Palestine, where France and Russia assert their "rights" to protect the Catholic or Orthodox holy places, it is considered a brown zone. And, given the role of Jerusalem for the three monotheistic religions, the city would be subject to an international administration, the form of which would have to be decided after consultation with the Allies (which at that time included Russia, which would be excluded after the October 1917 Revolution), as well as with the sheriff of Mecca[9] . These agreements were ratified by an exchange of letters between Paul Cambon, French ambassador in London, and Sir Edward Grey, British Minister of

Foreign Affairs (May 1916). They were presented to the Tsarist government and to Italy, who obtained in return the recognition of their interests and zones of influence in the perspective of the dismemberment of the Ottoman Empire. They were denounced and made public a few months after the October Revolution by the Bolsheviks.

However, these framework agreements were subject to changes dictated by the new political context and the balance of power on the ground. Thus, for example, France was forced, after hard fighting against Kemalist forces who put up bitter resistance, to cede Cilicia to Turkey, and it had to renounce, at the Treaty of San Remo, the wilayet of Mosul in favour of England. In return, in his negotiations with Lloyd George, Clemenceau had obtained, for the benefit of the French Oil Company, a 23.7% stake in the IPC, the company exploiting Iraqi oil, thus guaranteeing its energy independence. Sykes-Picot is therefore a symbol, and the map drawn by these agreements is very far from the final map of the region. After the war, they led to the formation of the "Levant" states (Palestine, Transjordan, Iraq, Syria and "Greater Lebanon"). The latter only came out of the Ottoman yoke to fall under colonial tutelage, and it took them many decades to gain their national independence. The Palestinians and the Kurds were the main losers. "Arbitrary territorial divisions have been imposed on populations and peoples have been forgotten", according to Jean Paul Chagnolaud, according to whom this route has led to nationless states, such as Jordan or Iraq, or nations without a state, such as the Palestinians and the Kurds[10] . The denial of the national and even cultural aspirations of the latter, who are present in Turkey, Iraq, Syria and Iran, is at the origin of Kurdish irredentism. This will arise above all in Turkey and Iraq, where they are the most numerous. With the exception of Palestine and Transjordan (now Jordan), which were affected by the creation of the State of Israel, and the Alexandria Sandjak, detached from Syria and ceded to Turkey by France in 1939, the borders of the other states in the region remained unchanged until the present day. This, despite the fact that they are all ethnic-religious mosaics and the attempts of the proponents of pan-Arabism to challenge them. On the centenary of the Sykes-Picot Agreement, the wars in Syria and Iraq and the creation of a so-called "Islamic State in Iraq and the Levant" seemed for a moment to call into question the borders drawn at that time.

The Balfour Declaration

On November 2, 1917, British Foreign Secretary Balfour wrote to Lord Lionel Rothschild, President of the Zionist Federation of Great Britain, that "His Majesty's Government favourably contemplate the establishment of a national home for the Jewish people in Palestine and will use every effort to facilitate the attainment of this objective, it being understood that nothing will be done to prejudice the civil and religious rights of the non-Jewish communities existing in Palestine. The Arabs, who constituted more than 90% of the Palestinian population, were thus reduced to an aggregate of "non-Jewish communities" to whom no national rights were recognized, even though President Wilson was about to proclaim the right of peoples to self-determination. There were two main reasons why the British government made this commitment, despite its efforts to win Arab sympathy. On the one hand, it was to conciliate the Zionist movement, which enjoyed a growing influence among Jews in Europe and America, where they could weigh in favour of its entry into the war. On the other hand, it was a question of the advantage that could be gained by the presence of a friendly European community on the route to India, in an essential strategic sector, while at the same time thwarting France's hold on Palestine, especially since the latter had rights over the Suez Canal. The natural sympathy of the Bible-loving Anglo-Saxon Protestants also influenced the decision of Lord Balfour, who was himself very religious. This support from Protestantism would not be denied when the United States, taking the lead of the "free world" in 1945, put all its weight behind the emergence of the State of Israel in 1948. With this declaration, "one nation," wrote Arthur Koestler, "solemnly promised a second the territory of a third[11] .

The Hussein-McMahon match

While in Egypt, which they had already occupied since 1882, the British had just suppressed Egyptian nationalism in 1914, they were going to encourage the national claims of the Arabs of the Hijaz and the "Fertile Crescent" whom they succeeded in inciting against the Ottomans. It was Sir Henry McMahon, the British High Commissioner in Egypt, who took the initiative in July 1915. But the main architect of this rapprochement was the famous Lawrence of Arabia, who was sent by the British authorities from Cairo to Hedjaz to meet Sherif Hussein. A representative of the Hashemite lineage, which takes its name from Hashem, the great-grandfather of the Prophet, Hussein had been appointed by the Ottomans as governor of this province, with authority over the holy cities of Mecca and Medina and the port of Jeddah. He was more sensitive to the betrayal of Islam by the Young Turks than to the idea of Arab unity. But in early 1915, he had been visited in Mecca by an emissary of Al Fatat, one of the clandestine societies engaged against the Ottoman Empire, to try to rally him to the Arab cause. Hussein hesitated to commit himself but sent his son, Faysal, to Damascus where he met Arab nationalists who mandated his father to negotiate an alliance with Great Britain in return for the recognition of the right of Arabs to independence. The contact between the British and the sheriff resulted, until January 1916, in an exchange of eight letters between him and McMahon. The correspondence was conducted in Arabic, which excluded any ambiguity in translation. To the first letter written by Abdallah, son of Hussein, which defined the Hashemite claims, McMahon replied on October 24, 1915 that "His Majesty the King of Great Britain would be very happy to see the Caliphate returned to a genuine Arab; and that Great Britain and her allies would recognize the independence of the Arabs. However, he remains vague about the boundaries of the future Arab kingdom. The vagueness mainly concerns the "purely Arab" character of the Syrian coastline (thus including Palestine and the future Lebanon). This lack of clarity was to be the source of many misunderstandings, notably between the Cherif and France. Without revealing to him the content of the Sykes-Picot agreements, Mc Mahon had nevertheless mentioned France's rights in one of his letters, specifying that they concerned "the two vilayets of Mersin and Alexandrette as well as maritime Syria". But Hussein categorically replied that he would not let "France or any other foreign power occupy an inch of Arab territory[12] ". As for Palestine, the British denied having promised it to Hussein, the Arabs maintained the opposite.

The Arab revolt and the conquest of Palestine and Syria

In March 1916, the British, who had concentrated enormous resources in Egypt, began the conquest of Sinai. Jamal Pasha, Ottoman governor of Syria, reacted with a brutal repression of Arab agitation, with the deportation to Anatolia of hundreds of Syrian and Lebanese families. On 6 May 1916, twenty-one Arab personalities were hanged in Beirut and Damascus, becoming emblematic martyrs of Arab nationalism. These executions precipitated the decision of Sherif Hussein to rise up in June 1916 against the Ottoman authority. Described by the Ottomans as a "stab in the back", the Arab revolt was led by Emir Faysal, advised by Lawrence. The rebels numbered between 30,000 and 40,000, but they had only about ten thousand guns and no artillery. Great Britain and France each sent a military mission to them. The pilgrimage (*hajj*), which took place in October 1916, was an opportunity for Sherif Hussein to receive delegations from all over the Arab world with the encouragement of the French (for North Africa) and the British (for Egypt). From Mecca, the "Cherifian" forces cut the railway from Mecca to Medina, isolating the Turkish troops garrisoned there, and then moved northwards towards Palestine. The stubborn resistance of the German-Turkish forces enabled them to block in Gaza the great offensive launched from Sinai by the British army supported by a French contingent in March 1917. "Sykes and Georges Picot, received by Hussein in May 1917, guaranteed him his future authority over "Muslim Syria". Indeed, the Allies did not want to compromise this Arab revolt, which had succeeded in eliminating, capturing or neutralizing tens of thousands of Turkish soldiers by besieging them[13] . In July 1917, Faysal's Arab cavalrymen seized Aqaba. The Allied forces, commanded by General Allenby, then launched a powerful offensive on Palestine in October. They entered Jerusalem on December 11, 1917 where they were welcomed as liberators. But the Palestine front came to a standstill for nine months. On September 18, 1918, the Allied troops, having received reinforcements, resumed the offensive and managed to drive the German-Turkish forces out of northern Palestine, while on their eastern flank, the Arab troops led by Faysal and Lawrence marched towards Damascus. On October 1er 1918 the Allies made a triumphal entry into Damascus where they were greeted by a frenzied crowd; General Allenby having had the skill to let the Arab horsemen of Emir Faysal precede him. Arab insurgents play a major role in the capture of Aleppo in late October 2018. The Cherifian troops also occupy the Bekaa included in the blue zone that was intended to be administered directly by France according to the Franco-British agreements. Finally, despite British advice to be cautious, Rida al-Rikabi, appointed governor of Syria by Faysal, sent a handful of Arab horsemen to Beirut to take power in his name and present France with a fait accompli. But on October 10 the arrival of French troops forced them to withdraw. In the weeks that followed, the British took control of all of interior Syria, which was to become the kingdom of Faysal, while the French were regrouped in Lebanon and along the Syrian coast. François Georges-Picot was appointed High Commissioner for the regions that were to be under French control. On October 30, the Anglo-Ottoman armistice of Moudros put an end to operations in the East.

The betrayal of the promises of independence.

In the Middle East, the contradictory British commitments to the French, the Jews and the Arabs, added to the power vacuum left by the collapse of the Ottoman Empire, were bound to raise enormous problems, the consequences of which, especially with regard to the Balfour Declaration, which was to promote the creation of a Jewish state in Palestine, are still felt today. The Balfour Declaration caused unrest in the Arab world. In addition, the Bolshevik revolution led to the revelation of the secret Sykes-Picot agreements. Sherif Hussein, who had risen against the authority of the Sultan and had proclaimed himself "King of the Arab countries" in accordance with the promises of the British, was naturally indignant at this betrayal, especially since the Allies only recognized him as King of the Hijaz. But this did not prevent Faysal from continuing his fight against the Ottomans. And it was only after his triumphal entry into Damascus that he and his friend Lawrence, who would be disgusted by the duplicity of his country, became aware of London's commitments to France. On November 7, 1918, in a declaration on the liberated Ottoman territories which will remain a dead letter, France and Great Britain affirm that: "their goal is the complete and definitive emancipation of the peoples oppressed for a very long time by the Turks and the establishment of national governments, drawing their authority from the initiative and the free choice of the indigenous populations. Far from wishing to impose on the populations of these regions such or such institutions, they have no other concern than to encourage and help the establishment of governments that they will have freely given themselves and agree to recognize them as soon as they are effectively established[14] ". But, contrary to this proclamation, the Arab peoples only came out of the Ottoman yoke to fall under colonial domination. The Arab states created on the ruins of the Ottoman Empire will be carved up largely according to the interests of the victors rather than on the basis of the rules of law, geography and history, and without consulting the peoples concerned. Only Lebanon was given preferential treatment. At the Peace Conference which opened in Paris, two divergent principles were confronting each other. One, the traditional one, was advocated by the Europeans: the victors shared the spoils of the vanquished. The other was defended by the American president Wilson: the right of peoples to self-determination. Wilson's departure, the rejection by the American Senate of the Treaty of Versailles (June 28, 1919) and the League of

Nations (League of Nations) pact marked the beginning of the isolationist withdrawal of the United States. They were therefore absent from this international organization created at their initiative, which left London and Paris free to reduce to its simplest expression "the right to self-determination of the Arab peoples." Clemenceau and Lloyd George would henceforth decide on the settlement of the "Question of the East," as well as the fate of the Ottoman Empire and its Arab provinces. Taking advantage of the power vacuum created by the defeat of Germany and the collapse of Russia, France and England seemed more determined than ever to impose their order and hegemony on Europe and the Mediterranean world. But, Benoist-Méchin will say, they did not only inherit the spoils of the Ottoman Empire, but also its problems. Realizing the lies of the British government, Lawrence will denounce in *The Seven Pillars of Wisdom* the fact that: "the Arab revolt was started by fraudulent means and that [...] the promises made by the British government would be a rag[15] .

The imposition of Anglo-French domination

At the end of the First World War, political identities were still weak, and it was not until 1918-1920 that we began to hear about the Syrian Arab nation and 1921 for the Palestinian Arab nation. The latter was essentially built in opposition to the Zionist danger. Indeed, Palestine, which was to be internationalized, was now claimed by the British, who decided to make it a "national home for the Jews", a notion unknown to international law, which only knows about states or the need to protect individuals. The former Arab provinces of the Ottoman Empire were initially organized as "administrations of occupied enemy territories" (OETA). They were placed under the supreme authority of the British command, thus invested with political power. Palestine was under British authority, which decided unilaterally to keep it. France, whose armies bore the main burden of the struggle on the European front, was in a position of military inferiority in the East. It therefore had to bow to this decision, even though it enjoyed great cultural and religious influence in Palestine. Maritime Syria, including Lebanon and Cilicia, was administered by the French and interior Syria by Faysal. The French administration had to comply with British military laws and France had no military presence in interior Syria. The French High Commissioner to the Levant, François Georges-Picot, was subject to the authority of General Allenby. He had all the trouble in the world to thwart the British machinations which sought to cancel the Sykes-Picot agreements (which he himself had negotiated). London already regretted them. Lord Curzon, Minister of Foreign Affairs, declared in the House of Commons: "If the agreements of 1916 were to be redone, we would not sign them[16] ". Also, the discussions between the British Prime Minister and Clemenceau, who reproached him for not respecting his commitments, often gave rise to lively quarrels.

The Peace Conference which opened in January 1919 in Paris lasted more than a year and a half. The rivalry between France and England, which was already regretting the commitments made to its ally, did not fail to manifest itself in

Syria. It took all of London's insistence for France to agree to invite Emir Faysal, who had been installed in Damascus by the British. Received at the Peace Conference on February 6, 1919, he demanded the constitution of an Arab kingdom including all the Arab provinces detached from the Ottoman Empire. As for Mount Lebanon, he considered it essential that it be part of a federal union with Syria. He did not even consider the possibility that the coastal cities of Beirut, Tripoli and Saida could be attached to it. This memorandum infuriated the French. To counter his claims, they obtained that a Syrian delegation be admitted to appear before the Conference. The concept of a Greater Arab Syria, defended by the Emir, was echoed by that of a Greater Syrian Syria under the aegis of France, advocated by a committee formed by a group of Parisian Syrian-Lebanese, chaired by Chukri Ghanem. But his position came up against both the rejection by the majority of Lebanese Christians of the idea of integration with Syria and the aspirations of Syrian nationalists who did not want French tutelage. On 3 January 1919, Weizman and Faysal met in London at the initiative of the British and signed an agreement in which the latter declared himself in favour of Jewish immigration to Palestine. However, the Emir followed this text with an important reservation: "If the slightest modification is made to the program of Arab independence which I have presented to the British government, I shall not be bound by a single word of the present agreement[17] ". By June, the few sympathies he had for Zionism had turned to prevention. The al-Fatat secret society, whose ranks Faysal had joined in 1915, formed itself into the Arab Independence Party. In June 1919, this party organized elections in the "three OETAs", which were followed by the holding of a Syrian General Congress in Damascus. The Congress called on Faysal to head a constitutional monarchy based on the principles of a democratic and largely decentralized government to guarantee the rights of minorities. Syrian nationalists categorically rejected any dismemberment of geographic Syria, as well as Zionist settlement in Palestine. To counter the Syrian claims, the Administrative Council of Mount Lebanon, which had unanimously proclaimed Lebanon's independence on May 20, decided to send two successive delegations to Paris. Led by the Maronite patriarch Howayek, the second delegation pleaded with Clemenceau to return Lebanon to its pre-1860 borders and to obtain independence under French protection. While in Mount Lebanon and Beirut, the principle of French protection was well received by the Francophile Christian population, in Syria, where the reaction was strong among the Arab nationalists, France met with strong opposition. As the traditional protector of the Christians of the East, France tried to reconcile the need to protect its relations with its protégés, while not alienating the Muslim majority. Clemenceau, an old secular radical, anti-colonial and anti-clerical, was on the verge of succeeding in this challenge when he signed a provisional agreement on January 6, 1920 with Emir Faysal, who had been installed in Damascus by the British. By virtue of this secret agreement, the Emir committed himself on the one hand to recognizing the independence and territorial integrity of Lebanon under the mandate of France, and on the other hand to asking the government of the French Republic alone for the advisers necessary to administer Syria. In return, it was agreed that France would recognize the authority of the Emir over internal Syria. But a few weeks later, Clemenceau left power, after the victory in the legislative elections of January 1920 of the conservative right that favored colonization. Faysal's failure to impose the terms of this agreement on the Syrian nationalists, combined with the change of government, and therefore of policy, in Paris, was the starting point for the deep mistrust that settled between Syria and France, which increasingly favoured its preponderant role in Lebanon. While the negotiations were taking place in Paris, President Wilson, who advocated the principle of the right of peoples to self-determination, had the peace conference agree to send a commission to gather the opinion of the populations of the Levant on the regime of their choice. The only communities to have pronounced themselves in favor of a French mandate were the Catholics and its principle was categorically rejected by the vast majority of Muslims. Designated as the King Krane Commission, it pronounced itself in favor of the unity of Syria within which Lebanon should be able to keep its autonomy. Finally, the commission expressed a very unfavorable opinion on the question of a Jewish national home in Palestine. Its recommendations were naturally completely ignored by England and France. Aware of the Muslims' rejection of the principle of French trusteeship, the French Minister of Foreign Affairs, Pichon, declared to Emir Faysal, during one of his visits to plead his case in Paris: "France has abandoned its ancestral mission of protecting the Christians. The Republic is secular. For her, all religions are equal. This is an established principle. France is no longer Christian except in the eyes of Muslims[18] . But this declaration does not prevent the mistrust of French decision-makers towards Arab nationalism and their prejudice towards "Muslim fanaticism".

The creation of the Greater Lebanon and the division of Syria

Meanwhile, Georges-Picot was replaced in November 1919 by General Henri Gouraud. He was both High Commissioner and Commander-in-Chief in the Levant. His political advisor, Robert de Caix, convinced of the need to rely on minorities in order to better preserve French influence, had a determining influence on the shift in French policy towards Faysal and the division of Syria, as well as on the creation of Greater Lebanon that Gouraud undertook in 1920. The minority option that he advocated contrasted with that of Louis Massignon who tended to favour an agreement with the Sunni majority. In his eyes, the latter would be better able, both to establish French interests and influence in Syria in the long term, and to ensure the defense of minorities. In March 1920, the Syrian Congress rejected the agreement between Clemenceau and Faysal concerning the principle of a French mandate. Recognizing the Emir as constitutional king under the name of Faysal 1[er] , it unanimously proclaimed the independence of Syria within its natural borders, including Palestine and Lebanon. The Congress also provided for a political and economic union with neighbouring Iraq, headed by Emir Abdullah, Faysal's brother, for whom it also requested independence. The two colonial powers took no notice of this and the

International Conference held in San Remo in April 1920 granted mandates from the League of Nations to France over Syria and Lebanon and to Great Britain over Palestine and Iraq. The Treaty of San Remo stipulates that the wishes of their populations must be taken into consideration in the choice of the mandate holder. But, apart from the Christians of Lebanon who opted for the protection of France, the Arabs rejected the trusteeship that was imposed on them. The withdrawal of Clemenceau from politics and the growing influence of the French colonial party contributed to aggravating the climate of mutual suspicion between Syrians and French. Tempted for a moment by a compromise agreement with Emir Faysal, who had been proclaimed King of Syria, France, as the Mandatory Power in Syria, decided to put an end to the country's desire for independence. On July 14, 1920, General Gouraud sent an ultimatum to Faysal. Making him responsible for the incidents provoked against the French posts by bands coming from Syria, he summoned him to evacuate the Bekaa and to accept the mandate. Faysal, who wanted to avoid a confrontation with the French and a popular uprising in Damascus, tried a final negotiation. But he came up against the intransigence of Gouraud, who had a division commanded by General Goybet occupy the Bekaa. And, on July 24th, advancing in the Anti-Lebanon, the French division crushed the Syrian troops in Maysaloun. The next day, French troops entered Damascus, then detachments deployed in the north of Syria occupied Aleppo, Homs and Hama without encountering any resistance, putting an end to two years of Arab dream. Driven out of Damascus, the short-lived king of Syria was installed on the throne of Baghdad by his British friends. But he gave up neither Damascus nor Beirut. From Baghdad, he called relentlessly for the union of the Fertile Crescent of which he had always dreamed. As a sign of the gap between the religious communities, the news of the battle of Maysaloun was received with consternation by the Muslims and with joy by the Maronites of Lebanon who saw the ordeal of a new Islamic domination moving away from them. On August 10, 1920, the Treaty of Sèvres recognized France as a proxy power in Syria. It did not mention Lebanon, which did not yet exist. For its part, England obtained a mandate over Mesopotamia, the Hijaz and Palestine. This treaty was officially ratified in 1922 by the League of Nations. A new concept in international law, the mandate was theoretically to be exercised under the authority of the League of Nations. The mandates having been classified into three categories A, B, and C, Syria and Lebanon belonged to category A which article 22 of the SDN statute presented as follows: "Certain communities which formerly belonged to the Ottoman Empire have attained such a degree of development that their existence as independent nations may be provisionally recognized, provided that the advice and assistance of a Mandator shall guide their administration until such time as they are able to conduct themselves. The wishes of these communities must be taken into consideration first in the choice of the mandatary. The mandatary power was thus bound by obligations limiting its powers over the country placed under its trusteeship. Each year it had to report to the General Assembly of the League of Nations, assisted by the Permanent Commission on Mandates in Geneva, on the progress of its work. But the practice proved to be different. For Paris, the mandate resembled a protectorate, and the time allowed to prepare for independence was constantly extended.

On September 1[er] 1920, General Gouraud, surrounded by the Maronite Patriarch and the Grand Mufti, solemnly proclaimed the creation of Greater Lebanon from the porch of the Residence of the Pines in Beirut where the High Commissioner for Syria and Lebanon had taken up residence. Its boundaries extended far beyond the predominantly Maronite Mount Lebanon to include Beirut, the four "casas" of the predominantly Shiite Bekaa, detached from the *vilayet of* Damascus, as well as the largely Sunni cities of Tripoli and Saida and their hinterlands. By acceding to the demands of the Maronites for an economically viable country, France incorporated into the country regions with a large Muslim population, the majority of whom would have liked to be part of a Greater Syria. Introducing a split between central and peripheral Lebanon, this decision was very badly received by the Sunnis and Shiites living in these regions, as well as by the Syrian nationalists who refused to recognize Lebanon's independence. Then, applying the tactic of divide and rule, Gouraud split Syria into two states: those of Aleppo and Damascus, later organized into a Syrian Federation. A Territory of the Alawites was also created, which was transformed into a state in 1924, and an autonomous Druze region. As for the Sandjak of Alexandrette, it was attached to the governorate of Aleppo but retained administrative autonomy. The Kurds and Christians (mostly Jacobites and Armenians) of Jezirah demanded autonomy similar to that enjoyed by the Alawites and Druze. But their claims are not taken into consideration.

The evacuation of Cilicia and the new Armenian exodus

The territories under French mandate included Cilicia, the seat of the ancient medieval kingdom of Little Armenia, and southeastern Anatolia, which had a large Christian Arab and Armenian minority. France had transferred there several tens of thousands of Armenians still surviving in the deserts of Syria. It intended to rely on them and other non-Turkish minorities to govern. However, it soon encountered strong resistance from the Turks, who were fighting for the very survival of their nation. The French troops had to hold a 500-kilometer front stretching from Mersin in Cilicia to Ourfa in southeastern Anatolia. The campaign against the troops rallied to Mustapha Kemal was extremely hard during the harsh winter of 1919-1920. On October 20, 1921, the French government concluded a secret treaty with Mustapha Kemal, renouncing the Treaty of Sevres and recognizing the government of Ankara. Leaving the Armenians behind, the French army evacuated Cilicia and the territories of south-eastern Anatolia, abandoning to their fate the Armenian populations placed under its protection, many of whom were massacred by the Turks. A new exodus of population followed. A part of the population was evacuated on French ships to Marseille and the other part to Lebanon and Syria. For their part, the British, who had encouraged the creation of an Armenian Republic, soon left the Caucasus without a second thought. This cynicism made the former Prime

Minister of this short-lived Republic say: "They came to us by calculation, and this calculation not being verified, they left as they had come, leaving us to fall at the most difficult moment. We were left without assistance and all alone[19] ". In June 1939, a few weeks before the outbreak of the Second World War, France signed an agreement with the Turkish Republic ceding the Sandjak of Alexandrette to it in order to ensure its neutrality in case of war with Nazi Germany. This marked the beginning of an exodus of Christians from Antioch, one of the most important places of Eastern Christianity, in particular Armenians who had survived the massacres of which they had been the victims.

Countries under British mandate

Following the Treaty of Sèvre (1920), which gave them a mandate over Palestine and Mesopotamia, the British created two states from scratch: Iraq and Transjordan. Born of the reunion by the British of the three Ottoman vilayets of Mosul, Baghdad and Basra, Iraq is an artificial state grouping together three major ethnic-religious communities: the Kurds and the Shiite and Sunni Arabs. Alongside them, there are also Christian, Turkmen and Yazidi minorities. And 250,000 Jews lived in Iraq until the creation of the State of Israel. Tribal structures remain important and the population is predominantly Shiite. In May 1920, Shiites and Sunnis were united in an uprising, first military, then civilian, against the British occupiers. It took the British army several months to put down the revolt, which resulted in some 10,000 deaths. Meeting in December 1920 in Cairo around Sir Winston Churchill, British experts on the Arab world awarded thrones and crowns to the sons of the Hashemite House. Faysal, who had been ousted from Syria by the French, was given Iraq as a kingdom. The amalgamation of the country's three major communities in an Iraq dominated by Sunni Arabs is a source of both regional and sectarian tension. The Shiite clergy refused this power, which was too closely identified with England, but their resistance was broken by force. Discrimination against other communities by Sunnis under the Hashemite dynasty and then the Baathist dictatorship was followed by discrimination against Sunnis under the Shiite-dominated regime put in place by the Americans after their invasion of Iraq in 2003, proving that the formal secular nature of institutions does not prevent the sectarian seizure of power.

Created from scratch by the British, the kingdom of Transjordan, which escaped Jewish colonization, fell to Abdallah, brother of Faysal, who had first been placed on the throne of Iraq. A very poor country, it was totally dependent on the subsidies granted to it each year by the British. Its armed forces, the Arab Legion, were staffed by British officers and commanded by an English general: Glubb Pasha. Its original Bedouin population coexisted with a majority of Palestinians when it took the name of Jordan after the annexation of the West Bank in 1948. As for Sherif Hussein, he had to be content with the title of King of the Hijaz. Having given up his dream of an Arab kingdom, he claimed the title of Caliph in 1924 as a descendant of the Prophet. But he was driven from his throne the following year by the Bedouin troops of Ibn Saoud. This colonial division was completed in 1922 with the incorporation of the Balfour Declaration into the British Mandate over Palestine, which led to a boycott of the Mandate institutions by leading members of the Arab population.

The imposition of the British protectorate in Egypt

Since 1882, Egypt has been occupied by the British, while remaining an Ottoman province. The occupation was motivated by their desire to take control of the Suez Canal, a vital milestone on the route to India. The pretext was a nationalist movement led by Orabi pasha against the control of the country's finances by a Public Debt Commission managed by English and French commissioners. Anti-European riots having broken out in Alexandria in June 1882, Great Britain landed troops in Suez and imposed its domination on the country. France, which also had interests in the Suez Canal, refused to intervene militarily and let England occupy the country. However, it kept a strong cultural influence. In 1899, Sudan was set up as an Anglo-Egyptian condominium. Having proclaimed himself Mahdi, a religious leader led an uprising that massacred the British garrison in Khartoum and was finally crushed by an expeditionary force commanded by Lord Kitchener. The year 1907 saw the birth of Egyptian nationalism with the foundation of the country's first two political parties, the National Party (*watani*) and the Party of the Nation (*ummah*), "a term chosen for its polysemy because it can refer to the Arab 'nation' as well as to the community of faithful Muslims[20] . Claiming to be a follower of Mohammad Abdo's ideas, he shows himself to be the opponent of all religious fanaticism, in particular pan-Islamism, and distrusts the masses, considering that the role of the elites is to educate them.

In October 1914, taking advantage of the Ottoman Empire's entry into the war against the Entente powers, London abolished the nominal suzerainty of the Porte and proclaimed its protectorate over Egypt. It acted unilaterally without basing its right on a legal agreement. The British Consul General became High Commissioner. The British army imposed martial law. Khedive Abbas II, who was close to the nationalists, was deposed and succeeded by his uncle, Abbas Kamel, who took the title of Sultan. He had no real power and upon his death in 1917, his brother Ahmad Fouad became sultan. On November 13, 1918, Saad Zaghloul, posing as the spokesman for the Egyptians, led a delegation to the High Commissioner, Wingate, to ask for Egypt's independence (with the acceptance of continued British military control of the Canal Zone). But Wingate replied that the Egyptians were not yet ready for independence, which was considered insulting by the Egyptian elites. While the Peace Conference was taking place in Paris, Egypt, which intended to assert its right to independence, was in turmoil. Saad Zaghloul founded the Wafd ("Delegation") party, whose mission was to plead this cause. Arrested by the British authorities in March 1919, he was deported to Malta along with three other party members. These arrests, far from calming Egypt, provoked a real popular uprising. Nearly a thousand Egyptians were killed in the British repression of this "revolution" (*thawra*). "This revolution of March 1919 will become the major national reference of the contemporary Egyptian history[21] . Appointed High Commissioner in Egypt, Marshal Allenby decided, in May 1919, to release the imprisoned Wafdists. Saad Zaghloul and his companions went to France in the hope of participating in the Paris Conference. But the brutal crushing of the Egyptian protest did not prevent the Allies from confirming Britain's protectorate over the country.

The other countries under English rule

Apart from northern Yemen, which remained free of foreign domination, and Saudi Arabia, where Abdel-Aziz drove the Hashemites out of the Hijaz in 1924-1925, the rest of the Arabian Peninsula was under British rule. Aden, which controls the Bab el-Mandeb strait, a strategic milestone on the sea route to India, has been occupied since 1839 by the British, who have subjected the tribes of the interior to their influence. Yemen was thus divided in two: a southern region controlled by the British and an independent northern region. The other states of the southern and eastern coast of the Arabian Peninsula, from the Sultanate of Oman to Kuwait, via the emirates of the Persian Gulf, were subjected in various forms to the British protectorate. The latter was all the more accepted by the local potentates as it constituted an insurance against the territorial ambitions of their neighbors, Saudi Arabia, Iran and Iraq.

The Italian occupation of Libya

The last Ottoman province in North Africa to escape European colonial imperialism, Libya was occupied by Italy in 1911, despite strong resistance from Turkish troops and the forces of the Senoussi religious brotherhood. Tripolitania was transformed into a settlement, while a 1920 agreement on the autonomy of Cyrenaica was not respected, forcing King Idriss al-Senoussi into exile in Egypt. Benito Mussolini came to galvanize the 20,000 or so Italian settlers in Tripoli in April 1926. Sheikh Omar al-Mukhtar led the resistance in the name of King Idriss. The total conquest of the country was completed in 1926 with the conquest of Fezzan and the Gulf of Sirte. General Graziani launched the final phase of pacification in 1930 by interning half the Bedouin population of Cyrenaica in concentration camps. Tens of thousands of people died in these camps, which fascist propaganda presented as centers for adaptation to sedentary life. The guerrillas led by Omar al-Mokhtar continued to oppose the Italian occupation. The capture of the sheikh and his hanging in 1931 marked the end of the movement. "However, it took Italy two decades to complete its conquest of the country. The cost inflicted on the population will have been even more exorbitant than that, already terrible, of the conquest of Algeria by France in the previous century[22] .

1 *The New Question of the East,* Georges Corm, La Découverte 2017.

2 *Pour une lecture profane des conflits, Sur le " retour du religieux " dans les conflits contemporains du Moyen-Orient*, Georges Corm, La Découverte, 2012, p. 185.

3 *Lebanon between Islam, France and Arabity,* Abbot Y. Moubarak, Pentalogie maronite, tome I. Publication of the Lebanese Cenacle, p. 1221.

4 *La nouvelle question d'Orient*, op.cit. p. 70.

5 ibid.

6 *Victims, A Revisited History of the Arab-Zionist Conflict,* Benny Morris, ed. Complexe 2003, p. 22.

7 ibid. p.26.

8 *Le Proche-Orient éclaté*, Georges Corm La Découverte 1983, p. 54.

9 *La France et l'Orient arabe, naissance du Liban moderne,* Gérard D. Khoury, Armand Colin edition, 1993.

10 *The Arabs their fate and ours.* Jean-Pierre Filiu, La Découverte 2017, p.15.

11 *La France au Levant*, Pierre Dufour, Pygmalion éditions, 2001, p.403.

12 *Lebanon-Syria, the mandate, (1919-1940),* Henri de Wally, Perrin 2010.

13 *The Arabs their destiny and ours.* op.cit. p. 52.

14 *L'Orient arabe arabisme et islamisme*, Henry Laurens, Armand Collin, 1993, p. 162.

15 *The Seven Pillars of Wisdom*, T.E. Lawrence, quoted by H. de Wally, *Lebanon-Syria, the mandate,* p. 86.

16 *Lebanon-Syria, the mandate,* op.cit, p, 87.

17 *Les Arabes ou l'histoire à contresens*, Charles Rizk, Albin Michel, 1992, p.58.

18 *Lebanon-Syria, the mandate,* op. cit. p.114.

19 *L'Europe et l'Orient*, Georges Corm, La Découverte, 1999, p. 99

20 *Les Arabes leur destin et le nôtre*, op. cit. p. 37.

21 *Orientales III*, Henry Laurens, CNRS éditions, 2004, p. 165

22 *Les Arabes leur destin et le nôtre*, op. cit. p. 76

Chapter 2. The Arab Near East until 1945

The creation of new states by the colonial powers called into question the functioning of all Arab societies. The question of the construction of national identities, still uncertain, became central and remains so today. The existence of the nation-states created a century ago has been challenged by three types of forces. The first are embodied in the failed attempts at Arab unification. The second is the withdrawal of communities, the desire for independence on the part of peoples such as the Kurds, and the attempt by the Islamic State to abolish the borders of the Levantine states. Finally, the third is pan-Islamism, which aims to deconstruct modern nation-states in order to restore the Muslim "ummah. "At first, it was difficult to distinguish Islamism from Arabism. It was not until the interwar period that the two were clearly distinguished, and it was not until the 1950s, after Gamal Abdel Nasser took power, that the two movements clashed. Their opposition would reinforce their respective radicalizations and further thwart the construction of nation-states in the region[1] . At the end of the first world conflict, the Arab Near East was entirely under Franco-British colonial rule, with the exception of Saudi Arabia and Yemen. It would take half a century to gradually achieve the independence whose dream had inspired the Arab revolt of 1916. For the Arabs, the refusal of the two colonial powers to treat them on an equal footing, even though they had loyally joined them against the Ottomans, left a deep sense of injustice. Their frustration and resentment towards Western imperialism will lead to protest movements and uprisings that will not fail to be severely repressed.

During this period, a muted rivalry developed between France and Great Britain. In the struggle for influence between them, it was systematically the latter that had the upper hand by posing as the champion of Arab nationalism and by granting independence, albeit in the guise of a façade, to the countries placed under its tutelage. France, on the other hand, refused to do so and adopted a policy of fragmentation and encouragement of minorities against the Sunni majority; a policy that the British did not fail to exploit by turning Arab opinion against French colonialism. Until the outbreak of the Second World War, the domination of London and Paris, favored by the isolationist withdrawal of the United States, was exercised without division over the region. But from the mid-1930s onwards, the region ceased to be their preserve and two new players emerged: Italy and above all Germany, which was to exploit Arab resentment against Franco-British imperialism. As for the United States, it enjoyed great popularity in the Arab world. Their assertive anti-colonialism and their humanitarian and educational undertakings contrasted with the desire of France and Great Britain to consolidate their imperial dominance. This period also saw the installation of large American oil companies in the region. At the end of the Second World War, which had established the preponderant weight of the two Great Powers, France and Great Britain ceased to be great powers. But unlike France, which was forced to renounce treaties with Syria and Lebanon, Great

Britain remained present in the Middle East, among other places militarily, in Egypt, Aden and the Persian Gulf. Exhausted by the war, it was nevertheless forced to play second fiddle to the United States. Since its emergence as a superpower, the latter had alternately adopted an isolationist and interventionist foreign policy. Having renounced, since its entry into the war in 1941, the isolationist policy that was theirs in the interwar period, they were led to multiply their interventions in Middle Eastern affairs to counter the USSR. "Their foreign policy has its roots in Calvinist notions of election and predestination. The United States is the new "chosen people" whose mission is to bring justice and freedom to the world. This mission was invoked when it entered the war in 1917 and 1941 on the side of the Allies, and again during the Cold War[2] .

Egypt under British rule

In June 1920, negotiations began in London between the British government and an Egyptian mission led by Saad Zaghloul and Adli Yeghen in order to reach an agreement on the replacement of the protectorate by a treaty of alliance. However, these negotiations ended in failure. In March 1921, Yeghen, more moderate than Zaghloul, formed a new government and began new negotiations in London. But they came up against the intransigence of Winston Churchill, who had in the meantime been appointed Colonial Minister. Churchill referred to Egypt as part of the British Empire, provoking protests from Egyptians. The Wafd launched a new campaign of agitation. The violence culminated on May 20-22 in Alexandria, where rioters attacked foreigners (Greeks and Italians). The British authorities imposed martial law and expelled Zaghloul again in December 1921. This measure led to new demonstrations of violence in Egypt.

Faced with rising nationalism and at the suggestion of the High Commissioner, Lord Allenby, the United Kingdom finally recognized the "independence" of the Egyptian state in February 1922. The country became a constitutional monarchy where Sultan Fouad 1[er] , who took the title of king, recognized the sovereignty of the people through universal male suffrage. The British, however, placed serious restrictions on this theoretical independence, in terms of defense, communications, protection of minorities and protection of their interests, both in the "Anglo-Egyptian" Sudan and in the Suez Canal. On March 15, 1922, the king asked Tharwat pasha, a moderate who headed the Liberal-Constitutional Party, to form the first government of "independent" Egypt. In September 1923, Saad Zaghloul returned to Egypt amidst a frenzy of popular emotion. The nationalist Wafd Party won a landslide victory in the January 1924 elections and formed the first representative government. Parliament met for the first time on March 15, 1924. In 1925, Allenby was replaced by George Lloyd, who intended to restore British prestige and authority. When a coalition between the Wafd and the constitutional liberals won the 1927 elections, he refused to allow Zaghloul to lead the new government. "This marked the beginning of a triangular political game that characterized Egyptian political history until 1952. England played the Palace against the Wafd while preventing the king from becoming too powerful. And when the Wafd wins the elections and becomes too demanding of the British, the latter push the king to dismiss their government and form a government of minority parties. This game completely distorts the normal functioning of the parliamentary system[3] . The local political scene was dominated by Saad Zaghloul, who died in 1927, and then by Mustapha Nahhas, who succeeded him as head of the Wafd. But the latter's submission to the occupier led to the birth, in 1928, of the Muslim Brotherhood movement. Founded by Hassan al-Banna, this formation which was at the beginning only a religious brotherhood, became a powerful political movement. It categorically rejects the motto of the Wafd "Religion is for God and the party for all". For Hassan el-Banna, Islam has an explicitly political dimension and it is the brotherhood of the faithful that is the foundation of authentic nationalism. It is an Islamo-nationalist ideology that claims to be more patriotic than the Wafd. The Islamist sentiment that developed played against the Wafd, a secular party in which Muslims and Copts worked closely together. In 1928, the king dissolved the Parliament (House and Senate). Then, the application of several articles of the constitution was suspended and the desire to revise the constitution was evident. The ministry chaired by Nahhas pasha was dismissed in June 1928. The cabinets followed one another, presided over by Mohammad Mahmud, then by Adli Yeghen, then again by Nahhas pasha, who resigned after six months in the chair. The king then called a strong man, Ismaïl Sidqî. From June 1930 to September 1933, he formed a government of independents. He modified the Constitution and the electoral law. This allowed elections to be held in 1931, which the Wafd boycotted. So, for the first time, victory went to another party, the People's Party, recently formed to support the government. For thirty-nine months, Sidqi imposed a semi-dictatorship on the country, punctuated by financial scandals. Supported by him and then, after his resignation and until 1935, by puppet cabinets, the king exercised his personal power by playing on intrigue and favours distributed, withdrawn or promised, with the tacit agreement of England. But England, in order to calm political irritation, forced the king to reinstate the 1923 constitution, to remove his favourites from the government and to hold general elections in 1936. In August 1936, the Egyptian government, once again led by Nahhas pasha, signed an Anglo-Egyptian treaty which, although recognizing Egypt's international sovereignty, was only an eminently London-friendly rearrangement of the status of the occupation, notably through the maintenance of a British force in the Suez Canal zone and a military alliance between the two countries. But it allowed the development of the Egyptian army, which until then had been limited by England. The abolition of the capitulations was made concrete by the disappearance of the mixed courts, and laws for the Egyptianization of the executives of foreign companies were passed. As a sign of its newfound independence, Egypt joined the League of Nations. Despite this, the treaty contributed to the discrediting of the Wafd, which went from being a symbol of independence to becoming a party of collaboration. King Farouk, who had succeeded his father Fouad 1[er] in 1936 and initially enjoyed a certain popularity, took advantage of this to make the throne the rallying point for nationalist forces. He skillfully manipulated the rising religious sentiment in Egypt. The Palestinian revolt of 1936-39 reinforced this trend. The religious movements organized active propaganda in favor of the Palestinians. At the League of Nations, where it had just returned, Egypt defended the Palestinians. In December 1937, the king dismissed the government formed by the Wafd and adopted a policy favourable to Islamism and Arabism which greatly worried the British.

At the outbreak of the Second World War, the Egyptians hoped for an Axis victory which, they hoped, would mean their liberation from the British presence. They were encouraged by the initial victories of the German-Italian forces commanded by Rommel in Libya. Young officers, such as Anwar Sadat, who was arrested and imprisoned, tried to make contact with the Germans. Faced with this double threat, the British chose the hard way. On July 4, 1942, their tanks surrounded the royal palace and the British ambassador imposed on the king the dismissal of the government and the appointment of Nahhas pasha as prime minister. The country was humiliated and the monarchy was discredited because it had given in. King Farouk was to lead a life of debauchery which caused him to lose his popularity. The hostility between him and the Wafd led to the dismissal of the Wafdist government in October 1944. The Wafd, which was once again in opposition, saw its influence undermined by new anti-parliamentary political forces that challenged narrow Egyptian nationalism: "Young Egypt" (Misr al Fatat), a right-wing paramilitary movement that sought to make Egypt the center of the Arab East, and above all the Muslim Brotherhood, which, with hundreds of thousands of militants, had become a major force. Because of Egyptians' feelings of solidarity with the Palestinians, the Palestinian question became increasingly important in Egyptian politics. In February 1945, Nukrachi pasha succeeded Ahmad Maher as prime minister, who was assassinated by a young nationalist. After the end of the war, the Egyptian government asked, in December 1945, for the revision of the 1936 treaty and the annexation of Sudan. Negotiations began in London with the Labour government, which was supposedly less attached to the imperial idea than the Conservatives it had succeeded. In October 1946, an agreement was signed providing for a gradual withdrawal of British troops. But London rejected Egypt's request for the annexation of Sudan, so the agreement was not ratified. Nukrachi then took the matter to the United Nations Security Council, but Great Britain intended to maintain its presence in Egypt, whose strategic value was essential for it to remain a great power. Egypt played a leading role in the creation of the Arab League. Despite the unpreparedness of his army, King Farouk decided in May 1948 to intervene in the war in Palestine. Egypt's defeat increased popular discontent and discredited the king and his government. In December 1948, the Muslim Brotherhood assassinated Prime Minister Nukrachi Pasha. And in retaliation, the Palace had the Brotherhood's leader, Hassan al-Banna, assassinated in February 1949. In early 1950, the Wafd, which appeared to be the only recourse, returned to power. And in October 1951, the Egyptian Parliament unilaterally abrogated the 1936 treaty, which meant that, from the Egyptian point of view, the maintenance of British troops in the country was now illegal.

The pseudo independence of Iraq

Following the Iraqi revolt of 1920, the British colonial authorities felt that a more effective and less costly way to run the country was to create a local government so as to make British rule less visible. With this in mind, Sir Percy Cox took office in Baghdad as the first High Commissioner. Faysal, who had been chosen by Churchill at the Cairo conference on Lawrence's recommendation to rule Iraq, was proclaimed king by referendum in July 1921. The British lightened their military presence in favor of a tightly controlled local armed force composed of Assyrian Christians. The new ruling class was mainly composed of Sunni Arabs and included former officers of the Ottoman army, including Nuri Said. The latter had the ambition to create a strong state on the Turkish model. There were two political currents, one pro-English, with Nuri Said as the leading figure, and the other nationalist, with Rashid Ali Al-Gaylani as the main representative. Faisal favored the formation of a modern national army. While the Shiites represented 50% of the population, they had only 15% of the positions in the administration. From its creation, the kingdom had to face ethnic and religious revolts from the Kurds and the Shiites of the south, whose uprising was supported by the clergy. British authority was based on two pillars, the Hashemite monarchy and the Anglo-Iraqi treaty of 1930, under which Iraq was recognized as "independent. "This is obviously a truncated independence, there is an Iraqi ambassador only in London, in other countries Iraq is represented by the British ambassador. But for the states under French mandate, it constituted a model to which they aspired to accede one day, especially after Iraq became the first Arab country to accede to the League of Nations in 1932[4] . Nuri Said was the architect of the treaty and served as Prime Minister fourteen times between 1930 and 1958. He implemented a coherent policy of building a strong state linked to Britain and was deeply hated by a large part of the Iraqi population. The British no longer openly meddle in domestic politics, but retain important military and commercial interests in the kingdom, where the question of minorities is already raised. Sunnis and Shiites clashed strongly, and Kurds and Assyrians wanted their own autonomous states. An Assyrian squadron (*Assyrian Levies*) had helped the British to suppress Shiite and Kurdish Arab nationalist insurrections, but at the end of the mandate in 1932, the United Kingdom abandoned its allies. The Assyrian crisis broke out in the summer of 1933, leading to the massacre of several thousand Assyrians by the Iraqi government. Two years later, it was the turn of the Kurds, who refused to be integrated into an Arab state, to revolt, but they too were killed in their thousands by the Iraqi army. When the second king, Ghazi, died, his son Faysal II was a child and his uncle Abdul Ilah became regent of the kingdom.

At the beginning of the Second World War, Iraq became a place of refuge for

Arab nationalists hostile to Britain. In 1939 Germany secretly promised the Iraqis to recognize their independence if they rebelled against the British. The Prime Minister, Rashid Ali Al-Gaylani, refused to comply with the latter's request to declare war on Germany. He was removed from power and in April 1941 led an anti-British coup d'état supported by Germany. But the Iraqi army was defeated by British forces from India and Transjordan. The government of Rashid Ali was overthrown and the pro-British party of Nuri Said took over. The latter dominated Iraqi political life until the 1958 revolution. The British reoccupation marked the limits of the independence granted in 1932. The Iraqi uprising also had repercussions in Syria and Lebanon under the French mandate. The Vichy government having acquiesced to the Reich's request to use Syrian and Lebanese airfields to help the Iraqis, the British army and the Free French Forces dislodged the Vichy administration in these two countries.

Lebanon under French mandate.

"The period of the French mandate over Syria and Lebanon (1919-1945) reflects the communitarian vision that presides over French policy in the Levant. The creation of Greater Lebanon in September 1920 responded as much to the wishes of the Christian population as to France's desire to create a solid bastion to defend its interests[5] . France's decision to amalgamate into the hard core of the Mountain peripheral regions whose population, mostly Muslim, wished to be part of a Greater Syria was however very badly received by the Sunnis and Shiites living in these regions. For a long time, the proxy authorities came up against their irredentism. And Lebanese political life was marked, until the eve of independence, by opposition between supporters of French protection and Arab nationalists. When the mandate was established, Lebanon was administered directly by the French. There was no legislative power, the right to legislate being reserved for the High Commissioner. Certain administrations such as customs as well as the "Service des intérêts communs" in Lebanon and Syria depended directly on him. He appointed a governor of Greater Lebanon, responsible to him, who exercised executive power. Until 1926, when a constitution was voted, the country saw four successive governors, all French. An administrative commission of a strictly consultative nature was created. It was composed of ten Christians and seven Muslims (six Maronites, three Greek Orthodox, one Greek Catholic, four Sunnis, two Shiites and one Druze). The High Commission alone retains the prerogative of appointing civil servants, and it alone decides on the budget for the year. It controlled the press, the economy, diplomacy and the armed forces, and concentrated all executive power in its hands. In 1922, the Administrative Commission was replaced by a Representative Commission elected by universal suffrage on a two-tier basis combining community and territorial representation. But legislative power continued to be vested in the High Commissioner, and the post of governor remained in the hands of a Frenchman. The bitterness is deep among Lebanese politicians, even the most Francophile, who recall that they must be associated with the government of their country.

At first excellent, relations with the High Commissioner deteriorated when the members of the Commission learned that an organic statute for the mandated states was being drawn up in Paris without them. Gouraud's successor, General Weygand, who remained in office from May 1923 to January 1925, was appreciated by the population. In Syria, it was he who put an end to the fragmentation of the country by proclaiming, in May 1924, the merger of the states of Damascus and Aleppo into a single federal state. This initiative earned him a grandiose reception in Damascus, which regained its status as the capital, where he was acclaimed by prominent figures and the Muslim and Christian population. General Sarrail who replaced him dissolved the Representative Council and suppressed the freedom of the press. Cassant and authoritarian, he managed to displease everyone. His behavior provoked the revolt of the Druze in Syria, leading to his hasty recall. His successor, Henry de Jouvenel, was for the first time a civilian. Then, until 1940, there was a succession of civilian High Commissioners: Henri Ponsot (1926-1933), Damien de Martel (1933-1938) and Gabriel Puaux (1938-1940).

The Mandate Charter obliged the Mandatory Power to provide Lebanon with an "organic status" within three years. Great Britain, which had the same obligation in Iraq and Transjordan, fulfilled it more quickly, appearing more liberal than France in the eyes of the Lebanese. When Aristide Briand became President of the Council in 1925, he decided to hasten the drafting of a Lebanese constitution. As soon as he was appointed high commissioner, Jouvenel, surrounding himself with French and Lebanese advisors, including Michel Chiha, set about this task. The Constitution with which the country was endowed in 1926 guaranteed in its title V the interests of the Mandatory Power. Although inspired by that of the Third Republic, it differed in its recognition of religious communities and the sharing of power among them according to their demographic weight. Article 95 stipulates that "as a transitional measure, the communities will be equitably represented in public employment and in the ministries without this harming the good of the State. It was supposed to protect the interests of all communities, but was never repealed, hindering the building of a true Lebanese nation. The Constitution was placed under the guarantee of France, which was equivalent to an official recognition of the mandate. And a law defined the prerogatives of the Mandatory Power, namely: the defense of the Lebanese territory, the control of the General Security services, the diplomatic representation of Lebanon and the right of the High Commissioner to annul laws and decrees contrary to the letter and spirit of the mandate. Two amendments to the Constitution, in 1927 and 1929, strengthened the prerogatives of the President of the Republic and extended the presidential term to six years.

The first President of the Republic, Charles Debbas, as well as the Prime Ministers who succeeded him during his two successive mandates, were all Christians. Until 1934, Lebanese political life was dominated by two currents, that of the supporters of Greater Syria, and that of those who believed that the

French presence guaranteed the existence of Lebanon. The elections of 1934 brought to the Chamber of Deputies deputies belonging to a single list practically imposed by the High Commissioner. The High Commissioner appointed Habib pasha al-Saad as President of the Republic by decree. When his term expired, Émile Éddé was elected President of the Republic in January 1936, beating his rival Béchara el-Khoury thanks to French support. Very Francophile, Edde saw in the Franco-Lebanese friendship a guarantee for the preservation of the identity and independence of Lebanon. The arrival in power in July 1936 of the Popular Front government presided over by Léon Blum led to the opening of negotiations between France and Syria, and then Lebanon, with a view to the establishment of friendship and alliance treaties intended to replace the mandates. The start of the Franco-Syrian and then Franco-Lebanese negotiations did not fail to give rise to different positions on the part of the Lebanese communities. The Maronite delegates demanded the maintenance of an independent and sovereign Lebanon, while a manifesto addressed to the High Commissioner de Martel declared that: "the Muslims claim national sovereignty within the framework of Syrian unity, however, in view of the difficulty of achieving it in the present circumstances, they decide to adhere to the principle of negotiations with France, with a view to a Franco-Lebanese treaty which will have to pave the way for the achievement of political unity with Syria[6] ". On November 13, 1936, a text providing for the independence of the country accompanied by a treaty of friendship and alliance between France and Lebanon was signed in Beirut. Lebanon gained sovereign independence and diplomatic relations were established between the two countries. It reserved for France the right to station military forces and economic benefits. Despite reservations in some Muslim circles, it was unanimously approved by the Chamber and in January 1937 the Constitution was fully restored. But the treaty was opposed by French colonialist circles. And, after the fall of the Blum government and the return of the Right to power, it was not ratified by the French Parliament.

Two groups of deputies were then formed in the Chamber: the first, gathered around Béchara el-Khoury, advocated the rapid advent of total independence and demanded the full restoration of the Constitution, hence its name of "Destour" (constitutional) party; as for the second, led by Émile Éddé, it took the name of National Bloc and considered that the mandate should be made more flexible without calling into question its principle. The opposition between the pro-mandate, anti-Arab National Bloc and the pro-independence Destour would mark Lebanese political life until the 1950s. Two other parties were created at the same time: the Najjadés and the Kataëb (the Phalanges) of Pierre Gemayel, whose supporters were recruited respectively from the Muslim and Christian middle and working classes. In 1937 Émile Éddé entrusted the presidency of the Council for the first time to a Sunni notable, Khayr al-Din al-Ahdab, inaugurating a practice that was to be confirmed by the national pact of 1943 concerning the sharing of power between the Lebanese communities. From 1938 onwards, he had increasingly difficult relations with the High

Commissioner of Martel who never wanted to grant him full authority. At the end of the year, the latter was replaced by Gabriel Puaux who remained in office until November 1940.

The difficult exercise of the mandate in Syria

While in Lebanon the mandate was exercised without major difficulty, the same was not true in Syria, where it was imposed by force. This resistance reinforced France's deep mistrust of Arab nationalism, in which it tended to see a British plot to threaten its strategic positions in the Middle East and a risk of contagion for its possessions in North Africa. Gouraud's division of Syria into two states: those of Aleppo and Damascus, as well as the creation of an Alawite Territory and an autonomous Druze Region favored these minorities at the expense of the Sunnis, who were the most hostile to French domination. The mandate finally allowed the Alawites, who had always been despised by the Sunnis, to raise their heads. At first the Druze, and especially the Alawites, welcomed the autonomy granted to them.

But the clumsiness and authoritarianism of the French administration, led for the first few years by the military, eventually made them disappointed. The states of Damascus and Aleppo were each endowed with a representative council and an indigenous government flanked by French advisors. Two great notables were appointed governors: Hakki bey el-Azem in Damascus and Kamil pacha el-Koudsi in Aleppo. But behind a façade of "indigenous government", the French officials monopolized all the powers. As for the Druze and Alawite regions, they were administered directly by the French military authority. The Alawite behavior went through two phases: the first in the 1920s was characterized by isolationism and the temptation of an Alawite state distinct from the rest of Syria; the second, from the end of the 1930s, went in the opposite direction of integration and Syrian centralism in reaction to the clumsiness of the Alawite policy of the French who behaved as if they were in a conquered country. The French High Commission, based in Beirut, is the common organ existing between Lebanon and Syria. The choice of Beirut as the seat of the High Commission offended the Syrians and the business community resented the fact that most Syrian trade passed through Beirut and Tripoli. The new currency, the Syrian-Lebanese pound, common to both countries is based on the French franc which is not convertible into gold, which increases their discontent.

In 1924, on the initiative of General Weygand, the States of Damascus and Aleppo were replaced by the Federal State of Syria. And the Alawite Territory was transformed into a state with Latakia as its capital. The representative councils of the two states were merged into a single chamber, the Federal Council. The executive was entrusted to a president elected for four years, assisted by five ministers responsible to him and the Federal Council. Diplomacy and defence remained the responsibility of the Mandatory Power. This decision was well received and, on 1er January 1925, Soubhi bey Barakat became the first president of the Republic. But the climate of trust that was beginning to develop between the French and the Syrians was soon compromised. The replacement of Weygand by General Sarrail, who believed only in the strong way, poisoned relations between France and Syria. He declared to Paul de Reffye, who succeeded Robert de Caix as Secretary General: "this backward country must be led harshly and administered like a colony, ignoring the notion of a mandate[7] ". A People's Party, radically opposed to the mandate, was founded in 1925. A Hashemite party that had established itself in Syria organized itself as the Independence Party.

Although the country was supposedly "pacified", a revolt led by the Druze leader Soltan el-Attrache broke out in July 1925. Starting in Druze Hauran, the revolt was supported underhandedly by King Faysal of Iraq, eager to take revenge for his ouster from Syria, and his brother, Abdallah, King of Transjordan. A small French detachment was massacred by Druze horsemen, and the citadel of Soueïda, capital of the Druze Jebel, was besieged. A relief column of 3000 men did not manage to lift the siege. This setback, which undermined French prestige, prompted Abderrahmane Chahbandar, leader of the People's Party and virulent opponent of the government installed by France, to form an alliance with Soltan el-Attaché. His supporters wanted to drive the French out of Damascus. The independence of Syria was proclaimed by a National Council of the Revolution, with equality solemnly consecrated between citizens of all confessions. The insurgency gradually spread throughout the country and will remain in the collective memory of Syrians as the "Great Syrian Revolution". The garrison of the citadel of Soueïda, which had been under siege for two months, was liberated on September 25, 1925, but the fighting in Damascus intensified. The French troops were also harassed from Ghouta. On October 25, Sarrail ordered the bombardment of the city, which they had to partially evacuate. The city was retaken, but the high number of victims and the extent of the destruction caused considerable emotion in Syria and Europe. The ferocious repression culminated in a large-scale military offensive on the Druze region. Sarrail, whose blunders had provoked the conflagration, was replaced by Henry de Jouvenel with conciliatory instructions. But his promise that no retaliatory measures would be taken against the chiefs who rallied did not succeed in putting an end to the revolt. A rebellion, which occurred in the mountain of the Alawites was hardly repressed. April 26, 1926. Soueïda, reoccupied by the Druze for six months, was reconquered. The fighting continued throughout the year and was accompanied by mass reprisals against the population and dozens of executions. At the beginning of 1927, the Druze threw their last forces into the battle, but were definitively put out of action. Soltan el-Attrache took refuge in Transjordan. He returned to Syria in 1936 and was welcomed in triumph as a hero of independence.

After the crushing of the "Great Syrian Revolution", the Syrian notables had come to admit that a confrontation with France had failed to advance their cause. They held the first congress of the Syrian National Bloc, which succeeded in becoming the first political formation in Syria in 1928. In May

1930 a new assembly gave Syria a republican constitution, but it remained unimplemented because of the intractable opposition of the nationalists. In Paris, some people began to think that the French mandate over Syria cost more than it brought in. But to give it up, according to the French government, would be to let England impose its influence on the Levant. As for Charles de Gaulle, stationed in the Levant at the time, he was critical of the management of the mandate. France, according to him, "has not yet seen by which end it was appropriate to take its mandate and is conducting a hesitant policy, oscillating between the principle of direct administration and a de facto protectorate[8] ". In his "*Histoire des troupes du Levant*", he wrote in 1931: "We have been in the Levant for ten years. My impression is that we hardly penetrate there and that the people are as foreign to us and, conversely, as they ever were. For me, our destiny will be to arrive at the constraint or to leave from here[9] ". In 1936 violent demonstrations broke out against the proxy power. Many insurgents were killed under the fire of the French troops. The Syrian nationalist leaders demanded that France grant Syria the same rights as those granted by England to Iraq.

In September 1936, after six months of difficult discussions, a draft treaty of alliance and friendship to replace the mandate was signed in Paris. Syria was reunified and the autonomy of the Jebel Druze and the Alawite territory was ended. Hafez el-Assad's father was among the group of six Alawite leaders who wrote to the President of the Council, Léon Blum, to have their state preserved. On November 22, the treaty was ratified by the Syrian Parliament. But an opposition grouping military, religious and economic circles formed in Paris. The conservative press spoke of "selling out the Empire". After the return of the Right to power and the replacement of Léon Blum by Édouard Daladier, the government decided not to submit the treaty to the French Parliament for ratification. The head of the Syrian government, Jamil Mardam bey, is dismayed by this about-face. After a vain attempt to find common ground with the nationalists, the new High Commissioner, Gabriel Puaux, opted for a policy of force. Death and prison sentences were handed down. In 1938, he established a regime of exception, dissolved the Chamber and suspended the Syrian Constitution. And in 1939, to the great displeasure of Syrian nationalists, France ceded the Alexandria Sandjak to Turkey. The decision of Paris was contrary to international law, France did not have to cede to a third country, a province of a state on which the League of Nations had given it a mandate.

The outbreak of the Second World War and the fate of the Levant

When the Second World War broke out in September 1939, the countries of the eastern Mediterranean basin were not directly involved in the hostilities, with the exception of Italian Libya and British-occupied Egypt, for whom control of the Suez Canal was of vital strategic importance. Until the summer of 1940, when Germany burst into this theater of operations, the confrontation mainly concerned Italian and British land and naval forces. But the end of the Battle of Britain made the Middle East the main battlefield between the British and the Axis forces. The region was a strategic crossroads, both for the Axis, who hoped to link the theaters of operations opened in 1941 (Libya, Egypt, the Balkans, then the USSR and in particular the Caucasus), and for the Allies, whose communication routes they depended on. Not to mention the fact that the Iraqi oil wells of Mosul and Basra were attracting interest. On the western front, the Wehrmacht went on the offensive on 10 May 1940. On June 14th the Germans were in Paris. General de Gaulle launched his call for resistance from London on the BBC on 18 June. Marshal Pétain signed the armistice, with the Germans on the 22nd and with the Italians on the 24th. Two rival powers were now in conflict. By denouncing collaboration with the invader and leading the resistance, de Gaulle represented legitimacy in the face of the legality of Vichy. Following the collapse of France, which undermined its image in the eyes of the peoples it dominated, he had the greatest difficulty in defending his positions against the British and the Americans. The Franco-German and Franco-Italian armistices left France with its empire and the forces necessary to maintain order within it, and implied the obligation for it to defend its overseas territories against any aggressor, whoever he might be. The integrity of the empire was, along with the refusal to deliver the fleet, one of the points on which the Pétain government had shown itself to be firm. While not wanting to be drawn into a war against France's former ally, Vichy was just as determined not to hand over these territories and the fleet to Great Britain or Free France in order not to give the Germans a pretext for occupying the free zone. From 1942 onwards, the Americans became aware of the strategic importance of the Middle East, hence the landing in North Africa in November, in order to catch Rommel at his rear and secure the Allies' position in this region. But while coming to Britain's aid in the name of defending democracy, Roosevelt did not want to present himself as the guarantor of the British Empire. Despite protests from Vichy, the Americans gave their political support to the entry of British and Gaullist forces into Syria and Lebanon.

The independence of Syria and Lebanon

Just after the declaration of war, the High Commissioner had taken over the legislative power and the executive power, and the Lebanese and Syrian Constitutions were suspended. In 1940-1941, the Levant was under the authority of the Vichy regime. General Dentz was appointed to replace Puaux as High Commissioner and was also Commander-in-Chief of the troops in the Levant. On April 9, 1941, Dentz appointed Alfred Naccache as head of the Lebanese state, replacing Émile Éddé. And in Syria, he replaced Bahige Khatib with Khaled el-Azem as head of state. The defeat of France in 1940 made his position very precarious in the face of the British who spared no means to oust him from Syria and Lebanon. As early as the summer of 1940, the question of the presence of Vichy forces in Lebanon and Syria was raised with the British government. But as long as the Battle of Britain lasted, during which the country was fighting for its survival, it could not afford a large deployment of forces outside the European theater. Once the threat of a Nazi invasion had been averted, its concern to ensure the security of the Suez Canal and the route to

India made intervention inevitable. In Iraq, the coup d'état of Rachid Ali Al-Gaylani in April 1941 heightened the British fear of being caught by the Germans. By virtue of an agreement with the Vichy regime, the Germans obtained permission to use Syrian airports to transport weapons, supplies and specialists to Iraq. On May 9, German planes began landing in Aleppo to assist the Iraqis. But on May 30, the government of Rashid Ali was overthrown. Despite the failure of the Iraqi revolt, the British considered the use of Syrian airfields by the German air force to be too great a threat to the Middle East, to its oil and to its communications. They then decided, in agreement with Free France, to invade Syria and Lebanon. Three main reasons pushed General de Gaulle to engage the Free French Forces in this fratricidal struggle: the desire to wrest control of a strategically important territory from Vichy, which would increase the human and material resources of Free France and strengthen its own authority; the fear of letting the British oust France, whose presence in the Middle East they had never willingly supported; and finally, the hope of obtaining the support of the British in the Middle East.finally, the hope of obtaining the rallying of the French army stationed in Lebanon and Syria, whose numbers reached 30,000 men.

In June 1941, a British army and the Free French Forces (FFL) attacked the Vichy army in Lebanon and Syria, which was forced to capitulate after five weeks of fierce resistance. This fratricidal battle between French soldiers left deep resentments. Very few French troops from the Levant joined the FFL. On September 9, 1941 Winston Churchill declared in the House of Commons: "We have no ambition whatsoever in Syria, we are not seeking to replace or supplant France, we are in Syria only to secure the war[10] ". The question of the independence of Syria and Lebanon was to become one of the main bones of contention between Great Britain and Free France. General de Gaulle appointed General Catroux Delegate General to Lebanon and Syria, a title that replaced that of High Commissioner for the Levant. After the eviction of the Vichy administration, the British and the Free French undertook to grant Lebanon and Syria their independence. But while London took independence for granted, the Free French, citing the imperatives of war, were reluctant to keep their promise. In fact, everything was going on as if the mandate was continuing. It was only on November 26 that General Catroux recognized Alfred Naccache as President of the Lebanese Republic. However, his letter specified that "the rights and prerogatives of the Lebanese state should be subject to the restrictions imposed by the current state of war and the security of the territory[11] ". Catroux had to face both British interference and Lebanese national demands. With the presence of the British army in Syria and Lebanon, the British representative, Edward Spears, openly played the independence card against the French. In fact, the mandate had become a Franco-British condominium which itself reflected the balance of power between the two allies. Controlling the supply of Syria and Lebanon and superior in numbers after having encouraged the repatriation of the Vichyists, the British had every opportunity to turn the independence demands in their favor. But the ambiguity of the French position is not in doubt. Not to mention that General de Gaulle's intransigence did not help matters. In his mind, it was a question of postponing the deadline for independence until the end of the war by subordinating it to a treaty. More open to the demands of the Syrian and Lebanese nationalists, Catroux felt that giving a liberal response was the best way to preserve France's traditional interests. But he faithfully applied the policy of the leader of Free France. However, true to his liberal convictions and in order to cut the ground from under Spears' feet, he proposed in May 1942 to de Gaulle to re-establish in Lebanon and Syria the Constitutions suspended since the beginning of the war and to consider the treaties of 1936, once ratified by France, as a provisional charter for relations with these two states. But he was refused by the General who replied: "one does not organize a ballot in the middle of a battle[12] ". From July 28 to September 13, 1942, General de Gaulle spent five weeks in the Levant. This trip enhanced the prestige of France and its leader. He received an even warmer welcome as the populations and leaders expected him to announce concrete measures for the promised independence. But in making his tour his aim was not to hasten independence but to consolidate the French Empire which he could not afford to be accused of selling off by Vichy. Disappointed, the nationalists turned to the British who supported them, accentuating the General's suspicions.

In 1943 the Allied victories on all fronts made it less justifiable to invoke external perils to justify the postponement of constitutional life. Under British and Lebanese pressure, General Catroux officially announced on March 8 the restoration of the Lebanese Constitution and his decision to form a provisional government to prepare free elections. The legislative elections took place from August 29 to September 5, 1943. Émile Éddé wanted to negotiate the independence of Lebanon with France, in order to preserve the traditional links and avoid a Franco-Lebanese divorce which risked subjecting the country to Syrian hegemonic aims. Bechara el-Khoury was determined to wrest it at all costs. On September 21, 1943, Bechara el-Khoury was elected President of the Lebanese Republic, with Riyad el-Solh heading the government. They concluded an unwritten "National Pact" between them whereby the presidency of the Republic would be given to the Maronites, the presidency of the Council to the Sunnis and the presidency of the House to the Shiites. It was also agreed that the number of deputies would be in the proportion of six Christians to five Muslims. This pact, concluded between the President of the Maronite Republic and the President of the Sunni Council, constituted a compromise between the two parties based on the renunciation of French and Western protection for the Christians and the demand for integration into a larger Arab state on the Muslim side. The Lebanese government decided to abrogate the articles of the Constitution that were in contradiction with national sovereignty. And on October 25, 1943, it delivered to Jean Helleu, representative of Free France, a letter demanding the conversion of the general delegation into a diplomatic representation, the transfer of the Special Troops of the Levant to the Lebanese

State and the retrocession of the services of the common interests between Lebanon and Syria. Faced with this challenge, Helleu had the President of the Republic, the President of the Council and the members of the government arrested. These actions provoked a huge indignation and numerous demonstrations of protest. But it was Great Britain that played a decisive role in resolving the crisis. It demanded the recall of Helleu and the immediate release of the prisoners. When Catroux arrived in Lebanon, he considered that it was better to settle the crisis immediately in order to appear to be acceding to the will of the Lebanese rather than to appear to be giving in to British pressure. On his recommendation, Helleu was recalled to Algiers. He was replaced in March 1944 by General Beynet as General Delegate and Plenipotentiary of France in the Levant. On November 22, 1943, Catroux had the prisoners of Rachaya released. Lebanon had finally gained its independence. Its commemoration will henceforth take place on November 22 and no longer on September 1er , the anniversary of the proclamation of Greater Lebanon by General Gouraud.

Negotiations concerning the independence of Syria opened in Damascus at the end of August 1941. Sheikh Tajeddine was appointed President of the Republic on September 27. But de Gaulle wrote to Catroux: "I invite you to be very careful when it comes to the practical realization of Syria's independence. To give it without any simultaneous counterpart would be extremely dangerous[13] ". The elections of 1943 confirmed the push of the nationalists of the National Bloc, who had been ousted in 1939, and who obtained a strong majority. Like Lebanon, Syria gained its independence in November 1943. Choukri Kouatly became the first president of the Republic of Independence. It was by acceding to the French request to formally renounce Lebanon that the Syrian nationalists obtained this independence. But this renunciation, which muted Arab unitary aspirations, was far from unanimous. The sovereignty of Syria and Lebanon was officially recognized on January 3, 1944, but the French army remained in place. France continued to insist that Syria and Lebanon sign agreements affirming its privileged role, without concealing the fact that this would be the condition for evacuating its soldiers. But demonstrations broke out in Damascus against the retention of French troops, and the city was bombed by their artillery and air force on 29 and 30 May 1945. Winston Churchill sent an ultimatum to de Gaulle demanding an immediate ceasefire and the withdrawal of French soldiers to their barracks. The British forces in Syria made a spectacular entry into Damascus and surrounded the barracks of the French troops. This unprecedented humiliation was followed by the ruthless expulsion of the French from Damascus. Furious, de Gaulle summoned the ambassador of His Majesty in Paris to whom he declared: "We are not in a position, I recognize, to wage war against you, but you have outraged France[14] . The enormous emotion caused by this aggression and the intervention of the British army forced the French forces to withdraw to Lebanon and they ended up evacuating Syria and Lebanon in 1946. One can only deplore the French obstinacy in holding on to the mandate over Syria and Lebanon. Few, like General Catroux, were aware that the new international context made this system obsolete. "We could have left with dignity, instead we were thrown out" wrote Alfred Fabre Luce in "*Deuil au Levant*[150] " where he evoked "the blunders of France which did not measure the strength of Syrian-Lebanese nationalism, nor the British will to appear as the protector of the independence of these two countries in order to consolidate its position in a strategically very important region. French intransigence meant that, at the end of the war, Lebanon and Syria were completely independent, while the former British protectorates (Egypt, Iraq, Transjordan) were linked to Great Britain by treaties.

The creation of the Arab League

In 1944, the search for a confederation of Arab countries, encouraged by the British, led to the creation in 1945 of the Arab League. When the talks for its creation began, a struggle for influence pitted Egypt against the Hashemites of Iraq and Transjordan, who presented themselves as the natural defenders of Arab union projects. In the end, Cairo won and was chosen as the headquarters of the organization. In Lebanon, Christian circles were apprehensive about any project that might promote Arab unity. The same was true of certain Arab regimes that were not at all willing to integrate into a larger entity. To allay these concerns, the Pact of the League of Arab States, signed in March 1945 in Alexandria, was based on respect for the sovereignty and independence of member states. The seven founding members are: Egypt, Saudi Arabia, Transjordan, Syria, Lebanon and North Yemen. Palestine is only represented by a "Liberation Organization". Of these seven countries, only Arabia and Yemen are free of colonial subjugation. The world conflict further strengthened British control over Egypt, Transjordan and Iraq. As for France, it continued to militarily occupy Syria and Lebanon, despite their formal independence in 1943. The association aimed to affirm the unity of the Arab "nation" and the independence of each of its members. From its inception, the League, far from reflecting these aspirations, was the closed field of intrigues of the regimes to ensure a relative supremacy. It was divided into two camps with opposing political aims, the Egyptian-Saudi entente favouring independence projects opposing the Jordanian-Iraqi Hashemite axis more inclined to cooperation with Great Britain. The only consensus that emerged was hostility towards the Jewish state and the takeover of the Palestinian cause. The years following the independence of the Arab states in the Middle East saw several failed attempts at Arab unity that challenged the borders inherited from the colonial era. They were driven by the ideological current of Arab nationalism that dominated political thought in the Arab world in the aftermath of World War II. This current can be divided into two main trends. The first is composed of local or regional nationalisms, such as the Syrian nationalism of the Syrian Popular Party (SPP), which exalts the rebirth of the Syrian nation within the framework of "Greater Syria". The second trend, embodied by the Baath (Arab Socialist Renaissance Party) and Nasserism, wanted to bring all Arabs together in a single political entity. Their failures show that the borders drawn by France and

England were not totally artificial. And, in any case, that local nationalisms - Iraqi, Syrian, Jordanian and Lebanese - have developed, supplanting the feeling of belonging to a mythical Arab "nation" which, moreover, will be challenged by the pan-Islamic current carried by Saudi Arabia.

Christian communities after independence.

With the accession of Arab countries to independence, the situation and attitude of minority communities, which had been favored by France and England, varied according to the country. In Lebanon, an unwritten compromise was reached in 1943 between the Sunnis and the Maronites who renounced French protection. In Egypt, the monarchy, faced with popular pressure, allied itself with the Coptic, Syrian-Lebanese and Jewish upper classes. The Wafd party, which dominated the post-war political scene, included important Coptic personalities who chose, not without ostentation, to endorse all the nationalist claims, to the point that one of them went so far as to declare: "I am a Christian by religion, but a Muslim by nationality[16] ". In Syria, which has remained little permeable to foreign influences, the same cultural difference between Muslims and Christians has not been created as in Lebanon. At independence, the Christian Farés el-Khoury became one of the country's leading political figures and was successively President of the House and Prime Minister. Many Christians are proud of their Arab personality. Political developments in the Arab world, starting with the Franco-English aggression and the Israeli attack on Egypt in 1956, with all the popular and nationalist upheavals that they raised in the Arab countries, recreated community tensions. The virulent anti-Westernism and the rise of unionism provoked by this last manifestation of colonialism aroused the fear of the Syrian and Egyptian upper bourgeoisie whose prosperity was largely due to the development of Western interests in the region. This fear was heightened by the spread of socialist ideology. So when nationalization measures were taken in Egypt, Copts, Egyptian Jews and Syrian-Lebanese Christians belonging to this class interpreted it as being directed against them, while at the same time an agrarian reform affected the great Muslim feudalists. Jews and Syrian-Lebanese emigrated en masse from Egypt, as did a good part of the Syrian Christian upper class who settled in Lebanon. These events and the union between Egypt and Syria rekindled a feeling of fear and a mentality of being under siege among the Christians of Lebanon, which was matched by the growing assertion of political claims by Lebanese Muslims. They explain the crisis and the confessional troubles of 1958, provoked by the pro-western policy of President Chamoun.

The creation of Saudi Arabia

Saudi Arabia is one of only two Arab states, along with the medieval kingdom of Yemen, to have escaped Western domination. And it is the only state in the world whose citizens are referred to by the name of the dynasty, thus underlining its patrimonial character and its anti-nahda ideology. The kingdom was officially founded in 1932 by the merger of the provinces of Najd and Hijaz by King Abdel Aziz Al-Saud (Ibn Saud). He is a distant descendant of another Ibn Saud, the one who, together with Ibn Abdel-Wahhab (the founder of Wahhabism), had created the first Saudi state in 1774. In January 1902, the support of the Bedouins of the Ikhwan order had allowed Abdel Aziz to expand his domain. He entered Riyadh victoriously, consolidating his control over the Najd province, the heart of central Arabia. In 1910, he repelled a military expedition led by Sherif Hussein to remove the threat he posed to the Hijaz. With the outbreak of World War I, Abdelaziz gradually moved closer to the British. He received support from the agents of the Viceroyalty of India (notably St. John Philby), while the Hashemites were supported by the agents of the British administration in Cairo (T.E. Lawrence and Gertrude Bell). Despite the British preference for an alliance with Sherif Hussein, a treaty of protection was signed between Sir Percy Cox, the future High Commissioner in Iraq and Abdelaziz in 1915. The British wanted him to cooperate with the sheriff, or at least not to hinder his action. Instead of bending to their will, he adopted an ambiguous attitude. His troops attacked the tribes submitted to the Sherif. In 1924, he started the conquest of the Hedjaz. In the autumn, he seized Mecca (where his troops entered with their rifles turned towards the ground) and then Medina. It was only after a long siege that Jeddah fell in 1925. Modest king of the Hijaz, Sherif Hussein had seen his dream of a unified Arab kingdom fade away, although two of his sons were installed on the thrones of Iraq and Transjordan. Failing that, he believed he could claim the caliphate as an Arab descendant of the Prophet. In that same year, 1924, this institution had indeed been abolished by the Turkish Republic. But the conquest by Abdel Aziz of the Hijaz also destroyed this illusion. Forsaken by the British, Hussein was forced to abdicate on October 3 in favor of his eldest son, Ali, and took refuge in Amman where he died in June 1931. On February 20, 1930, on board a British warship, Ibn Saud and Faisal of Iraq reconciled and concluded a treaty of friendship and good neighborliness. Pragmatism took over, to the detriment of the claims of the Hashemite family on the Hijaz.

Saudi Arabia is an absolute monarchy based on a pact between the throne and Wahhabism, a doctrine preaching an ultra-fundamentalist version of Islam. "In this country, ultraconservative puritanism serves as a screen for the power of the royal family and a tyranny characterized by a denial of humanist principles on democracy, freedom, human rights and gender equality. This tyranny was based on a strict control of morality (a moral police, the *moutawa'a*)[17] . The discovery of oil in 1938 led to the beginning of a strategic alliance with the United States. The pact was sealed on 14 February 1945, during a meeting between the king and President Roosevelt on board the cruiser Quincy, stationed in Egypt. This meeting should be seen in the context of the emerging American-British rivalry on which Ibn Saud, as a cunning old king, knew how to play. The United States undertook to protect the Saud dynasty. In return for this protection, the kingdom ensured the continuity of oil supplies to the West. And it reinvested a large part of its petrodollars, either in arms orders for the sole benefit of the American protector, or in financial investments in the United States or Europe. However, until the agreement establishing a 50% share of the profits from oil exploitation, the kingdom received only a minimal share. And pilgrimage taxes were its main resource. The kingdom aspires to play the role of a flagship state in the Muslim world, justified by its status as the cradle of Islam and the seat of its holy places. Its king bears the caliphal title of "servant of the two Holy Cities of Islam": Mecca and Medina. The theory that every civilization needs a beacon state was supported by Samuel Huntington. According to him, four states could claim this role in the Muslim world: Iran, Egypt, Saudi Arabia and Turkey. Since the quadrupling of the price of crude oil in 1974, the Kingdom has put the loot from its oil revenues at the service of the global spread of Sunni fundamentalism. It finances the construction of dozens of mosques and Koranic schools, both in Muslim countries and in Christian lands. Wahhabism has thus gone from being a sect adhered to by a handful of tribes, established in the Najd, from the end of the XVIIIe century to the beginning of the XXe century, to a belief shared by tens of millions of people today. Riyadh also played a leading role in the founding of the Organization of the Islamic Conference (OIC), the only international institution that brings together states on a religious basis and not on the basis of language or belonging to the same region.

1 http://orientxxi.info/le-moyen-orient-1876-1980/moyen-orient-une-geographie-qui-a-une-histoire-ii,1986

2 *History of political ideas*, Jean Touchard, Presses universitaires de France, p.103

3 *Le Grand jeu, Orient arabe et rivalités internationales*, Henry Laurens, Armand Colin, 1991, p. 21

4 ibid.

5 *France in Lebanon and the Near East.* Ibrahim Tabet, ed. of the Revue Phénicienne, 2012, p.194

6 *Histoire du Liban contemporain*, Denise Amoun, Fayard 1997. p. 28

7 *France in Lebanon and the Near East,* op. cit. p. 217

8 *Lebanon, Syria, the Mandate,* Henri de Wally. Perrin, 2010, p.292

9 Charles de Gaulle. *Histoire des troupes du Levant,* quoted by Alexandre Najjar. *De Gaulle and Lebanon,* p 25

10 *France in the Levant,* Pierre Dufour, Pygmalion 2001

11 *Selim Takla, a contribution to the independence of Lebanon*, Gérard Khoury, Kathala-Dar el-Nahar, 2004, p. 355.

13 *Le général de Gaulle et le monde arabe, Jean-Paul Bled* (dir.) éditions dar el-Nahar, 2009, p.86

14 *France in Lebanon and the Middle East,* op.cit p. 236

15 *France in the games of influence in Syria and Lebanon*, Anne-Lucie Chaigne-Oudin, l'Harmattan, 2009, p. 100

16 *Deuil au Levant*, Alfred Fabre Luce, Fayard 1950, p.89

17 *History of religious pluralism in the Mediterranean basin*, Georges Corm, Geuthner 1998, p.238

18 *Le Monothéisme, le pouvoir et la guerre,* op. cit. p.262

Chapter 3. The Creation of the State of Israel

The British mandate in Palestine.

Endorsed by the San Remo Conference of April 20, 1920, the British Mandate in Palestine is the corollary of the Balfour Declaration, which aimed to establish a "National Home" for the Jewish people in Palestine. Its preamble affirmed "the historic link between the Jewish people and Palestine". Article 2 stated that the purpose of the Mandate was to introduce into the country the "political, administrative and economic conditions which would ensure the establishment of the Jewish National Home. It was therefore naturally more favorable to the Jews than to the "existing non-Jewish communities in Palestine", a term which in the declaration refers to the Arab people of Palestine. Unlike the other mandates, it did not recognize the country's vocation for independence because this could only lead to Arab sovereignty, which at the time represented the vast majority of the population. Throughout their presence in Palestine, the British played the role of pyromaniac firefighter, trying unsuccessfully to control the fire they themselves had started. In June 1920, Sir Herbert Samuel (a committed Zionist) was appointed High Commissioner to Palestine, a position he would hold until 1925. He adopted a policy of creating favorable conditions for Jewish settlement. At the same time, he worked to improve the living conditions of the Arab population. From 1920 onwards, Palestinian notables asserted their opposition to the Zionist project. Anti-Jewish violence broke out in 1921. But until 1926, Palestine was relatively calm, despite the growing concern among Arabs about the arrival of new waves of Jewish immigrants.

At the end of the war, the representatives of the Zionist organizations set up the basic structures of the "Yishuv", a term that designates the entire Jewish community in Palestine. In addition to the World Jewish Organization, which continued to work in the diaspora, the Jewish Agency in Palestine was charged with administering the material interests of the Yishuv and representing it before the British authorities. In the early 1920s, the future Israeli Prime Minister, David Ben Gurion, became the head of Mapai, a political formation that gave rise to the Labor Party and the Histadrut, the main Zionist union. His position also allowed him to control the Haganah, a clandestine militia for the defense of the Jews. Ten years later, he became the strong man of the Yichouv, being elected president of the Jewish Agency, the matrix of the future Israeli government. He also took control of the World Jewish Agency. Within the Zionist movement, the socialist wing dominated the political scene. There is also a far-right movement, led by Vladimir Jabotinsky, which became, after 1948, the Herut party, which in turn gave rise to the Likud.

In 1922, Winston Churchill, then Minister of Colonies, stated in a White Paper that there was no question of converting all of Palestine into a Jewish homeland, a position that implied the possibility of partitioning the country. The document formalized the split of Transjordan from Mandatory Palestine. After the publication of the White Paper, the League of Nations ratified the British mandate over Palestine. The first British census recorded the presence of 84,000 Jews and 760,000 Arabs at the end of 1922. In 1925, Sheikh Izz al-Din al-Qassam led a movement to end the British Mandate. Killed in 1935 in a battle against the British, he is considered one of the fathers of the Palestinian resistance.

These years saw the formation of the main Zionist settlements. The purchase of land by the Jews resulted in the expulsion of tens of thousands of Arab peasants. In 1929, anti-Jewish riots broke out while the British had only a small garrison in the area, forcing the Haganah to defend the Yishuv on its own before British reinforcements were sent in. As a result of these events, a new British White Paper was published in 1930, which for the first time limited Jewish immigration. However, the waves of Jewish migration accelerated after Hitler came to power in 1933. From 1922 to 1948, the Jewish population in Palestine increased from 84,000 to 650,000. The majority of the Jews were of European education. The Yishuv had high-class educational institutions, while 60% of the Arab population was poorly educated and lived in miserable villages. The Arabs were gradually dispossessed of their land. Increasingly violent clashes broke out between the two communities. The Jews' contempt for the Arabs was matched by the latter's growing hatred for the invaders. The Arabs, although divided, categorically refused the idea of establishing a Jewish Home.

Between 1936 and 1939, a great Arab rebellion against the British occupation broke out. Its main instigator was Hajj Amin al-Husseini, Grand Mufti of Jerusalem, spiritual leader of the Muslim community in Palestine. This revolt witnessed the birth of a Palestinian nationalism, in opposition to Zionist nationalism. In April 1936 a general strike, proclaimed by an Arab High Committee, was savagely repressed by the occupying forces. It was suspended in October after a thousand Arabs were killed (eighty Jews and thirty-seven British). But only civil protest came to an end, while an unprecedented guerrilla war developed. Faced with the Arab guerrillas, who gathered some 2,000 insurgents, the British sent 20,000 soldiers as reinforcements.

Learning the lesson of these events, London published in July 1937, on the recommendation of the Peel Commission, a plan for the partition of Palestine into a Jewish and an Arab state. Despite the amputation it brought to the project of "Eretz Israel" (the biblical land of Israel), the partition, which had the inestimable advantage of historically enshrining the principle of the Jewish state, won the support of the Jewish Agency. In the Palestinian camp, however, the partition project deepened the opposition between the two rival formations. The one led by the Nachachibi, supported by King Abdullah of Transjordan, who approved it. And that of the Husseinis, led by Mufti Hajj Amin. The latter's rejection of the plan revived the uprising. Armed Arab groups attacked the British and the Jews. The latter committed attacks against the Arabs in retaliation, while the British carried out a harsh repression. The Mandatory Power mobilized veterans of the counter-insurgency in Ireland and enlisted thousands of Jewish auxiliaries. While the Arab resistance was exhausted in local battles against a superiorly armed and organized enemy, the Zionist movement grew stronger. After three years of Arab revolt, the nationalist elite was liquidated by executions, imprisonment or exile. The repression resulted in more than 5,000 deaths and its military failure led to the dismantling of the Arab paramilitary forces and the strengthening of the Zionist paramilitary forces with the support of the British. "To the modern and efficient organization of the Jewish community (the Yishuv), the Palestinian movement opposes an emotional Arab nationalism tinged with religious demagoguery and archaic Islamic institutions led by Hajj Amin al-Husseini[1] . Forced into exile in Iraq, he took refuge in Germany in 1941. He took the side of Nazi Germany, whose victory he hoped would expel the Jews from Palestine.

On the eve of the Second World War, in order to allay Arab fears, London published a third White Paper in 1939 limiting Jewish immigration to Palestine to 75,000 people for the next five years, prohibiting land transactions between Arabs and Jews and promising the country's independence within a unitary framework within ten years. Zionist leaders have often compared this text, which they see as a capitulation to Arab demands, to the Munich Agreement, which was also the work of Neville Chamberlain. But the reality is that the Arab cause was already lost, even before 1948.

During the Second World War, the British did not loosen their grip on immigration, despite the Nazi policy of exterminating the Jews. Ben Gurion declared: "We will help the British in the war as if there were no White Paper and we will fight the Book as if there were no war[2] ". Clandestine Jewish immigration was organized, causing clashes with the British navy and the sinking of refugee ships like the Exodus. Zionist movements became more radical, in particular the Irgun, led by Menachem Begin, which carried out attacks against the Mandate and the Palestinians. The Jewish Agency, which benefited from growing American support, defined the new Zionist objectives at a conference held at the Biltmore Hotel in New York in May 1942: the establishment of a Jewish state throughout Palestine. This conference consecrated the passage from the official theses of the 1929 Zionist Congress, which aimed at the creation of a bi-national state, to a Hebrew state proper.

By 1945, Ben Gurion was convinced that the struggle against the British and the Arabs was inevitable. The Haganah (embryo of the future Jewish army) and its elite unit, the Palmach, fought not only the Arabs but also the British army. While the extremists of the Irgun and the Lehi (acronym for "Fighters for the Liberation of Israel", also called the Stern group) led by Itzhak Shamir used the weapon of terrorism against them. The most spectacular operation was the assassination in Cairo on November 6, 1944 of Lord Moyne, the British resident minister in the Middle East and personal friend of Winston Churchill.

In the aftermath of the war, the Jewish revolt against the British occupation intensified. While the violence between the British and the Zionists increased, the Palestinian Arab population remained calm during the period 1945-1947. In May 1946, Mufti Amin al-Husseini, who was kept under house arrest by the French, managed to take refuge in Egypt. The Palestinian representative to the Arab League had proposed a series of aid measures to enable the Palestinian Arabs to cope with the economic superiority of the Yishuv. The return of the Mufti, who was recognized as the main spokesman for the Palestinians at the League conference in June 1946, ruined his efforts. The British Labour Party, which came to power in July 1945, maintained the White Paper policy of 1939. The new U.S. president, Truman, who was sympathetic to the Zionists, asked the British to scrap the White Paper. But London refused his request to grant immigration visas to 100,000 European Jews in Palestine. On July 22, 1946, the Irgun blew up part of the King David Hotel in Jerusalem, headquarters of the British army, killing 92 people.

A real climate of hatred was established between British soldiers and the Jewish population. As the British authorities sentenced Irgun militants to death, this group took hostages and executed prisoners in retaliation.

The breakdown of the Jewish-Arabic struggle

Faced with rising violence, Britain decided to abandon the mandate and turn the Palestinian issue over to the UN. Important factors motivated this decision. Financially, materially, and humanely, Great Britain was completely exhausted from the Second World War. More than 80,000 British soldiers were present in Palestine and engaged in an armed conflict with Jewish militias. This situation became unbearable for British public opinion, which began to demand withdrawal from Palestine. With the Second World War, the British relationship with Zionism evolved. In 1939, Great Britain had imposed on the Zionist movement the White Book, which provided for an independent Palestine with an Arab majority in 1949. With the war and the genocide, the perspective changed: the idea that the Jews needed a state to live in peace gained ground with international opinion. The Arab League stuck to its proposal for a unitary Palestinian state. London submitted a partition plan, which gave 56% of the territories to the Zionists and 43% to the Arabs, who made up two-thirds of the total population, with the internationalization of Jerusalem. The vote took place on November 29, 1947. The partition plan provided for three distinct zones: a Jewish state including the coastal plain, the eastern Galilee and part of the Negev; an Arab state including the rest of the Galilee, the West Bank, the Gaza Strip and part of the Negev; and an international zone including the Holy Places and extending over Jerusalem and Bethlehem. All the Arab nations opposed it, either on principle or because it gave the Jewish state more than half the territory (and the best land). The plan was supported by the United States, despite the opposition of the Secretary of Defense and the oil lobbies, as well as by the Soviet Union. It was adopted by thirty-three votes to thirteen, with ten abstentions, including Great Britain. France, which had planned to abstain, finally voted in favor. The Zionist movement accepted the plan, with the exception of the extremist groups Irgun and Stern. Although the Jewish Agency accepted the principle of partition, Ben Gurion knew that war was inevitable. The acceptance of partition was only a diplomatic way to prepare for war against the Palestinians and the Arab states.

The Arab population of Palestine felt the partition was a real injustice to them. But it was divided between supporters and opponents of the Mufti, who also faced hostility from the Arab states, particularly Transjordan. He ordered a general strike throughout Palestine on December 1[er] 1947. This movement was accompanied by violent clashes with the Jewish population which led to a real war. The Yishuv, invoking the danger of a new Holocaust, aimed to establish territorial continuity between its various enclaves. While affirming their attachment to the division provided for in the partition plan, the Zionists prepared additional annexations which they justified on security grounds. They also sought to force the departure of as many Arabs as possible from the part allocated to them, where the Arabs made up nearly 50% of the population and owned most of the land. This is the Dalet plan, drawn up by the head of Haganah operations.

The hostilities, which broke out even before the British left, pitted the Haganah, the Irgun and the Stern group against Palestinian fighters commanded by Abdel Qader al-Husseini, nephew of the Mufti, and the undisciplined volunteers of the "Arab Liberation Army" commanded by Faouzi el-Kaoukji. The Arab fighters, two to three times less numerous, soon gave up ground. The Arab population felt that they had been left unarmed by the Zionist troops. In the coastal towns, part of the Arab population fled the fighting. The first Arab city to fall was Tiberias. The greatest disaster occurred in Haifa, taken on April 22. Of the 70,000 Arab inhabitants of the city, only 3 to 4,000 remained. Jaffa and Acre suffered the same fate. Most of the Arab villages located in the territory devolved to the Zionists were destroyed after the expulsion of their inhabitants, and those in Deir Yassin were massacred. This defeat and the exodus of the population made the Arab High Committee realize that the only hope lay in the military intervention of the Arab states.

The first Arab-Israeli war (1948-1949)

At midnight on May 14, 1948, the British mandate over Palestine officially ended and the State of Israel was proclaimed by David Ben-Gurion. The American president, Harry Truman, recognized it the same day. The Arab League then decided to intervene directly in the conflict and the armies of neighboring countries invaded Palestine. The Palestinian Arab forces were dissolved or integrated into the Egyptian and Syrian armies. The Arab troops totaled 24,000 men: 10,000 Egyptians, 5,000 Jordanians, 3,000 Syrians, 3,000 Iraqis and 3,000 Lebanese and volunteers from the Arab League, against 30,000 men on the Israeli side. On May 28, Ben Gurion issued an order to group all the more or less independent defense organizations into a single army: Tsahal, headed by Haganah cadres. It took six months for this integration process to be completed. There is virtually no coordination between the Arab armies, so that

Israeli forces can fight each of them, one by one, without another coming to attack at the same time. Moreover, they are poorly prepared, with the exception of the Transjordanian troops. And there is mutual distrust between the Arab states, especially towards King Abdullah of Transjordan, whose aim is to prevent the establishment of an independent Palestinian state. Egypt, Saudi Arabia and Syria, enemies of the Hashemite clan, opposed Abdallah's policy in the name of the refusal of partition. The war was therefore as much an Arab-Zionist confrontation as it was an issue of inter-Arab quarrels. King Abdullah secretly negotiated with Golda Meir. The strategic objective of his Arab Legion commanded by Glubb Pasha was not so much to defeat the Zionist troops as to conquer as much of the territory as possible that the partition plan had included in the Palestinian Arab zone. The latter seized the old city of Jerusalem and, with the addition of an Iraqi contingent, the West Bank. On May 17, it took control of the Latroun position, threatening to lay siege to West Jerusalem, but the Israelis managed to bypass it, thus opening up this part of the city. For their part, the Egyptians took Gaza and the Negev and the Syrians a few kibbutz in the extreme north of the Galilee. Skirmishes also took place on the Lebanese border between the Haganah and the small Lebanese army.

On June 11, 1948, a mediator appointed by the UN, Count Bernadotte, got all the adversaries to agree to a cease-fire. He proposed a new partition of Palestine, which was rejected by both parties. Both sides tried to take advantage of the truce to strengthen their forces. Czech weapons were delivered by the Soviets to the Israelis. The latter also managed to obtain Spitfire fighters. The Arab forces, on the other hand, were unable to circumvent the UN arms embargo, which was essentially favourable to the Israelis. At the end of the truce, which expired on 8 July, the Israeli forces, which had reached 60,000 men, found themselves superior in both numbers and equipment to their opponents, who were militarily and politically divided. They launched a series of offensives interspersed with cease-fires until March 1949. On July 12, they seized the towns of Lydda and Ramleh, which the Arab Legion had left uncovered to defend Jerusalem; then the position of Latroun. The part of the Galilee that had been allocated to the Palestinians, including Nazareth, was captured on July 14. The IDF's advance was accompanied by forced expulsions and a campaign of terror against the Palestinian population.

On 15 July the Security Council voted for a second ceasefire. But on the 27th the Israelis went on the offensive again. On 17 September, Bernadotte was assassinated by the Stern group. The assassination of the Swedish diplomat provoked an international outcry, forcing Ben Gourion to proclaim this group and the Irgun outlawed and to dissolve these two organizations. In October 1948 Israeli troops, commanded by General Ygal Allon, took back the northern Negev from the Egyptians. In early 1949, the conquest of the rest of the Palestinian territory continued. Taking advantage of the ceasefire that was maintained with the Transjordanians on the central front, the Israelis eliminated a pocket that had remained in Syrian hands in the north of the Galilee. And they seized the southern Negev in March. On March 10, 1949, the Israeli conquest of Palestine was completed, with the exception of East Jerusalem and the West Bank, annexed to the Transjordan, and the Gaza Strip occupied by Egypt.

If we add the period of civil war that preceded it, the first Arab-Israeli war of 1948-1949 caused about 5,800 deaths on the Israeli side, a quarter of them civilians. It was the bloodiest war of the Arab-Israeli conflict for the Israelis. On the Palestinian side, the number of victims has never been accurately counted, with estimates varying between 12,000 and 20,000 dead. As for the Arab armies, Egypt had 1,400 dead and the Jordanians, Iraqis and Syrians several hundred each. The main victims of the Israeli policy of ethnic cleansing and of Arab disunity were the Palestinians, 700,000 of whom took the road to exodus. For them it was the "Nakba", literally the catastrophe. While they represented two thirds of the territory's population in 1948, i.e. about 1.3 million people, they are now divided, in addition to refugees in neighboring Arab countries, into four groups: 160,000 remained in Israel where they lived as second-class citizens, 80,000 in the Gaza Strip, 300,000 in the West Bank and East Jerusalem, which was part of Jordan. Only the Gaza Strip, 1% of the territory of the original Palestine, where a quarter of the country's Arab population is now concentrated, escaped the expansion of some and the absorption of others.

The UN resolution 194 of December 11, 1948 decides in its article 10 "that refugees who so desire should be allowed to return to their homes as soon as possible and to live in peace with their neighbors, and that compensation should be paid for the property of those who decide not to return. But it will remain a dead letter. The Arab states signed armistice agreements with Israel that did not amount to recognition, but they did not give the Palestinians any representation of their own. The Palestinians disappeared from the front of the stage. "From being a people who aspired to be sovereign over their land, the majority of them were reduced to being nothing more than refugees taken in charge by UNRWA (the United Nations agency responsible for their assistance), awaiting a hypothetical "right of return" that would never see the light of day; while some acquired Jordanian nationality .[3]

Israeli intransigence and Arab refusal

Israel refuses any return of refugees and pursues a policy of irreversible displacement of the Palestinian population. In addition to security considerations, this policy is based on the Zionist doctrine which considers the Holy Land to be the exclusive land of the Jewish people. Drawing its legitimacy from the religious myth of the "Promised Land", the Hebrew state adopted as its symbol the Star of David: a six-pointed star, made up of two intersecting triangles: the point of one points upwards, the sky; the point of the other downwards, the land. The new state enjoyed the sympathy and support of the West. The transformation of European anti-Semitism into support for the Jewish state is explained by the horror of the Nazi genocide during World War II. It gave rise to a bad conscience and a feeling of guilt within Christian Europe, which Israel benefited from for a long time and which it did not fail to exploit. The Holocaust occupies a central place in the collective memory and the Western imagination. The slightest questioning of the extent of the genocide, or even the slightest criticism of the State of Israel, risks being branded as anti-Semitism. The media spread the image of a heroic and democratic pioneer country surrounded by backward and aggressive Arab neighbors. While Israel's founding fathers established the principle of secular citizenship, the law takes religion into account by facilitating the fulfillment of rituals such as the Sabbath or those related to education.

The Law of Return of 1950 granted Israeli nationality to any Jew who requested it. Beyond the human and political dimension, the goal of the Israeli authorities was above all to strengthen the demographic weight of a Jewish population that was much smaller than the neighboring Arab populations. In November 1949, an airlift allowed the repatriation of 50,000 Yemeni Jews to Israel. A few months later, 130,000 Iraqi Jews and 250,000 other Jews from all over the world arrived in Israel. Mostly European, i.e. Ashkenazi, immigration (aliyah) was to involve Sephardic Jews from Arab countries on a massive scale in the 1950s and 1960s. These "mizrahims" (the name given to Oriental Jews in Israel) were, however, discriminated against. To this day, there is still a significant gap between the Mizrahim and the Ashkenazim, in almost all areas: education, salaries, employment, representation, living areas, etc. And the place of religion in politics has been affirmed since the birth of the country, mainly through the religious parties that have become unavoidable in elections. In *How the Jewish people was invented*,[4] Shlomo Sand defends the idea that the construction of the State of Israel was based on a mythical founding narrative, making the Jewish populations a people, united by the same origin and possessing a common national history, going back to the land of Israel. Sand denies the reality of this common origin, emphasizing the importance of conversions in the constitution of populations of the Jewish faith. On the other hand, for him, until the advent of Zionism, these populations defined themselves only through their common religious affiliation and therefore did not perceive themselves as a people.

As for the newly independent Arab countries, they had just suffered the first of a series of bitter failures, not only military but political, in the face of Israel. Outclassed in terms of technology, leadership and modernism, they had only one weapon: the veto. The armistice agreements with Israel signed by the four neighboring states (Egypt, Jordan, Syria, Lebanon) put the region in an unstable situation of neither war nor peace. In contrast to their diplomatic clumsiness and their inability to realistically take into account the balance of power and the international context of the time, the Israeli government made the United States its main ally from 1967 onwards. Strengthened by this support, Israel refused to make any concessions on the territorial level or on the question of refugees. For its leaders, only the maintenance of the faits accomplis of 1948-1949 and absolute military superiority would ensure the security of the Jewish state. Any Arab attack will be followed by crushing Israeli reprisals, since, according to them, "the Arabs know only force". The latter, for their part, reject the argument of the martyrdom of the Jewish people during the Nazi era. "For them, this is a crime of Christian Europe in which they had no part. If the Jews have the right to demand reparation, it is unjust to offer them an Arab land as compensation. They analyze the Zionist enterprise as purely colonial. Nor do they remember the UN vote of 1947, arguing that at that time the UN was an instrument of the great powers and that the colonized countries were not yet represented there. This argument forms the basis of the Arab attitude of refusal[5] . Each side relies on a resolution of equivalent value adopted by the UN General Assembly a year apart. Israel uses Resolution 181 of November 1947, which divides Palestine into a Jewish state and an Arab state, as the basis of its legitimacy. As for the Arabs, they have placed themselves in an untenable position. They are now demanding that the UN implement the partition plan that they rejected when it was adopted. And they demand the implementation of Resolution 194, adopted on 11 December 1948. This demand for the implementation of the "right of return" of Palestinian refugees is posed by the Arabs as an imperative condition for the recognition of Israel. In reality, the Palestinian question in the Arab world is no longer a question of national liberation where the Arabs and the Jewish immigrant population form a single country. It is no longer a question of an Arab-Muslim refusal of the Jewish presence in Palestine. This refusal, labelled as anti-Semitism, will not fail to be exploited by the Israelis and to serve the Arab cause in the eyes of Western opinion. And when Egypt, Jordan and the PLO finally resolved, in the 1970s, to recognize Israel, it was at the cost of a de facto renunciation of the right of return. That said, the Arab world and, more generally, the Muslim world did not experience the anti-Judaism of Christian Europe and then racist anti-Semitism. The idea of an alleged "world Jewish conspiracy" only spread with the development of Jewish colonization in Palestine and the creation of the State of Israel.

1 *Les Arabes ou l'histoire à contre-sens*, Charles Rizk, Albin Michel, 1992, p.220

2 ibid. p.64

3 *Les Arabes, leur destin et le nôtre*, Jean-Pierre Filiu, La Découverte 2017, p. 83

4 *Comment le peuple juif fut inventé*, Shlomo Sand, Fayard 2008,

5 *Les Arabes, leur destin et le nôtre*, op. cit. p. 89

Chapter 4. The birth of modern Turkey and Iran

Led by two strong men with quite similar visions, Turkey and Iran had a very different destiny than the Arab countries in the interwar period. In Turkey, Mustapha Kemal succeeded in liberating his country from foreign occupation to build an independent nation state. The transformation of Turkey into a nation-state, however, led to population exchanges, ethnic cleansing and the virtual disappearance of its remaining Christian population, prepared by the Armenian genocide of 1915. "The empire and the nation-state are in fact based on different logics. Empires have a universal vocation, whereas the ambition of nation-states is to bring together a homogeneous population united by the same identity and the same desire to live together within borders that are as natural as possible. The old multi-ethnic and multi-confessional empire of the Osmanlis had, as best it could, allowed different peoples to coexist in an astonishing mix and a cosmopolitanism of which Constantinople and Salonika gave the example[1] . Like Kemalist Turkey, the other non-Arab state in the region, Iran, also embarked on a policy of modernization and secularization from above under the rule of Reza shah Pahlevi. And both countries have sought to rebuild their national identities on the glorification of their pre-Islamic past.

The Turkish War of Independence

Turkey did not escape the aims of European imperialism determined to complete the dismemberment of the Ottoman Empire by cutting up the very heart of Anatolia. After the armistice of Moudros, defeated and ruined, the Ottoman Empire must accept the occupation of Istanbul and the Straits by British and French troops. In February 1919, General Franchet d'Esperay, mounted on a white horse, made a triumphal entry into the capital at the head of his troops where he was acclaimed by the Christians. A demonstration which stimulated the hostility of the Turkish population. In addition to the zones of influence granted to Paris, London and Rome, the French occupied Cilicia and the Italians Antalya and its region. The Greeks dreamed of a "Greater Greece" encompassing Thrace, Eastern Greece, Western Anatolia and, why not, Istanbul where a quarter of a million Greeks lived. In 1919, they occupied Izmir and its region. Considered a slap in the face, this occupation, accompanied by abuse and humiliation of the Muslim population, deeply outraged Turkish public opinion and rekindled the spirit of resistance. The Armenians and Kurds, strengthened by the promises of the Allies, demanded their own states in north-eastern and south-eastern Anatolia. As for the Turks, they were supposed to be satisfied with central Anatolia. Responsible for this disaster and for the massacre of Armenians in 1915, for which they feared paying the price, the main Young Turk leaders fled, leaving a weak and powerless government that gave in to all the Allies' demands. While Mustapha Kemal fought against the occupier, the Istanbul government bowed to the Entente's diktat by signing the ignominious Treaty of Sevres in August 1920, which was practically a death sentence for

Turkey. It provides that the entire eastern part of the country will be erected into a Republic of Armenia, that an autonomous Kurdish territory will include the lands southeast of the Euphrates. It confirms the attribution of zones of influence to Italy over the Antalya region and southwestern Anatolia and to France over Cilicia where an Armenian home would be established under its protection. It also stipulated that Izmir and Gallipoli would return to Greece. Istanbul would be demilitarized and the Straits placed under international control. Additional constraints were superimposed on the old capitulations. All that remains for Turkey, in the center of Anatolia, is a territory of 120,000 km^2 of arid land deprived of any possibility of economic development. Foreign commissions had to administer the country's finances, which had to be allocated in priority to the costs of the occupation. Finally, the army was to be replaced by a limited gendarmerie. In Paris, several voices were raised against the harshness of the conditions imposed on Turkey.

As was to be expected, this treaty arouses immense indignation in the country. In Anatolia, General Mustapha Kemal, hero of the Dardanelles, raised the banner of revolt. He calls the Turks to the defense of the fatherland against three enemies: the Greeks in the west, the Armenians in the east and the French in the south. He whom his comrades nicknamed "the Grey Wolf" obtained the support of several military leaders, including General Kazim Karabekir, commander of the main Turkish army based in Eastern Anatolia, and Ali Fuad, commander of the 20^e corps based in Ankara. In July 1919, in Erzurum, he convened a congress of delegates who, opposing all foreign occupation, declared themselves ready to take charge of the affairs of the state if the sultan's government proved incapable of safeguarding the independence of the nation and its integrity. A second congress held in Sivas a month later resulted in a national pact affirming the rights of the Turkish nation clearly distinct from the Ottoman Empire and elected Mustapha Kemal to head a representative committee. He had to fight against both internal and external enemies. The Sultan-Caliph argued that he had spiritual authority to present the nationalists as "enemies of God. Approved by the Allies, his Minister of War raised an "army of the Caliph" and the *Sheikh ul Islam* issued a fatwa asking religious leaders to urge the population to take up arms. In Anatolia, the masses fanaticized by the local clergy rose up at the call of the commander of the believers. But the troops who remained faithful to Mustapha Kemal eventually won.

At the end of 1919, the Ottoman government organized general elections in the hope of cutting the ground from under Kemal's feet. But the new House was mostly composed of nationalists opposed to the Entente's takeover of Turkey. Kemal was elected deputy for Erzurum. The British finally decided to strike a blow. Their troops occupied Istanbul on March 16, 1920 and arrested one hundred and fifty deputies in the middle of a session, many of whom were in favour of Mustapha Kemal. Those who managed to escape, joined by deputies from new elections, held a "Great National Assembly" in Ankara on April 23, 1920. It decided to hold executive and legislative powers until the sultan, declared a "prisoner of the Allies," was fit to resume his duties. Executive power was delegated to the Council of Ministers, whose president was also the president of the Assembly. Mustapha Kemal was unanimously elected to this post. Although he was personally in favour of the establishment of a republic, he decided not to rush things, knowing that most of the deputies were loyal to the sultan.

Now embodying the rejection of the diktat imposed on the Turkish nation, Kemal then launched the war of independence. Despite his opposition to Bolshevik ideology, he decided to seek the support of the Republic of Soviets, which was fighting against the same adversaries as Turkey and which wanted neither a Greek empire, a client of the English, nor a "Great Armenia". In September 1920 the Kemalist troops entered the Republic of Armenia and crushed its small army. The Armenian government was forced to renounce the application of the Treaty of Sevres, and the country, reduced to its Transcaucasian part, became a Soviet Republic. The Kurds, who had initially sided with the nationalist troops in the "war of independence" against the Armenians and Greeks, rose up in 1921. He dislodged the Italians from the regions of Konya and Antalya and fought hard against the French army in Cilicia and in the territories of south-eastern Anatolia. While these battles were taking place, the Hellenic forces occupied Eastern Thrace and Bursa. During this time, the English, in a hurry to demobilize their army, left Anatolia. Lacking troops, they allowed the Greeks to occupy also a vast region around Izmir and their forces advanced to seventy-five kilometers from Ankara. In spite of their numerical superiority, they did not manage to break the resistance of the Turkish army. Both adversaries are exhausted and the front stabilizes for a year.

In October 1921, France signed a secret treaty with the government of Ankara in which it renounced the Treaty of Sevres and undertook to evacuate Cilicia and the territories of south-eastern Anatolia. Of capital importance, it induces its recognition of the government of Ankara and the promise of independence of the Turkish nation. By a protocol annexed to the agreement regulating this evacuation, French arms and ammunition were supplied to the Kemalists. During this time the Greek troops remained inactive. They were stretched out on a front of almost four hundred and fifty kilometers extending from the Sea of Marmara to the valley of the Meander. Confident in victory, Mustapha Kemal issued a brief proclamation to his troops on 26 August 1922: "Soldiers! Forward! Objective the Mediterranean[2] ! Massing all his forces in front of the Greeks, he launched a victorious offensive against them. Cut in two sections, the Hellenic forces flee towards Izmir... On September 10th, Izmir is liberated, while the population and the Greek soldiers in rout are evacuated by the ships of the allies. Shortly afterwards the Greeks were forced to evacuate Eastern Thrace.

Awarded the title of Ghazi following these victories in the war of liberation, Mustapha Kemal hung the name of Atatürk (the father of the Turks). He made vote in an authoritarian way, on November 1er 1922, a law abolishing the sultanate and expelling Mehmed VI from the country. But he did not yet dare to abolish the caliphate, while reducing it to a purely religious power that would be devolved to a member of the Osmanli house chosen by the Assembly. The choice fell on Abdlülmecid, a prince respected by all and cousin of the deposed sultan. The cancellation of the temporal attributions of the head of Islam, reduced to a purely spiritual function, led to an outcry from Turkish clerics and the rest of the Muslim world, who considered it a heresy. The abolition of the sultanate also upset those among the nationalist deputies who believed that the raison d'être of the war of independence was the liberation of the sultan and the fight against the occupying forces, not the transformation of the country. Even his most devoted comrades-in-arms did not want to touch the monarchical institution which was, in their eyes, sacred. The struggle of Ghazi with the representatives of Islam and the nostalgics of the imperial system will be tumultuous. As the dictatorial powers granted to Mustapha Kemal by the law of 5 August 1921 expired, the opposition would now like to establish more democratic standards. Determined to keep all the powers and to have the Republic proclaimed at last, the latter precipitated the resignation of the government and decided to proceed to new elections from which he hoped to obtain a new House more docile to his wishes. On October 29, 1923, the Turkish Republic, with Ankara as its capital, was proclaimed. Mustapha Kemal became its first president. At the same time head of state and of the army, president of the Council, of the Assembly and of the People's Party, invested with the totality of the executive power, he established an authoritarian, dictatorial regime. He entrusted Ismet Inonü (named after his victory over the Greeks) with the task of forming a ministerial cabinet. He obtained at the treaty of Lausanne (1923) the evacuation of Istanbul by the Allies and the recognition of Turkish sovereignty over the whole of Anatolia and Eastern Thrace. The humiliation of the Treaty of Sevres was erased, the creation of a Kurdistan forgotten, as well as the internationalization of the Straits.

Kemalist Turkey

Atatürk's creation of modern Turkey marked a sharp break with its imperial, multi-ethnic and multicultural past. Rejecting Ottomanism, Panturanism and pan-Islamism, Kemalism is based on an ultranationalism fuelled by the traumatic memory of the dismemberment of the Ottoman Empire. This logic of ethnic homogenization led to the almost total expulsion of non-Muslim minorities from the country, transforming Turkey into a 99% Muslim state. About three million Orthodox inhabitants of Turkey had to join Greece, while half a million Muslim inhabitants of Greece had to join Turkey. And as a result of the struggle led by the Kemalist forces against the French occupation of Cilicia and southern Anatolia, almost the entire Christian population, Armenian or Arab, of these regions was forced to evacuate.

Kemalism is based on a radical secularism and violently anti-Islamic. Islam is for Kemal a foreign graft, thanks to which the Arab clergy, defeated by the Turkish warriors, has slyly put its hand on the soul of the victors. He also had a particular hatred for the imams and sheikhs who propagated a religion that he believed to be contrary to the values of a virile people. Rejecting all that was oriental in its culture, Kemalist Turkey wants to create a new Turkish man stripped of all external signs reminding his kinship with Islam. Considering that Islam was responsible for the delay of Turkey on the West, Mustapha Kemal, undertakes to change its identity by imposing a forced westernization and by repressing any religious demonstration and of its Ottoman past. Contrary to other Muslim reformers, there could be, according to him, no modernization without Westernization. "To the question asked for centuries to the Muslim world: why are Muslims behind the West? He brings a radical answer: According to him the education and the morals that the men of religion inculcate to the people led the Muslim world to obscurantism and submission. Their influence must therefore be stopped. Religion as a political force is completely dismantled[3] .

In March 1924 the Turkish Parliament abolished the caliphate. A law decreed the total secularization of the state. In 1926, the religious courts were replaced by civil courts. Ottoman legislation, which continued to govern certain aspects of civil life, was replaced by the Swiss Civil Code. A Commercial Code and a Penal Code inspired by European models were introduced. With all these measures the reign of the Sharia is definitively closed. Finally the Sufi brotherhoods are forbidden and will live from now on in clandestinity. But Turkish secularism has nothing to do with the French law of separation of Church and State. The creation in 1924 of the *Diyanet* (Directorate of Religious Affairs) corresponds in fact to a domestication of Islam by the state. This secularism has another paradoxical aspect. The Kemalist power expels religion from public life only after having set it up as an essential component of Turkish identity. Mustapha Kemal himself agrees with this inextricable link between nation and religion, saying: "since we are all Turks, and therefore all Muslims, we can and must all be secular"[4] .

In April 1924, the new Republic adopted a constitution. It stipulated that Islam was the religion of the state, which was not abolished until 1928. In 1925, a Kurdish revolt led by Sheikh Said, hereditary leader of the Nakshibendye dervish brotherhood, was ruthlessly crushed. Fanatical Muslims, the Kurds, who still live as in the Middle Ages, did not accept the abolition of the caliphate and the secularization of the state. Their crushing was intended to dissuade them from considering themselves as a distinct ethnic group within the Republic. "Before the Turkish majority, the other elements have no other influence. We must absolutely Turkify all the inhabitants of our country. We are going to annihilate those who oppose Turkisation[5] ". says Ismet Inonü. But the Kurds are not the only targets of this exacerbated nationalism. All non-Turkish speaking minorities are persecuted. Drastic measures penalizing the oral use of languages other than Turkish are taken. Greeks, Armenians, Arabs and Jews were episodically described as enemies from within. The Greek-speaking Muslims expelled from Greece were also seen as a threat and everything was done to stifle this foreign language. Opposition to the new Turkey is numerous. Some were non-violent, such as that of the *Nursis* (partisans of the light), founded in 1930 by Sheikh Said Nursi, who advocated a new Muslim faith and established itself as a real parallel society that the government did not manage to dismantle. The most serious violent opposition occurred when insurgents belonging to one of the millenarian currents that agitated Anatolia slit the throat of an officer, the incarnation of the hated Republic, to the applause of the crowd. The government took advantage of this to pass a law to restore public order, eliminate all opposition and establish a single party regime: the Republican People's Party or CHP (*Cumhuriyet Halk Partisi*).

After the political reforms that marked the transition from a cosmopolitan empire to a nation-state, a series of radical cultural and social reforms were initiated. In 1925, Mustapha Kemal decided that the change of mentality of the Turkish people must begin with a change of dress and campaigned in favour of the hat, used in so-called "civilized" countries. He banned the old Ottoman headgear with a law called "hat law". This law was followed by the emancipation of women, which remains undoubtedly one of the greatest achievements of Kemalism, the prohibition of the veil, the replacement of the Arabic alphabet by the Latin alphabet, the closure of religious schools and the multiplication of secular schools.

On June 15, 1926, an attempted assassination attempt in Izmir offered Mustapha Kemal a new opportunity to consolidate his power and, above all, to settle his accounts with the former unionists. The trial of the conspirators was staged in a manner inspired by the great Soviet trials, with the accused, deprived of a lawyer, having to prove their innocence themselves. The military, including General Kazim Karabekir, were sentenced to degradation and national indignity for life. The court, in view of their services and in order not to upset the army, released them. The civilian defendants were not as lucky. All of them, some of whom were not accomplices in the attack, but refused to convert to Kemalism, were eliminated (nineteen death sentences).

In 1927, Mustapha Kemal delivered a speech (*Nutuk*) hailed as "The Holy Book of the Turks" in which he set out the six ideological foundations (called "arrows") of Kemalism, which are Turkish ultranationalism, republicanism, secularism, statism (or dirigisme), progressivism and populism. The first of his six arrows is nationalism, but unlike Panturanism, Kemalist nationalism is limited to the defence of Turkey, and it is only on the cultural level that it claims a pre-Ottoman heritage. "It is to this nationalism that we must link the reform of the language, the replacement of Arabic and Persian words by ancient Asian words, but also the rewriting of history and the will to reappropriate Anatolia by adopting Hittite or Sumerian ancestors[6] . "The Ottoman centuries were reduced to a long parenthesis marked by corruption. The true Turkish history included only two phases interspersed by the "Ottoman decline": *the Ergenekon,* the golden age of Turkishness, and the Republic announcing a radiant future[7] ". This famous speech was followed by a brief pluralist experiment that lasted only three months. The cult of the personality of Ghazi proclaimed "Eternal Leader" develops.

In 1929, a new Kurdish revolt was violently repressed. Ignored in their cultural and linguistic specificities, the Kurds will not stop rebelling. After the extermination of the Armenians during the Great War, followed by the annihilation of their last strongholds in eastern Anatolia, the expulsion of the Greeks and the crushing of Kurdish attempts at autonomy, Turkey finally became the homogeneous nation of which Mustapha Kemal dreamed. In 1933 the call to prayer is turquified despite the vehement opposition of religious circles. In 1937, the "six arrows" were incorporated into the Constitution, a date that also marked the transition from a single-party regime to a party-state.

In foreign policy, Atatürk wanted to be realistic. He had no territorial ambitions at the expense of Turkey's neighbors, with the exception of Alexandrette, which he hoped to take back. In 1925, the League of Nations confirmed the possession of the Mosul vilayet by Iraq, which had been placed under British mandate. In compensation, Turkey obtained 10% of the royalties on the extraction of oil from the region for twenty-five years. Turkey is totally disinterested in its Arab neighbors and Ankara turns its back on the Arab and Muslim world for fifty years. The Turks believe that the Arabs betrayed them by siding with the British in the First World War. When Atatürk died in 1938, Ismet Inonü, hero of the war of independence and Prime Minister from 1925 to 1937, succeeded him. He continued the Ghazi's anti-religious policy until 1945. At the outbreak of the Second World War, he adopted a policy of neutrality between the Axis and the Allies, while leaning towards Germany because of the enmity between Turkey and the USSR. But seven months after the defeat of the Wehrmacht at Stalingrad, Turkey broke off diplomatic relations with Nazi Germany in August 1943. And in February 1945, it declared war on Germany for the sole purpose of participating in the founding of the UN.

Persia becomes Iran

Heir to a thousand-year-old civilization, Iran is a mosaic of populations which, alongside an Iranian-speaking majority, includes a large Turkish-speaking minority, as well as Arabs and Kurds who are also present in Turkey, Iraq and Syria. The country experienced a constitutional revolution in 1906.

This followed popular discontent caused by the signature by the Shah of a leonine contract granting the Anglo-Persian Oil Company a 60-year concession for all the country's oil reserves. In 1907, an Anglo-Russian agreement divided the country into two spheres of influence: Russian in the north and British in the south. The First World War saw the influence of the British grow as they became more and more interested in its oil resources. In August 1919, Great Britain recognized Iran's full independence and began to evacuate it. It left it in total decomposition. In 1921, the USSR withdrew from Iran, while the Qadjar dynasty was overthrown by a coup led by a Cossack guard officer, Reza Khan, who seized power in Tehran. Taking the lead of the army, he crushed the Gilan rebellion, a nationalist movement following the constitutionalist revolution which founded the short-lived Socialist Republic of Gilan (1920-1921) with the help of the Soviets. However, the USSR signed a treaty with London in 1921 agreeing to withdraw from Iran, which weakened the Gilan Republic.

After assuming the post of Prime Minister, Reza Khan first considered making Persia a Republic, following the model of Atatürk, but gave up in the face of opposition from the clergy. On 12 December 1925, the Parliament, meeting as the Constituent Assembly, appointed Reza Khan Sardar Sepah as the new Shah of Persia. He was crowned on April 25, 1926 under the name of Reza shah Pahlavi. "Pahlavi is the old term that he exhumes from a distant pre-Islamic past to adorn the dynasty he founds, which denotes his desire to revive those ancient times, beyond all the centuries of Islam, and meets the wish of the modernist fraction of the nation[8] . One of the first acts of the new sovereign is to annex Arabistan located east of the Shatt el Arab to strengthen the Iranian presence on the Gulf. He hastened to Iranize the province and renamed it Khûzistân. He thus opened a long and painful dispute with Iraq which will be quantified, during the eight-year war (1980-1987), in hundreds of thousands of deaths. During the First World War, a group of intellectuals in exile in Berlin, including former leaders of the Constitutionalist Revolution, had founded modern Iranian nationalism, advocating the Westernization of the country and its secularization. Aryanism, the idea of belonging to the Aryan race, was already well established among them. They felt that Islam and its laws had disastrous effects on society and advocated the replacement of Islam with nationalism. Referring to the phrase "the Aryan nation," they dreamed of the resurrection of Iran's glorious past and opposed the decadent Qadjar dynasty. Alongside Aryanism, the other pillar of secular Iranian nationalism was the Persian language (Farsi). Identity-based nationalism was consolidated by Reza shah's modern state-building. Like the secular intellectuals, Reza shah believed that Islam was the main obstacle to the progress and development of society and, like Mustapha Kemal, he tried to build a national identity from above. The Persian language became compulsory in the administration and educational institutions, and in 1923 the use of other languages was banned. The aim was to erase ethnic identities in favor of belonging to the Iranian nation. He undertook in an authoritarian way to modernize Iran at a forced march on the European model. The privileges granted to foreigners were cancelled. Justice, until then controlled by the Shiite clergy, was reformed and a civil code was promulgated. Polygamy was abolished. The wearing of the veil by women was prohibited and men were required to wear "Western" clothes. At the same time, he undertook the development of industry and the construction of a trans-Iranian railroad. In 1935 he officially asked the international community to stop using the term Persia and to use the name Iran to designate his country (which is his name in the local language). Despite the progress he made in the country, his dictatorial style of government and his fight for the modernization of Iran despite the positions of the clergy earned him the resentment of the population.

In 1941, Reza shah declared Iran's neutrality and refused the expulsion of

German nationals, even though the United Kingdom had control of its oil and its territory was of vital importance for the supply of the Soviet Union. British and Soviet forces occupied the country and forced the Shah to abdicate in favor of his son Mohammed Reza Pahlavi. In January 1942, by an agreement with Great Britain and the USSR, in which the United States joined, Iran placed its land and resources at the disposal of the Allies in exchange for the solemn promise that its territory and independence would be preserved and that all occupying forces would be recalled at the end of hostilities. At the end of November 1942, the Tehran conference was held between Roosevelt, Churchill and Stalin, who promised their help in the reconstruction of the country. When the war ended, Iran was threatened with disintegration. On November 13, 1945, with the support of the Soviet Union, Iranian Azerbaijan proclaimed itself a democratic republic, and the Kurds founded a republic in Mahabad. The Iranian army supported by the British entered the secessionist territories. The Iranian-Soviet crisis, the first of the Cold War, ended in December 1946 with the collapse of the republican governments having lost the support of the USSR.

1 *Monotheism, power and war*, Ibrahim Tabet, l'Harmattan, 2017, p. 19

2 *Le loup et je léopard, Mustapha Kemal*, Benoit Méchin, Albin Michel, 154, p. 275.

3 *History of Turkey from Altai to Europe,* Ibrahim Tabet, l'Archipel, 2007, p.313

4 *Histoire de la Turquie contemporaine*, Hamit Bozarslan, La Découverte, 2004, p. 35.

5 ibid. p. 36

6 ibid. p.92

7 ibid. p. 33

8 *History of Iran and Iranians*, Jean-Paul Roux, Fayard 2006, p.424

Chapter 5. Egypt and the shattered dream of Arab unity

"A century for nothing"?

As the evocative title of a recent book, *Un siècle pour rien. Le Moyen-Orient arabe de l'Empire ottoman à l'Empire américain*[1] , the history of the Arab world since the fall of the Ottoman Empire has been a long series of failures and disappointments. The hope for the rebirth of the Arab nation and societies that the *Nahda gave* rise to has come to nothing. This failure is almost as much the responsibility of its secular and modernist component as that of its Islamo-nationalist opponents. The dream of a unitary Arab nation collapsed first when it led, after the First World War, to balkanization within the framework of the mandates, and a second time, in 1970, with the death of Gamal Abdel Nasser, when secular Arab nationalism was supplanted by political Islamism. "Until the emergence of this ideology in the 1980s, the vast majority of Arab states had joined the Non-Aligned Movement in the 1950s and 1960s, whose language was entirely secular and whose agenda was a more just international order.......the decisions of the Movement were never concerned with religious considerations relating to Islam or other religions, much less with conflicts of civilizations or values.[2] "Islamism, which emerged on the ruins of Arab nationalism, perceived the secular model as a danger to the social body and the supposed solidarity of Muslim peoples in the international order. It resulted in a deadly cultural regression while the absence of freedoms made the Arab societies lose the thread of their struggle for emancipation and miss the train of modernity once again. "At the time of independence, after the Second World War, however, the liberals seemed to triumph. Countries such as Egypt and Syria experienced a phase of parliamentary life and partisan pluralism. Parliamentary elections are held regularly, led by political parties with a strong secular bias: the Wafd in Egypt and the two major Syrian parties, the People's Party and the National Bloc. The parties that claim to be Islamic fundamentalists are considered by large sections of the public to be obscurantist[3] . But in Egypt, Iraq and Syria, the *Nahda* elites were removed from power by the social-military regimes that were put in place shortly after independence. "The succession of coups d'état that took place between 1949 and 1970 resulted in the repression of any form of opposition, accompanied by a militarization of political life based on close collaboration between the intelligence services and the single party. This culture of arbitrariness and the trivialization of violence attacked the very root of politics. Everywhere, the great hijacking of Arab independence by military cliques is leading to an absolutely tragic intellectual regression[4] . It is reflected, among other things, in the attachment to a charismatic leader (*zaim) who is* supposed to give the Arabs a sense of dignity and enable them to regain their former greatness. One cannot understand otherwise the popular fervor and the cult of personality attached to dictators like Gamal Abdel Nasser, Saddam Hussein or Hafez el-Assad. "They consolidate their absolute power in a logic that is both patrimonial in terms of monopolizing the country's resources and paternalistic in terms of infantilizing the people, who are called together at regular intervals for confirmation plebiscites[5] .

The pan-Arab secular and socialist nationalism championed by the military regimes reached its peak between 1950 and 1963. However, it was weakened by their rivalries, partly caused by the Cold War. A lasting polarization was established between the regimes allied with the United States and subject to its influence and those whose non-alignment tended to bring them closer to the USSR. The failure of the ephemeral Syrian-Egyptian union shattered the dream of Arab unity, forcing Nasserism and the Ba'ath, whose promoters they were rivals, to fall back, unwillingly, on a nationalism limited to their respective countries. The humiliation of the 1967 Arab defeat by Israel and their poor economic performance discredited them. Since 1949, the military balance of power between the Arab states and the Jewish state has been tilted in favour of the latter. Nothing illustrates this evolution better than the victories of the Tsahal in 1956 and 1967, which were much faster and less costly in terms of losses on the Israeli side than those of 1948-1949. Oil revenues, rather than ensuring the socio-economic, technological and scientific development of Arab societies, have been spent on fabricating religious radicalism claiming to be Islam.

The defeat of 1967 consecrated the general impotence of the Arab world, faced with a country infinitely less populated. For the lucid minds, its military inferiority was due to the cultural, scientific and technological underdevelopment of Arab societies. Whereas for the Islamists, "if the Arabs were defeated by Israel, it was not because of their attachment to the supposedly archaic and retrograde Islamic tradition, but on the contrary because of their abandonment of this tradition for the chimeras of secular nationalism[6] ". In addition to the internal causes of the failures of the Arab states, there were external factors related to the interventions of foreign powers that did not cease with their accession to independence. While these interventions continued to be carried out by London and Paris, they were now mainly in the context of the Cold War, with each of the two superpowers seeking to enlist the various Arab states in its camp. This clientelism was also encouraged by the Arab ruling classes, which themselves sought external protection, whether to maintain their power or to thwart their Arab neighbors' attempts. "This is how the outside uses the inside, but the inside also uses the outside[7] . Leaders like Nasser did struggle to free themselves from the tutelage of "Western imperialism", but it was only to fall into the orbit of Moscow. As a result, the Arab world, which for a time appeared to be the master of its own destiny and an actor in international politics, fell back under foreign domination.

The 1960s were dominated by the opposition between Nasser's pan-Arabism, increasingly dependent on Soviet aid, and the pan-Islamism of King Faysal of Saudi Arabia. The latter was the great organizer of Wahhabi preaching, which he saw as a means of combating Nasserian Arabism. The polarization between Arab nationalism and political Islam degenerated into a veritable "Arab cold war[8] ". In the 1960s, the United States supported this preaching, which was seen as an instrument to combat revolutionary Arabism and communism. A shift occurred in the 1980s. Coinciding with the fall of communism and the Soviet Union, both a model and an ally, it consecrated the failure of unitary Arab nationalism and the social-military regimes in the region. These failures paved the way for political Islamism. The movements claiming to be Islamist occupy the space and hinder the emergence of any other ideology. While most Muslim countries had restricted the application of sharia law to family law, and adopted modern Western-inspired laws for the rest, the Islamists set out to reverse the secular reforms of the past 100 years, including the legal emancipation of women that has been achieved in some countries. Intellectual and cultural life shows the same regression. The Shiite movements are supported by the Iranian mullahs, who in 1979 established the only theocracy in the world. And the Sunni movements are supported by Wahhabi Saudi Arabia and Qatar.

The new international context

Since the end of World War II, Britain and the United States, which have a special relationship, have regarded the Middle East as a priority region for their national interests. "Britain's support for the Lebanese and Syrian independence parties greatly enhanced its prestige in the Arab world. In particular, it made people forget the way in which, as the champion of independence in the French mandates, it had crushed the independence movement in Iraq[9] . In the aftermath of El Alamein, it triumphed not only militarily, but morally, by the idea it had managed to spread in the Arab world that its imperial interests were identified with those of Arab nationalism. This identification was to be taken further when it championed Arab unity by promoting the creation of the Arab League. This policy and its military presence, in Egypt, Aden and the Arab monarchies of the Gulf, strengthened its influence, which was preponderant in the region after the war. But, as early as 1948, this influence was shaken by the collapse of the British mandate in Palestine. And the Arab nationalism that it had itself encouraged finished undermining it. Nevertheless, it tried to make its hegemony over the Arab East last as long as possible.

For their part, "the new global responsibilities of the United States and oil issues had pushed them to take an interest in the Middle East. The real contact dates from 1945 when Roosevelt, on his return from Yalta, spoke with Abdel Aziz Ibn Saud and King Farouk and exchanged correspondence with the heads of the Arab states. The American president pledged not to do anything that would help the Jews against the Arabs[10] . But Truman, who was sincerely moved by the tragic fate of the Jewish people and needed the Jewish vote, adopted a policy increasingly favorable to the Zionists. In July 1945, he asked the British to lift restrictions on Jewish immigration to Palestine. The State Department, for its part, pushed for a conciliatory policy towards the Arab states because of the risks of Soviet expansion in the Middle East. Nevertheless, in the words of Truman to American diplomats, "Arabs don't vote in the United States[11] ". He was the first head of state to recognize the State of Israel, on the very day of its proclamation on May 14, 1948.

In 1951, the Cold War took on a new dimension in the region when Washington and London proposed a common anti-Soviet defense policy to the states of the region and President Truman promised them military and economic aid in case of Soviet aggression. At the beginning, a division of influence was established between London and Washington. Since the meeting between President Roosevelt and King Abdel Aziz ibn Saud in February 1945, the United States had made Saudi Arabia a preserve, agreeing to allow British predominance in Iraq, Iran and the Gulf. The United States also relied on Turkey, which became a member of NATO in 1952. But, heavily involved in East Asia and Europe, they were not prepared to ensure a military presence in the Middle East, which was left to the British. In 1955, they allowed Great Britain to take the initiative of the Baghdad Pact. With this text signed by the United Kingdom, Turkey, Iraq, Iran and Pakistan, the aim was to contain the communist threat: this was the strategy of *containment*. This pact became the cornerstone of Anglo-Saxon policy in the Middle East, although the United States, while associated with it, was not part of it. It was seen as a new manifestation of Western imperialism and aroused the animosity of the Arab peoples, and was violently opposed by Egypt and Syria. Even Jordan, although closely linked to Great Britain, refused to join.

Opposition to this pact opened the door of the Middle East to the USSR. The Cairo-Damascus axis (left-wing republican) opposed the Baghdad-Amman axis (right-wing royalist). In 1955, the purchase of arms by Egypt and Syria for the Eastern camp raised strong feelings in the West and in the region. Saudi Arabia denounced the danger of "atheistic communism". However, if at first the United States relied on its British ally, the Suez crisis in 1956 changed the situation and London would henceforth play the second role. In the context of the Cold War, where the Middle East became one of the main theaters of the American-Soviet confrontation, a new order in which Washington posed as the leader of the "free world" replaced the old order based on European predominance, particularly British. The arrival in power of President Lyndon Johnson at the end of 1963 marked a change in the American policy of neutrality towards the Arab-Israeli conflict. The president had never hidden his sympathies for Israel, which he perceived as a valuable ally in the global anti-communist crusade led by the United States. Israel became the United States' main ally in the Middle East. The country received significant economic and especially military aid. This protection was coupled with a diplomatic component, since the United States systematically used its veto in the United Nations Security Council to prevent any condemnation of the Jewish state. For its part, the USSR, in order to gain a foothold in the region, supported Arab nationalism against the colonial powers. As for the United Kingdom, its failure to enlist other Arab countries, even Jordan, in the Baghdad Pact, followed in 1956 by the Suez affair, and the dismissal in March of the same year by King Hussein of the British commander of the Arab Legion, are signs of the decline of its regional influence.

The oil question

It is impossible to understand power rivalries in the Middle East without taking into account the oil question, which has become a major geopolitical issue since the First World War. Great Britain was the first power to exploit oil in the region, of which Iran remained the only producer until 1927, when oil production in Iraq began. The capital of the company exploiting Iraqi oil (the IPC, *Iraq Petroleum Company*) was divided between Shell (Anglo-Dutch), BP (English), the Compagnie Française des Pétrole and a consortium of five American "majors". The latter then obtained exclusive rights to exploit Saudi oil through Aramco (*Arab American Oil Company*). At the end of the Second World War, the oil resources of the Middle East took on vital strategic and economic importance for both producing and importing countries. Their control will play a very important role in the political crises and conflicts of which the region will be the scene. Europe's energy dependence on the Middle East means that it is highly vulnerable to these crises. The oil market is dominated by the seven sisters (five American, one Anglo-Dutch and one English) and the share of profits received by the producing countries is reduced to a minimum. However, this share tends to be 50% with the appearance of independent oil companies in the Middle East. The *Anglo Iranian Oil Company* refused to apply this new contract model, which led to the nationalization of Iranian oil in 1951. The issue of oil nationalization will thus be an integral part of the struggles for independence of producing countries, both economically and politically. It was followed by the creation of OPEC in 1960, at the initiative of the Shah of Iran. And in 1973, the Arab exporting countries will not hesitate to use the oil weapon as a means of political pressure on the West.

French policy in the Middle East until 1973

For a France that came out of the Second World War very weakened, the colonial empire was the instrument of its maintenance as a great power. This empire is for a large part Muslim. Everything was therefore pushing to spare Muslim interests. After the evacuation of Syria and Lebanon, France tried to maintain a political presence there. A fundamental principle inspired its policy: the attachment to maintaining Syrian independence in the face of the unionist project of the Hashemite States, which would have tipped it into the orbit of the British. In April 1947, a family pact was signed between the kings of Jordan and Iraq, whose objective was the unification of the countries of the Fertile Crescent, of which Syria is a part. In the same year, the Fourth Republic was faced with a difficult choice concerning the plan to divide Palestine between Jews and Arabs. Its status as a "Muslim power" in North Africa led it to spare the interests of the Muslims. But there was a natural sympathy for the Jews, victims of Nazi barbarism. And the great powers, the United States and the Soviet Union, had openly taken sides in favor of Zionism. So, in November 1947, when the partition plan was voted on, it initially opted to abstain. But a call to order from Washington led her to vote in favor.

Unlike Great Britain, which had supported the founding in 1944 of the League of Arab States, which would nevertheless become a forum for nationalist one-upmanship, France developed a hostile attitude to Arab nationalism. And it saw

Egypt as the heart of Arab nationalism, making it responsible for the nationalist movements that shook the protectorates of Morocco and Tunisia and the Algerian uprising. In 1955, France was hostile to the extension of the Baghdad Pact, which it equated with the Fertile Crescent project dear to the Hashemites. It initiated a rapprochement with Egypt, which was short-lived. From 1954, it drew closer to Israel. A very sustained diplomatic and military cooperation was established between Paris and the Hebrew state. Indeed, given the declining French influence with the end of the trusteeship over Lebanon and Syria, the pan-Arab ambitions of Abdel Nasser's Egypt and the competition with the United States and the United Kingdom, it was necessary to rely on a state that would allow it to keep a foot in the region. A strategic alliance was established between the two countries. The Fourth Republic helped build Israel's nuclear arsenal. Shimon Peres, then Israeli Minister of Defense, had his access to the French Ministry of Defense. This alliance was to unravel with the readjustment of French foreign policy decided by General de Gaulle. The fallout from the Algerian war and the Suez expedition in 1956 led to the ruin of French positions in the Arab-Muslim world.

When General de Gaulle returned to office in 1958, he defined an ambitious policy in the Middle East, with the aim of "re-establishing France's position in a region where her business had been at a low ebb since the Algerian crisis and the Suez crisis, whereas she had always been present and active. Nourished by history but also by political and economic realism, Gaulli's vision laid the foundations of France's "Arab policy" which was pursued by most of his successors. While American policy was linked to its strategic alliance with Israel and to a project of hegemonic domination of Arab countries, French policy in the Middle East was based on a balanced position with respect to the Arab-Israeli conflict. "It seeks, within its means, to represent a recourse by counterbalancing Washington's blatant bias in favor of Israel. One cannot understand this policy without taking into account the influence of the major options of the General's foreign policy, which embodies a certain distrust of the United States and a desire for independence based on the search for a third way between the two superpowers[12] . At the end of the Algerian War, the Arab countries that had broken off diplomatic relations with France re-established them between 1962 and 1963. One of the reasons for this was the desire to diversify their partners. Cooperation with France was seen as a way to break the monopoly of the United States (and for some their dependence on the USSR) and to strengthen their ties with Europe. During the Arab-Israeli war of June 1967, General de Gaulle condemned the Israeli aggressor, and denounced the occupation of Arab territories. Before the outbreak of hostilities, he had clearly expressed France's position, namely that "the State which first used weapons would have neither its approval, nor a fortiori its support[13] ". Immediately after the war, French diplomacy clearly proclaimed two fundamental principles: the right of all states in the Middle East, including Israel, to live within secure and recognized borders, and the refusal to endorse all "changes achieved on the ground through military action. During a historic press conference in which he described Israel as a "self-confident and domineering people", de Gaulle reaffirmed that the occupation was illegal, that it would necessarily generate resistance which the occupier described as terrorist, that there could be no solution other than an international one, and finally that Jerusalem should be given international status.

The Pompidou and Giscard d'Estaing presidencies only confirmed this line. It was Georges Pompidou who integrated the Palestinian national fact into the formulation of France's "Arab policy". For him, the Palestinians must be considered as a people deprived of its state, its freedom and its national identity and not as mere refugees. France, which imports 75% of its oil from the Middle East, has an even greater interest in being gentle with Arab countries since the 1973 oil crisis. Giscard d'Estaing authorized the opening of a PLO office in Paris and had the European Community adopt a declaration in favor of the right of the Palestinian people to self-determination. The use by the Arabs of the weapon of oil confirmed in the eyes of the government the need to strengthen Franco-Arab relations in view of France's strong energy dependence.

The establishment of the Free Officers' regime in Egypt

"Egypt, by its demographic weight, its cultural influence and its political will, is one of the essential actors on the political scene of the Arab East. Its revolutionary choice in the early 1950s was imitated or rejected by the other Arab states. His fight for a true independence of his territory and of the whole region, and the personality who led it, Gamal Abdel Nasser, were the political reference in an Arab East, still divided and subject to foreign influences[14] . The years following the end of the Second World War were marked by serious unrest, internal disorders and crises. Demonstrations, strikes and attacks followed one another. The demonstrators demanded the withdrawal of British troops. Great Britain decided to withdraw from the Delta, Cairo and Alexandria, and planned to leave the Canal Zone in 1949. But it wanted to ensure that the Sudanese could choose the future status of their country. To calm the riot, the king called Ismail Sidqi to power in February 1946. He could not prevent demonstrators from ransacking the property of foreigners in Cairo on 21 February, causing many injuries and deaths. On 4 May 1946, the uprisings were renewed in Alexandria. Sidqi resigned in December 1946. On June 19 of the following year, Sudan promulgated a draft constitutional reform that was a first step towards independence. It was practically lost to Egypt. In 1950, following general elections, the Wafd returned to power. In a bid to regain its popularity, it became increasingly anti-British. In the name of neutralism, Egypt opposed in 1951 the joint defence plan by which the United States and Western European countries would extend the NATO Atlantic Pact by forming a chain of alliances on the southern borders of the USSR.

When the Free Officers movement was born, the Egyptian monarchy was discredited by its submission to the British and the humiliating defeat in the

Arab-Israeli war. A wind of revolt blew over Egypt. The Egyptians embarked on a guerrilla war against the British forces that remained in the Canal Zone, despite the Egyptian government's denunciation of the 1936 treaty. The revolt broke out in 1952, after dozens of Egyptian policemen were killed by British artillery in Ismailia. This violence led to riots in Cairo, killing dozens of people. Gamal Abdel Nasser (a colonel at the time) called for an end to British interference in an article published by the weekly *Rose al-Youssef.* But he learned that King Farouk intended to have him and other members of the movement arrested. On July 23, 1952, the Free Officers group overtook him and took power. They put the very popular General Naguib at their head, but the real strongman of the group was Nasser. The aim of the coup was to purge Egypt of Farouk and the corruption of the pashas and to reform it. The monarchy was maintained but King Farouk, who was exiled, had to resign in favor of his son, who was six months old, under the supervision of a regency council. It was not until June 18, 1953 that the Republic was established. The Free Officers had neither a common ideology nor a detailed political program apart from nationalism and a certain solidarity with the peasant masses.

Unlike the Baathists, there was no mention of pan-Arabism or Israel in their first proclamations. A government composed of traditional politicians, headed by Ali Maher, was set up. But the Revolutionary Council, made up of the main Free Officers, held the real power. And in September, Ali Maher resigned and Naguib formed a new government of which he became president. This marked the disappearance of the traditional politicians and the emergence of a new political class. During the first two or three years, the new regime was rather well regarded by the British, the French and the Americans. In January 1943, a new constitution formally established the Republic. Its first president was General Naguib and Gamal Abdel Nasser became President of the Council. The former advocated the establishment of democracy and the return of the army to its barracks, while the latter refused. They also clashed over the Muslim Brotherhood, which Nasser wanted to crush and Naguib to spare. In January 1954, Nasser decided to dissolve the Brotherhood without consulting Naguib. He strengthened his control over the army by having Abd al-Hakim Amer placed at its head and organized demonstrations by his supporters who brandished the slogan: "No parties, no parliament, no elections[15] ". The struggle for influence between them turned to the advantage of Nasser who dismissed Naguib in November 1954 and took power. The fall of Naguib, who was placed under house arrest, led Sudan to give up the idea of merging with Egypt and to move towards total independence. Political parties were dissolved, trade unions were banned, and the new regime took an authoritarian stance, with the secret services (the *moukhabarats*) working to suppress all forms of opposition, which were seen as "imperialist" manipulations.

In order to consolidate his power, he needed the success of prestige that only the evacuation of British troops could provide. On 27 July 1954, a new Anglo-Egyptian agreement was signed, under which Great Britain undertook to evacuate the Suez base within twenty months. The agreement, reached after two years of negotiations, also provided for the independence of Sudan, which until then had been jointly administered by Britain and Egypt. This agreement strengthened Nasser's popularity. On October 26, 1954, in Alexandria, he participated in a celebration of the agreement on the evacuation of British troops. While delivering a speech to tens of thousands of people, he escaped an attack by a member of the Muslim Brotherhood. Without losing his composure, unharmed, he shouted to the crowd: "the life of Egypt does not depend on Gamal's life! It depends on you, on your courage, on the fight that you lead! Fight! And if Gamal dies then, let each of you be a Gamal! A few words that are enough to conquer the hearts of millions of Egyptians[16] . The revenge of the raïs is not made wait. He ordered the arrest of thousands of members of the Brotherhood who were thrown into prisons and concentration camps where mistreatment and torture were part of the daily life of the prisoners.

In June 1956, the Constitution that brought Nasser to the presidency of the Republic was approved by 99.99% of the people. Before aspiring to the leadership of the Arab world, at the beginning his action was located inside Egypt. "It is only afterwards that he elaborates with his friend Haïkal the theory of the three circles: the Egyptian circle, the Arab circle, the Muslim circle[17] . His main goal was to fight against foreign influence in his country and against those in the Arab world whom he considered allies of imperialism. The Palestinian problem and revenge against Israel were not high on his agenda. However, the Israeli attack on Gaza in February 1955 marked a turning point. Some 40 Egyptians were killed and Nasser, for the first time, showed real concern for the Palestinian problem. The new regime applied a socialist economic policy. It nationalized industry, carried out land reform, and implemented major public works projects, notably the Aswan Dam. This economic policy, due in part to the social origin of the officers, who came from peasant families or small civil servants, favored the emergence of a middle class at the expense of the Egyptian or Syrian-Lebanese rich class. Although the country is benefiting economically from certain modernization efforts, poverty remains striking. Corruption and clientelism are not diminishing.

In his negotiations with London, Nasser had benefited from the support of Washington, which wanted to enlist Egypt in the anti-Soviet camp. But two developments would henceforth give Nasserism an anti-Western orientation: the Baghdad Pact, to which it was radically opposed, and the new policy of the Soviet Union towards the Third World, whose importance it realized in its confrontation with NATO. It is from this period that the Soviet commitment in the Arab world dates. The Bandoeng conference in Indonesia, held in April 1955 and attended for the first time by some thirty African and Asian countries, really propelled Nasser onto the international stage. The final resolution of the conference denounced colonization and called for a peaceful struggle for independence. It advocated non-alignment in relation to the two blocs that were facing each other, led by the United States and the USSR, then in the midst of the Cold War. After his participation in the conference, the Egyptian president became one of the main leaders of the Third World, and thus of the fight against Western imperialism. No Arab leader had his charisma. A good orator, eloquent, he galvanized the crowds by expressing himself mostly in Egyptian popular language. The violent anti-colonialist propaganda of the "Voice of the Arabs" broadcast from Cairo was heard throughout the Arab world. The Algerian war having just begun, this worried France to the utmost, especially since it was noticed in Paris that a Maghreb office was operating in Cairo which maintained contacts with Algerian independence fighters. French hostility towards Egypt strengthened Franco-Israeli military cooperation. Israel acquired Mirage fighter planes manufactured by Dassault.

Non-alignment will not resist the imperative of the fight against imperialism. Although he was one of the promoters of the non-aligned movement, Nasser drew closer to the USSR, on which he relied to modernize his army. In September 1955, an arms agreement was concluded. As the Soviet Union was in a phase of détente with the West, Czechoslovakia was to make the deliveries. The Western monopoly of armaments no longer exists. The Soviet Union became a major partner on the regional scene where the arms race began in the context of the confrontation between East and West. The Arab states will find in the USSR the arms supplier that will enable them to challenge the Israeli faits accomplis. In the long term, Moscow was preparing the possibility of having naval facilities for its fleet, intended to compensate for the American naval presence in the Mediterranean. The Soviets also provided Egypt with arms for the Algerian National Liberation Front (FLN), then in the midst of a war of independence against France. Nasser saw in Ben Bella, a refugee in Cairo, the man who would wrest independence from Algeria and make it Egypt's ally. This support for the Algerian nationalists threatened French interests, while the United Kingdom was irritated by Nasser's opposition to the Baghdad Pact, which, according to London, "endangered Arab unity. All this contributed to making him the bête noire of the West and put him in the line of fire of the United States. The Czech arms deal heightened Israel's fears. Ben Gurion and Dayan prepared a plan to invade the Sinai and waited for the right opportunity to unleash it.

The evolution of the Arab-Israeli conflict

At the end of the first Arab-Israeli war, Israel was firmly established. But the Israeli population considered its territory extremely vulnerable and regarded the Arab population within it as a foreign body. The Arab states were waging an economic, diplomatic and propaganda war against the new nation. The plight of the Palestinian refugees, which reflected the humiliation suffered by the Arab world, fuelled its animosity towards Israel. The years 1951-1953 were marked by infiltrations and reprisals along the Israeli-Jordanian border. The most deadly was carried out in October 1953 by Unit 101, a commando unit led by Major Ariel Sharon against the border village of Qibya. After this raid, a wave of international condemnation swept over the Jewish state. Although the Egyptian regime that emerged from the 1952 revolution did not adopt extremist positions on the Palestinian question during the first months of its existence, the dispute with Israel became more acute. Israel's conquest of the Negev in 1949 and the establishment of Israeli access to the Red Sea on the Gulf of Aqaba were considered illegal by Egypt. It did not win its case at the UN on this issue, but prohibited the passage of Israeli ships through the Suez Canal. Incidents in the Gaza Strip sector degenerated into small-scale fighting. In Israel, Ben Gurion, a supporter of a policy of force towards the Arabs, temporarily withdrew from political life in November 1953. His replacement at the head of the government, Moshe Sharett, while not a dove, adopted a less aggressive foreign policy, which helped avoid an armed confrontation between the two countries. However, in July 1954, the Israeli secret service tried to foment a plot in Egypt, which was foiled. This crisis led to the recall in February 1955 of Ben Gourion who took over the Ministry of Defence. He wanted to seize the Gaza Strip and provoke a civil war in Lebanon to install a Christian-dominated government, but Sharett opposed his plans. One of the factors in the Arab-Israeli conflict is the possession of water. Negotiations on the sharing of the waters of the Jordan River and its tributaries between Israel and Jordan were not successful. From 1951, clashes took place between Israeli and Syrian forces over a disputed area of the border along Lake Tiberias and Lake Huleh. From the 1960s, the Syrian army bombed Israeli positions from the Golan Heights. Israel retaliated with retaliatory operations. Israeli officials believe that the 1949 armistice lines are far from secure and that tensions with its Arab neighbors may provide opportunities to realize their territorial ambitions. The United States having refused to deliver arms to Israel, a first major arms contract was signed with France for hundreds of tanks and several dozen Mystères IV fighters. Between June and October 1956, French and Israeli leaders secretly agreed on a joint action aimed at overthrowing Nasser and destroying the Egyptian armed forces,

The Suez crisis (1956) and its consequences

For years, Nasser had been negotiating with the West to finance the Aswan High Dam, which was vital for the Egyptian economy. But for the American Secretary of State, Foster Dulles, a visceral anti-communist, the purchase of arms from the East by Egypt was a crime. In July 1956, he announced the refusal of the United States to finance the construction of the Aswan High Dam, "given the catastrophic state of the Egyptian economy. President Nasser was informed of this refusal in a press release. The affront, which is added to the draconian conditions of the World Bank, recalling the hours of British tutelage, is that of too much. Following this humiliating refusal, the Egyptian raïs made a real gamble. On July 26, 1956, in Alexandria, he announced, in a memorable speech, before an incredulous crowd, the nationalization of the Universal Suez Canal Company. Poverty is not a disgrace, it is the exploitation of peoples that is," he declared. We will take back all our rights, because this canal is the property of Egypt [...] no sovereignty will exist in Egypt, except that of the people of Egypt, a single people who are advancing in the path of construction and industrialization, in a block against all aggressors and imperialist plots [....] With the 100 million dollars in profits that the company makes every year, we will build the Aswan Dam" announced the head of state to the cheering crowd with a great burst of laughter[18] . Broadcast live by the "Voice of the Arabs", the impact of the speech was immense in the country and in the Arab world. For Egypt, this nationalization had two objectives: to finance the construction of the high dam thanks to the income from the canal; and to get rid of the Western presence on its territory, which was using the internationalization of the canal zone as a pretext to constitute a state within a state. But, in addition to seriously damaging their economic interests, it represents an unacceptable political challenge for London and Paris. Also, in a neo-colonialist vision that took no account of the changes that had occurred on the international scene, Guy Mollet and Anthony Eden opted for a military response. The French press raged against Nasser, compared to Hitler, and warned the Western democracies against a new Munich. At the end of September, a resolution of the UN General Assembly accepted most of Egypt's demands. But the aim of Franco-British policy was to get rid of the Nasserite regime. For his part, Ben-Gurion had long been ready for a preventive war against Egypt. Eden insisted that there should be no sign of collaboration with the Israelis.

According to a plan drawn up jointly by Paris, London and Tel Aviv, the Israelis were supposed to attack first; then the British and the French would intervene under the pretext of protecting the canal against the belligerents. French fighter planes were sent to Israel to help protect its airspace. The Israeli troops, commanded by Moshe Dayan, launched their attack on October 29, 1956, occupied Sinai in a few days, and stopped on September 3 15 kilometers from the canal zone, which was then occupied by Franco-British forces (November 5-6). However, they had to quickly put an end to the operation under pressure from the USSR and the United States. Eisenhower did not forgive Eden and Mollet for having deceived him. Moscow sent an ultimatum to France, England and Israel in which they alluded to the possible use of nuclear weapons. The UN demanded the departure of British and French forces and the evacuation of Sinai and the Gaza Strip by Israel. Speculation was unleashed against the pound sterling. Eden was the first to give in, ordering a ceasefire to the great displeasure of the French. After having considered delaying the acceptance of the cease-fire in order to extend their occupation to Suez, they in turn bowed down. Only France supported the Hebrew state, but its position became increasingly weak in the face of the United States. The French-English troops remained on the canal until December 22, 1956. Finally Israel had to evacuate the Gaza Strip and the Sinai. UN forces took up positions in Egyptian territory along the border with Israel.

If Nasser lost on the military front, he won masterfully on the political front. The Franco-Anglo-Israeli attack on Egypt aroused a wave of popular indignation in the Arab world and provoked a series of diplomatic ruptures with France and Great Britain. The Suez crisis symbolized the loss of influence and, above all, a real transfer of power from the traditional colonial powers in the region (France and Great Britain) to the new world powers (United States and USSR). It pushed the United States to redefine its policy in the Middle East. In March 1957, the Eisenhower Doctrine considered that the American presence in this strategic region with its immense oil resources was absolutely essential to fill any power vacuum caused by the disappearance of the role of France and Great Britain and to counter the rise in prestige of the USSR. It authorizes the President of the United States, in addition to economic aid, "to use, if he deems it necessary, armed force to assist any nation or group of nations requesting such assistance against armed aggression from any country controlled by international communism[19] . This interventionist policy was manifested as early as 1958 when American and British troops were sent to Lebanon and Jordan to protect the pro-Western regimes in those two countries.

After the disastrous Suez campaign, which highlighted its retreat, France lost any possible political role in the Middle East, which it would not regain until 1959 with the return of General de Gaulle to power. The Suez crisis did not interrupt cooperation between France and Israel, and Paris very discreetly provided the Hebrew state with the technology to build a nuclear reactor in Dimona, which was considered to be a nuclear weapons manufacturing site. However, the Israeli government has always refused to comment on the subject, sticking to a policy of deliberate ambiguity. In parallel with the construction of the Dimona site, in which French engineers participated, Israeli scientists are suspected of having been invited to participate in French nuclear tests in the Algerian desert. The political outcome of the war was marked by a radicalization of the Arab-Israeli conflict. If the Arab states had not previously pursued the destruction of the Jewish state as a matter of policy, this was the case after 1956. Although border incidents remained very limited between 1957 and 1962, Israeli collusion with the former imperialist powers and the attack on Egypt only increased the political desire for belligerence in the Arab world. The Arab leaders had one more "proof" that Israel was the imperialists' staging ground in the Middle East .[20]

Nasserite Egypt

The role of the United States in the Suez affair did not win Nasserism. Israeli aggression against Egypt forced it to accept Soviet offers of alliance and to move further and further away from the West. Egypt's diplomatic success over Western imperialism made Gamal Abdel Nasser the undisputed leader of pan-Arabism and revived dreams of Arab unification. His speeches galvanized crowds throughout the Arab world. "Prussia of the Arab world, Nasser's Egypt wanted to be the pole of attraction around which it hoped, from 1956 onwards, that the Arab world would cluster[21] . The "Voice of the Arabs", which appealed to the "Arab people" over the heads of governments, raised the hope of a united Arab nation, regenerated by a genuine social revolution and recovering under energetic leadership its rightful place in the world. In February 1958, when Nasser's prestige was at its zenith, he accepted the proposal of the Syrian Baath to merge Syria and Egypt. He was welcomed in Damascus by a frenzied crowd. Following the merger, joyful demonstrations broke out in many Arab countries. In Iraq, demonstrators demanded the end of the Baghdad Pact, the resignation of Nuri Said and the integration of the country into this new Republic. In Lebanon, more than 300,000 supporters of pan-Arabism travelled to Damascus to celebrate the proclamation of the UAR, undermining the country's communal balance. In South Yemen, a unionist revolt broke out, but was severely repressed by the British. North Yemen considered joining the union for a while before changing its mind. In the end, attempts to extend the union to other Arab countries failed, weakening the enterprise. Despite the overthrow of the monarchy, Iraq quickly emerged as Nasser's rival in the Arab world. Soon the realities of unity proved to be different from the Syrian dream. The reality of local power in Damascus was in Egyptian hands. In the two "provinces" of the United Arab Republic (UAR), the repression led by the special services (*moukhabarates*) fell on the opponents. The Muslim Brotherhood is the target of a particular relentlessness. This short-lived union was dissolved at the initiative of the Syrian Baathists who revolted in September 1961 against the Egyptian rule over the country.

Beyond the Syrians' rejection of Egyptian domination, the failure of the RAU underlines the limits of Egypt's power, which suffers from a double economic and geopolitical fragility. At the same time as its ambitions were growing, its socialist economic policy and its galloping demography condemned it to poverty. This disparity between its political objectives and its underdevelopment accounts to a large extent for the failure of the Nasserite experiment. The second weakness of nasserism is geopolitical, and results from the fact that the configuration and balance of the Arab world evolved, starting in the 1960s, to the detriment of Egypt. With their accession to independence, the Maghreb countries took on a new dimension, while the oil power of the Gulf States, particularly Saudi Arabia, emerged. This change diminished Egypt's relative weight in the Arab world, where it could no longer claim to exercise its former domination.

Nasser responded to the breakdown of the union with Syria by radicalizing his domestic policy. He attributed the failure of the RAU to reactionary forces. Accentuating the socialist orientation of the regime, he accelerated the process of nationalization of the economy. "After the Western economic interests, it was the turn of the Syrian-Lebanese bourgeoisie established in Egypt for a long time. The foreign colonies, like those of the Greeks, were dispossessed of their property and had to emigrate. Egypt closed itself to foreigners after having been for a century a country of international economy. The Egyptian capitalism knows the same fate. [...] This orientation marks the completion of a secular movement of reconquest of Egypt by the Egyptians[22] . A new single party replaced the National Union of 1958: the Arab Socialist Union (ASU) chaired by Ali Sabri. This new orientation of the regime was the subject of the "National Action Charter" of May 1962, which was supposed to found a "scientific Arab socialism". If Nasserism took a socialist orientation in Egypt, on the inter-Arab level, it was led to oppose Baathism even more vigorously while fighting against conservative forces. He attributed the collapse of the coup d'état in Syria in 1961 that ended the UAR to the support he received from King Faysal of Saudi Arabia. Following the overthrow of the Yemeni monarchy in September 1962, Nasser decided to send an expeditionary force to help the new Republic. His intervention in the civil war was countered by Saudi support for his royalist opponents. The stalemate of the Egyptian army in Yemen weakened Egypt's power. On December 23, 1963, he proposed the first summit of all Arab heads of state in Cairo to reaffirm his leadership. The most important decision of the summit was the creation of a representative body for the Palestinians: the Palestine Liberation Organization (PLO). As part of his overall strategy, the Egyptian president sought to use the Palestinians to achieve his own goals. Nasser accuses the Muslim Brotherhood of having revived their secret organization. Since its dissolution in 1954. Since then, their ideology had become more radical. Freed at the end of 1964 after ten years of captivity and ill-treatment, their theorist, Sayyid Qotb, called for a fight against Egyptian society, described as *jahili* (ignoring God), in order to establish an Islamic society. His book *Milestones on the Trail* is a real condemnation of the Nasserite regime and especially the basis for an Islamic revolution. He was hanged after a summary trial in August 1966. Under the presidency of Lyndon Johnson, the United States became more clearly committed to Israel, which led Egypt in February 1966 to sign an agreement strengthening its military cooperation with Moscow.

The Six-Day War (June 1967)

From 1964 onwards, tensions relating to disagreements over the use of the waters of the Jordan between Israel and Syria had not ceased to rise. Border incidents, in which several Syrian Mig 21 fighters were shot down, increased. In early 1967, Israel's threats against Syria intensified. In May the Soviet Union informed Egypt and Syria of the existence of Israeli military concentrations on the Syrian border. Nasser was forced to go to Syria's aid. In May, he recklessly embarked on the fatal spiral that would lead to the Six Day War. On May 15 he ordered the Egyptian army to take up positions in the Sinai and asked the UN to withdraw its forces from the international border with Israel. Perhaps he thought that the United States would intervene at the last moment to negotiate a political settlement, but he was sadly mistaken. His decision to remilitarize the Sinai and block Israeli ships from entering the Straits of Tiran was a casus belli for Israel. King Hussein of Jordan came to Cairo to sign a defence agreement comparable to the one already binding Egypt and Syria. He even entrusted the command of the Jordanian army to an Egyptian general. On June 4, Iraq joined the pact with Egypt. In reality, Egypt, whose army was partly immobilized in Yemen, did not have the means to wage war. Nasser thought that Israel would not attack and he counted on American mediation to negotiate from a position of strength. France, which was still the main external supporter of the Hebrew state, tried to dissuade it from attacking and decided to impose an arms embargo on the Middle East, where it was its only client. The consequence of this decision was to make the United States the preferred supplier of arms to Israel. In Israel, the Prime Minister, Levi Eshkol, was accused of indecision by the Chief of Staff of the Israeli Defense Forces (IDF), Yitzhak Rabin, and the Commander of the Air Force, Ezer Weizman. He was forced to accept the formation of a government of national unity where Moshe Dayan became Minister of Defense. Believing that it was too dangerous to wait for the Arab offensive, he favored a preventive attack.

On 5 June, Israel, determined to break the Arab encirclement, took the initiative in hostilities by concentrating its efforts on the Egyptian front. The armies involved had no common ground. The Egyptian army was poorly trained and weakly mechanized. Because of its politicization, many of the higher echelons of command were occupied by incompetent officers. Its air force was inefficient and its radar system was unable to detect low-level flights. Extremely well trained and prepared for this operation, Israeli airmen destroyed most of the Egyptian air force in a surprise attack. The Egyptian military authorities covered up the disaster. The Syrian air force and the small Jordanian air force suffered the same fate. With complete control of the air, the Israeli army launched a ground offensive against Egyptian forces in Sinai on the 6th. Three armoured columns supported by the air force, overturning their defensive positions, rushed towards the Suez Canal and the southern tip of Sinai (Sharm el-Sheikh). During the first day, the fighting was very violent and the Egyptian army managed to hold out. But on the 7th, the Egyptian army retreated in disorder, and the Israelis reached the canal on the 8th. Although Israel informed King Hussein that it had no intention of attacking Jordan, the latter, deceived by false claims of Egyptian success, decided to go to war. On the Jordanian front, where ground engagements began on the 6th, the Jordanian army, deprived of air support, was forced, despite fierce resistance, to withdraw from the West Bank to defend the Transjordan. The Israelis seized East Jerusalem on the 7th and reached the Jordan River on the 8th. Defense Minister Moshe Dayan was initially opposed to the plan to attack Syria, for fear of direct Soviet intervention. But, Igal Allon, obtained the decision by stressing the need to defend the Galilee against Syrian bombing. The conquest of the Golan Heights began on the 9th and ended on June 10. Damascus is only 45 km away. In two days of fighting, the geostrategic situation that had prevailed for two decades was exactly reversed to the detriment of Syria. The Egyptian, Syrian and Jordanian armies were crushed in just 6 days of lightning war. Having seized the Golan Heights, Israel accepted the ceasefire. Nasser accused the United States of direct involvement in the Israeli offensive, triggering an outbreak of anti-American violence throughout the Arab world.

The Six Day War (5-10 June 1967) changed the geopolitical situation in the Middle East. Israel had tripled its territory, Egypt lost the Sinai and the Gaza Strip, Syria the Golan Heights and Jordan the West Bank and East Jerusalem.

On June 27, the Arab part of the city was annexed to Jewish Jerusalem, which was not recognized by the United Nations. "On the strength of its crushing victory, Israel is seeking a global settlement of the Arab-Israeli conflict on the basis of the recognition of all the facts accomplished since 1948. All that Israel is implicitly proposing is a pure and simple capitulation of the Arabs in exchange for the conditional return of a fraction of the occupied territories[23] . In the Arab world, the Egyptian and Syrian debacles significantly undermine the "progressive" camp and strengthen the conservative one. The Soviet Union broke off diplomatic relations with the Hebrew state, condemned the Israeli aggression and called for the immediate withdrawal of Israeli forces from the occupied territories. France condemned Israel for having attacked first, and urged the Arab states to accept Israel's right to exist and Israel to withdraw from the occupied territories. For the Americans, the responsibility for the war was due to the closure of the Gulf of Aqaba by Nasser. The United States accepted the principle of an Israeli withdrawal but within the framework of a global settlement ensuring a lasting peace. On November 22, 1967, the UN Security Council adopted Resolution 242, which called for an Israeli withdrawal from the territories occupied during the recent conflict and a settlement of the refugee problem. But the United States declared that it would not pressure Israel to withdraw without a comprehensive settlement. Egypt, Jordan and Lebanon accepted the resolution, while Syria and the

Palestinians refuse it. "The main reason for the failure of the Arab armies on the battlefield was the cultural and technological gap between the competing societies, which resulted in huge discrepancies in levels of organization and national mobilization. Other factors also played a decisive role: a glaring difference in the quality of armaments (the Israelis had much more sophisticated weapons than the Arabs), a gap between the military competence of the two sides, and incomparable degrees of political and military unity[24] . While the Arabs will prove incapable of developing a weapons industry, Israel will manufacture and export state-of-the-art weapons systems. Not to mention the fact that the Hebrew state has a nuclear capability born of its cooperation with France at the end of the Fourth Republic and the beginning of the Fifth. Israel's possession of atomic potential places de facto Arab-Israeli negotiations under the unequal ratio of the Israeli atomic threat.

From 1967 to the death of Nasser

Egypt's defeat was not only due to its military weakness but also to its economic, social and political fragility. It had been preceded by the setbacks inflicted on it by Nasser's Arab adversaries: the anti-Nasserite regime of Kassem in power in Baghdad and above all King Faysal of Saudi Arabia. Following the catastrophic defeat by Israel, Nasser announced his resignation, but eventually acceded to the street demonstrations, imploring him to remain in power. He dismissed the main Egyptian generals, including Marshal Amer, who committed suicide. Their elimination and the formation of a new team of officers willing to prepare the revenge allows him to take control of the army and make it more professional. A summit of Arab heads of state meeting in Khartoum, Sudan, decided that the rich oil-producing countries would pay the three countries of the so-called "confrontation" (Egypt, Syria, Jordan) substantial subsidies to rebuild their destroyed military potential. This summit can be called the summit of the three "no's": "no to negotiation, no to surrender, no to peace". Struck to death in Egypt itself, the Egyptian army evacuated Yemen in August 1967, as Nasser had pledged during the Arab summit in Khartoum. As Israel refused to accept the principle of withdrawal from all the occupied territories, the mission of Ambassador Jarring, appointed as mediator under the terms of Resolution 242 by the UN Secretary General, ended in 1968 in failure.

Aware that Egypt was in a weak position vis-à-vis Israel, the raïs practiced a political and military escalation aimed at internationalizing the conflict. With Nasser's acquiescence, the Soviets considerably increased their military presence in Egypt, which could only worry the Americans. The Egyptian president sought both to have a card vis-à-vis Washington and to make Egyptian territory safe from possible Israeli attacks. The new American president, Richard Nixon, was convinced at the beginning of the need for a global settlement that would avoid the domination of the Soviet Union over the region. But for Henry Kissinger, the absence of a solution would force the Arabs to renounce Soviet protection and resort to American intervention to break the current deadlock.

Nasser understood that only military pressure on Israel and indirectly on the great powers would make it possible to obtain an Israeli withdrawal. From March 1969, he began a war of attrition on the Suez Canal. Based on intensive bombardments by Egyptian artillery on the line of fortified Israeli positions on the canal (the Bar Lev line), this war was also punctuated by commando raids beyond the canal. In retaliation, the Israeli air force, to whom the Americans had just delivered Phantom fighter-bombers, launched a campaign of aerial bombardments aimed at the Egyptian batteries and the towns located along the canal. In a second phase the Israelis carried out aerial bombardments in depth, reaching the Nile valley and the surroundings of Cairo. This escalation pushed Nasser to ask for a direct Soviet intervention. 15,000 Soviet troops were sent to Egypt, to whom Moscow delivered new Sam 2 and Sam 3 anti-aircraft missiles to protect its airspace. There were even air battles between Israeli planes and "Egyptian" fighters piloted by Soviets. Neither the Soviets nor the Israelis wanted total war. The Americans intervened to prevent the situation from escalating further. In August 1970, a peace plan proposed by U.S. Secretary of State Rogers was accepted by Egypt, Jordan and Israel. A cease-fire was established between the two belligerents in the war of attrition that caused as many casualties as the 1967 war. On the other hand, the Rogers plan was rejected by the Palestinians. In September 1970, violent fighting between the Palestinian resistance and the Jordanian army broke out (Black September) and Nasser imposed his mediation. But he died on 28 September, the day after a small Arab summit he had convened in Cairo for this purpose. He was then an exhausted and bruised man, whose prestige had been definitively damaged. And the last three years of his presidency had reflected Egypt's loss of influence in the Arab world. The disaster of 1967 decapitated the Arab nationalist movement and favoured the Islamist current by bringing down Nasser. While the Palestinian organization tried to take advantage of the vacuum created to take away the role he had played. Nasser's funeral, which took place on 28 September 1970, was attended by millions of grieving Egyptians. However, this tremendous crowd demonstration marked the end of an era; that of the Arab revolutions confiscated by regimes infinitely more repressive than those they had replaced. As for the masses, they will only play a role on the stage of History in 2011, during a certain "Arab Spring".

1 *Un siècle pour rien. The Arab Middle East from the Ottoman Empire to the American Empire,* Ghassan Tuéni, Gérard Khoury, Jean Lacouture, Albin Michel, Dar el-Nahar 2002

2 *The new question of the East*, Georges Corm, La Découverte, 2017, p.116

3 *Pour une lecture profane des conflits*, Georges Corm, La Découverte. 2012, p. 191

4 *Les Arabes, leur destin et le nôtre,* Jean-Pierre Filiu, La Découverte, 2015, p.123

5 ibid.

6 *Les Arabes ou l'histoire à contresens*, Charles Rizk, Albin Michel 1992, p.183

7 *The new question of the Orient* op. cit. p. 88

8 The expression is by historian Malcon H. Kerr in his book *The Arab Cold war, Gamal Abdel-Nasser and his rivals,* 1958-1970, Oxford University Press, N.Y. 1965 s

9 *Les Arabes ou l'histoire à contresens.* op. cit. p. 37

10 *Le grand jeu, Orient-arabe et rivalités internationales*, Henry Laurens, Armand Colin 1991, p.63

11 ibid. p. 67

12 *France in Lebanon and the Middle East,* Ibrahim Tabet, Phoenician Review, 2011

13 *Le Général de Gaulle et le Monde arabe*, Proceedings of the colloquium organized by the Paris-Sorbonne University of Abu Dhabi, Dar el-Nahar, 2009, p. 22

14 *Le grand jeu*, op.cit. p. 9

15 *The Arabs, their destiny and ours,* op.cit. p.103

16 *The Egyptian Eagle*, *Nasser*, Gilbert Sinoué Taillandier, 2015

17 *Un siècle pour rien,* op. cit.

18 *Suez*, Marc Ferro, éditions Complexe, Brussels, 1982, p.120

19 *Le grand jeu,* op. cit. p. 151

20 *Victimes, histoire revisitée du conflit arabo-sioniste*, Benny Morris, éditions Complexe, 199 p. 330

21 *Les Arabes ou l'histoire à contresens, op. cit.*

22 *Le grand jeu,* op.cit. p.186

23 ibid. p. 213

24 *Victims,* op.cit. p. 741

Chapter 6. Other Arab countries (1945-1970)

Lebanon from independence to 1975

The country's accession to independence in 1943 was facilitated by the conclusion of a national pact between the President of the Maronite Republic, Bechara el Khoury, and the Sunni Prime Minister, Riyad el Solh. It was the result of a compromise between the Muslims, who finally accepted it as their definitive homeland, and the Christians, who in return recognized its Arab face and renounced French protection. The only Arab country to have a truly pluralist political system reflecting the pluralism of its society, Lebanon is an example of a state resulting from the association of minorities and where the very notion of a majority is non-existent. But some, like Georges Naccache, founder of the French-speaking daily "l'Orient", think that the problem is not solved. In a famous article, he wrote premonitory on March 10, 1949: "the famous pact of November 1943, which is the fundamental pact of independence, carries within it the contradictions that make any government impossible. Neither the West nor Arabization: it is on a double refusal that Christianity and Islam have concluded their alliance. What kind of unity can be derived from such a formula? A state is not the sum of two impotencies and two negations will never make a nation[1] ". In 1950, the customs union with Syria established by the mandate was broken. It was dictated by the dirigiste orientation of the Syrian economy while Lebanon opted for an ultraliberal economic policy.

After the war, Lebanon experienced a period of unprecedented prosperity. The Arab revolutions: Syria (1949 to 1960), Egypt (1952) and Iraq (1958), which adopted regimes of economic dirigisme, gave Beirut a sort of monopoly of regional economic liberalism. Until 1975, Lebanon lived its golden age. The Lebanese model was an exception in its Arab environment and appeared to be an undeniable success. The "laissez-faire" approach could have been a sustainable solution had it not been for Lebanon's internal contradictions and the regional context. The war in Palestine had a serious impact on the country with the influx of some 150,000 refugees in 1948-1949, the majority of whom were Muslims, who brought the seeds of future conflicts, both social and political. Thereafter, each Arab-Israeli war was accompanied by a new stream of refugees, reaching a figure of half a million in the 1980s. This growth worried the Christians who feared a reversal of the confessional balance, especially since the Muslims saw in the Palestinian militias that were beginning to

to organize an appreciable reinforcement. In 1949, a coup d'état by the PPS (Syrian People's Party) advocating union with Syria was foiled, and its leader Antoun Saadé was executed. In retaliation, Riyad el-Solh was assassinated by his supporters. The nepotism, clientelism and corruption of the regime provoked a general strike which forced President Bechara el-Khoury to resign in 1952. Camille Chamoun was elected president on 23 September in an atmosphere of almost general optimism. During his term of office (1952-1958) the economy experienced a remarkable boom. It is from this period that the nickname of "Switzerland of the Middle East" given to Lebanon dates. The Suez crisis and the Israeli-French-English aggression against Egypt provoked a new split between the pro-Western camp and the pro-Arab camp. Lebanon refrained from breaking off its diplomatic relations with France and Great Britain. In France, "the political wisdom of Lebanon" was praised, and according to an article in "Le Monde", it appeared to be "the last remaining French influence in the Middle East[2] ". In 1957 the Lebanese government decided to adhere to the "Eisenhower Doctrine" promising American military and economic assistance to the "free countries" of the Middle East that would accept to counter the Soviet penetration.

The national pact was shaken for the first time when President Chamoun's pro-Western policy provoked a confessional insurrection in May 1958. The merger of Egypt and Syria into a "United Arab Republic" (UAR) further widened the gap between the Sunnis, who were attracted by the triumphant Arabism represented by Nasserism, and the Maronites, who saw it as a threat to the independence of Lebanon. Chamoun complained to the UN about the real interference of the RAU in supporting the insurgents and asked for the application of the Eisenhower doctrine. The American president hesitated to intervene. But on July 14, the pro-Western Hashemite monarchy was overthrown. To protect the pro-Western regimes in Lebanon and Jordan, 5,000 Marines from the US 6th Fleet landed in Lebanon on the 15th and British soldiers were sent to Jordan on the 17th. General Fouad Chehab, who had preserved the neutrality of the army during the conflict, succeeded Camille Chamoun as President of the Republic. His election, made possible by an agreement between Abel Nasser and the United States, represented a new compromise. Wisely, he maintained a middle ground between the two blocs in the quarrel between Arab political regimes. He undertook administrative and economic reforms, aiming to mitigate the strong social and regional inequalities. An IRFED study on the needs and possibilities of development in Lebanon led to the first five-year plan of integrated and harmonized development of the country (1964-1968). Finally, neglecting the politicians and the clientelist circuits, he called upon technocrats to modernize the country. His work, although promising, was unfinished and quickly called into question. For Nadine Picaudou, "The chehabism represents the missed opportunity of a real national integration around a strong power that is neither the instrument of the dominant oligarchy, nor a simple union of community interests[3] . Traditional politicians, aggrieved by certain reforms, accused the Second Office of preventing the normal functioning of democracy. If the mandate of President Camille Chamoun was characterized by the erasure of French influence to the benefit of American influence, those of General Fouad Chéhab and Charles Hélou, which coincided with the return of Charles de Gaulle to power in France (1958-1969), were to see a revitalization of relations between France and Lebanon. Charles Hélou, elected in 1964, was the continuator of the policy of the Chehabists. The Shiite community woke up under the impulse of Imam Moussa Sadr. He founded the Movement of the Disinherited, from which the political organization Amal emerged, allowing an affirmation of the Shiite social claim which, until then, had only been able to express itself through the left-wing parties. The latter have as their leader Kamal Joumblatt who allies himself with the Palestinians.

The 1967 Arab-Israeli war widened the gap between the two wings of the country. It gave a new impetus to the Palestinian resistance, which seemed an attractive alternative to the inefficiency of the Arab governments. In December 1968, a Palestinian attack against Israel from Lebanese territory provoked an Israeli raid on Beirut airport which destroyed eight civilian planes of the MEA company. The reaction of the Sunni street was violent, demanding the resignation of the government and arms to fight the Zionist enemy. Furious, President de Gaulle decided in January 1969 to apply a total embargo on arms deliveries to Israel, including spare parts. For him, Israel, under the guise of punishing Lebanon for the aid it was giving to the Palestinian resistance, wanted in reality to force it to distance itself from the Arab world, at the risk of breaking its national unity. In October 1969, the Lebanese army tried unsuccessfully to take control of the camps held by the armed Palestinian groups. This clash led to the resignation of the President of the Council, Rachid Karamé. The ministerial crisis, which lasted nine months, revealed once again the depth of the confessional divide between the Muslim camp in favour of the Council President and the Christian camp in favour of the President of the Republic. It ended with the intervention of President Nasser and the signing of the Cairo Agreement by General Emile Boustany, Commander-in-Chief of the Lebanese Army, and Yasser Arafat, leader of the Palestine Liberation Organization (PLO). Establishing the freedom of movement of the Palestinian resistance on the Lebanese territory, its consequences proved disastrous for the country which thereby abdicated its sovereignty. Faced with this situation, Christian self-defense militias began to form. The most powerful was the Phalanges (Kataëb). In August 1970, a coalition of the three largest Christian parties, the Kataeb, the National Liberal Party (NLP) and the National Bloc, allowed the election of Sleiman Frangié to the presidency of the Republic. After the PLO's power was broken in Jordan in 1970 during the "Black September", where it had tried to take power, it strengthened its presence in Lebanon. The escalation of PLO terrorist attacks against Israel was matched by a parallel increase in Israeli reprisals against southern Lebanon. Israel's strategy, by making the Palestinian presence intolerable, aimed to destabilize the Lebanese state in order to force it to fight the resistance. From 1973 it became clear that the Palestinian armed presence represented a mortal danger of destabilization of the country. The Lebanese army, paralysed by the differences undermining political power, was unable to oppose it, so the Christian Phalangists and the Palestinian federates took up arms. This was the case on April 13, 1975, which marked the beginning of the Lebanon war, in which all the major political forces in the Middle East were involved: The Arab states, the PLO and Israel as well as France and the superpowers. It would last fifteen years, causing the ruin and the break-up of the country, a frightening number of victims and the collapse of the Lebanese state.

Jordan

After the annexation of the West Bank and East Jerusalem, Palestinians form the majority of Jordan's population and some of them are granted Jordanian nationality. But their loyalty to their new homeland was far from assured. In July 1951, King Abdullah, accused of having "sold Palestine", was assassinated. His son Talal succeeded him but the new king was deposed by parliament after only one year of rule. Abdullah's grandson, Hussein, nicknamed the "little king", was 16 years old when he took the throne in August 1952. Pending his majority, a regency council was established. He came to power in a difficult political context. Although he could count on the loyalty of the Bedouin population, the undeclared British tutelage, particularly over the Jordanian army, increasingly irritated the Palestinian population of the country. Syria and Egypt accused him of being "an agent of imperialism. The Nasserite radio propaganda of the "Voice of the Arabs" broadcasting from Cairo raged against him and called for his overthrow. And he escaped various assassination attempts, probably fomented by the Egyptian and Syrian secret services. Despite its links with Britain, Jordan did not join the Baghdad Pact in 1955. After the Suez crisis in 1956, Hussein was forced to distance himself from the British and accept the formation of an Arab nationalist government. In March 1956, yielding to pressure, he dismissed General John Bagot Glubb (Glubb pasha) as commander-in-chief of the Jordanian army. But the creation of the RAU in 1958 increased his isolation and, since the overthrow of the monarchy in Iraq in July of the same year, he was the only Hashemite ruler still in power. Saudi Arabia, forgetting the quarrels that had so long opposed the two ruling families, now actively supports Jordan. The two kingdoms, which opposed the Nasserist current, supported the coup in Syria that put an end to the UAR. This alliance between the two kingdoms is reinforced by the fact that the Muslim Brotherhood is well established in both Aman and Riyadh, where thousands of Islamists, survivors of the repression in Egypt and Syria, have found refuge.

In 1964, Hussein dealt with the newly formed PLO, but when it sought to control the West Bank, he banned the organization from the country. However, on the eve of the Six Day War in 1967, Hussein concluded a military alliance with Nasser that proved disastrous for the kingdom. Although Israel informed him that it had no intention of attacking Jordan, he did not want to appear to be a traitor to the Arab cause and decided to enter the war. The king had obviously been lured into aggression by inaccurate and misleading information. It seems that he was persuaded to act by false Egyptian reports of initial victories, and losses in the Israeli air force. When the fate of the Egyptian army was sealed, the Israeli army's defensive approach was replaced by an offensive perspective. On June 7, the Israelis conquered the old city of Jerusalem and seized the Temple Mount and the Wailing Wall. The conquest of Nablus and other West Bank cities, including Nablus, the largest of them, was completed on the 8th. The defeat of the Jordanian army caused it to lose the West Bank and East Jerusalem. On June 27, the Arab part of the city was annexed and integrated into Jewish Jerusalem, which was not recognized by the United Nations. The kingdom welcomed 300,000 Palestinians who fled the fighting. Unable to stir up an anti-Israeli uprising inside the occupied territories, the Palestinians hoped to infiltrate their commandos from Jordan, to whom they made pay the price of their powerlessness against Israel. The Israeli army responded with incursions into Jordanian territory, as in the battle of Karame in 1968, when the Jordanian army supported the Fatah federates. All PLO organizations, including Fatah, wanted to impose their influence in Jordan, with the PFLP and DFLP even favouring a confrontation with the Jordanian throne. Faced with the destabilization caused by the Palestinian movements and the attempted putsch against the Hashemite government, the latter launched a crackdown on them and drove the armed groups out of the country (Black September 1970). King Hussein, who had legal sovereignty over the West Bank, launched a project in 1972 to federate the two sides of the Jordan River. But in 1974, he renounced all claims to the West Bank, reconciled with the PLO and recognized it as the sole legitimate representative of the Palestinian people.

The Syria of repeated coups

Syria is a mosaic of populations that includes, alongside the Sunni majority, Alawite, Christian, Armenian, Kurdish, Druze and Shia minorities. But, unlike Lebanon with its plural identity, it wants to be resolutely Arab. It even considers itself to be, before Egypt, the spearhead of Arab nationalism after having been "the beating heart of Arabism" at the end of the Ottoman era. Her Umayyad past, her conviction that Palestine was part, along with Lebanon, Transjordan and the Sandjak of Alexandria, of the Great Natural Syria or "Bilad al-Sham", explains her resentment towards the "eternal plot of imperialism". It accuses the latter, after having reduced it to its current size (185,000 km2 against 300,000 km2) of having weakened it to prevent it from playing its essential role as a unifying pole of the Arabs and of having tried to break it up. Not to mention that, when the mandate was established in 1920, the French authorities favored the Christian, Alawite and Druze minorities to the detriment of the Sunni majority. It was by formally renouncing Lebanon that the Syrian nationalists of the National Bloc obtained independence in 1943. The new generation found the compromises made by the Sunni bourgeoisie that came to power at the proclamation of independence unacceptable. They opposed the Syrian homeland to the Arab homeland and their ideology was the basis of the Ba'ath ("resurrection"). This was created in 1943 by Michel Aflak and Salah Bitar. A secular Arabist and socialist movement, it aims to re-found Arab society and culture, and its ultimate goal is the total merger of the Arab states into a single entity. It is led by a national command for the entire Arab world and regional commands for each country. Established since the 1930s in Syria and Lebanon, the Syrian People's Party (SPP) combines a unitary aspiration with an uncompromising secularism. Rejecting both Arabism and confessionalism, it advocates vast social reforms in a unitary "Greater Syria" including Lebanon and Palestine. Founded in 1945 by Akram Hourani, the Arab Socialist Party supported the struggle of the poor peasants and became a real local power in the Hama region. It was the first to try to infiltrate the army. Finally, there is also a Syrian Communist Party led by Khaled Bekdache. These formations were at the origin of the series of military coups that followed one another from 1949 onwards. The last one in 1963 allowed the Baath Party to take power.

Posing as the fiercest opponent of Israel, Syria participated in the first Arab-Israeli war of 1948. But the disappointment of the Syrians following the defeat of the Arab armies by the new Hebrew state was immense. The regime of the notables who had neglected the army after independence paid the price. The discontent of the latter led, in March 1949, to the coup d'état of Colonel Husni Zaïm against the National Bloc party and President Choukri Kouatly. "The coup may have been bloodless, but it was the first time an Arab army had seized power directly - previous interventions by the Iraqi military had never challenged the constitutional monarchy in Baghdad[4] . Establishing a military dictatorship in Damascus, Zaim implemented modernizing reforms and adopted a pro-Western policy. After encouraging him, he handed over to the Lebanese government the leader of the PPS, Antoun Saadé, who had fled to Syria after his failed coup in Lebanon. He was in power for only 134 days and was assassinated by an officer belonging to the PPS. There were two other military coups during the year. The first was led by a pro-Iraqi general, Sami Hinnaoui, suspected of being manipulated by the British. Everything seemed to be moving towards a union with Iraq, but the Ba'ath and Akram Hourani, who was very influential in the army, were opposed to it, and he remained in power for only a few months. The second putsch was that of Adib Chichakli, who had a different scope and remained in power for four years. He established a military dictatorship, dissolved the political parties, abolished all forms of political confessionalism, strengthened the public sector in the economy and dealt a heavy blow to the economic and political power of the big notables. In July 1953, feeling the need to adorn himself with legitimacy, Chichakli was "elected" president of Syria with 99.7% of the votes. During this period, Syria, plagued by chronic instability, always suspected Lebanon of harboring regional or international plots against it. It also had to guard against Hashemite ambitions that did not abandon their Fertile Crescent project. Shishakli, increasingly isolated, was eliminated without bloodshed in 1954 and took refuge in Lebanon and then in France. During the Zaïm era, in 1949, and the Chichakli era, from December 1949 to 1954, Syria rejected any alliance with Great Britain, which was close to the Hashemite kingdoms of Iraq and Transjordan. On the other hand, France was in a better position. It maintained a certain influence through economic and military relations and, to a lesser extent, cultural relations, which it kept until 1954. The Syrian army was equipped with French weapons and France continued to sell arms to Damascus. However, the fall of Shishakli marked a clear cooling of Franco-Syrian relations for a long time. The Franco-Israeli rapprochement and the beginning of the war in Algeria provoked the divorce between Syria and France.

After five years of dictatorship, elections were held to restore democracy. The 1954 elections marked the electoral success of the independents at the expense of the People's Party, which supported a union of the Fertile Crescent, and the National Party, as well as the rise of the Baath. The latter, with which the Arab Socialist Party founded by Akram Hourani had merged in 1952, became increasingly influential. After the signing of the Baghdad Pact in 1955, which it denounced vigorously, Syria distanced itself from the Western camp and, under the government of Khaled el-Azm, nicknamed the "Red Billionaire", adopted a neutral stance that leaned more and more towards Moscow. Shukri Kouatly, deposed in 1949, became head of state again in 1955. Moving closer to Nasserite Egypt, Damascus violently condemned the Franco-British expedition to Suez in 1956. For Syrian public opinion, Nasser became the Arab hero par excellence. But the Syrian government was unable to cope with the successive crises that hit the country following the adoption of the Eisenhower doctrine by the United States in March 1957. The pro-Western regimes of Turkey, Iraq, Jordan and Lebanon surrounded a completely isolated Syria whose unstable political system was in the eye of Washington's sights. In August 1957, Azm signed an important economic and technical cooperation agreement in Moscow, which also allowed him to finance arms purchases. The American press was threatening: the United States could not tolerate Syria becoming a Soviet satellite. The CIA fomented a plot to overthrow the Syrian government and Damascus expelled three American diplomats. Turkey concentrated troops on the Syrian border. Faced with the external threat represented by the pro-American and Hashemite axis and the internal danger represented by the Communist Party, the Ba'ath Party worked for a union with Nasser's Egypt, which was the undisputed leader of the Arab world and of the resistance against Western imperialism. The main architect of this initiative was Michel Aflak, who managed to convince the President of the Republic, Choukri Kouatly, of the necessity of the union despite his reluctance. Nasser accepted the principle of unity but demanded a highly centralized state. The democratic parenthesis closed when, in February 1958, the Syrians, alienating their sovereignty, voted by referendum for this unity, within a United Arab Republic (UAR) composed of the northern province, Syria, and the southern province, Egypt, with Cairo as its capital. Nasser became the new president, assisted by four vice-presidents: two Egyptians and two Syrians. At first, the union aroused great popular enthusiasm in Syria. The population saw in the union the means to put an end to the permanent instability that Syria had experienced and the Syrian bourgeoisie was in favour of it for economic reasons. Nasser imposed the depoliticization of the Syrian army, and the extension to Syria of the one-party system in force in Egypt. The Ba'ath, which had worked for union, agreed to merge into a single party, but the Communists, whose party had been abolished, appeared to be the most resolute opponents of the RAU. The Egyptians were arrogant and ignorant of the Syrian reality. Nasser appointed General Amer as proconsul in Syria and his control over the country turned into a police dictatorship. Colonel Abdel Hamid Sarraj's special services reign terror. The new state looked more and more like a large Egypt, entirely governed by Cairo. The Baath Party and National Party cadres were quickly removed from power. The authoritarianism of Nasser's regime led to the flight abroad of the great Syrian families, which caused serious economic difficulties. Businesses were overwhelmed by a fussy and corrupt bureaucracy. As early as 1959, Baathist officers opposed to the UAR formed a clandestine military committee. They reproached the civilian leadership of their party for its blindness towards Nasser. Its three main members, Mohammed Omrane, Salah Jédid and Hafez el-Assad, all came from the Alawite minority, which made up a large part of the army's workforce and officers. The union experiment was short-lived, and in September 1961, a coup d'état by the Syrian army put an end to it.

From 1961 to 1963, the political climate was relatively liberal. With Nazem el-Koudsi as President of the Republic, the old People's Party returned to power. But on March 8, 1963, a military coup led by the Military Committee formed in 1959 brought the Ba'ath to power. Salah Bitar was Prime Minister, but the strong man of the new regime was General Hafiz. He declared a state of emergency that was never lifted. Since then, Syria has not had any democratic elections. On July 18, 1963, the Arab Nationalist Movement (ANM), founded by George Habash, and the Nasserites tried to stage a new coup. They were completely eliminated, which confirmed the break with Egypt. In April 1964, the Muslim Brotherhood started riots in Hamah, which were mercilessly repressed. A new military putsch, in February 1966, saw the ousting of the party's historical leaders (Salah Bitar and Michel Aflak) by Salah Jédid and Hafez el-Assad. Omrane, supported by the civilian leaders of the Ba'ath, who had denounced the leftist drift of his comrades in the plot, was imprisoned. The national (pan-Arab) command of the Baath, headed by Aflak, is dissolved and replaced by the Syrian regional command. Aflak and Bitar were forced into exile. The Baathists who took power in Iraq in 1968 adhered to the line advocated by Aflak, which deepened the division between the Syrian and Iraqi branches of the party. The new leaders claimed to be hard-line socialists. A major train of nationalizations was launched, affecting industry, oil, the banking sector and big business. The agrarian reform initiated at the time of the United Arab Republic was radicalized. The nationalizations, the closure of private schools and the arabization of education provoked an exodus among the upper middle class, especially Christians, some of whom settled in Lebanon. Priding itself on being at the forefront of the fight against imperialism and drawing closer to the USSR, Syria became the bête noire of the West. It called for a popular war to liberate Palestine and offered aid to the PLO. The first commando attacks against Israel from Syrian territory put Damascus in the line of fire of Tel Aviv, which blamed it. At the beginning of May 1967, Damascus warned Cairo of concentrations of Israeli troops on its border, which triggered the fatal spiral of hostilities. The Syrian army took part in the 6-day war (June 1967) which led to the loss of the Golan Heights.

This was the beginning of a long political crisis during which Hafez el-Assad did not stop plotting against his opponents as well as his allies and gradually extended his control over the party and the army. Only two obstacles remained on his way to absolute power, Noureddine Atasi and especially Salah Jédid, leaders of the hard wing of the Baath. Minister of Defence, Assad refused to send his squadrons to the rescue of the Palestinians during the events of Black September 1970. He was convinced that Syria had allowed itself to be drawn into the 1967 war by the Palestinians and did not want to repeat the same mistake. The Syrian policy towards the Palestinian resistance is based on supporting the organizations outside and strict control inside. There is no question of any autonomy of action, let alone the use of Syrian territory for operations against Israel without the approval of the Minister of Defense. Having removed his rivals, whom he threw into prison, Assad took power on 13 November 1970. Domestically, the previous regime had frightened a large part of the population by its leftist overbidding. On the regional level, Assad proclaimed his desire to reconcile Syria with the other Arab countries. Finally, at the international level, the Americans could not but be satisfied with the ousting of the regime that had emerged from the February 1966 coup d'état, which was very close to the Soviet bloc for their taste, and thought they could rally Syria to the Arab countries

"Moderates". As for the Soviets, fearing to lose a country in which they had invested heavily, and perhaps also tired of the adventurism of the team in power, they ended up supporting Assad's coup d'état. For form's sake, he organized a plebiscite on March 12, 1971, in which 99.2% of voters said yes to his presidency. The same masquerade was repeated every seven years. The Constitution of March 13, 1972 explicitly gives the Baath Party the function of dominant party, and this, until the referendum of 2012. The Baath Party dominates the Parliament (People's Council). Parliamentarians do not initiate laws, so it serves as a registration chamber. "According to its ideology, Arabness should take precedence over any other affiliation. Communitarianism was not supposed to exist and was considered an obsolete residue of old traditions. But the reality turned out to be quite different. The party actually achieved the opposite of its ideology. While it advocated the abolition of sectarianism and communalism, it based its repressive power on communal loyalty[5] . The main positions in the army and the government were taken by the Alawites, who thus took their revenge after centuries of domination and humiliation by the sunnis. Prior to the Basist coup of 1963, the Sunnis had known nothing but persecution from the dominant Islam, Sunnism. Until the 1960s, Sunni bourgeois still bought young Alawite maids by notarized contract. Hunted and persecuted for centuries, the Alawites had to take refuge in the arid coastal mountains between Lebanon and present-day Turkey, while giving their belief a hermetic and esoteric side. They even allowed themselves lies and dissimulation (*Taqqiya) to* escape their torturers. If they came to power it is because, at the time of independence, the Sunni bourgeoisie of Syria made the mistake of relegating the profession of arms to the poor. The army was therefore mainly made up of minorities, especially Alawites.

The establishment of the Baathist regime in Iraq

At the end of the Second World War, the country was bloodless. During the following years, the resolutely pro-Western policy of the Iraqi government led to riots, which were still violently repressed. In January 1948, the regent negotiated a new alliance treaty with Great Britain in Portsmouth. The British agreed to evacuate their military bases, but the British army could reoccupy them in case of war. But violent demonstrations forced him to renounce this treaty, which would have led to the perpetuation of the British presence. Nuri Said hoped that the Baghdad pact would ensure Iraq's preponderance in the Arab world. Egyptian propaganda presented him as a traitor to the Arab nation. When the Suez Canal crisis broke out in October 1956, and Israel, France and Britain attacked Egypt, Nuri Said was jubilant. But the opinion of the street pushed him to officially condemn the Suez expedition and to take sides with Egypt. The proclamation of the United Arab Republic on February 1, 1958 - linking Egypt and Syria - led to the creation of the Arab Federation of Iraq and Jordan two weeks later.

This merger of the two Hashemite kingdoms came to an end five months later, with a military coup initiated by General Abdel Karim Kassem on 14 July 1958. He overthrew the pro-Western Hashemite monarchy and proclaimed the Republic. King Faisal II, Regent Abdul Ilah and Prime Minister Nuri Said were assassinated. The government remained dominated by Sunni Arabs, and its aim was to maintain Iraqi unity in the name of Arab nationalism, at the cost of terrible repression of the Kurdish and Shiite movements. "Much more than in Syria, terror has become an instrument of government: the physical elimination of opponents is no longer enough, the senior members of the party and the army are regularly purged in order to mark the exclusivity of the leader's power at the cost of eliminating part of the ruling elite[6] . The regime received support from Moscow and from the outset took an anti-Nasserite orientation. The army was divided into two groups, that of Kassem, who, while proclaiming himself an Arab nationalist, wanted to maintain Iraq's independence, and that of Abdel Salam Aref, who advocated union with the UAR. After the proclamation of the UAR in February 1958, riots broke out in Baghdad demanding the integration of Iraq into the new Republic. Agreements to achieve this membership were not followed by effect in the face of Kassem's obstruction. In March 1959, a coup attempt supported by the RAU failed. Qasem, who had the support of the Soviet Union, initially relied on the communists before distancing himself from them.

In 1961 the proclamation of Kuwait's independence provided Baghdad with the opportunity to claim the emirate as an integral part of Iraq, but its independence was recognized by the Arab League and the UN. The same year, the first Kurdish insurrection led by Mustapha Barzani broke out. Weakened internally, the regime was isolated externally. On 8 February 1963, Kassem was overthrown by a bloody Baathist coup. A month after taking power in Iraq, the Ba'athist regime launched a coup in Syria. But this extension of Ba'athist power into Iraq and Syria was short-lived, and on November 18, the Ba'athists were removed from power in Baghdad by President Abdel Salam Aref. This development put an end to negotiations aimed at unifying the two countries, which soon became brothers in arms. In July, the Iraqi Baathists took over and repressed the Nasserite and communist opponents. Their leader, General Ahmad Hassan Al-Bakr, became president, but his lieutenant, Saddam Hussein, was in fact the strong man of the country. He relied on the Republican Guard and other special forces that constituted the regime's praetorian guard. In June 1972 the Iraqi government nationalized *the Iraq Petroleum Company in* order to finance the modernization of the country. Presenting itself as the champion of the liberation of Palestine, it sent part of its army to fight the Israelis on the Golan front during the October 1973 war. "Iraq is gradually moving away from the leftist orientation it has had since the overthrow of the Hashemite monarchy in 1958 and ceases to appear as a subversive state seeking the overthrow of the status quo in the Gulf[7] . It normalized its relations with Saudi Arabia and Oman. While maintaining its strategic alliance with the USSR, with which a treaty of friendship and alliance was signed in 1972, it adopted a more balanced policy that won it new friendships in the West.

Saudi Arabia

The first son of its founder, Saud bin Abdel Aziz, became king in 1953. Since the Saudi system of succession is adelphic, that is, it is passed down from brother to brother in order of primogeniture, his brother, Faysal, became crown prince and was appointed head of government. But the king's reckless spending brought the Saudi state to the brink of financial collapse. And the attempted overthrow of the Yemeni monarchy by officers inspired by the Nasserian example in 1962 put the kingdom in a difficult situation. Nasser immediately supported the new Republic and sent an expeditionary force to Yemen, which soon became bogged down in war. Faced with this new danger, in November 1964, Faysal became sovereign after having removed his brother, King Saud, from the throne, who was considered incompetent. During his ten-year reign, he undertook several modernizing reforms aimed at bringing the country out of the Middle Ages despite opposition from conservative circles and the religious establishment. Education for girls was introduced and the country's first television station was authorized. It was also during his reign that slavery was formally prohibited. The kingdom changed from a union of several tribes to a strong and centralized state. His fear of communism led him to choose the Western camp. Posing as a rival to Nasser, he called for a gathering of all Muslims in the world. The Yemen war, which weakened the power of Egypt, increased the political importance of Saudi Arabia, which also benefited from the rise in oil revenues. After the Six-Day War in June 1967, he agreed to bail out Egypt's coffers. The Egyptian defeat and its dependence on Riyadh allowed King Faysal to take the lead in the Arab world. He adopted an uncompromising attitude towards Israel and worked to use his influence internationally to support the Palestinian cause. Since the Khartoum summit of September 1967, Saudi Arabia has taken a growing place in Arab politics. Faysal did not abandon his old plans for Islamic unity. On August 21, 1969, an unbalanced person set fire to the Al-Aqsa mosque in Jerusalem. The entire Muslim world accused Israel of being responsible for the sacrilege and Faysal took advantage of this to implement his idea of an Islamic summit. The summit was held in Rabat from 22 to 25 September 1969 and decided to set up a permanent consultation structure, the "Islamic Conference", which would periodically bring together the heads of Muslim states or their representatives in Islamic summits. At the Rabat summit, the PLO was for the first time admitted on an equal footing with sovereign states. In October 1973, in response to the Yom Kippur War, Riyadh played a leading role in the announcement by the Organization of Arab Petroleum Exporting Countries (OAPEC) of an embargo on oil shipments to countries supporting Israel. These countries also demanded a complete withdrawal from the territories occupied by Israel. At the end of 1973, Faysal clearly explained his policy to Saudi diplomats: never harm American interests, fight against communist influence in the Middle East, and make the Arabs understand that their salvation would not come from Moscow but from Washington. But in 1974 the pro-Israeli positions of President Ford, who replaced Richard Nixon in the White House - he recognized Jerusalem as the capital of the Hebrew state - caused tension between the United States and Saudi Arabia. In retaliation Riyadh reduces the volume of oil extraction and withdraws the Saudi gold reserves stored in the United States. An agreement is finally reached. The king will end up recruiting a thousand American military advisors to train the Saudi army. With this strong gesture, he placed the fate of the dynasty and the kingdom in the hands of the Americans. In March 1975 King Faysal was assassinated and the throne went to his half brother Khaled.

The Gulf emirates

Great Britain granted independence to Kuwait in 1961. Iraq did not recognize this independence. For the Iraqis, the state of Kuwait was artificial, created by the British from scratch. Moreover, Kuwait, rich in oil, is the natural access to the sea of Iraq. The Kuwaitis appealed to Great Britain, which sent military contingents to defend the emirate in July 1961. They were replaced in September by an Arab intervention force. In October 1963, Iraq recognized the independence and sovereignty of Kuwait. The country where the Al-Sabah dynasty reigned became a constitutional monarchy. But until 2005, only 15% of the population had the right to vote. In 1968, London announced its disengagement east of Suez, and its intention to withdraw its troops in 1971 from the Persian Gulf emirates, known as the Truce States. Before the discovery of oil, the most important of them, Abu Dhabi, had as resources only the products of fishing and pearl trade. In 1968, its emir, Sheikh Shakhbout, who absolutely refused to modernize the emirate, was removed from power by the family clan and replaced by his younger brother, Sheikh Zayed bin Sultan al-Nahyane. The latter was the architect of the formation, on December 2, 1971, of the United Arab Emirates, which grouped Abu Dhabi, Dubai, Ajman, Charjah, Fujairah, Umm el-Qiwain and Ras el Khaimah. It took him two years of negotiations to overcome the reluctance of the Bedouin sheikhs of these neighbouring emirates, who were opposed to each other and had never worked together. The hardest to convince was his main rival, Sheikh Rached al Maktoum, Emir of Dubai, the second largest emirate after Abu Dhabi. To get them to form a federation, he offered to share Abu Dhabi's oil revenues with them, provided that each emirate worked on its own development. Two days before the creation of the UAE, Iran took control of three small islands in the Persian Gulf that were part of it. Sheikh Zayed was elected the first president of the United Arab Emirates (UAE) and remained so until his death in 2004.

The United Arab Emirates, the Sultanate of Oman, Qatar, and Bahrain gained their independence from London in 1971. Sheikh Zayed made the UAE the most modern and tolerant country in the Arabian Peninsula in a few decades. He enjoyed great prestige on the international scene. Under his influence, the UAE experienced rapid economic growth. Believing that all citizens have a role to play in building the country, he is taking steps to improve the status of women in society, facilitating their access to education, and giving them a more important place in the political life of the country. "On the international level, the UAE president was careful throughout his reign (1968-2004) to cultivate valuable alliances. With the United States playing the Saudi card and the United Kingdom being the former colonial power, Zayed turned to France, which became a privileged partner[8] . Oman, where Sultan Qaboos has reigned since 1970, has been in the grip of a communist insurrection in Dhofar since 1965, which was finally put down in 1976 by British and Iranian troops. The sultanate will then enjoy great prosperity thanks to its oil resources.

Yemen

Yemen is divided in two. Having known neither the Ottoman nor the colonial domination, North Yemen is a medieval monarchy of Zaydi obedience, a sect of Shiite Islam. The south with the port of Aden was controlled by the British. On September 27, 1962 the Imam King, Mohammad al-Badr, was overthrown by Arab nationalists. Abdallah Sallal took power in Sana'a and established the Republic. But the Imam's son took refuge in Saudi Arabia, from where he led a monarchist insurrection. Nasser dispatched an Egyptian expeditionary force to support the republican camp in the face of fierce resistance from royalist tribes supported by Riyadh. But he was forced to withdraw his troops in 1967 after the Six Day War. Nevertheless, the republicans eventually won and North Yemen became the Yemen Arab Republic. After withdrawing its support for the royalists, Saudi Arabia officially recognized the Yemen Arab Republic in 1970. In 1967, Great Britain withdrew from South Yemen, which was renamed the

People's Democratic Republic of Yemen (P.D.R.Y.). In 1970, the latter became part of the Soviet orbit.

The Libyan revolution

In September 1969, King Idris 1er , leader of the Senoussia religious brotherhood, which had ruled Libya since 1954, was overthrown by a coup d'état led by a group of officers. The main members of this group, who came from several tribes, were General Haftar, Commander Jalloul and a young 27-year-old captain, Muammar Gaddafi, who quickly established himself as their leader. He succeeded in taking over the Libyan tribal system, composed of 30 tribes, and remained in power for 41 years. Iraq was the first country to recognize the new regime in place, quickly followed by the United Arab Republic. Gaddafi became chairman of the Revolutionary Command Council and began nationalizing various enterprises. The Republic adopted the slogan of the Baath Party: "Arab unity, freedom, socialism". Decisions were taken at a rapid pace. Gaddafi, who had proclaimed himself colonel, dismissed the Italian colonists, as well as the British and American troops present on Libyan territory. He is gradually removing the tribes that are plotting against him. He uses the oil money to build infrastructure in the country and modernizes agriculture. He skilfully rides the wave of pan-Arabism and the Palestinian cause. He was even endorsed by Nasser himself, who declared that he was "the repository of Arab nationalism, of the Arab revolution and of Arab unity[9] ". After the death of the Egyptian raïs in 1970, Khadhafi's ambition was to collect his legacy. The Union of Arab Republics, comprising Egypt, Syria and Libya, was proclaimed in April 1971. But it never materialized because of the differences between the Libyan leader and Sadat, who distrusted him.

1 *Histoire du Liban des origines au XXe siècle*, Boutros Dib (direction) Philippe Rey éditions 2006

2 *Le Liban et la Syrie au miroir français,* (1946-1991) Marie-Thérèse Oliver-Saïdi, l'Harmattan 1993, p.300

3 *La déchirure libanaise*, Nadine Picaudou, éditions Complexe 1989, p. 107

4 *The Arabs, their destiny and ours*, op. ct. p. 101

5 *The Syrian exception, between modernization and resistance*, Caroline Donati, La Découverte 2009

6 *Orientales III. Parcours et situations*, Henry Laurens, CNRS editions, 2004, p, 298

7 *Les Arabes ou l'histoire à contresens.* op. cit. p. 320

8 *These fifteen men who changed the face of the Middle East, Sheikh Zyed, the visionary Bedouin*, Anthony Samrani, L'Orient-le Jour, special issue of November 2, 2017

9 ibid. *Muammar Gaddafi, evil genius or pathetic clown?* Julie Kebbi.

Chapter 7. The Arab Near East after Nasser

Gamal Abdel Nasser, a charismatic leader adored by the masses, had embodied the dream of Arab unity, which died with him. Between 1970, the year of the death of nasserism and pan-Arabism, and the attacks of 11 September 2001, the internal contradictions and rivalries of the Arab countries of the Middle East, which had not ceased to affect the course of its history, became more acute. The decline of Arab nationalism led to a growing polarization between progressive regimes and their equally authoritarian conservative rivals. The global democratization process that began in the 1990s all over the world, from Eastern Europe to Latin America, did not affect the Arab world. "The contrast between the political turmoil and repeated coups of the 1950s and 1960s and the stability of the political regimes in place in the last three decades of the century is striking. When Nasser died in 1970, power passed smoothly to Sadat, who was succeeded by Mubarak. In Syria, Hafez el-Assad retained power until his death in 2005 and passed it on to his son. Saddam Hussein is the undisputed master of Iraq until 2003. The same is true of Gaddafi who will remain in power in Libya until 2012. The Arab monarchies that may have seemed threatened during the previous period of revolutionary and republican turmoil are surviving the storms very well[1] . Until the fall of the USSR in 1990, Arab dictatorships took advantage of the struggle for influence between the two superpowers to stay in power. Syria was supported by the USSR and Egypt, from 1973 onwards, by the United States, which had little regard for the lack of democracy in the country. The West uses the defense of democracy and human rights to selectively threaten regimes whose policies it does not like. Israel, meanwhile, continues to ignore UN resolutions, fuelling Arab resentment of an international order based on double standards. The US-Israeli military alliance is strengthened and institutionalized. As for the Arab peoples, they are treated as a negligible quantity on the great international chessboard.

The explosive mixture of these endogenous and exogenous factors of tension led to a succession of crises and wars that spared almost no country in the region. The Palestinian revolution resorted to terrorist operations against the West and threatened the stability of Jordan and Lebanon. Between 1970 and 2001, the Middle East was the scene of four major wars: the Arab-Israeli war of 1973, the "civil" war in Lebanon (1975-1990), the Iraqi-Iranian war (1980-1988), followed in 1991 by the second Gulf War to liberate Kuwait from Iraqi occupation ("Operation Desert Storm")

These conflicts made the Arab-Israeli conflict lose its centrality. In launching the October 1973 war, the priority objective of Egypt and Syria was to recover the Sinai and Golan Heights lost in 1967. Although the Syrian and Egyptian armies were eventually driven back, the Fourth Arab-Israeli War allowed Egypt to achieve this goal through American good offices. But Cairo had to give up its demand for a similar withdrawal from the occupied Palestinian territories. The separate Camp David peace agreement between Egypt and Israel consecrated the disintegration of the Arab front and the supremacy of the Jewish state. No Arab state will now have any inclination for military confrontation with Israel. Washington imposed itself as the main mediator in the Israeli-Palestinian conflict.

The new oil situation resulting from the quadrupling of the price of crude oil in 1973 gave the oil-producing countries a greater say in the affairs of the region. But the financial windfall was not just a blessing, as it was used to finance Muslim fundamentalism and jihadist groups. The soaring price of oil increased the economic and geostrategic importance of the Middle East and provided an additional pretext for interference, often destabilizing, by the great powers. Control of the Persian Gulf, through which most of their hydrocarbon imports were channelled, became of vital geostrategic importance for the Western powers, led by the United States. Until the fall of the Shah, Iran played the role of gendarme of the Gulf and protector of the oil wells of the Arabian Peninsula on behalf of the Americans. But the Iranian revolution of 1979 changed all that. In January 1980, Jimmy Carter issued a new doctrine of containment in which he stated that any attempt by any force to seize the Gulf region would be considered an attack on vital U.S. interests and could be repelled by any means necessary, including military force. To show his determination, he announced the creation of a *Rapid Deployment Force* to defend American interests in the region. Oil became a political weapon. It was used in 1973 by the Arab countries as a means of putting pressure on the West so that it in turn would pressure Israel to withdraw from the occupied territories. Washington did not hesitate to use the economic weapon against its adversaries either. In June 1985, the United States and Saudi Arabia agreed on a new oil strategy to suffocate Iran and the Soviet Union. Riyadh opened the floodgates of its oil production, causing the price of crude oil to collapse. The year 1979 was marked by two major events: the Soviet invasion of Afghanistan and the Iranian Islamic revolution. The establishment of the Khomeini dictatorship in Iran was a turning point and had major international and regional repercussions. It was indirectly the cause of the Iran-Iraq war and the invasion of Kuwait by Iraq (1989). From being an ally of the West, Iran became its bête noire while pursuing the hegemonic ambitions of the imperial regime in the Middle East, under the guise of the anti-imperialist struggle. Under the presidency of Ronald Reagan, the Arab allies of the United States rallied to the fight of the "free world" led under the American banner against the Soviet "evil empire" in Afghanistan. The rout of the Red Army in Afghanistan undermined the already shaky edifice of the Soviet Union, which collapsed ten years later. The other consequence of the war in Afghanistan was the birth of Al Qaeda, which would become an international terrorist organization after Operation Desert Storm.

The rise of pan-Islamism

In the 1970s, Arabism was supplanted as the dominant ideology by pan-Islamism, the founding act of which was the creation, on 29 September 1969, of the Organization of the Islamic Conference, on the initiative of Saudi Arabia and Pakistan. [e]The Middle East was the region where the worldwide phenomenon of the "return of religion" affecting all religions, which began in the last quarter of the 20th century, had the greatest repercussions. Described by Gilles Kepel as the "revenge of God[2] ", it resulted in the increasing irruption of religion in the political sphere, which led Georges Corm to write that it was, in this case, less a "return" than a "recourse" to religion. Religion serves as an instrument of internal domination of societies as well as an extension of influence, even domination over other societies. The rise of political Islamism posed a serious threat to existing Arab regimes. The confrontation between the increasingly powerful Islamist movements and these regimes led, from the 1980s onwards, to an upsurge in violence and open or latent civil wars. The global phenomenon of the return of religion was reflected in the re-Islamization of Turkey and the establishment of the only theocracy in the world in Iran. It was instrumentalized by Washington to bring down the USSR and by Ayatollah Khomeini to bring about an Islamic revolution in the Muslim world. With American support for the Afghan mujahideen and the Iranian revolution, demonization of the adversary became a common practice in the discourse of international and regional powers. The United States refers to the USSR as the "evil empire," a term with biblical connotations; and America is referred to by Iranian mullahs as the "great Satan," with the term "little Satan" reserved for France. Despite this example of recourse to a religious vocabulary, the foreign policy of international and regional powers essentially obeys a logic of influence and geopolitical ambitions. Whether it is Iran's support for Hezbollah, Qatar's funding of the Muslim Brotherhood, Saudi Arabia's funding of their Salafist rivals, or Bashar al-Assad's cleverness in posing as a defender of minorities and waving the Islamist scarecrow to ensure the continuity of his regime. The desire of the Iranian Islamic Republic to export its revolution will cause great concern among its Sunni neighbors. "The idea that a common destiny exists between the Iranian and Palestinian revolutions is pushing Arab militants who have long been nationalists to rally to Islamism, not so much out of religious conviction as to erase past defeats[3] . Syria, governed by an Alawite minority close to the Shiites, will be the only Arab country to take sides with Iran, although this choice is also dictated by geostrategic considerations. While Iraq, where the Shiites are subject to Sunni domination, will be, along with Saudi Arabia, one of its fiercest opponents. This situation fuelled the confrontation between Damascus and Baghdad, which were nevertheless governed by two branches of the same party (the Ba'ath). The secular ideology of the party did not prevent Saddam Hussein from supporting the Syrian Islamists against Assad and the latter from supporting the Iraqi Islamists against him.

The failure to impose a "new order" in the Middle East

In the mid-1980s, the loss of influence of the Soviet Union, weakened by the failure of Perestroika and its rout in Afghanistan, is evident in the Middle East. The collapse of the USSR in 1989 marked a major turning point in international relations and a new phase in the tormented history of the region. The Non-Aligned Movement faded away, deprived of its raison d'être between the two superpowers, since one of them had disappeared. The end of the USSR, both model and ally, weakened the social-military regimes in the region. The United States' military involvement in the first Gulf War (1991), inconceivable when the USSR was still a great power, is a sign of this. Since that war, the United States has maintained a massive military presence in the region, making it less dependent on Israeli military support. The end of the Cold War and the accession of the United States to the status of sole superpower led it to want to lay the foundations of a "new order" in the Middle East. The Madrid Conference, convened at their initiative to finally establish an Arab-Israeli peace, and the Israeli-Palestinian agreements of Oslo in 1993 brought a wind of optimism to the region. "Between February 1991 - the month of the liberation of Kuwait - and October 1994 - the month of the signing of the Israeli-Jordanian peace treaty and the holding of the Casablanca economic summit - everything seemed to converge towards the definitive appeasement of the Middle East conflicts[4] . In Casablanca in 1994, and then in Amman in 1995, the United States brought together Arab, Israeli and international political and business leaders to build peace and economic development in this region of the world after all those years of war and instability. But the reality on the ground turned out to be different. The occupied Palestinian territories are subject to regular closures by the Israeli army, which has only deployed outside the major urban centers. In Lebanon, Hezbollah's armed resistance to the occupation of the south of the country provoked two Israeli reprisal operations in 1993 and 1996. Saudi Arabia was the scene of attacks against American troops. The Gulf War destabilized Iraq, which was subjected to a total economic embargo, causing suffering among its population. "As the achievement of peace became elusive, Washington opted for a policy of pacification, favouring support for authoritarian Arab regimes and aiming to eradicate all forms of violent protest against the new regional order. Stability is becoming the watchword of Western policy in the region, which is muffling its calls for more freedom in the Arab world[5] . Priority is given to the fight against terrorism, which will be the subject of the summit held in Sharm el-Sheikh in Egypt in March 1996. The same year a military agreement was concluded between Turkey and Israel under the sponsorship of the United States. Intended to consolidate Western hegemony in the Middle East, the agreement only fanned the flames of resentment among the enemies of the United States, particularly Islamists. Under American domination, the region was the scene of an escalation of violence and Islamist terrorism that culminated in the attacks of 11 September 2001.

Post-Nasserian Egypt

Nasser's death on September 28, 1970 marked the end of an era. For more than fifteen years, he was the "voice of the Arabs". The news of his death was like a bomb in the Arab world. "One hundred million human beings - the Arabs - are orphans" wrote the Lebanese daily "Le Jour". On October 1er his mortal remains were followed by more than five million grieving Egyptians in the streets of Cairo[6] . His successor, Anwar Sadat, would take Egypt in a very different direction. The only candidate, although not a natural heir in the eyes of the nasserites, he was elected president on 15 October 1970 with 90% of the votes. Following a power struggle, he managed to eliminate the left wing of the regime led by Ali Sabri and had his opponents arrested for conspiracy (May 1971), which worried the Soviet leadership. Determined to maintain privileged relations between the two countries, it forced Sadat to sign a treaty of friendship and cooperation with the Soviet Union. The fragility of Egyptian-Soviet relations became apparent, however, when Egypt and Libya intervened to suppress a pro-communist coup in Sudan. Ostensibly, Sadat presented himself as Nasser's heir. But his policy marked the affirmation of the Egyptian specificity, the abandonment of previous unionist and socialist ambitions and the beginning of an economic liberalization placed under the sign of openness (*Infitah*). This turn will allow a caste to get rich without succeeding in lifting the country out of poverty. Economic liberalism was accompanied by a relative political liberalism. The press was freer to express itself than before. A multiparty system is allowed, but within the limits that ensure the preponderance of the president's party. Both conservative and modern, he wanted to make Egypt the "country of science and faith". A deeply religious Muslim, he fought atheistic Marxism and encouraged moderate Islamist currents. The Muslim Brotherhood found the word. Playing with fire, he used them to counterbalance the extreme left and he promised them the future integration of Sharia in Egyptian laws. "He would later confide, at the time of the fall of the Shah of Iran, that the latter "had lost the game, because he had attacked the clerics[7] ". In 1977 he dispersed the followers of Shukri Mustapha, who sought to live as "true believers" on the bangs of society in order to better conquer it when the day came. In 1980, following a constitutional reform, Islamic law became the main source of legislation. This reform detached the Coptic population from the regime.

Sadat continued the war of attrition against Israel begun by Nasser, whose objective was limited to altering the balance of power that was too favorable to the Hebrew state. "Desiring above all to restore the territorial integrity of his country, he was convinced that only the United States could obtain a retrocession of the Sinai and that only the West, accompanied by the Arab oil-producing countries of the Gulf, had the financial means to get Egypt out of its economic disaster[8] . Drawing closer to the United States, he sent back Soviet military experts in July 1972, as a prelude to the October 1973 war. One of his objectives was to break the political deadlock that Kissinger had managed to maintain. Both he and Assad know that the consolidation of their regimes depends on erasing the humiliation of 1967. However, their war aims are different. For Sadat, the confrontation was aimed at forcing the Americans to resume negotiations; the matter was primarily political. For Assad, the Arabs must regain as much of their lost land as possible in order to force Israel to withdraw from all the occupied territories, including the West Bank and Gaza. While the priority of the Egyptian president is to recover the Sinai.

The October War

The failure of UN and US sponsored peace proposals had demonstrated that Israel would not cede any territory through negotiations. Golda Meir, who took over the Israeli government in March 1969 after the death of Eshkol, reinforced her inflexible attitude. The Israelis and their government were convinced of their superiority over the Arab armies. For their part, Sadat and Hafez el-Assad were convinced that war was the only option. Their intention was to reconquer the territories lost in 1967. But while Syria hoped to recapture the entire Golan Heights, Sadat wanted to seize a strip of territory on the eastern bank of the canal, in order to encourage the Jewish state and the international community to find a way out of the political impasse. The Egyptians and Syrians invested a great deal of effort in order to create a tactical and strategic surprise effect. This was aided by the Israelis' underestimation of their military capability.

Launched on October 6, 1973, the Jewish holiday of Yom Kippur, the surprise offensive of the Egyptian and Syrian armies initially overwhelmed the Israeli troops stationed on the canal and the Golan Heights. For a moment the situation seemed desperate to Dayan, the Israeli Minister of Defense, and the Chief of Staff, Yitzhak Rabin. The Syrian attack was intended to overwhelm the then outnumbered and outfitted Israeli troops and reach the Jordan River. The battle that took place over the next four days was the most important tank battle since the Second World War. The IIe and IIIe Egyptian armies that had crossed the canal were content to occupy a strip of land on the eastern bank of the Sinai and did not push their offensive to the line of the strategic Gidi and Mitla passes. The United States then established an air bridge with Israel, providing it with exceptional military and financial aid. Tanks and ammunition were landed directly on the Sinai battlefield. For their part, wanting to mark their role in the war, the Soviets organized an airlift to Egypt and Syria, despite the dismissal of their advisers by Sadat. Massive deliveries of American weapons enabled the Tsahal to restore the situation. On 14 October the Israelis, who had completed their mobilization, launched a counter-offensive against the Syrian army which, despite fierce resistance, was pushed back beyond the Golan Heights. In the meantime, in order to reduce the pressure on the Syrian front, the Egyptian armies had advanced beyond the protection zone of their Sam missile batteries, becoming vulnerable to attacks by Israeli aircraft. The Tsahal took the offensive on 15 October; many reinforcements had been brought in from the north following the recapture of the Golan Heights. The Egyptians suffered heavy losses. Forced to withdraw near the canal, they left the area of the weir where the canal enters the bitter lake uncovered. Disobeying the orders of the general staff, Ariel Sharon, who commanded the Israeli forces on the ground, seized the flaw in their system and launched a daring counter-offensive, making his troops cross the canal behind the Egyptian lines. On 16 October, the Israeli army established a bridgehead on the western bank of the Suez Canal. Over the following two days, in a turning movement, it destroyed the Sam missile batteries and surrounded the Egyptian IIIe army that had remained on the other side. In reaction to the American intervention, on 17 October, Saudi Arabia, followed by the other Arab oil-producing countries, decided to impose an embargo on oil deliveries to Western countries. Arab oil production was reduced by 10% with the threat of a 5% monthly reduction until an agreement was reached on the return to the 1967 borders and the recognition of Palestinian rights. The price of oil quadrupled in a few weeks. Negotiations between the two superpowers led to the drafting of a joint text, voted on October 22 by the UN Security Council, under the name of resolution 338, calling for an immediate ceasefire. The resolution was immediately accepted by Sadat, provoking a crisis in his relations with Assad. Israel decided to complete its encirclement maneuver, but on October 24, the nuclear threat posed by the USSR forced it to accept a cease-fire decreed by the UN. The war ended with an Egyptian half-victory, mostly moral. Sadat, whose army was encircled east of the canal, certainly lost out militarily, but he proved that Tsahal was not invincible and the October war gave him the legitimacy he lacked.

The Secretary of State, Henry Kissinger, then undertook numerous shuttles in the region. On November 11, 1973, an agreement of disengagement of the Israeli-Egyptian forces concluded thanks to his mediation allowed the supply of the 3rd Egyptian army. The Israeli army completed its withdrawal from the western bank of the canal on 3 March 1974. Due to Assad's intransigence, the Israel-Syria agreement was more delicate and on May 31, 1974, Israel, where Rabin replaced Meir as Prime Minister, withdrew from the area that its forces had conquered beyond the old 1967 ceasefire line, including the city of Quneitra. As in Sinai, a buffer zone with UN forces was established between the two armies. The general negotiation was supposed to take place at an international conference in Geneva in December. But nothing came of its first session. Rather than attempting to tackle the overall settlement of the conflict, Kissinger opted for a step-by-step approach, seeking limited agreements on issues that arose as the negotiations progressed. Through the bilateral disengagement agreements he had obtained in 1974, he excluded the USSR, Europe and the United Nations from the diplomatic game and made the United States appear to be the only actor capable of bringing about positive change in the Arab-Israeli dispute. By negotiating separately with Syria and Egypt, he broke the Egyptian-Syrian coalition of October 1973. He skilfully convinced Israel that limited concessions would allow it to remain inflexible on the essentials, while telling the Arabs that these agreements were only a first step towards a comprehensive settlement.

In June 1975, the Suez Canal was reopened to navigation. But Israel refused to withdraw its army beyond the Sinai passes. And it was not until September 4, 1975 that it agreed to do so after having obtained a commitment to increase American aid. The peace efforts were interrupted by the resignation of President Nixon, following the Watergate scandal, and only resumed with the election of

Jimmy Carter as President in November 1976. In June 1977 the coming to power of Menachem Begin's right-wing alliance dominated by the Likud ended three decades of Labor's political dominance in Israel. While Labor accepted, at least in theory, the notion of territorial compromise, as well as the formula of "land for peace", Begin did not and would govern Israel for six years until 1983.

Camp David

The absence of a political solution to the Arab-Israeli conflict proved dangerous when, following pressure from the International Monetary Fund, the Egyptian government reduced subsidies on basic products, which triggered popular riots. On November 19, 1977, in order to break the deadlock in the Geneva peace negotiations, Sadat caused a political earthquake of regional proportions by becoming the first Egyptian head of state to make an official visit to Israel. During this historic visit, he met with Prime Minister Menachem Begin, who hailed him as "the most valuable guest Israel has ever hosted[9] . And he addressed the Knesset in Jerusalem where he made a speech pleading for peace with justice and defending the rights of the Palestinians. But he did not obtain any concession from Begin, who remained unmoved by his plea and provoked the hatred of the Arab peoples and the anger of their leaders, who cried treason. Sadat's courageous initiative encouraged the new American president, Jimmy Carter, to distance himself from Kissinger's policy of a partial approach to the Middle East problems. He wants to achieve a comprehensive settlement of the Arab-Israeli conflict, which requires a resumption of the Geneva conference, at least as a framework for negotiations.

But Israeli reluctance, the formation of a strong Arab front at the Arab summit in Algiers in February 1978, and Egypt's isolation led him to sponsor bilateral negotiations between Egypt and Israel. In the early months of 1978, Arab opponents of rapprochement, both inside and outside Egypt, put more pressure on Sadat to abandon the peace process. In Israel, on the other hand, a peace movement called "Peace Now" organized a rally of 100,000 people in Tel Aviv on September 2, 1978. The demonstrators sent a clear message to the Prime Minister to encourage him to make concessions in order to conclude the peace.

On September 5, 1978, Begin and Sadat went to Camp David, at the initiative of President Carter. The latter hoped that the Americans would extract from Begin the promise of an evacuation of the occupied territories. Initially, he demanded that the fate of all the occupied Arab territories and that of the Palestinians be linked to the Sinai question. But Begin did not give an inch on the issue of the occupation of the West Bank and Gaza. At most, he agreed to grant limited autonomy to the Palestinians. He also began by refusing to evacuate the Israeli settlements in the Sinai, for fear of creating a precedent. It took Carter to force Begin and Sadat to agree on September 17, after 13 days of negotiations, on the principle of a peace treaty between Egypt and Israel. It is also supposed to include a framework for peace in the Middle East. But the Palestinians perceive the agreements as a betrayal of their interests. For them, the term "autonomy" merely camouflages the continued occupation of the West Bank and Gaza. And on November 5, the Arab summit in Baghdad threw anathema on the Camp David agreements. The treaty was formally signed in Washington on March 26, 1979. The Israeli Prime Minister refused the slightest concession on the Palestinian question. It was therefore a separate peace that gave free rein to Israeli colonization and completed the isolation of Syria. Egypt, for its part, obtained the restitution of the Sinai Peninsula in three stages spread over three years and significant American aid paid annually to its army. This separate peace, which dealt a fatal blow to Arab solidarity, led to Egypt being ostracized from the Arab world. The Arab League left Cairo for Tunis and several Arab states broke off diplomatic relations with Egypt. It consecrated the supremacy of the Hebrew state, which obtained de jure recognition by the most powerful Arab state and got rid of the southern front, which had always been the main concern of its staff. Sadat and Begin receive the Nobel Peace Prize. A cold peace was established between Egypt and Israel.

The last years of the Sadat presidency

In Egypt, the Islamists, who had been spared by Sadat until then, are now a real threat. In addition to condemning peace with Israel, they vehemently attack the Westernization of the country and the corruption of those who profited from the economic opening. For their part, the Copts are vigorously opposing Sadat's religious policy, which has increased concessions to the Islamists. In September 1981, Sadat launched a violent repression targeting Nasserites, communists, Islamists and intellectuals. He also put the Coptic Orthodox Patriarch, Shenouda III, under house arrest in a monastery. This repression, which resumed the practices of his predecessor, added to an economic crisis, increased his unpopularity. On October 6, 1981, one month after the wave of arrests, he was assassinated during a military parade by soldiers belonging to an Egyptian Islamist millenarian group opposed to the peace treaty signed with Israel and who did not forgive him for having reached out to the Jewish state. Sadat's detractors in the Arab world do not hide their joy. Appreciated by the West, hated by the Arabs, he has never managed to equal the aura of Nasser in the eyes of Egyptians. But while Nasser's pan-Arabism is now dead and buried, Sadat's political legacy will live on in Egypt.

The Mubarak era

The uprising that broke out in the wake of Sadat's assassination in Asyut, Upper Egypt, was quickly crushed by Hosni Mubarak, who succeeded him. Militants and Islamist sympathizers were rounded up by the thousands, and sometimes deported after years of detention and torture. Mubarak was an air force commander during the 1973 war and had been appointed vice-president by Sadat. He practiced a policy of appeasement aimed at inspiring a climate of confidence and restoring national unity, which had been severely damaged by Sadat's assassination. When he came to power, he enjoyed the full support of the Reagan administration. While maintaining privileged ties with the United States, which provided him with significant economic and military aid (2e rank after Israel), he managed to reintegrate Egypt into the Arab world. He confirmed the multiparty system established by Sadat, but the National Democratic Party (NDP), founded in 1978 by Sadat, is still the president's party and retains hegemony over political life. "Heir to the successive single parties of the nasserite era, and of the early years of his successor, it is a loose collection of urban bureaucrats and rural notables. Virtually all senior officials are required to belong to this organization, whose main function is to provide a parliamentary majority for the president in every election[10] . The Wafd, the voice of the old bourgeoisie that was victimized by the Nasserite regime, is allowed to reconstitute itself. Among the authorized formations is the Socialist Labor Party, representing the left of the political spectrum. But the Muslim Brotherhood was excluded from the multiparty system and was not allowed to stand for election as such. In 1984, the government recognized the Brotherhood's status as a religious organization, but refused its participation in politics. The Muslim Brotherhood circumvented this ban by running "no-label" candidates in the elections and by entering parliament through alliances with other parties. But the secular regime of Hosni Mubarak has blocked most of its political manoeuvres. The organization remains banned but is paradoxically tolerated. To better combat it, the regime appealed to the institutional Islam represented by the religious university of al-Azhar, which posed as a censor of morals and ideas. "Police repression and the decline of freedom of thought have caused a backward step compared to the 1980s, which had seen real progress towards political and intellectual liberalization[11] . In the 1987 elections, the opposition parties won 22 per cent of the seats without challenging the dominance of the NDP.

The main problem remains that of poverty and population growth. The Mubarak regime is trying to deal with these difficulties by building infrastructure. But the population continues to grow at a rate of over one million per year. The government is continuing the liberalization of the economy begun by President Sadat. The policy of subsidizing agriculture and basic foodstuffs became unsustainable for public finances, so these were reduced and prices were liberalized. A series of privatizations increased the importance of the private sector and large parts of the public sector were dismantled. This policy, which increases inequality and leads to a deterioration of public services, is causing growing discontent among the poorer classes. The Muslim Brotherhood took advantage of this to offer its own social services to the population, while intensifying its propaganda. Despite the opening up of the economy, and the income generated by the Suez Canal and tourism, the millions of workers who have emigrated to Iraq and the Gulf countries are one of Egypt's main resources. So the country was hit hard when the oil counter-shock reduced employment opportunities abroad and when Iraq expelled Egyptian workers at the end of its war with Iran in 1988.

In foreign policy, Mubarak is pursuing a clever policy of making Egypt the pillar of "moderation" in the Arab world in the eyes of Washington. He sought to restore Egypt to a prominent role in Arab politics, while maintaining the gains of Camp David, which implied a cold peace with Israel. The final phase of the evacuation of Sinai by Israeli forces, in application of the clauses of the Washington treaty, took place in March 1989 and Egypt recovered the small enclave of Taba, near Aqaba. It re-established relations with the PLO. The Arab summit in Amman in November 1987 consecrated the reintegration and the end of Egypt's boycott. And on March 11, 1990, the decision to return the headquarters of the Arab League to Cairo was taken by the Council of Arab Foreign Ministers. The Egyptian army trained regularly with the American rapid intervention force. Its participation in 1991 in the coalition gathered under the American banner to liberate Kuwait made Egypt the preferred Arab partner of the United States. Half of the country's foreign debt was cancelled.

On May 4, 1992, Islamists attacked Copts in Upper Egypt, in Asyut. On June 8, the writer Farag Foda, hostile to the fundamentalists, was assassinated in Cairo by Islamists. On October 21, Western tourists were targeted. The aim is to ruin the tourist activity which is a vital resource for Egypt. This strategy culminated in the attack perpetrated in Luxor in 1997 by Islamists: 57 tourists and four Egyptians were killed. The terrorists demanded the release of Sheikh Omar Abdel Rahmane, who had been detained in the United States since the 1993 attack on the World Trade Center. From March 1992 to June 1997, Islamist terrorism claimed nearly twelve hundred lives. Violent clashes broke out in Cairo between the police and the Islamists. On October 4, 1993, Hosni Mubarak was re-elected president for six years. On June 26, 1995, he escaped an assassination attempt in Addis Ababa, Ethiopia, claimed by the Gamaa al-Islamiya. Mubarak was again elected president in 1999. However, his fall in popularity accelerated with the exposure of his son's corruption. Alaa, during public procurement and privatization deals. Towards the end of 2000, it was his other son, Gamal, who made the news by rising through the ranks of the National Democratic Party. Gamal succeeded in integrating a new generation of liberals. As his influence grew, there were rumors that he was being groomed to succeed his father as head of state. In the "multi-party" elections of April 2002, President Mubarak's National Democratic Party won 99 per cent of the votes cast! The ruling party controls the majority of seats in both houses of parliament (People's Assembly and Consultative Council). The opposition parties combined (Al Wafd, the National Progressive and Unity Party, the Nasserite Arab Democratic Party and the Liberal Party) have only 17 of the 454 seats in the Assembly. Of the 37 "independent" deputies, 17 are close to the Muslim Brotherhood.

Mubarak opposed the American-led war against Iraq in 2003, arguing that the Israeli-Palestinian conflict had priority. Public opinion was very anti-American and the press celebrated the actions of Hamas or the resistance in Iraq. The American ambassador protested, which led to him being accused by the newspapers of interfering in Egypt's internal affairs. Under pressure from the

United States, which claimed that one of the goals of its intervention in Iraq was to promote democracy in the region, Mubarak posed as a champion of political reforms, but these must, for him, come from within and not be imposed from abroad (implying that the United States was exerting pressure in this direction). In March 2004, he organized a conference in Alexandria on the theme of the challenge of Arab reforms. The conference emphasized the need to take into account the Arab cultural and religious context. The United States should set an example by applying democracy in international relations, i.e. by respecting other countries. The foreigner is referred to his responsibilities in Palestine and Iraq. But a trip by the president to the United States, after a frank discussion with G. W. Bush, reaffirmed the strategic partnership between Egypt and America, which actively resumed its mediation in the Palestine question. In July 2004, Mubarak appointed a new Prime Minister and a new government. However, this government was not perceived positively by many Egyptians, and the economic conditions of the country did not improve. In December 2004, a movement called *Kifaya* (enough!) emerged to organize demonstrations against Mubarak's possible re-election to a fifth term or his succession by his son Gamal. The president held a referendum that introduced a certain level of facade competition into the Egyptian political system. "Whereas before the president was voted in by the people after being "elected" by a parliament that he controlled, now there is a supposedly pluralistic presidential election. But only candidates approved by that same parliament are allowed to run[12] . The opposition called it a farce and called for a boycott of the referendum. But on May 25, 2005, the referendum received a 93% yes vote. The creation of a new party named *al Ghad* (tomorrow) is authorized. In any case, the elections are rigged. Hosni Mubarak accuses the opposition parties of being financed by foreign money. Ayman Nour, the leader of the al Ghad party, was arrested and later released on bail. He ran in the first officially multiparty presidential election on September 9, 2005, which Mubarak won with 88.5% of the vote.

The deviation of the Palestinian Resistance

The defeat of the Arab armies in 1967 led to a radicalization and a rise in power of the "Palestinian Revolution" whose "sacred" cause enjoyed more support than ever from Arab public opinion. Arafat took over from Nasser the role of hero of the anti-imperialist struggle and of resistance to Israel. This popularity did not fail to arouse the suspicion of several Arab states, especially as the federates claimed a freedom of movement that threatened the stability of Lebanon and Jordan in particular. In 1969, the Lebanese state was forced to sign the Cairo agreements, which granted the PLO extraterritoriality in the refugee camps and on the border with Israel. This was the beginning of "Fatahland" and the reign of Palestinian militias in southern Lebanon. At the same time, the Fedayeen launched a wave of terrorist operations targeting not only Israel but also Western interests. In this escalation of violence, Yasser Arafat was outflanked by his rival, PFLP leader George Habash. In September 1970, the PFLP hijacked British and American Swiss airliners at an airport in eastern Jordan and held their passengers hostage. Georges Habash proclaimed that "the Resistance is ready to make the Middle East a hell[13] ". During this "Black September", Habash and the PFLP led the PLO into a suicidal confrontation with the Jordanian army. The only hope for the Fedayeen was for the Syrian army to intervene on their side. Salah Jedid had his tanks cross the border, while Hafez al-Assad refused to provide them with air cover, forcing them to withdraw after a bombardment by Jordanian fighters. Nasser finally imposed a cease-fire on Arafat and King Hussein, but died shortly afterwards. The Palestinian federates who fled Jordan were not welcome in Syria, where Assad had just taken power. Arafat and his supporters, armed to the teeth, moved to Lebanon to the great misfortune of the country. For years, the multiple terrorist actions of the fedayeen from various radical Palestinian organizations, the most spectacular of which was the hostage-taking of Israeli athletes at the Munich Olympics in 1972, discredited the Palestinian resistance in the eyes of international opinion and greatly destabilized the region.

The Arab countries sought to take up the Palestinian cause, but they came up against Arafat's determination not to put himself at their service, which earned him the hostility of Nasser and especially of Assad. In 1974, measuring the danger that extremist factions posed to the Resistance, Arafat endorsed the principle of a Palestinian Authority over "any proportion of liberated Palestinian territory". The PFLP condemned this move towards coexistence with Israel and formed a Palestinian "Refusal Front". But the PLO was admitted as a full member at the Arab Summit in October 1974 and the following month Arafat was invited to the UN General Assembly. In a famous speech, he did not speak of national liberation but advocated the formation of a single country where Jews, Christians and Muslims would live on an equal footing within a democratic framework. He declared: "I have come bearing an olive branch and a fighter's rifle. Do not let the olive branch fall from my hand. The war is burning in Palestine, but it is also in Palestine that peace will be reborn[14] ". But in Lebanon, where he ran a state within a state, he allowed himself to be drawn into the civil war that broke out in April 1975. The PLO was defeated by an intervention by Assad's Syria in 1976 against the "Palestinian-progressive" coalition. It suffered an even more serious defeat when it was expelled from Lebanon in 1982, following Begin and Sharon's decision to invade the country in order to destroy it. Its departure will be under French protection. The misfortunes of the Palestinians gave rise to dissent within the PLO, encouraged by Hafez el-Assad. Clashes between dissidents and supporters of Arafat took place in the Syrian-controlled Bekaa. The PLO leader, who had returned to Lebanon from exile in Tunisia, and his supporters were besieged in Tripoli by the Syrian army and pro-Iranian militias. France intervened a second time in December 1983 to save Arafat and the French operation enabled them to be evacuated. Arafat's departure to Tunisia meant that he lost contact with the population of the occupied territories where the Muslim Brotherhood was developing its networks. The latter were favored by Israel at the expense of the nationalists in order to divide the Palestinian resistance.

The evolution of Jordan.

After the tragic episode of Black September, King Hussein reconciled with Yasser Arafat in 1982, even if a mistrust persisted between the two men. Jordan had refused to accept the role reserved for it in the Camp David agreement, but wishing to participate in the peace process, the king could not act alone. He knows that he needs a Palestinian guarantee for this. But the first Jordanian-Palestinian dialogue ran into opposition from the hardliners in the PLO and the principle of a future Jordanian-Palestinian confederation, approved by Arafat in December 1982, was finally abandoned. In 1987 Hussein began secret talks with Shimon Peres in London. In November 1989 Jordan held its first free elections in a quarter of a century. This election was more or less imposed on King Hussein by the agitation of the tribes, dissatisfied with the nepotism and corruption of the regime. The Muslim Brotherhood, which won a relative victory, entered a coalition government for the first time. When the 1991 Gulf crisis occurred, King Hussein had to take into account the feelings of the

of the Jordanian population behind Saddam Hussein. Jordan did not participate in the war led by the United States to liberate Kuwait, which led Washington to deprive the kingdom of its financial aid because of its support for Baghdad. The kingdom also suffered the ire of Saudi Arabia and the Gulf monarchies, which were angered by its attitude during the Iraqi occupation of Kuwait. Palestinians also paid the price and tens of thousands of them, expelled from the emirate, flocked to Jordan.

Jordan participated, along with Israel's other Arab neighbors, in the Madrid conference which was the beginning of direct peace negotiations, supported by the United States and Russia. In Jordan's case, this put an end to hostilities with Israel. On July 25, 1994, an Israeli-Jordanian peace treaty was signed in Washington by King Hussein, Israeli Prime Minister Yitzhak Rabin and Bill Clinton. The agreement gives rise to minor changes on the borders pending a final settlement of the Israeli-Palestinian conflict. Amman maintains relations with both the Jewish state and Palestinian organizations and assures the PLO of its commitment to defend "an independent Palestinian entity. In November 1997 a Mossad commando sent to Amman to assassinate Khaled Mechaal using a slow poison was intercepted by the Jordanian services. King Hussein was furious and threatened to abrogate the peace treaty with Israel if Netanyahu did not deliver the antidote that would save Mechaal. The latter's initial refusal led the king to increase his demands and he obtained, in addition to the antidote, the release of Sheikh Yassin. King Hussein died on 7 February 1999. Some time before his death, he dismissed his brother Hassan, heir to the throne since 1964, to entrust the country to his son Abdullah II. Abdullah II is continuing the political and economic reforms of the country, which began in the 1990s, towards greater liberalism. Moreover, the Jordanian government has shown its concern to remain at peace with its neighbors, despite the events affecting the region, notably the outbreak of a second intifada by the Palestinians in September 2000. From the 2000s onwards, it has had to deal with the threat of destabilization from Islamist networks that have taken root in the country. The latter claimed responsibility for the attacks of 9 December 2005 in Amman.

Since the beginning of the Syrian conflict, Jordan has been faced with managing a major crisis just across its long northern border. Although Amman has agreed to receive hundreds of thousands of refugees, the security issue has remained central to the handling of this border. A system for controlling Syrian refugees was put in place by Jordan during the first two years of the conflict, and in 2013 it closed its border to refugees. It must contain the Islamist contagion, while a fringe of its population is ideologically close to these political movements, while maintaining its strategic relations with its American and Gulf allies - who are also its main financial backers. Support for forces opposed to the Syrian regime from Jordan began as early as November 2012, and the American secret service trained ASL rebel fighters on Jordanian soil. But Jordan plays a kind of double game, supporting the ASL while continuing to maintain political and commercial ties with neighboring Syria, with whom it shares a common enemy: radical Islamism. In 2014 it joined the international coalition to fight Daech in Syria. In March 2015 a Jordanian pilot was burned alive by this terrorist organization after his plane was shot down while conducting a raid against its positions in Syria.

"Assad's Syria[15] "

In Syria, Hafez al-Assad, who seized power in November 1970, succeeded in turning an unstable, medium-sized country with no particular resources into a regional power capable of interfering in the affairs of its neighbors. All of his most important political choices were, in some way, influenced by the three great frustrations and obsessions of his youth, which shaped his besieged mentality: the marginalization of the Alawite community, the instability of the Syrian state, which had been weakened by ten coups d'état, and successive defeats by Israel. "A formidable strategist, which earned him the nickname of "Bismarck of the Middle East", he became a key player in the Middle East, justifying the formula: "no war without Egypt, no peace without Syria. He will impose himself as the arbiter of regional situations, and will consider Lebanon as his preserve. Superiorly intelligent, perfectly in control of himself, which earned him the nickname of "Sphinx of Damascus", he was endowed with considerable working power and a formidable thirst for power, while leading a simple life. He is also a pragmatist who does not bother with theoretical debates[16] . His arrival in power suits everyone a little. The Americans are rid of a dogmatic regime close to the USSR, the Egyptians and the Saudis are renewing their relations with Damascus, and Israel can only note that the new power is more pragmatic than its predecessors. In Assad's mind, it is better not to provoke the enemy into launching a battle for which Syria is not ready. The slogan "the people's war is the only way to liberate Palestine" disappears from Baathist phraseology. By claiming to be an anti-imperialist and anti-Zionist regime, it enjoys the support of the vast majority of the left, in the Arab world and elsewhere. By claiming to be the ultimate protector of minorities, it gets the panicked support of these minorities, as well as of the West. He reinforces the dictatorial character of the regime. A cult of his personality is organized, describing him as a just, wise and powerful leader whose influence extends beyond Syria. Relying on his Alawite community, the Ba'ath Party, the army and the security services, he ruled the country undivided for 30 years, from 1970 until the end of the century. As the Alawites were not considered Muslims, he obtained a religious consultation from Imam Moussa Sadr who recognized them as belonging to Shiite Islam. Controlling society through clientelist networks, he tolerated no opposition. The system of power based on fear that he instituted and the imprisonment, sometimes accompanied by torture, of his opponents was described as a "state of barbarism" by the researcher Michel Seurat, who was to become its victim. The state of emergency established in 1963 was maintained throughout his presidency. Under this law, the press was limited to three newspapers controlled by the Party, and dissidents were judged by special courts when they were not imprisoned or liquidated without trial. An estimated 17,000 people "disappeared" between 1980 and 2000. Sponsoring state terrorism has always been part of its strategy, as it is with its Iranian ally. Although it does not directly sponsor all operations, it is more often than not content to control them and direct them in its own interests. While reinforcing political authoritarianism and the personalization of the regime, he distanced himself from the radicalism of his predecessor and initiated a certain economic opening that would be called the era of "rectification. But the results were far from meeting the expectations of the population, which faced numerous shortages. This encouraged smuggling, particularly from Lebanon, from which those close to the president, particularly his brother, were the main beneficiaries. The resentment of a large part of the Sunni community and his difficulties in domestic politics led him to attach great importance to foreign policy.

During his 30 years of rule, Assad did not really confront the Israeli army until 1973, preferring to fight against it by proxy. After 1967, his foreign policy aimed to break Syria's isolation and to get closer to Egypt in view of a possible confrontation with Israel. He joined, with Egypt and Libya, the stillborn project of the Federation of Arab Republics. He emerged politically strengthened from his participation alongside Egypt in the Yom Kippur War in October 1973, despite his military defeat and his failure to retake the Golan Heights. In 1974, he negotiated an agreement to disengage his armed forces from the Golan Heights, under the leadership of the American Secretary of State Henry Kissinger, which allowed Syria to recover the city of Kuneitra and normalize its relations with the United States. This negotiation will prove to be one of the main foundations of the regime's survival. The Syrian president's negotiating skills, fueled by his scheming mentality, would earn the admiration of Dr. Kissinger, a master in the field. As a sign of the importance of his role on the regional scene, he welcomed President Nixon who visited Damascus in 1974 to re-establish diplomatic relations between the two countries. From that moment on, Washington will consider Damascus as a stabilizing element with which it can sometimes work. Assad met President Carter in Geneva in 1977, who considered that the Syrian President had a great role to play in the search for a peace settlement in the Middle East. After the Kipur War, Assad developed the concept of "strategic parity with Israel". Dreaming of taking his revenge against the Hebrew state, he believes that it is necessary to wait until the two armies are on the same level before resuming hostilities. Except that after having dangled this possibility in front of him for a decade, the Soviets made their closest ally in the Middle East understand that strategic parity was a utopia. Israel being too strong for Syria, it will try to impose its hegemony on its neighbors. Its first concern is to bring the Palestinian resistance to heel. It will take turns arming and repressing the federatists according to its interests. By taking care to divide them in order to weaken the one who dares to challenge his supremacy: Yasser Arafat.

The outbreak of the war in Lebanon in 1975 provided him with the opportunity to impose his domination there. "Believing, like most Syrians at the time, that Lebanon had been detached from Syria by the colonial powers, he summed up his vision of the situation in the following words: "one people in two states[17] ". His plan could not but provoke frequent clashes with France, which, for him, was Syria's historical adversary in Lebanon. He took advantage of the outbreak of the Lebanese war in 1975 to act as an arbiter in the conflict. His intervention in Lebanon allowed him to make Syria a real regional power. He will show the same ferocity as in Syria, not hesitating to order the bombing of civilian populations and the physical elimination of anyone who stands in his way, from Walid Jumblatt to Béchir Gemayel, including the French ambassador to Lebanon, Louis Delamare. Sadat's visit to Jerusalem in 1977, which he considered a betrayal, pushed him to strengthen his control over Lebanon and the PLO and to get closer to Jordan. After the Camp David agreements (September 1978) and the defection of Egypt, Syria became the pillar of the "Refusal Front" against America and Israel. At the same time, in Lebanon, the Syrian regime, which had allied itself with the Christian camp at the beginning of the war to counter the "Palestinian-progressive" camp, became its opponent. Once defeated, following the Israeli invasion of Lebanon in 1982, it made a strong comeback on the Lebanese scene. And the elimination of the resistance in the Christian area in 1989 will allow him to extend his domination to the whole country, except for the border area between Lebanon and Israel. Although Assad capitalizes on his "resistance" to Israel, the Golan front remains as quiet as the Sinai front. And he is careful not to allow the Palestinian federates to launch operations against Israel from Syrian territory. While respecting the ceasefire line under the control of the United Nations, it chooses an indirect policy of pressure on Israel through support for various Arab movements hostile to the Jewish state, such as the Lebanese Hezbollah and the Palestinian Hamas. And it refuses to recognize the existence of Israel, officially described as a "Zionist entity".

Following the Iranian Revolution, the competition between the Syrian and Iraqi branches of the Ba'ath led Assad and Khomeini to form a strategic alliance in 1979 in the name, officially, of the fight against Israel, but, in fact, of the shared hostility against Saddam Hussein. Islamist hostility to what they saw as an Alawite stranglehold on power led to a major crisis when, in June 1979, an Islamist commando broke into the Aleppo air force cadet school, sidelined Sunni cadets, and massacred 80 Alawite cadets in application of a fatwa by Ibn Taymiya. The regime responded by intensifying repression. In 1982, an uprising by the Muslim Brotherhood in Hamah, the Brotherhood's stronghold, was mercilessly crushed by special forces commanded by Rifaat al-Assad, the president's brother. It is estimated that more than 20,000 people died as a result of the unleashing of the regime's special forces on the city, some of whose districts were completely razed. The Islamist threat was removed, but at the cost of real terror. The mistake is to think that the country entered into civil war in 2011. Inter-communal violence has in fact never ceased, but the West was not interested because at that time there was no oil and gas agenda concerning Syria, nor any agenda against Iran. When the president fell ill in 1984, Rifaat kept order in the country, which, without a leader, was in danger of falling into civil war. He was accused of trying to seize power. When the president recovered, he forced his brother to go into exile because of diverging political opinions, and the latter settled in France. In 1999 his supporters were arrested and imprisoned. These measures were related to Hafez's succession, as Rifaat began to reposition himself as his brother sought to eliminate any potential competition to his designated successor, his son Bashar al-Assad. The latter had originally had little interest in politics. His father had prepared his eldest son, Bassel, to succeed him as head of the regime. When his eldest son died in a car accident in 1994, Hafez el-Assad called upon his youngest son to take over.

The wise policy of the Syrian president contrasts with the adventurism of Saddam Hussein. Unlike the latter, he understands the importance of the implosion of the USSR and takes a calculated step towards the Western camp. After supporting Iran in its war against Saddam Hussein's Iraq, his sworn enemy, even if it meant alienating the Arabs, he joined the international coalition against Iraq after the invasion of Kuwait. The removal of Iraq, his eternal rival after the Iraq-Iran war and the Gulf war, was a revenge for Assad. The Syrian regime then became more "acceptable" and obtained the American green light to put an end to the Lebanese resistance and consolidate its hold on Lebanon. However, it had to take into account the Iranian influence, which relied on Hezbollah, and accept the appointment of Rafik Hariri as Prime Minister, an ally of Saudi Arabia. Hariri, with the support of Jacques Chirac, encouraged Assad to normalize his relations with the West. Throughout the 1990s, he became a party to the Middle East peace process. Not wanting war, but not really wanting peace either, he will play the game while remaining inflexible. He then agreed, under pressure from the United States, to enter into negotiations with Israel, which failed.

During the last years of his presidency, the balance of power in the Middle East deteriorated considerably for Syria. At the head of an economically dilapidated state, weakened by the fall of the Soviet protector and, since 1996, by the formation of an Israeli-Turkish strategic partnership, neighbouring an ideologically hostile Saddam, as well as a Jordan at peace with a Jewish state that was more powerful than ever, Hafez el-Assad hardly took the full measure of the impoverishment of his game. A dispute with Turkey over the use of the waters of the Euphrates has led Damascus to put pressure on Ankara by discreetly supporting the Kurdish PKK in the Bekaa. In the autumn of 1998, when Ankara threatened Damascus with open conflict if the Kurdish rebel leader of the PKK, Abdullah Ôcalan, was not extradited as soon as possible, the "Bismark of the Middle East" capitulated and let go of his protégé within a few days. When he died on 10 June 2000, Syrian television announced: "the Syrian president died after fighting for more than half a century for the honour of the Arabs". The propaganda that was blasted for almost 30 years has had its effect. By conviction or fear of reprisals, many Syrians are crying out their pain. In a country where silence reigns, the demonstrations of mourning seem deliberately exaggerated. But foreign leaders are not rushing to his funeral. Jacques Chirac was the only Western leader to attend the ceremony, along with a few Arab leaders, including Yasser Arafat, who had a bad relationship with the deceased. The ceremony resembled more a handover to his son than a funeral. Slogans such as "By our soul and by our blood, we will sacrifice ourselves for you Bashar", or "There is only God, Syria and Bashar" are chanted in the street as the coffin passes. The young ophthalmologist has the reputation of being a modern man, wishing to bring Syria into the internet age. But although he has succeeded in imposing his power on the old guard, he is far from having the skill and stature of his father whose legacy he will squander.

Saudi Arabia

In the 1970s, a religious-political movement called Al-Sahwa Al Islamyia ("the Islamic Awakening") emerged in Saudi Arabia. Its members called for a greater role for the clergy in governance and control of the royal family's privileges, more transparency in the management of public funds, and a more conservative and Islamic society to counteract Western cultural influence. The fact that Arabia defines itself as an Islamic state whose only constitution is the Quran should protect it from an Islamist claim. But it is weakened by the life of the members of the ruling dynasty, which is not compatible with official puritanism. A major crisis erupted when, on November 20, 1979, a group of millenarian exalts seized the Great Mosque of Mecca, the holiest place in Islam, to proclaim their leader mahdi (a man guided by God to lead the Muslim community and fight its enemies). It took two weeks for the Saudi authorities, with the help of the GIGN (elite anti-terrorist unit of the French Gendarmerie), to take back the shrine from the exalted ones. A few days later, the rebels were beheaded with swords in the main squares of eight different cities in the kingdom without any judgment being passed on them. This affair dealt a terrible blow to the Saudi regime, which bases part of its legitimacy on the custody of the Holy Places. It made some concessions to the Wahhabis and the Soviet invasion of Afghanistan, which occurred three weeks later, provided it with an opportunity to prove, by proclaiming jihad, that it remained faithful to the values it claimed. This commitment certainly brought the Saudi population together around the regime, but it represented a real danger for it. Once on the ground, the Saudi mujahideen asserted their autonomy.

In 1981 the Crown Prince, Fahd, proposed a peace plan for the Middle East based on UN resolutions and American pressure on Israel. The Western powers showed interest in what they saw as a real opening on the part of the Arab world. The Fahd plan was accepted at the Fez summit. But it came up against the intransigence of Israel and the Arab refusal front. On the death of King Khaled in 1982, Fahd, who succeeded him, tried to bring the Wahhabi institutions under his authority. The threat to the kingdom posed by the invasion of Kuwait by Saddam's army in August 1990 forced King Fahd to call on the Americans. The massive arrival of American troops in the country was an intolerable cultural trauma and sparked the dissent of Osama Bin Laden that would shake the world. The invasion of Kuwait by Iraq followed by the reception of the coalition troops on the soil of the kingdom provoked a shock in the Saudi society. "King Fahd's refusal of Osama bin Laden's proposal to use his militia to defend the kingdom against a possible Iraqi invasion caused a rift between the leader of al-Qaeda and the Saudi dynasty. The American presence is more and more contested among the population. The Sahwa movement, which opposes it, is banned and several of its members are arrested by the Saudi authorities .[18]

Until the early 1990s, the Saudi government maintained close relations with the entire Islamist movement. The kingdom had given refuge to thousands of Muslim Brothers persecuted by nationalist regimes in the Arab world. In the 1980s, more radical Islamists also enjoyed the protection of the kingdom, especially when they were fighting the communists and Soviets in Afghanistan. When King Fahd called in hundreds of thousands of foreign, mainly American, troops in 1990 to protect the kingdom and liberate Iraqi-occupied Kuwait, these militants led a broad-based opposition to the royal family. In February 1991, Saudis signed a petition calling for liberal measures, including reform of the religious police and the creation of an advisory council. Internal tensions continued. The denunciation by the Muslim Brotherhood of the Saudi alliance with the United States during the Gulf War in 1991 sealed the rupture of the good relations that Riyadh initially maintained with the Brotherhood. A growing mistrust between the Saudi regime and the local Islamists then set in. In 1994, the main figures of the protest were thrown into prison. To the point that in 2002, Prince Nayef, Minister of the Interior, made the Muslim Brotherhood "the source of all the kingdom's ills. Prince Abdullah bin Abdul Aziz became regent of the kingdom in 1996 after King Fahd suffered a stroke. he initiated some timid political reforms by organizing municipal elections and limiting the privileges of some 25,000 members of the royal family. In 1995 and 1996, attacks were carried out against American soldiers and civilians. Following these attacks, the main American military installations in Arabia were moved to Qatar in 2003. In 2004, following the American invasion of Iraq, a series of bombings took place, mostly targeting buildings housing expatriates, particularly Americans.

United Arab Emirates

The increase of the oil price in 1973 conferred an important weight to the Arab emirates of the Gulf. However, they feel threatened by the double danger of Iran and Iraq. Their human resources are limited and they have to call upon a large immigrant population which sometimes constitutes the majority of the inhabitants of their countries. The Islamic revolution in Iran in 1979 increased their concerns. In 1981 the UAE, Bahrain, Qatar and Oman formed the Gulf Cooperation Council with Saudi Arabia. The new organization has a permanent structure, consisting of a higher council, a council of ministers and a secretariat, but in reality it is dominated by Saudi Arabia. The danger of revolutionary Islamism is countered by a strengthening of Islamic puritanism. During the Iraq-Iran war (1980-1988), the Arab monarchies of the Gulf were allies of Iraq, to which they provided considerable financial support, while being wary of its hegemonic ambitions. This mistrust was to be confirmed when, at the end of the war, Iraq invaded Kuwait, with which it had a financial and oil dispute. Following Iraq's invasion of Kuwait in 1990, the UAE maintained good relations with its Western allies in the military field. It cooperated with Western forces to liberate Kuwait and signed defense and military cooperation treaties with France and the United States, which provided military aid and equipment. Recently, a military defense treaty was signed in which France pledged to protect the UAE in the event of an attack on its national sovereignty. France has also opened a military base in the UAE capital and the two countries have signed a civilian nuclear agreement. When Sheikh Zayed died in 2003, his eldest son, Sheikh Khalifa bin Zayed Al Nahyane, succeeded him as president of the UAE and ruler of Abu Dhabi. The UAE's wealth comes mainly from Abu Dhabi and its hydrocarbon resources. In 2009, the emirate had to come to the rescue of Dubai, which was in trouble as a result of the 2008 financial crisis, with a stimulus package of some $20 billion.

The emergence of Qatar

A small emirate with a small population, Qatar enjoys colossal wealth thanks to its gas exports, of which it has the third largest reserves in the world. It is ruled by the Al-Thani family, and professes the same Wahhabi faith as Saudi Arabia. From 1995, this tiny state began to emerge as a major player on the international scene. In June of that year, Emir Hamad overthrew his father and took power in Doha. Determined to assert his country's influence over neighboring Arabia, he launched the satellite channel Al Jazeera in November 1996. This television channel, which has been broadcasting continuously since 1998, brings a new style: information produced by Arabs of all nationalities targeting a global audience. It became the platform for opponents of Arab regimes, mainly Islamists, but also jihadists and more generally of the protest against the established order. Al Jazeera and the other Arab satellite channels broke the propaganda monopoly of the official television stations and played a decisive role in the awakening of political consciousness and the "Arab Spring". Where the Sauds support the apolitical Salafists, Qatar supports the Muslim Brotherhood in opposition to secular Arab dictatorships, while maintaining good relations with their leaders. From the 2011 Arab revolutions onwards, Qatar will be the main provider of funds to the Tunisian and Egyptian Muslim Brotherhood and to the Islamist insurgency against the Syrian regime. In parallel to this political activism, it practices a soft power policy, investing a significant part of its considerable revenues in operations aimed at improving its image in the Arab-Muslim world and in Europe. These operations of seduction can range from aid to the population of Gaza to sponsorship of the Paris-Saint Germain soccer club. But they will not prevent the frequent denunciations by the Western media of the financing of radical Islamist movements by Qatar (and Saudi Arabia), even if the lure of juicy contracts leads European leaders to turn a blind eye to these actions.

Yemen

In 1978 Ali Abdallah Saleh became president of the Republic of North Yemen. A remarkable maneuverer, he purged the armed forces in favor of his relatives and tolerated the Muslim Brotherhood, while counterbalancing their influence with that of the Salafists. The civil war that devastated Aden in 1986 favoured his aims for South Yemen. And. in 1990, he became the first president of a unified Republic of Yemen. The zaydites are a minority in a country with a sunni majority. It was in 1990 that the beginnings of the Houthi rebellion emerged through the Zaydi party Hizb el-Haqq (the Party of Truth) and the group al-Shabab al-mu'minin (The Young Believers). The group then followed the influence of Hussein Badreddine al-Houthi, who would later found the Houthi movement. In 2004, tensions with Saleh marked the beginning of a long armed confrontation with the regime's forces. The discourse of the Houthis is not originally that of a community movement. The rebels' motto is clear: "God is great, death to America, death to Israel, curse on the Jews, Islam will win." The movement is fundamentally anti-imperialist, while Yemen has been engaged in counterterrorism since 2001 alongside Washington.

The Libyan "Jamahirya

In 1976 Colonel Gaddafi published *The Green Book* (like Mao Tse-tung's Red Book), whose color refers to that of Islam. An unpredictable character, with a willingly extravagant behavior, he proposed a third way rejecting capitalism and communism. Founded on a model of direct democracy, it is presented as the only valid state organization based exclusively on popular committees. The book is distributed throughout the country, almost acting as a constitution. Gaddafi proclaimed the "Jamahirya" (State of the masses) which replaced the Republic in 1977. Having concentrated power in his own hands, in 1980 he gave himself the title of "guide of evolution". He relied on the power of the tribes to govern and consciously maintained the disorder of the institutions through constant reforms, thus preventing the emergence of any counter-power. He works to ensure a form of stability by funding generous social policies with oil resources, and by developing the Libyan education and health systems. But at the same time, he relies on a repressive apparatus that uses the most brutal methods, regularly executing real or supposed conspirators. Advocating equality between men and women, he opened a military academy exclusively for women in 1983. Nicknamed the Amazons by the media, they served as his bodyguards, and for some as sex slaves.

Libya being a major exporter of oil to Europe, the European states that he courted initially turned a blind eye to the antics and abuses of the Libyan dictator. However, his relations with several Western countries, in particular the United States, were very tense from the beginning of the 1980s, and resulted in the sacking of the American embassy in Tripoli in 1980. At the end of the 1980s, Gaddafi allowed the Palestinian extremist group Abu Nidal to open training camps in Libya. In August 1981, manoeuvres by the American fleet in the Gulf of Sirte led to an incident in which two Libyan fighter planes were destroyed in flight. In 1986 Washington decided to impose a total embargo on Libya, accused of harbouring terrorist groups. The Libyan "mad dog", according to President Reagan, became the pariah of the international community. On April 5, Libya was involved in an attack against American soldiers in Berlin. In retaliation, the American air force bombed Tripoli and Benghazi. Two years later, on December 21, 1988, an American civilian plane exploded over Lockerbie, Scotland. None of the 259 passengers on board survived the attack, which was attributed to the Libyan secret services. The following year, an attack on a flight of the French company UTA caused 170 victims. Libya was again singled out and years later had to pay billions of dollars to the families of the victims of both attacks. After the September 11 attacks, Gaddafi calmed down and tried to improve his image in the international community. Several heads of state or government followed one another to Tripoli, signing trade agreements in several key areas. He himself is welcomed with open arms in several European capitals, including Paris and Rome by Nicolas Sarkozy and Silvio Berlusconi. And on every official visit, he brings his tent with him as if to taunt the host country. In 2009 Gaddafi was elected to the presidency of the African Union. His son Saif al-Islam Gaddafi advocates political and economic reforms but he is not listened.

1 *Le Proche-Orient éclaté II 1990-1996,* Georges Corm, La Découverte 1997, p. 20

2 *La revanche de Dieu, chrétiens juifs et musulmans à la conquête du monde*, Gilles Kepel, Seuil 1991

3 *Les Arabes, leur destin et le nôtre*, Jean-Pierre Filiu, La Découverte 2015

4 *Le Proche-Orient éclaté II*, op. cit. p. 5

5 *Les Arabes, leur destin et le nôtre*, op. cit.

6 *These fifteen men who changed the face of the Middle East*, L'Orient-le Jour of November 2, 2017

7 ibid.

8 *Le grand jeu, Orient-arabe et rivalités internationales*, Henry Laurens, Armand Colin 1991, p. 299

9 *Ces quinze hommes qui ont changé la face du Proche-Orient,* op.cit.

10 *Le grand jeu,* op. cit. p. 363

11 *L'Orient arabe à l'heure américaine*, Henry Laurens, Hachette-Pluriel 2005, p. 63

12 *The Middle East powder keg,* Noam Chomsky, Gilbert Achkar, Fayard 2006

13 *Le Proche-Orient éclaté II*, op. cit.

14 *The New Question of the East*, Georges Corm, La Découverte 2017, p. 36

15 Slogan posted on road signs in praise of the Syrian president.

16 *General Assad's Syria*, Daniel le Gac, Complexe Editions 1991

17 *Les Arabes, leur destin et le nôtre*, op. cit. p. 187

18 *Saudi Arabia at war*, Antoine Basbous, Perrin 2004

Chapter 8. The Israeli-Palestinian conflict

The rise of the Palestinian resistance

The 1948 war had seen the collapse of the traditional Palestinian leadership led by Hajj Amin al-Husseini under the Arab High Committee. The West Bank was merged with Transjordan and the Gaza Strip was administered by Egypt. In the 1950s, the Palestinian question fell victim to Arab rivalries, particularly that between Egypt and Iraq. The Palestinians had long held the view that the liberation of Palestine would require the achievement of Arab unity. As this became less and less feasible, the new generations decided to take their destiny into their own hands. This was the case of Yasser Arafat, who founded the Palestinian Liberation Movement (Fatah) in Kuwait at the end of the 1950s. Palestinian nationalism, which was forged in the 1960s within Arab nationalism, initially claimed a secular and democratic Palestine where Jews, Muslims and Christians would live on an equal footing. But this demand clashed with both Zionists and Muslim fundamentalists. For their part, the Arab states, particularly Egypt, intended to put the Palestinian cause at the service of their own aims. In May 1964, at the Cairo summit, the PLO (Palestine Liberation Organization) was created under the aegis of Nasser. Its presidency was entrusted to Ahmed Choukeiry who organized a Palestinian National Congress (PNC). The latter adopted the first Palestinian charter and decided to set up a Palestinian Liberation Army (PLA) integrated into the regular Arab armies. The Palestinian radicals were not satisfied with speeches about their cause and decided to take action by launching commando operations against Israel. The Palestinian resistance was born. To counter Nasser's influence on the PLO, King Faysal encouraged Yasser Arafat and his movement, Fatah. The instrumentalization of the rivalry between Shukeiry and Arafat by Egypt and Saudi Arabia prevented the Palestinian cause from freeing itself from inter-Arab clashes. The Six-Day War (June 5-10, 1967) allowed Israel to complete its occupation of the whole of Palestine, seizing the West Bank, Gaza and the Arab part of Jerusalem, causing a new wave of refugees. More than one million Palestinians, spread across the West Bank and Gaza, fell under Israeli occupation. Israel officially annexed East Jerusalem and its environs, which were declared part of the city's greater municipality and where Jewish settlement began in the early days of the cease-fire. Within two or three years a settlement enterprise was established in the rest of the occupied territories. Wildcat settlements established at the initiative of religious activists sprang up alongside government-authorized settlements. Since then, Israel has refused to implement UN Security Council Resolution 242 calling for Israeli withdrawal from the occupied territories and a just settlement of the Palestinian refugee problem. This refusal, as well as the oppression and humiliation suffered by the Palestinian population, could only exacerbate their will to resist.

In December 1967, Shukeiry, who had distinguished himself by making inflammatory statements, including calls to "throw the Jews into the sea", resigned from the PLO. A Fatah congress held in Damascus decided, under the impetus of Yasser Arafat, to intensify the armed struggle. Arafat and Fatah established their headquarters in Karameh, Jordan, and launched operations against Israel from Jordanian territory. Terrorist actions, to which Fatah did not hesitate to resort, were met with violent Israeli reprisals. Resistance operations were conducted under the political umbrella of the PLO, which included, alongside Fatah, founded by Yasser Arafat, Marxist movements: the Popular Front for the Liberation of Palestine (PFLP), founded by George Habash in December 1967, the Popular Front for the Liberation of Palestine-General Command (PFLP-GC) led by Ahmad Jibril, and the Democratic Front for the Liberation of Palestine (DFLP) of Nayef Hawatmeh. While Fatah is the largest organization and represents Palestinian nationalism above all, the ideology of the other three movements is more pan-Arab and anti-imperialist. This is particularly true of the PFLP, which emerged from the Arab National Movement (ANM) and disappeared in 1967. The Syrian Ba'ath, for its part, created its own Palestinian organization: La Sa'iqa ("the lightning"), for which the Palestinian revolution was inseparable from the more general Arab revolution. All these movements believe that the armed struggle is the only way to liberate Palestine. And they rejected UN Resolution 242 which "ignores the national rights of the Palestinian people". In March 1968, the Israeli army launched a large-scale operation to destroy the Palestinian camp of Karame in Jordan. In this way, the city's economy was transformed into an economic and social hub, and the city's economy was transformed into an economic and social hub, and the city's economy was transformed into an economic and social hub, and the city's economy was transformed into an economic and social hub. The camp was finally razed to the ground, but the battle was considered a victory by Fatah. This new situation allowed Fatah to emancipate itself completely from Egyptian control. Nasser recognized Fatah and its leader, whom he had tried to circumvent by all means. Arafat was elected head of the PLO in February 1969 and the Fatah formations took control of the organization. After Karame, the PLO moved its headquarters from Damascus to Amman and, because of its growing prestige, tended to become a state within a state in Jordan.

The religious dimension of the Israeli-Palestinian conflict

"Any analysis of the Israeli-Palestinian conflict cannot ignore the religious factor. The decision of the UN to endorse the proclamation of the State of Israel, based on a religious dimension, created a major theological-political problem. The inability of Western states to separate Jewishness and citizenship meant that a Polish Jew, a German Jew, a French Jew, an Italian Jew became first and foremost a Jew (with a capital letter, i.e. a people), who needed a land to live in, whereas, now aware of the horror of Auschwitz, they had a duty to include and reaffirm the primacy of citizenship "without distinction of origin, race or religion". From then on, through an identification between Palestinians and Muslims, any extension of Israeli territory at the expense of Palestinian territory becomes an expression of the religious domination of Judaism against Islam. And the Palestinian resistance against the occupation takes on the face of a struggle of Muslims against Jews[1] . The theological-political dimension of the State of Israel also has international repercussions. First, through the support of a large part of the international Jewish community for its Jewish character. Second, through the solidarity of Muslims with the Palestinian people. Their anti-Zionism goes as far as hatred of the Jews and calls for the destruction of the State of Israel among the most extreme. For their part, the religious Jewish nationalists consider the colonization and annexation of the occupied territories as a commandment from God. They see the 1967 victory as "miraculous" and the liberation of the territories as the beginning of divine redemption. In a sermon at the Wailing Wall, Rabbi Zvi Yehuda Kook said, "We inform the people of Israel and the whole world that, according to God's commandment, we have just returned home. [...]. We will never leave again[2] . In 1974, religious activists founded the Gush Emunim (Faith Bloc) movement, which was to determine right-wing activism vis-à-vis the territories. The religious dimension of the Israeli-Palestinian conflict is amplified by the sanctity of Jerusalem where the holy places of the three monotheistic religions are located. This is the case of the Al-Aqsa mosque, the third Holy Place of Islam, which came under the control of the Hebrew state in 1967, as well as the Wailing Wall and the Esplanade of the Mosques. Called by Muslims *Haran-al Sharif* (the Noble Sanctuary), it was built, according to the Jews, over the remains of the first Temple. "For the Jews, the Temple was *Beyt-ha-Mikdash* (the Holy House) which the Muslims adopted. They called the city itself *Bayt al-Makdis* ("the Holy House"[3]). The esplanade of the mosques has become the exemplary place of confrontations where the religious and the national sacred are inextricably mixed[4] . The existence of Jewish messianist groups demanding the destruction of "pagan temples" to allow the restoration of the Jewish temple aggravates the situation. Since the conquest of the Old City in 1967, Jews have not been allowed to pray in the Esplanade. The Jewish religious authorities had forbidden Jews to enter the esplanade anyway because they might step on a consecrated space, and thus commit sacrilege. But other rabbis claimed the right to pray on the esplanade. While, on the Arab side, the Islamic movement organized demonstrations in defense of the Al-Aqsa mosque. In August 2000, Israeli Prime Minister Barak (a secular Labor Party), made the request during the Camp David negotiations under American auspices. As for the Likud, supported by the religious parties, it made Jerusalem and the Temple Mount its hobbyhorse. It was in this explosive context that Ariel Sharon went to the Esplanade on September 28, 2000. This provocation triggered the second intifada. From then on, the conflict experienced an unprecedented escalation of violence.

The colonization of the occupied territories

From 1974 onwards, the movement to build Israeli settlements in the territories occupied since the Six Day War gained momentum. In Israel, the crisis of confidence caused by the Yom Kippur War led to the resignation of Golda

Meir's government, which was replaced by General Rabin, who in turn had to give way in April 1977 to Shimon Peres. But in the May 1977 elections, Labor lost the power it had held for 29 years to the Likud, founded in 1973 by Ariel Sharon and Menachem Begin. Led by Begin, the new government pursued an ultra-nationalist policy with the support of the religious parties and strongly supported settlement. Appointed Minister of Agriculture, Sharon accelerated the settlement process in the Gaza Strip, the West Bank and the Golan Heights. After Sadat's visit to Jerusalem on November 19, 1977, the PLO, realizing that the Egyptian president was moving towards a bilateral Israeli-Egyptian agreement excluding the Palestinians, tried to scupper the peace process. In order to embarrass Sadat, on March 11, 1978, it carried out a commando operation, killing 37 Israeli civilians. Three days later, the Israeli Defense Forces invaded southern Lebanon, destroying PLO bases as far as the Litani River. Public opinion in Israel feared that Begin would lose a historic chance for peace with Egypt by being inflexible. Israel's main peace movement, "Peace Now", took part in the largest political demonstration ever held in the country, in Tel Aviv on 1er April 1978. A petition with 100,000 signatures forced Begin, despite his own convictions, to take into account the desire for peace of a large part of the population. Other considerations also influenced his position: the threat of ministers belonging to a moderate party to leave the coalition if he missed the opportunity to conclude the peace. And the desire not to alienate the American ally. In view of the Camp David meeting, he was determined not to accept any settler withdrawals from the West Bank and Gaza and not to give in on the issue of Palestinian self-determination. Freed from the worry of the Egyptian front after the separate peace agreement reached with Sadat at Camp David in 1979, and assured of the unwavering support of American power, Israel had a free hand to do literally whatever it wanted. Begin had never seriously considered giving a large measure of autonomy to the Arabs of the West Bank and Gaza. Tripartite negotiations between the Americans, Egyptians and Israelis on autonomy began in late May 1979 and ended in 1982 in complete failure. Sadat broke off negotiations after the Knesset passed the Basic Law on Jerusalem on July 30, 1980. Proclaiming "Jerusalem reunited, the eternal capital of Israel", this law imposed Israeli law on East Jerusalem, whereas Sadat had demanded that this part of the city be attached to the autonomous West Bank. Further meetings failed to break the deadlock. Given the nature of the right-wing Israeli government and the Palestinian and Egyptian demands, the talks were doomed to failure. Israel had initially excluded the PLO, and neither the West Bank and Gaza residents nor Jordan had agreed to participate. While the negotiations were taking place, Israel authorized a series of new buildings in the West Bank and Gaza. While reflecting Begin's beliefs about Jewish rights to "Judea and Samaria," the settlement policy also served to deflect right-wing opposition to the peace treaty with Egypt and the withdrawal from Sinai.

In 1981, a plan for peace in the Middle East and for a just settlement of the Palestinian problem, based on UN resolutions, proposed by the Crown Prince of

Saudi Arabia, Fahd, was not followed up. Cautiously formulated, it only implicitly mentions the recognition of Israel. Anxious to preserve the unity of the resistance, Arafat, who feared being outflanked by the hard wing of the Palestinian resistance, took a wait-and-see attitude, while Hafez el-Assad immediately rejected it. This is obviously also the case of Begin, who, having won the June 1981 elections, set up a coalition of right-wing and religious parties. Having got rid of the "doves", he enjoyed much greater freedom of manoeuvre with his new Cabinet, dominated by Likud hawks, than with the previous government. Sharon was also appointed Minister of Defence. In July, the Israeli air force resumed its bombing of Palestinian targets in Lebanon. Palestinian rocket attacks on Israeli border towns, followed by an assassination attempt on June 3, 1982, against the Israeli ambassador in London by the Abu Nidal group, provided Begin and Sharon with the pretexts they were looking for to invade Lebanon in order to destroy the PLO and expel it from the country. Once the organization was crushed, the two men thought, Israel would have almost free rein to determine the fate of the West Bank and Gaza Strip. They also planned to restore Christian predominance in the country, after which Lebanon would sign a peace treaty with Israel. Sharon submitted two operational plans to the Israeli cabinet. The first envisaged a limited invasion of southern Lebanon and the second an advance to Beirut where the PLO headquarters were located. This would allow Israel to establish a link with the Christian enclave, cut the Beirut-Damascus road, and eventually expel the Syrian units stationed in Lebanon. Despite the strong reluctance of the Cabinet, he managed to wrest approval for the second plan. The invasion of Lebanon, called "Peace in Galilee", which began on 6 June 1982, succeeded in destroying the PLO's infrastructure, which had to be evacuated from Lebanon, but failed to achieve the other objectives set by the Begin-Sharon tandem. It pushed Washington to revive, to Begin's great displeasure, the issue of the occupied territories, and their annexation by the Hebrew state. This was the theme of the Reagan plan of 1er September 1982. The question," says Secretary of State George Shultz, "is how to reconcile concerns about its security with the no less legal rights of the Palestinians. And the answer can only be found around a negotiating table leading to a barter: land for peace. The Camp David agreement remains the foundation of our policy in this matter[5] ". While calling for a freeze on Israeli settlements in the occupied territories, and supporting the creation of a Palestinian self-government in that region, he spoke out against the establishment of an independent Palestinian state. But the Reagan plan was rejected by Israel and the Palestinian National Council held in Algiers in February 1983.

In Israel, the political failure of the invasion of Lebanon and the massacres at Sabra and Shatila caused an electroshock in public opinion. Faced with the rebellion, Begin had to resign in August 1983. Yitzhak Shamir replaced him as Prime Minister. Although he belonged to the extreme right, he remained more moderate and less dogmatic than his predecessor. Sharon, to whom the Kahane

Commission attributed some of the responsibility for this tragedy, began a long period in the desert. The Israeli elections of July 1984 failed to produce a majority and led to the formation of a government of national unity between Labour and the Likud. Shimon Peres and Yitzhak Shamir instituted a system of rotation whereby the latter succeeded the former as Prime Minister after two years. Itzhak Rabin held the portfolio of Defense from 1984 to 1990. Faced with the extremists within the Palestinian movement and the Syrian regime that wanted to impose its tutelage, Arafat moved closer to the "moderate" Arab camp formed by Egypt and Jordan. In the wake of his reconciliation with King Hussein, the principle of a future Jordanian-Palestinian confederation was even considered. But the Jordanian option, which was not unanimously supported by the Palestinians, was abandoned. In 1985, a series of disastrous incidents for the Palestinian cause, including the hijacking of a cruise ship by a Palestinian commando who murdered an Israeli passenger, interrupted the dialogue that had been initiated between the United States and the PLO through Jordan.

The first Intifada (1987-1993)

Caused by poverty, unemployment, pervasive humiliation and the subjugated state of the military occupation, a major revolt broke out in December 1987 in the occupied territories that took everyone by surprise. "It was not an armed rebellion, but a massive and sustained campaign of civil resistance, marked by strikes and business closures and punctuated by violent (though unarmed) demonstrations against the occupying forces[6] . This was the first Intifada, known as the Stone Revolt to emphasize the difference in means between the Palestinians, who had virtually no weapons, and the Israelis, who had a modern army with planes and tanks. In the beginning, there was no national umbrella for the movement and the refugees in the camps and the urban poor, mostly young, became the dominant force in Palestinian society. However, a national leadership of the uprising was formed in the West Bank with representatives of Fatah, the PFLP, the DFLP and the Communist Party, while the Islamists worked to take over the leadership in the Gaza Strip. Even though he had nothing to do with this spontaneous uprising, Abu Ammar, from his Tunisian exile, harangued the crowd, exalting the street to push it against the Jewish state. And Itzhak Rabin declares: "We will break the back of the revolt. The anti-Israeli attacks were met with brutal repression: the destruction of the demonstrators' homes and new collective sanctions. Hundreds of Palestinians were killed and thousands more were detained in Israeli jails, often without trial. The Israeli army and the internal intelligence services (the Shin Bet) were unable to break the Palestinian population's will to resist.

From this popular uprising against an intolerable occupation, the resistance of the Palestinians from the inside prevailed over external activism. The year 1987 marked the creation by Sheikh Yassin of Hamas. Born from the Palestinian branch of the Muslim Brotherhood, this Islamist movement poses as a rival to Fatah. Its charter includes as an objective the destruction of the State of Israel and the establishment of an Islamic state on all the land of the former Mandate

Palestine. This maximalist position earned him the support of Syria and Iran. On the other hand, Yasser Arafat understood that terrorist actions in all their forms had to be abandoned to please the Americans. In November 1988, the PLO proclaimed the State of Palestine at the Arab summit in Algiers and accepted UN Security Council Resolution 242, which recognized Israel and provided for the withdrawal from the occupied territories. It endorsed the principle of two states - Arab and Israeli - on the territory of Palestine. The Palestinian National Council is thus making an unprecedented concession on the road to peace and coexistence with Israel. Hamas, on the other hand, refuses any concession. Arafat's maneuver of declaring the PLO charter "obsolete" put the Israelis and the international community, which recognized the PLO as a partner for peace, in a corner. The intifada allowed the reappearance of the Palestinian problem and its placing on the agenda of the United Nations as a problem to be solved, which led the Israelis and Palestinians to the Oslo Accords signed in 1993, which put an end to the first intifada. But the PLO was put back on the ban of nations for its support to Saddam Hussein, which naturally played into the hands of Hamas and Israel.

The Oslo Accords

In the 1990s, one million Russian Jews emigrated to Israel. At the time, they represented a quarter of the country's population and increased its demographic weight in relation to the Palestinians. "The first Gulf War in 1991 seemed to pave the way for the establishment of a "pax americana" to which the administration of President George H. Bush was committed. The Madrid Conference, organized at the initiative of the United States and supported by the USSR, which was held in October 1991, was the first attempt to initiate a peace process in the Middle East involving Israel and the Arab countries[7] . In accordance with the conditions set by the United States and Israel, the PLO was excluded from the conference and the Palestinian representatives are part of the Jordanian delegation. The European Union had only observer status, and the USSR had only a formal co-chairmanship. The conference stated the principle that a stable and lasting peace must be based on a "territorial compromise", which is not the same as withdrawal from the occupied territories. Despite the anti-Arab diatribes and the rigid position of Israeli Prime Minister Yitzhak Shamir, the event was hailed by the media as a success of American diplomacy. It was followed by bilateral negotiations, under the aegis of the United States alone, between Israel on the one hand, and Syria, Lebanon, Jordan and a Palestinian delegation led by a non-PLO official on the other.

In 1992, Yitzhak Rabin became the head of the most pro-peace cabinet since the creation of the Jewish state. He was convinced that the Greater Israel policy advocated by the Likud would lead to a catastrophe: the continued growth of the Palestinian population would call into question the Jewish character of the state in the event of annexation, while violence would be permanent if political and military domination of the territories was maintained. It is therefore necessary to separate the peoples while defending Israeli interests. This hawk turned dove presents himself as the only one capable of bringing "peace and security". "In the inaugural speech of his second term as Prime Minister, Rabin recalled that "enough tears and blood have been shed. Interpelling the Palestinians: "We offer you the fairest solution: autonomy with its advantages and limitations[8] ". Secret negotiations between Israel and the PLO led to the Oslo Accords signed by both parties at the White House under the auspices of President Clinton on September 13, 1993, although the United States had no hand in it. After 45 years of conflict and five years of intifada the unthinkable happened: Rabin and Shimon Peres exchange handshakes with Arafat accompanied by Mahmoud Abbas, nicknamed Abu Mazen, the main Palestinian negotiator. This agreement recognizes the existence of Israel and its right to live in security and peace. The issue of settlement is not addressed, and the mutual recognition between Israel and the PLO is accompanied by a commitment to establish a "Palestinian Authority" in the territories to be evacuated by Israel. For having won his bet on peace, Arafat became the first president of the new Palestinian Authority and received the 1994 Nobel Peace Prize along with Shimon Peres and Yitzhak Rabin.

Hamas, which refused to recognize the existence of the State of Israel and opposed the concessions made by the PLO, rejected the Oslo Accords. It retaliated by carrying out the first of a series of suicide attacks in Gaza. The Palestinian Authority was established in July 1994, in the Gaza Strip and the town of Jericho, the only enclave in the West Bank that Israel had agreed to evacuate. The peace process opened with a profound misunderstanding in Gaza, where the PLO's central administration was set up. Its leaders, who had arrived from Tunis, boasted of having "liberated" the territory, while the local population considered that only their sacrifices during the intifada had allowed the return of exiled militants. After 27 years in exile, Arafat was allowed to return to Palestine where he received a triumphant welcome in Gaza. To win his bet on peace, he had to fight both the reluctance of some Arab countries, led by Syria, and the mutiny that was rumbling within his own troops. These agreements gave hope that peace would finally be established between the two enemy peoples. But it was not to be. Despite the Israeli withdrawal from part of the West Bank, the pace of Israeli settlement building in the occupied territories continues unabated and the Palestinian population, far from seeing the dividends of peace, sees its daily life worsen. The agreement divided the territory into Israeli and Palestinian areas, the latter intended to lay the foundations for a future Palestinian state.

Continuing his quest for peace, Yitzhak Rabin reached out to the Jordanians. A peace agreement was signed between Israel and Jordan on October 26, 1994. Then, in September 1995, the Israeli Prime Minister signed an agreement with Arafat called Oslo II, which divided the West Bank into three areas: the Palestinian Authority was to manage Area A, where 90% of the Palestinian population lived, while Area B was under shared jurisdiction and Area C under exclusive Israeli jurisdiction. In reality, in the name of security, the Israeli army is only redeploying itself by keeping control of the communication routes between the various Palestinian enclaves, which have been transformed into a series of urban ghettos, rendering the meaning of the word self-government meaningless. And Israel regularly carries out closures of the Palestinian territories. Rabbis proclaim that any cession of the Land of Israel is contrary to religious law. They call for civil disobedience. Rabin, a signatory of the Oslo Accords, was the target of a violent political campaign by the Likud leader, Benyamin Netanyahu. On November 4, 1995, after giving a speech in Tel Aviv to a jubilant crowd chanting "yes to peace, no to violence", he was assassinated by a Jewish extremist. Immediately belted, he told the policeman that he had no regrets and that he had acted "on divine orders". The assassination of the Prime Minister, which was a sign of the creeping radicalization of Israeli society, dealt a mortal blow to the hope of a compromise peace between Israelis and Palestinians. The advent of the Gush-Emunim movement (the Faith Bloc), with the arrival of the first settler parties in Israeli politics, completed the transformation of the original areligious Zionism.

Hamas then played the policy of the worst by multiplying the suicide attacks in Israel. The Israeli forces responded by destroying several hundred homes and intensifying the policy of eliminating the leaders of Hamas and Islamic Jihad. Tensions are rising. Hatred and mistrust became palpable. On February 25, 1996 a double suicide bombing killed 25 civilians in Israel. The Palestinian Authority and the Israeli army launched a vast operation of repression against the Islamist organizations. Peres, who succeeded Rabin as head of the government, set out to continue the work of his predecessor and began the withdrawal from Area A of the West Bank. But Labor was defeated in the May 1996 elections. Netanyahu, a historic opponent of the Oslo Accords, became Prime Minister in May 1996 and set about gutting them. The extreme position advanced by the Likud is summarized by the slogan "peace against peace", as opposed to "peace against the territories". For Ariel Sharon: "If the Palestinians want a state, they should take it from Jordan, where more than half the population is already Palestinian[9] ". As for Arafat, his authority and prestige are being challenged in Gaza by Sheikh Yassin, the founder of Hamas, who was released by Israel under pressure from King Hussein. He also has to deal with the movement's exiled leader, Khaled Mechaal. This disaffection is largely due to his nepotism, the corruption that reigns within the Palestinian Authority and the brutality of its police. Palestinian society, like all Arab societies, is increasingly Islamized. At the same time, the divide between secular and religious Israelis, which is gaining ground, is deepening. Suicide bombings against Israeli targets, sponsored by Hamas and Islamic Jihad, are continuing. The families of the suicide bombers are financed and supported by both organizations. In retaliation, Israel liquidated several of their leaders. In 1998, however, President Bill Clinton succeeded in getting Yasser Arafat and Benjamin Netanyahu to sign an agreement at the Wye Plantation summit on the evacuation of 31% of the West Bank by Israel.

The second Intifada

Labour's election victory in May 1999 created a climate of euphoria in Israel and revived Israeli-Palestinian negotiations. The new Prime Minister, Ehud Barak, made soothing remarks, even declaring that he wanted to "put an end to a hundred years of Arab-Israeli conflict[10] ". Nevertheless, years of negotiations about the 2500 prisoners held in Israeli jails have not led to their release. The Palestinian street, which no longer believes in peace, concludes that negotiations are useless. Violence broke out in mid-May 2000, during the annual commemoration of the Nakba, which represented for the Palestinians the creation of the Jewish state on May 14, 1948. The July 2000 Camp David II summit between Barak and Arafat was a failure. The differences over Jerusalem, the indivisible capital of Israel according to Barak, the capital of two states for Arafat, as well as over the question of Palestinian refugees, were insurmountable. The hope of reaching an agreement collapsed in the eyes of the Palestinian base, which launched, two months later, the second Intifada named Al-Aqsa Intifada. The spark that ignited the fire was the visit to the Esplanade of the Mosques in Jerusalem on September 28, 2000 by Ariel Sharon, who hoped to win the leadership of the Likud from Netanyahu. This provocation, undoubtedly deliberate, triggered deadly incidents that spread to all the Palestinian territories. Unlike the peaceful uprising of 1987-1993, they immediately took on a violent and militarized character. Marwan Barghouti, Fatah's leader for the West Bank, took over the leadership of the movement. But the leaders of the Islamist factions, Khaled Mechaal for Hamas and Ramadan Shalah for Islamic Jihad, played their own part. The brutality of Israeli repression plays into the hands of the Islamists, who have never believed in the peace process and are gaining in popularity with Palestinian opinion. "The Palestinians have not become followers of Sharia law [...] But in the face of F16 planes and Apache helicopters that fire on the cities, the population sees the actions of suicide bombers as legitimate resistance[11] ". Arafat swings between two positions. He remains committed to the agreements he signed with Israel. He cannot go back on the strategic choice he made almost ten years ago and which allowed him to return to his land. But he cannot ignore the anger of his people and appear as a traitor[12] . Without renouncing dialogue, he has tried to use violence as a means of political pressure against Israel. Not to be outdone by Hamas' Qassam Brigades, Fatah formed the Al-Aqsa Martyrs Brigades. Another armed force has emerged from its ranks: the "Tanzim". DFLP and PFLP militants joined the movement. On October 30, the violence escalated when Hamas and Islamic Jihad, soon followed by Fatah, launched a campaign of suicide bombings. Some forty attacks were carried out against settlers and in Israel itself until the end of 2001. The Israelis retaliated with massive reprisals and targeted eliminations of Palestinian activists. The Palestinian police could not remain insensitive when their compatriots were shot at and they in turn took part in the riots. In Israel, Israeli Arabs are demonstrating and blockading, being shot at.

At the political and media level, the first months of confrontation seemed to benefit the Palestinian Authority. The "excessive use of force" by Israel against the Palestinians was condemned by the UN General Assembly on October 21. At the same time, the Arab League states meeting in Cairo on 21 and 22 October condemned Israel and called for peace. On November 1, 2000, a ceasefire signed between Palestinian Authority President Yasser Arafat and Israeli Prime Minister Ehud Barak was about to be put in place, but the violence continued. Since the beginning of the intifada, approximately 360 people have been killed, the majority of them Palestinians. American President Bill Clinton intervened. On December 22, he proposed the establishment of Palestinian sovereignty in the Gaza Strip and most of the West Bank, the right of return for Palestinian refugees and the establishment of an international presence. Following the American proposals, negotiations between Palestinian and Israeli representatives took place under the aegis of the Americans and the UN Secretary General, Kofi Annan, in January 2001 in Taba, Egypt. They addressed the contours of a peace, dealing with the contentious issues: Israeli settlements, borders between the two states, the possible right of return and Jerusalem. In particular, it was agreed that East Jerusalem, where the holy places are located, would be shared between the two states, and that the city would become the capital of both Israel and the Palestinian state. But the two parties did not reach an agreement. Arafat made the mistake of not bringing the violence down soon enough, which contributed to Sharon's election as prime minister against Barak in February 2001. "By allowing the revolt to proceed, the PLO leader provided Sharon with the opportunity to implement his strategy of destroying the administrative structures of the Palestinians to ward off any prospect of statehood, which is his real objective. He does not hesitate to equate the repression of the intifada with the "global war on terror" proclaimed by George Bush after the September 11 attacks[13] . The latter, favouring an essentially security-based approach, refused to meet the head of the Palestinian Authority. Worse, he gave the green light to the responses decided by Ariel Sharon.

On May 21, 2001, the international commission chaired by former U.S. Senator George Mitchell and charged with analyzing the reasons for the conflict, issued its report. It called for an end to the violence, a freeze on construction in Israeli settlements, an end to the closure of Palestinian towns and the resumption of negotiations. These decisions were apparently approved by the Palestinians and the Israelis, but on the ground, new suicide attacks were carried out against Israeli civilians in the spring of 2001 by Hamas, Islamic Jihad and the al-Aqsa Brigades. These attacks wiped out much of the effect produced in international opinion by the images of Palestinian victims of Israeli fire. In addition to the disapproval they provoked, these crimes constituted a major tactical error for Yasser Arafat; by seeking to compete with Hamas on its own ground, that of "kamikaze" attacks, he alienated the Israeli left, which, in 2003, abstained or voted for Ariel Sharon. The pragmatic leaders of the Palestinian national movement, such as

Mahmoud Abbas, Yasser Abed Rabbo and Hanane Ashraoui, for their part, consider the attacks on civilians to be a disaster for the Palestinian cause. The cycle of suicide bombings/reprisals continued in 2002.

In the face of escalating violence, the Bush administration called for restraint on the part of the parties. On March 28, 2002, a summit of the Arab League held in Beirut updated the 1981 Fahd plan, this time including explicit recognition of Israel and normalization of relations with it. And UN resolution 1402, passed on March 30, called for Israel's withdrawal and mentioned for the first time a Palestinian state. But at the beginning of April, after calling up the reserves, the Israeli army launched Operation Defensive Shield to occupy the whole of Area A in retaliation for the suicide bombings in March. Tanks entered the cities of Kalkiliah, Tulkarem, Bethlehem, Jenin and Nablus. And the IDF operated for the first time in the refugee camps. During this operation, Marwan Barghouti was arrested. In Ramallah, the Israeli army besieged the headquarters of Yasser Arafat, the Moqatâ'a, from spring 2002, and bombed Palestinian ministries. Arafat called for an end to the violence with the armed groups in July 2002. But his appeal did not succeed.

At the beginning of June 2002, the deadlock was complete. A roadmap drafted by the Quartet (United States, European Union, Russia and the United Nations) provides for the creation of a Palestinian state, in three stages, before 2005. Initiated on June 4, 2002 in Aqaba, the discussions have stalled. At the same time, Ariel Sharon's government decided to build a separation wall along the green line separating Israel from the West Bank, in order to protect Israeli territory from suicide attacks. It will go deep into the West Bank to protect the main settler towns. This will involve further cuts into Palestinian space and further expropriation of land. "The construction of this wall further diminishes the space of Palestinians and locks them in a collective prison. It will be condemned in July 2004 by the International Court of Justice in The Hague as contrary to international law, without this decision dissuading the government from stopping this collective imprisonment of the indigenous population[14] . By the end of 2002, after 27 months of intifada, 685 Israelis and 2073 Palestinians had died. The latter included victims of inter-Palestinian clashes. In the early fall of 2003, no political solution seems to be in sight. The political decomposition of the Palestinian Authority progressed and the peace process was interrupted by the resignation of Palestinian Prime Minister Mahmoud Abbas on September 6, 2003. On the very day of his resignation, an assassination attempt on Sheikh Yassin, the spiritual leader of Hamas, organized by the Israelis, showed that the logic of violence had prevailed, with its infernal cycle of revenge and retaliation. Arafat, besieged in his home in Ramallah, did not come out until October 2004. Seriously ill, he was evacuated to France where he died shortly after in a military hospital. Mahmoud Abbas succeeded him as President of the PLO and of a Palestinian Authority that was largely weakened (discredited internally, internal dissension, American ostracism, European criticism). More seriously, the Palestinian population suffered a real disaster: in addition to the victims, the economic fabric was ravaged and the infrastructure destroyed.

The crushing of the Intifada in the West Bank did not stop the armed uprising in

Gaza, which was not discouraged by the systematic elimination of Palestinian leaders such as Sheikh Yassin. In May 2004, the Israeli army launched Operation Rainbow, which aimed to put an end to the guerrilla warfare in the Gaza Strip by weakening the infrastructure of the armed Palestinian groups and destroying the tunnels used by arms traffickers on the Egyptian border. On February 8, 2005, Sharon met with Mahmoud Abbas, Egyptian President Hosni Mubarak and King Abdullah II of Jordan. The negotiations aimed at stabilizing the situation. In October 2005, the Israeli army launched an offensive on the Gaza Strip called "eternal restart". The occupation of the Gaza Strip cost more than it brought in for Israel, so Sharon decided, in September 2005, to withdraw the Israeli army and the handful of Israeli settlers who had settled there. He then faced the rebellion of a part of the Likud, but created with Peres, a new party: Kadima. He was convinced that the decoupling of Gaza from the West Bank had blocked the way to a Palestinian state. Hamas was quick to take over the field to the detriment of an increasingly weakened Palestinian Authority.

The second intifada raised the prestige of Hamas at the expense of Fatah in the Gaza Strip. Benefiting from the rejection of Fatah's corruption, it won the Palestinian elections in January 2006. At the same time, he changed his objective to the establishment of a Palestinian state in East Jerusalem, the West Bank and the Gaza Strip. But the United States and the European Union demanded that the Islamist party explicitly recognize Israel in order to do business with it. As its leaders rejected this demand, the population of Gaza, which was deprived of European aid, was effectively punished for its vote. On January 4, 2006, Ariel Sharon suffered a cerebral hemorrhage that plunged him into a deep coma from which he would never recover. On March 28, 2006, the elections confirmed the victory of the Kadima party, which had been created by Sharon. A coalition government led by Ehud Olmert was established. On June 28, the kidnapping by Hamas of a French-Israeli soldier led to a new operation against the Gaza Strip aimed at recovering the kidnapped soldier and destroying the military infrastructure of Hamas. In response to the kidnapping of Israeli soldiers on the Syrian-Lebanese border by Hezbollah, Tsahal launched a violent bombing campaign in July 2006, followed by a ground offensive in Lebanon which ended in failure. The international community accuses the Hebrew state of totally disproportionate responses. In April 2007, an Israeli commission published a report denouncing the responsibilities of the Prime Minister, the Minister of Defence and the Chief of Staff in the failure suffered by the IDF, testifying to the vitality of Israeli democracy[15] . On November 27, 2007, U.S. President George W. Bush attempted to bring Israelis and Palestinians together in Annapolis to reach a new agreement. The meeting formalized the "two-state solution" for the first time. But Hamas refused to recognize the outcome of the negotiations before a solution was found. In 2008, Israeli Prime Minister Ehud Olmert proposed to Mahmoud Abbas to return most of the West Bank to the Palestinian Authority, but his offer, which ignored the issue of Jerusalem and the settlements, was rejected. In any case, the continuation of the settlements undermines the peace process, which is well and truly buried.

The Palestinian tear

For the Palestinians, the "drama within the drama" is their political, ideological and territorial division. On one side is Hamas and on the other the Palestinian Authority. Since the death of Yasser Arafat in November 2004, they have been unable to reconstitute the national unity that is essential to them. The tension that had been mounting between them erupted in June 2007. Following fratricidal and deadly fighting between Hamas and Fatah, Hamas seized power in the Gaza Strip. The Israeli government decided to blockade the territory. The refusal of the United States and Israel to recognize Hamas's electoral victory, and thus to recognize this group as the legitimate representative of the Palestinians, played an important role in the division between the Hamas-controlled territory of Gaza and the Fatah-controlled West Bank. This policy has encouraged Fatah to cede no authority to Hamas in the West Bank. The Gaza Strip, with its leaders boycotted by the European Union, is under full siege by Israel and Egypt (at the Sinai land border). Hamas and the even more radical Palestinian Islamic Jihad rain rockets on Israel from this suffocatingly blockaded territory, provoking massive Israeli retaliation, resulting in thousands of Palestinian civilian casualties and enormous destruction, notably during Operation Cast Lead launched in 2008. This military operation was widely condemned by international opinion because of the disproportionate nature of the Israeli response. And a UN commission accused Tsahal and Hamas of war crimes. In January 2009, Operation Cast Lead entered a new phase when the Israelis sent troops into the Gaza Strip. According to Palestinian sources, the operation resulted in over 1,300 Palestinian deaths. Following Hamas's refusal to sign the inter-Palestinian reconciliation plan negotiated under its aegis, Egypt undertook, in January 2010, the construction of an underground metal barrier to reduce the flow of contraband products transported by tunnels to the Gaza Strip. This initiative is part of the American desire to isolate the movement. Rocket fire against Israel from the Gaza Strip and Israeli retaliation continued in 2011 and 2012. These rocket attacks were mainly carried out by Islamic Jihad. In response In November 2012, the Israeli army conducted an operation called "Pillar of Defense" against Gaza.

On November 12, 2013, Palestinian President Mahmoud Abbas announced a plan to apply to the United Nations for recognition of Palestine as a "non-member state" within the pre-1967 borders. According to the Israeli government, this unilateral initiative is illegal and Hamas has accused it of treason. A new and even more deadly military operation against Hamas and Islamic Jihad in Gaza took place in July-August 2014. In 2017, 18 years after the 1999 date when the Oslo Accords provided for the end of the interim period, the two-state solution appears to be slipping away. Some say that a Palestinian state is already no longer viable, as all that remains are pockets, or "Bantustans," separated from each other. The situation is extremely serious. The most tragic is surely that of the population of Gaza, still under siege, starving, abandoned to its fate after three criminal wars in seven years, led by the Israeli army, and generous promises (five billion dollars) made by the Donors' Conference, but not realized. Israel is seeking to officially annex East Jerusalem, whose Palestinian population is caught in a vice-like grip by Israeli settlements that are springing up like mushrooms to the east of the city, but also in the middle of the Arab center, and a nine-meter high wall that isolates the city from the entire West Bank. The West Bank looks more like a series of besieged ghettos than the territory of a viable state. The Israeli-Palestinian peace process is well and truly buried. Israel faces two incompatible choices: to remain a Jewish and democratic state, or to continue to occupy the West Bank with an apartheid policy. And because of population growth, Arab citizens of Israel and Palestinians in the West Bank will eventually form the majority of the population of the territory of former Mandate Palestine. Palestinian dissension is seen as one of the main obstacles to resolving the Israeli-Palestinian conflict and one of the causes of the evils endured by the two million inhabitants of Gaza: war, the Israeli and Egyptian blockade, poverty and unemployment. Faced with this situation a rapprochement between Hamas and Fatah intended to put an end to a decade of devastating rifts, began in June 2017. Constituting a small glimmer of hope, an agreement was finally signed in Cairo, on October 11, 2017, between the two enemy brothers providing for the return of the Gaza Strip to the fold of the Palestinian Authority. Concluded under the aegis of Egypt, it was made possible by the weakening of Hamas, isolated on the Arab scene since the defeat of the Muslim Brotherhood and Islamist rebels in Syria and deprived of the financial support of Qatar. But an assassination attempt on March 13, 2018, in Gaza against Palestinian Prime Minister Rami Hamdallah shows that the rapprochement could fall apart at any moment. A new development in the conflict occurred at the end of March when the Israeli army fired on Palestinians peacefully demonstrating near the Gaza-Israel border killing several people and injuring over a thousand. With this peaceful march for the "right of return", reminiscent of the first Intifada, the Palestinians hope to awaken the conscience of the international community. But it is doubtful that it will make Israel bend.

The radicalization of Israeli society

"Israel's policy can only be understood in the light of the crushing weight of the Shoah in the collective memory. This deep, somewhat existential feeling of being in mortal danger as soon as tensions, let *alone* violence, arise is omnipresent. This is why, for example, the second Intifada was devastating for the peace camp in Israel. Since then, the fact that there has been an occupation since 1967 has been erased, concealed and denied by a large number of Israelis who see themselves primarily as potential victims, especially since the first years of the State of Israel's existence were marked by the violence of Arab refusal. All this remains indelibly engraved in the collective memory, which is constantly nourished by education and by multiple commemorations, the most impressive of which takes place every year at the Yad Vashem memorial[16] . If this capital dimension of Israeli society is inescapable, it must also be seen that the most nationalistic Israeli leaders do not hesitate to use it in many ways to serve their own political purposes and to try to camouflage their enterprise of colonizing Palestinian lands. This is at the heart of the Zionist ideology, which is in essence and by necessity an expansionist and colonizing movement. From the outset, its goal was to convert all of Palestine into a Jewish state. And the leaders of the time, led by Ben Gurion, coldly considered the necessity of a voluntary transfer or forced expulsion of as large a part of the Arab population as possible. In 1967, the conquest of the West Bank, Gaza and the Golan Heights gave new impetus to the great original dream of Zionism. From the 1970s onwards, the growing influence of the settlers and the evolution of Israeli society led to a turning point in political life with the rise of the right and religious parties, at the expense of the Labor Party. With the coming to power of the coalition government between the Likud and the religious parties in 1977, the Israeli position on negotiations with the Palestinians hardened considerably, and the pro-settlement parties dominated the political scene. The significant influence of the ultra-Orthodox Jews (*Haredin*), however, was due to the fact that their parties, such as Shas (representing Sephardic Jews) and the National Religious Party (representing Ashkenazi Jews), obtained the deputies needed for government majorities. Built on full proportional representation with a very low threshold, the Israeli electoral system encourages the fragmentation of factions represented in the Knesset and an exacerbated partisan pluralism. While observant Jews have remained cohesive behind their parties, secularists have dispersed into a multitude of left, right and center parties. The result is that no secular party has ever been able to form a coalition without the support of religious parties. This is the case of the National Home, an extreme right-wing party that emerged in 2008 from the National Religious Party. Led by Naftali Bennett, it represents the interests of settlers and modern orthodox Jews.

Today Israel is faced with a dilemma. Either it perseveres in its policy of occupation and colonization at the risk of losing its identity, threatened by Palestinian demographic growth, not to mention the little capital of sympathy it has left in the rest of the world. Or it resigns itself to withdraw from most of the occupied territories to the great displeasure of the settlers, with the risk of civil war that this entails. Its clear choice to intensify settlement undermines Israel's moral values and raises the question of whether it can be both a democratic, human rights-respecting state and an apartheid state. That said, the conviction and imprisonment of former Prime Minister Ehud Olmert in 2016 for corruption would have been unthinkable in any Arab country. It shows the vitality of Israeli democracy, at least in domestic politics, and is one factor among others in its superiority over authoritarian or dictatorial Arab regimes. The second intifada has accentuated an already evident evolution within Israeli society. The most notable trends are the growing political influence of the army and settlers; the increasing use of violence by settlers against Arabs; increasingly open racism; the decline of the peace movement; and a near internal consensus regarding the occupation and settlement of "Judea and Samaria." The polarization of society between ultra-Orthodox and secular Jews is increasing. The former are mainly recruited among Sephardic Jews, but also Ashkenazi, while the latter are mostly secular. Traditionally drawn from the reputedly elitist Israeli left of the Ahusalim (Hebrew acronym for Ashkenazi, secular, socialist, born in Israel), their ranks have been swollen by the arrival of Russian-speaking Jews who form a community that is both deeply secularized and ultranationalist. This nationalism is not the same as the territorial mysticism of the settlers, but it translates into a desire for separation from the Arabs. The party that represents them, Israel Beiteinou (founded by Avigdor Lieberman, a Moldovan-born Russian speaker), advocates a transfer of Israeli Arabs to the territories of the Palestinian Authority.

The West and Palestine,

In most Western countries, the Jewish lobby has a permanent campaign to portray Israel as "the shield of the West" and tries to convince elected officials to impose a policy favorable to the Israeli regime. In the United States, when the president tries to adopt a less biased attitude, he is held hostage by a Congress whose elected officials compete in servility to Israel. It is a race to see who will demand a more complete alignment of American policy with Israel's. In particular, Israel enjoys unconditional support among a majority of new American Christian evangelicals who have a literal reading of the Bible and call themselves Christian Zionists. Although more sensitive than the United States to the plight of the Palestinians, Europe seems paralyzed when it comes to Israel. It is as if it were incapable of respecting and enforcing its values (human rights and international law). There is a partner that is granted total impunity for violations of the law. A state that is placed above the law and has thus become an outlaw state is Israel! In practice, the EU adopts excellent resolutions at all its ministerial meetings, but refuses to implement them by taking the necessary measures to make the Israeli authorities apply them. Whether it is about the daily violations of the rights of the population under occupation, whether it is about the colonization that is annihilating the two-state project or whether it is about the

destruction of all that the EU has built over the past 25 years in the occupied territories for the infrastructure of a future state. And it is the same EU that is asking the Palestinian Authority to postpone the declaration of Palestinian statehood, telling it to do so "in due course". But when will that time come? When there will be no more territory available because the Israeli settlements will have devoured everything? However, since the second intifada, the brutality of the Israeli occupation, the rise in Europe of the extreme right, and the presence of a large Muslim community sensitive to the Palestinian cause have resulted in sporadic outbreaks of anti-Judaism. This is the case in France, where demonstrations in support of the Palestinian people have been marked by the burning of synagogues and cries of "death to the Jews! Mostly chanted by Muslims, they are probably as much an expression of anti-Israeli sentiments as of their frustration with French society.

The end of the two-state solution?

"Since the Oslo Accords signed in 1993, there has been an interminable and totally asymmetrical "peace process" between Israel and the PLO, the latter having no capacity to obtain concessions from the occupying party. The continuation of this process has become the objective of the European powers and the United States, thus replacing peace itself over the years[17] . The timid hopes for the resumption of peace talks between Israelis and Palestinians are in danger of being dashed by Donald Trump's historic decision on December 6, 2017, to recognize Jerusalem as the capital of the State of Israel and to transfer the U.S. embassy from Tel Aviv to Jerusalem. This recognition has no international legal standing and the UN considers Israel an occupying power in East Jerusalem. This recognition has no international legal value and the UN considers Israel to be an occupying power in East Jerusalem. It has caused a wave of disapproval in the Middle East and beyond, and has further distanced the prospect of the establishment of a Palestinian state and played into the hands of Hamas. Its leader, Ismail Haniya, has called for a new intifada. It puts Palestinian President Mahmoud Abbas in a difficult position, as he has always relied on diplomatic mediation to reach a solution in the Israeli-Palestinian conflict. Shortly after the announcement by the American president, the latter stated that "the United States could no longer play the role of mediator in the peace process. But this distancing from Washington is not enough to hide, in the eyes of many Palestinians, the feeling of a strategic failure on the part of the Fatah/PLO couple. Since the process that led to the Oslo Accords in 1993, the two organizations have relied on diplomacy, through American mediation, in the hope of advancing the peace negotiations. Despite the failures of the various attempts, and the continuation of Israeli colonization in the Palestinian territories, the PLO has never questioned its strategic course, continuing to insist on the need for dialogue to achieve "a two-state solution. But this now seems totally unrealistic. Although in a few years there will probably be more Arabs than Jews between the Jordan River and the sea, the one-state solution will probably end up being the de facto solution, albeit an apartheid state, for at least two reasons: the growing weight of ultra-Orthodox "Eretz-Israel" Jews in the Jewish population, and continued settlement activity. The most extremist Israelis are even toying with the idea of a new expulsion of part of the Palestinian population. Commenting on Donald Trump's decision, Leila Shahid, former Palestinian ambassador to the European Union, admits that "the strategy of non-violence adopted by the PLO in the early 1990s was a failure. But this failure must be seen in the context of history. We have reached the end of a stage for the Palestinian national movement, marked by several phases. The first was the armed struggle, led mainly by Palestinians in exile, which ended in 1974 when the liberation movement gained international recognition. Then there was a second phase that began with the recognition of the PLO, when Yasser Arafat gave a standing ovation at the United Nations. This was the first time that the Palestinians had a symbolic homeland. In 1987, during the first intifada, the entire population opposed the occupation. The negotiation phase, the third phase, began with Oslo in 1993, which was very important for Yasser Arafat, because it was the return of a homeland to a national soil. The diplomatic phase is now over. Oslo, in a way, trapped us in a cage, territorialized us. Oslo made us false promises to put us in a ghetto divided into several zones, where we do not have the same status. The two-state solution was a dead end even before Trump's declaration on Jerusalem. The one-state solution is even more unrealistic than the two-state solution because Israel does not want to live with the Palestinians and only wants to be a Jewish state. But that has not ended our right to self-determination, an inalienable right. What matters is that we have equal rights. Whether it is a one-state system, a two-state system, a condominium or a Middle Eastern Benelux is not important. But what is needed above all is political will on our part, but also on the Israeli side, and on the international community, to help us get there[18] ".The Trump administration's decision to unilaterally recognize Jerusalem as Israel's capital on December 6, 2017, has been called "the slap of the century by the Palestinians. It dealt the final blow to the Oslo process said President Mahmoud Abbas. And the leaders of the Palestine Liberation Organization's Central Council called for the suspension of the Palestinian side's recognition of Israel. They instructed the PLO executive committee to suspend recognition of Israel until it recognizes the State of Palestine within its 1967 borders, cancels the annexation of East Jerusalem and ceases settlement activity. But the Council's recommendations are not binding and the Palestinian Authority has very little room to manoeuvre. In any case, the American decision only confirms a state of affairs. The majority of Israeli political institutions are already located in Jerusalem. No government has concretely opposed the annexation laws passed by Israel in 1980, a Knesset vote that defined Jerusalem and the settlements built in East Jerusalem as the capital of the Jewish state. Nor was there any opposition, for that matter, to the policy of Judaization of Jerusalem, which, implemented over the years, has made it impossible to declare a Palestinian capital in the Arab part of the city. Nor to the draft laws debated in 2017 about the "Greater Jerusalem", to finish annexing to Israeli territory the settlement blocks built in Palestinian territory and close to Jerusalem.

1 *Le Monothéisme, le pouvoir et la guerre*, Ibrahim Tabet, l'Harmattan, 2011, p.263

2 *The Palestine Question - Volume 4, The Olive Branch and the Fighter's Gun,* Henry Laurens, Fayard 2011, p. 37

3 *Jerusalem*, Simon Sebag Montefiore, Calman Levy 2011, p.350

4 *Geopolitics of religions*, Didier Giorgini, PUF 2016, p, 106

5 *La France au Liban et au Proche-Orient*, Ibrahim Tabet, Revue Phénicienne, 2011. p. 334

6 *Victimes, histoire revisitée du conflit arabo-sioniste*, Benny Morris, éditions Complexe 2003, p 609

7 *L'Orient arabe à l'heure américaine*, Henry Laurens, Hachette littérature, 2005

8 *Victims,* op. cit. p. 668

9 ibid

10 *Le Monde*, July 7, 1999

11 *Des Pierres aux fusils, les secrets de l'intifada,* Georges Malbrunot, Flamarion 2002, p.96

12 *Les Arabes, leur destin et le nôtre,* Jean-Pierre Filiu, La Découverte 2015, p. 197

13 *From Stones to Guns,* op.cit, p. 12

14 *The New Question of the East*, Georges Corm, La Découverte 2017, p. 147

15 *Tsahal, a new history of the Israeli army*. Pierre Razoux, Perrin -Tempus, 2008 p. 548

16 *Intifada or liberation struggle*? Jean Paul Chagnollaud, Confluences Méditerranée, n.13, Spring 2001, pages 11 to 18.

17 *The New Question of the Orient*, op. cit. p. 157

18 L'Orient-Le jour of December 18, 2017

Chapter 9. Lebanon in turmoil

The Lebanese War (1975-1990)

The war in Lebanon, which began on April 13, 1975, was both a civil war and a proxy war on the Lebanese scene. "Several types of analysis are proposed to try to explain the causes and the stakes. Some emphasize the fact that the decomposition of the Lebanese state predates its outbreak and that the Lebanese bear a heavy responsibility for the misfortune they inflicted on their country: the Muslims who, by allying themselves with the Palestinians against their Christian compatriots, took the initiative to break the "National Pact" and the Christians who, in desperation, ended up throwing themselves into the arms of Israel. Others try to show that it was partly sponsored and managed by actors outside the Lebanese scene. There is also the thesis of a conspiracy, whatever its origin, which is mainly the work of some Lebanese who seek by this to minimize their own responsibility in the disaster[1] . The President of the Lebanese Republic at the beginning of the conflict, Sleiman Frangié, reported that there was an American plan to settle the Israeli-Palestinian conflict at the expense of Lebanon by making the country a substitute homeland for the Palestinians. And that Henry Kissinger would have proposed to him to welcome the Christians of Lebanon in the United States and Canada.

The war went through several phases and multiple twists and turns, involving in turn different local, regional and international protagonists. Between 1975 and 1989, more than ten foreign armies passed through the Lebanese territory, not counting various local militias. Its first phase (1975-1976) was essentially Lebanese-Palestinian. It opposed the Christian politico-military forces to the Palestinian armed formations, allied to the "National Movement", a group of "Islamo-progressive" militiamen, led by the Druze feudal leader, Kamal Joumblatt, who demanded greater participation of Muslims in power. Meetings between the "National Movement" parties, the Sunni leadership and the PLO were held openly under the chairmanship of Yasser Arafat. Faced with the Islamic-Palestinian coalition, the Christian "Lebanese Front" positioned itself as defender of the established order. It is especially opposed to the presence of armed Palestinian organizations on Lebanese soil. Its main leaders are the President of the Republic Sleiman Frangié, the former President Camille Chamoun and the leader of the "Kataëbs", Pierre Gemayel. Each of the protagonists finds arms and encouragement abroad: the Phalanges in the West and in Israel, and the "Palestinian-progressive" camp in Syria and in other Arab countries. On the side of the latter, the operations on the ground are directed by the commanders of Fatah and the Saïka, the latter being in reality only a label disguising the Syrian army.

The outbreak of the conflict

On April 13, 1975, following shots fired by "fédayins" at Phalangist sympathizers in front of a church in Ayn el-Remaneh, a town on the outskirts of

Beirut, several Palestinians were killed as their bus passed through this town in the Christian suburbs of Beirut. After this incident, fighting raged for control of downtown Beirut, from which the Christian militias were finally expelled in the summer of 1975. Fighting also took place in the Bekaa and in the north of the country between the Christian town of Zghorta and Palestinian fighters supported by Syria. But Damascus is not the only external player in the game being played on the Lebanese chessboard. The growing involvement of the great powers is a sign that the stakes are higher than local. The Soviet ambassador Soldatov regularly sits alongside Arafat and Jumblatt to follow the operations of Moscow's allies on the ground. And the French Foreign Minister Couve de Murville undertook mediation between Damascus and the Lebanese Front. The appointment on 30 June 1975 of a compromise Prime Minister, Rachid Karamé, to head a government of national unity, as well as the adoption in February 1976, under pressure from Damascus, of a "Constitutional Document" supposed to satisfy the demands for reform from Muslim circles, and which was accepted by the Christians, did not succeed in resolving the crisis. The issue is no longer the reform of the Constitution but the future of the territory. The Palestinian-progressive forces caught the Christian part of Beirut and its suburbs in a pincer movement between the Palestinian camps located within it, notably that of Tal el-Zaatar, and the regions under their control. Innocent civilians are kidnapped and coldly eliminated on both sides just because of their religious affiliation. Not content with killing each other, the militias of both sides reign anarchy and shamelessly loot the center and port of Beirut. Later, they will come to carry out all kinds of rackets and impose taxes to finance themselves. It is clear that they are working to achieve a separation between the predominantly Christian east of Beirut and the western neighborhoods with an initially more mixed population, but where the predominance of Muslims is growing as the Christians are leaving.

The state disintegrated and the army, which could not resist its collapse, broke up into partisan factions. Countless cease-fires were violated as soon as they were declared. Jumblatt dreamed of crushing the Christians, whom he described as "isolationists" (an allusion to the project of creating a Christian entity dreamed up by some of their leaders). And the Palestinian leader, Abu Ayad, proclaims that "the road to Palestine passes through Jounié[2] ". Playing the role of pyromaniac fireman, Hafez el-Assad, who had initially supported the adversaries of the Christians, turned against them to prevent the establishment of a competing Islamo-Palestinian power in Lebanon, risking to drag it into a war against Israel. He also fears a partition of Lebanon that would lead to the creation of a Christian state on part of the territory that would inevitably become a satellite of Israel.

The Syrian intervention

In April 1976, the Syrian army entered Lebanon and defeated the Palestinian-progressive forces. This intervention allowed the Christian forces to destroy the Palestinian camp of Tal el-Zaatar which was holding the eastern suburbs of

Beirut under its threat. In retaliation, the Christian town of Damour was taken by the Palestinians, some of its inhabitants massacred and the rest forced to flee. The reactions of the international community fell far short of the challenge posed by the Damascus power grab. France can only welcome the Syrian intervention in favor of the Christians. Washington's only concern is to keep the Syrian intervention within tolerable limits for Israel. Kissinger coordinates the agreement between Damascus and Tel Aviv. Syrian troops were not allowed to cross a red line to the south, delimited by the Litani River. Thus was established the policy known as "the good border": the Lebanese in the south would henceforth address Israel with their backs turned to Beirut from which they were cut off. A tacit separation of Lebanon into Syrian and Israeli zones of influence was thus established. The Soviets, who supported the PLO, expressed their disapproval. But they did not want to risk a break with Damascus for fear of strengthening the position of the United States. Elected President of the Republic in May 1976, Elias Sarkis had very limited power. The authority of the government had practically ceased to exist. The Christian militias that Béchir Gemayel, Pierre Gemayel's youngest son, had brought together within the Lebanese Forces governed the Damascus Road mountain in the north, the stronghold of the Frangié clan, the Syrian troops were in the east and the Chouf, the PLO dominated the south, and Beirut was divided between an eastern sector controlled by the Lebanese Forces and a western sector held by the PLO and its Muslim allies. Kamal Joumblatt, leader of the coalition uniting the PLO and the National Movement was assassinated, probably on Syrian orders. In accordance with feudal traditions, his son Walid succeeded him at the head of the Druze community and the Progressive Socialist Party. On the initiative of King Fahd of Saudi Arabia, an Arab summit was held in Cairo from 26 to 28 October 1976. A general cease-fire was established throughout Lebanon. It was accepted by the

Palestinians, the National Movement and the Lebanese Front. An Arab Deterrent Force (ADF), set up by the Arab League, with a Syrian contingent making up more than three quarters of its strength, was responsible for ensuring compliance with the ceasefire. Placed under the - purely theoretical - command of the Lebanese President, it began to be deployed from 14 November 1976 throughout the country, with the exception of the South. After a year and a half of war, which claimed some 65,000 victims, no one was opposed to it and a precarious calm was established. President Assad had maneuvered well: nothing was changed in his political-military set-up, except that the Arab states would assume collective responsibility for his actions, and that his occupation forces would be financed by Saudi Arabia and the Emirates. But the behavior of the Syrians, who behave worse than an occupying army, creates an atmosphere of growing hostility between them and the Lebanese population.

The confrontation between the Christian camp and Syria

In a second phase (1977-1978), the regional and international situation changed dramatically when President Sadat went to Jerusalem (November 19, 1977) and Egyptian-Israeli peace negotiations were opened. Lebanon then became for

Hafez el-Assad the ideal ground to fight the signing of a separate peace agreement between Cairo and Tel Aviv. He got closer to the Palestinian-progressives who shared the same opposition to Sadat. Moreover, as was to be expected, deep divergences soon appeared between Damascus and the Christian camp, which had initially welcomed the Syrian intervention with relief and was increasingly resentful of its armed presence. Faced with the new Syrian reversal, the Christian camp is divided into two trends. The first, represented by the Frangié clan, remains faithful to the Syrian alliance which it considers the best protection against the opposing camp. While the second is represented by the Kataeb and the supporters of President Chamoun who, distrusting the Syrian intentions, are getting closer to Israel. The latter, which has no intention of letting Syria control Lebanon, encourages Christian resistance to the Syrian occupation. Intensifying its military aid to Christian militias, it continues to maintain tension on the southern border. France and the United States tried to persuade the Christian leaders to give up the idea of throwing themselves into the arms of Israel. Following the signing of the separate Egyptian-Israeli peace agreement at Camp David, Syria, which was violently opposed to it, turned against the Christian "Lebanese Front" which, rejecting its occupation, resorted to Israeli aid. In early 1978, the non-Syrian contingents of the ADF were withdrawn by their governments and the force became exclusively Syrian. In February the war resumed in earnest. Christian areas were savagely bombed by the Syrian army. In Europe, demonstrations of solidarity and support for the victims of Syrian barbarism multiplied. In Paris they mobilize thousands of people. France and the United States decided to bring the case before the UN Security Council. On October 7, the Council adopted a resolution asking "all parties involved in the fighting to meticulously respect an immediate ceasefire". But the Syrians did not take this into account. Despite the hesitations of Pierre Gemayel, who was afraid of compromising Islamic-Christian relations and cutting himself off from the Arab world, the Lebanese Front resigned itself to asking for Israeli support. The year 1978 saw the direct entry into the fray of Israel, whose army penetrated into southern Lebanon in March to push back the Palestinians (Operation Litani). It withdrew only partially, leaving a border strip under its control defended by a Lebanese force: the South Lebanon Army, led by a dissident Christian officer, Major Saad Haddad. This situation led the Shiite Amal movement to form its own militia, which took control of the southern suburbs of Beirut, the northern Bekaa, and part of southern Lebanon. A UN force, the UNIFIL (United Nations Interim Force in Lebanon) has the mission to separate the belligerents, to ensure the Israeli withdrawal from southern Lebanon and to help the Lebanese authorities regain control: wishful thinking that will remain a dead letter like many UN resolutions.

In 1980, the regional context changed to Syria's advantage. In October, it signed a treaty of friendship and cooperation with the Soviet Union. For his part, Béchir Gemayel, head of the Lebanese Forces, who had imposed his domination on the Christian country in 1981, sought to include Zahle in the area controlled by the

LF, which triggered a violent Syrian reaction. The Begin government then decided to help its Christian allies in order to maintain the balance between the conflicting parties. On April 28, the Israeli air force shot down two Syrian helicopters over the Bekaa. But following this incident the USSR provided Syria with anti-aircraft missiles which it installed in the Bekaa. A cease-fire prevented a direct confrontation between Israel and Syria. Sent by President Ronald Reagan, the American envoy Philippe Habib entered the scene. His mission was both to defuse the missile crisis and to try to find a solution to the Lebanese problem. But he came up against Syrian and Israeli intransigence. The policy of Paris, increasingly worried about Syria's hold on Lebanon, is aggravating its already tense relations with Damascus. It was in this context that the French ambassador to Lebanon, Louis Delamare, was assassinated near a Syrian dam on September 4, 1981.

The Israeli invasion and the Western intervention

The Litani operation was followed in 1982 by a full-scale Israeli invasion which was a major turning point in the conflict. "From that moment on, the conflict became international. Lebanon became one of the theaters of the Cold War and the local parties that clashed had no autonomy. They are only extensions of regional forces that control them remotely[3] . Syria, which is the pillar of the Arab refusal to accept the Egyptian-Israeli peace treaty, has become the enemy to be destroyed for Washington and Tel Aviv. The Israeli government, having ensured the security of its southern border through the treaty with Egypt, now proposes to impose its own solution to the Palestinian question. It consists of destroying the military and political power of the PLO in Lebanon, setting up a friendly regime in that country, and then, with any effective Palestinian resistance eliminated, continuing its policy of colonizing the occupied West Bank. With some understanding from the United States, for whom the land of the cedars had become a mere arena, the Likud government decided to invade Lebanon. The pretext was an attack on the Israeli ambassador in London by a commando from the Abu Nidal group, a mortal enemy of the PLO.

On June 6, 1982, the Israeli army launched Operation Peace in Galilee. Crossing the lines held by UNIFIL (UN peacekeeping force), it advanced along three axes, along the coast, in the center and in the east, facing the Bekaa and the Syrian troops. With an overwhelming military superiority, it crossed the 40 kilometer line initially announced as an objective by Defense Minister Ariel Sharon. At the beginning, the Reagan administration, which fully endorsed the Israeli view of the need to crush the Palestinians, did nothing to stop the invasion. Palestinian forces were easily dispersed, but the refugee camps offered fierce resistance for several days, showing the Israelis that urban warfare would be difficult to wage. The Druze and the Shiites refrained from fighting the Israelis, and let them take over their regions, sometimes even welcoming them. This attitude can be explained, in the case of the Shiites, by the fact that they are tired of suffering reprisals in the South as a result of the actions of the Palestinian resistance. The only real Syrian reaction was a sortie of its air force over the Bekaa where it suffered a hecatomb, losing nearly 80 aircraft in a single day, after the destruction of its anti-aircraft missiles. Violent clashes on the ground nevertheless took place with the Syrian troops who suffered a crushing defeat. Then Tsahal reached the capital on June 14 where it joined forces with the Christian Lebanese Forces. Then began the long siege of West Beirut where the PLO found refuge among the civilian population. The savage bombardments of Tsahal by air, land and sea caused terrible damage: 7000 dead, 30,000 wounded, tens of thousands displaced and enormous destruction. The media impact of these scenes dealt a severe blow to the Israeli cause in international public opinion. At the same time, the Israelis began to destroy the civilian and military infrastructure of the PLO. Part of the camps were razed while several thousand people were arrested and transported to detention centers. The objective of this conduct, in which the Lebanese Forces were involved, was to lead to a new exodus of Palestinians.

There was then a reversal of American policy: President Reagan was now in favour of a global solution to the Lebanese and Palestinian problems. This was the theme of the Reagan plan of September 1er 1982. "Affirming that the war in Lebanon had proved that Israel's military supremacy alone could not bring about peace in the Middle East, he proposed to relaunch the process begun at Camp David with a view to establishing it. This plan, which would deprive Israel of the fruits of its victory, obviously arouses Begin's deep disappointment[4] . To his great displeasure, Israel was finally obliged to accept an agreement concluded at the initiative of France and the United States which provided for the cessation of hostilities, the evacuation by sea and land of West Beirut by Palestinian and Syrian fighters, and the establishment of a multinational intervention force (IMF). Composed of French, American and Italian soldiers, its mission was to enable and protect this evacuation. The withdrawal of Palestinians and Syrians from the capital took place in August. On September 1er nearly 14,000 Palestinian and Syrian fighters left Beirut, the latter by land with all their weapons. Then, their mission accomplished, all the contingents of the IMF left on September 13.

With American and Israeli support, Béchir Gemayel was elected President of the Republic on 23 August despite the reluctance of Muslim leaders. Aware that participation in the fighting by a Christian militia risked irreparably dividing the country and making any reconciliation with the Muslims almost impossible, he decided not to fight alongside the Israelis. He got closer to the Muslim leaders. Finally, to ensure his election, he began to show a certain independence from the Israelis, to whom he owed so much. And his statements during the three weeks of his presidency, in which he called for national understanding and spoke of his vision of the future Lebanon, raised immense hope in the country. But, abandoned by the Israelis and in the line of fire of the Syrians, he was assassinated on September 14th, three weeks after his election, by a member of the PPS (Syrian Popular Party). Immediately afterwards, in order to avoid a power vacuum, the deputies rushed to elect his brother, Amine, in his place. The

Israeli army used the assassination as a pretext to occupy West Beirut, dragging in its wake Christian militias. Drunk with grief and revenge, the militias went on to massacre Palestinians in the refugee camps of Sabra and Shatila under the complacent eye of the Israelis. These tragic events provoked demonstrations in Israel condemning the government's policy. And, following a report underlining the responsibility of the Israeli army, Ariel Sharon was forced to give up the Ministry of Defense in March 1983. This massacre led to the return of the Multinational Force to Beirut.

The West, led by the United States and France, tried to bring peace to Lebanon. At first the Western plan seemed to succeed. Order and security returned to Beirut. The crossing points between the different sectors were opened again. But the counterattack is being prepared, we can't see it. In the east and north of Lebanon, the Syrian army recovered from the terrible blows dealt by Tsahal and reconstituted its forces with Soviet help. And the delivery by France of Supertendards equipped with Exocet missiles to Iraq exacerbated Iran's animosity towards the French. Refraining from frontal attacks, these two countries subcontracted their operations to their local allies. The French military began to be the target of sporadic attacks by Islamist militiamen, who gradually began to appear again. On February 16, 1983, the Lebanese army, which had been reorganized and re-equipped, managed to penetrate the western districts, breaking the resistance of the Islamist militias. Driven out of Beirut and the south, the PLO was still present in Tripoli. Yasser Arafat, who had returned and formed an alliance with Islamic fundamentalist movements, was expelled in December 1983 by the Syrian army after bloody clashes. Once again, he was evacuated on a ship sent by the French government, which did not please the master of Damascus.

A draft Lebanese-Israeli agreement sponsored by the United States was endorsed on 17 May 1983 by the Lebanese deputies, but it was violently opposed by Syria, supported by the USSR, and its local Druze and Shiite allies. On September 2, 1983, President Gemayel, putting an end to a legal ambiguity, officially requested the withdrawal of Syrian troops and Palestinian fighters from all Lebanese territory. From that moment on, there should be in principle no difference in status in Lebanon between the Syrians and the Israelis, although there is still talk of Syrian "presence" and Israeli occupation. But at the same time, (an attitude that will be reproached to him by many Lebanese Christians) he hesitated to sign the Lebanese-Israeli agreement of May 17, rightly considering that it would lead Lebanon to a real economic suicide given the dependence of its economy on its Arab environment. This attitude led Ariel Sharon to make a threat to him that was to prove true: "Soon," he said, "the Lebanese president, if he refuses to accede to Israel's wishes to engage in a dialogue tending towards normalization, would no longer control anything but his own palace, a few neighborhoods in East Beirut and Jounié .[5]

The Israeli withdrawal and the return in force of Syria

The Israeli army having unilaterally withdrawn to South Lebanon, a "war of the mountain", opposing the Christian "Lebanese Forces" to the Druze, emptied the Chouf of its Christian inhabitants. This exodus is partly due to the double game of the Israelis who did not prevent the Syrian reinforcements to the Druze. The Syrian army, supported by the Druze militia, then attempted a breakthrough which was pushed back towards the presidential palace. It bombed the international intervention force in Beirut. In response, the American fleet and French aircraft bombed Syrian positions. The war threatened to resume on a large scale. Mediations supported by the presence in Beirut of the multinational force led on 25 September to the constitution of a "National Congress of Reconciliation" which met on 31 October in Geneva. In a now classic scenario, this prospect of appeasement provoked violence from extremists. The Shiite and Druze militias took control of West Beirut. On October 23, 1983, two simultaneous suicide bombings caused the death of 256 American Marines and 58 French soldiers (attack on the Drakar post). This first campaign of suicide attacks was claimed by the "Free Islamic Revolution Movement" behind which was hidden the Hezbollah, which was still only a small Shiite organization fanatical about the Iranian pasdaran. The first reaction of the United States and France was to proclaim their determination to maintain their forces in Lebanon. French President François Mitterrand went to the scene the day after the attack to pay a final tribute to the sacrifice of the French soldiers and to encourage their comrades engaged in a perilous mission. Yasser Arafat, who had been forced to leave Lebanon by the Israeli army's assault on Beirut, returned to Tripoli from where he was expelled by the Syrian army in December 1983. In 1984, the multinational force was forced to withdraw, capitulating in the face of terrorist attacks and Syrian bombings.

After the withdrawal of all Western troops, Lebanon sank into five more years of chaos. Pauperization, insecurity and population displacement forced tens of thousands of Lebanese to emigrate. On April 30, 1984, a government of national unity was formed. Headed by the leader of the opposition, Rachid Karamé, and composed mainly of warlords from both sides, it lasted until the assassination of the Prime Minister on 1er June 1987. But it was powerless to put an end to hostilities. "It was pretending to ignore the triple Syrian, Palestinian and Israeli occupation and believing that an agreement between the Lebanese, assuming it was possible, could bring peace[6] . On September 20, 1984, a bloody attack against the American embassy in Beirut decapitated the local branch of the CIA. From 1985, the kidnapping of Western hostages in Lebanon constituted a new stage in the Syrian-Iranian war against France and the United States. Among the Western hostages were several Frenchmen, victims of a serious dispute between France and Khomeini's Iran. They were kidnapped by the Islamic jihad. Its main demands are the cessation of French military aid to Iraq and the repayment of a billion dollars made by Iran to the nuclear consortium EURODIF. Hafez el-Assad exploited the tragedy of the French hostages for his own benefit and orchestrated their release according to his own interests. Eventually all the hostages were released, except Michel Seurat who died in custody. Hezbollah concentrated its attacks against the Israeli army, which did not prevent fratricidal fighting from breaking out between its militiamen and those of the Shiite movement Amal, less radical and close to Syria. It is also held responsible for several Western hostage takings. It was partly under pressure from Hezbollah and Amal that the Israeli forces decided in January 1985 to evacuate the whole of Lebanon, except for the border strip they had established along the southern border.

At the beginning of 1987, Syria, which had been driven out of most of its positions by the Israeli army, re-entered West Beirut thanks to the chaos caused by the fierce fighting between the Amal militia, which benefited from its support, and the left-wing militias and the Palestinian camps. When Amine Gemayel's presidency ended in the autumn of 1988, two thirds of the territory was occupied by Syria, and 10% by Israel in the south. He himself was only obeyed around his palace in Baabda and in his stronghold of Bikfaya. The control of the "Christian reduction" is shared between the "Lebanese Forces", commanded by Samir Geagea and the regular Lebanese army commanded by General Aoun, whose project is to maintain the independence and integrity of Lebanon against the militia order and foreign occupations.

The last phase of the war.

When Amine Gemayel's term expired, the Americans reached an agreement with the Syrian President to have Mikael Daher, a Damascus loyalist, "elected" to the presidency of the Republic. But this appointment was rejected by Samir Geagea and Michel Aoun. They received support from Iraq, which delivered considerable quantities of arms and ammunition. As the deputies could not agree on his successor, Gemayel appointed Michel Aoun as head of government in October 1989. Surrounded by a military cabinet, he was determined to impose his authority even on the Lebanese Forces. With the previous Chairman of the Governing Council, Selim el Hoss, remaining in his post in West Beirut, the division of the country was deeper than ever. In a headlong rush and despite the disproportion of forces, General Aoun, raging against Syria, proclaimed on March 14, 1989 "the battle of liberation" against the Syrian occupation in Lebanon. He received enthusiastic support from the Christian population and French public opinion. He was supported by France and Iraq, but came up against the United States. Syrian shells rained down on the Christian area (1,500 km^2 , 800,000 inhabitants) which was isolated. An attempt to restore peace led to the signing by Lebanese deputies, on October 22, 1989 in Taif, Saudi Arabia, of a "Document of National Understanding" instituting political reforms that were supposed to be a first step towards the abolition of confessionalism and deciding on the dissolution of the militias. It was rejected by Michel Aoun on the grounds that it enshrined the Syrian occupation. René Moawad was elected President of the Republic, but, showing signs of independence from Damascus, he was assassinated only 17 days later, on November 22. To avoid new clashes, the deputies immediately elected the Syrian candidate, Elias Hraoui, in his place. But a fratricidal battle between the "Lebanese Forces" militia and the Lebanese army weakened the Christian camp.

Assad seized this opportunity to end the resistance to his occupation and pocket the benefit of his participation in Operation Desert Storm. Having obtained a green light from the United States, Syrian troops invaded the Christian area on October 13, 1990, putting an end to the war. After the elimination of General Aoun, the difficult reconstruction of the state began. The country was materially and morally ruined after fifteen years of war. General Emile Lahoud, commander-in-chief, worked to reunify the army. The militias were dismantled, with the exception of Hezbollah, which kept its weapons under the pretext of resistance to Israel.

The French attitude during the war

"France was the only Western power where the government and public opinion felt truly concerned by the existence of Lebanon. While the interventions of the United States, for whom Lebanon is a bargaining chip, have always favored the interests of Israel, France has tried, within its means, to effectively help solve the Lebanese crisis[7] . Two presidents of the French Republic have, each in their own way, agreed to commit the diplomatic credit of France supported by military contingents: Valery Giscard d'Estaing and François Mitterrand. However, France was powerless in its attempts at mediation. During the first phase of the war, the French government adopted a position of strict neutrality because of its close relations with the Arab world and friendly relations with the Christian camp. Anxious not to appear to take sides with either side, French policy was timid and ambiguous. It even seems at times to be more concerned with appeasing its Syrian, Palestinian and "Islamo-progressive" adversaries, in a vain attempt to attract their good grace, than with supporting its traditional Christian friends fighting for the country's independence. However, when Christian areas were savagely bombed by the Syrian army, President Giscard d'Estaing played a leading role in the adoption of a UN resolution to put an end to it. During the second and third phases of the conflict, marked by the Syrian determination to subdue the Christian camp, and then by the Israeli invasion in 1982, France became more resolutely involved, under the presidency of François Mitterrand, in the defense of Lebanon's independence. But it paid dearly for its interventions. Its ambassador, Louis Delamare, was assassinated in Beirut in September 1981 at the probable instigation of Damascus; its embassy was the victim of a car bombing; 46 of its soldiers perished in a suicide attack by Islamic Jihad against their position in 1984; and sixteen Frenchmen were taken hostage by pro-Iranian armed groups. Faced with the implacable determination of its adversaries and its powerlessness to influence the course of events, official France was forced to accept Syrian hegemony over the country.

The role of Syria

In the Lebanese drama, Syria has even heavier responsibilities than Israel. Since

Lebanon's independence in 1943, it has tried to intervene in the internal affairs of Lebanon, whose sovereignty it has never formally recognized. Hafez el-Assad is probably less interested in annexing Lebanon than in satelliteizing it. The outbreak of the unrest that he had largely provoked would provide him with the opportunity to do so. Throughout the conflict, he maneuvers very skillfully. Firstly, to make his ambitions match American interests while taking care not to alienate Moscow. Then to turn the situation in his favor after each setback. "Syria's game in Lebanon stems from a hegemonic will in the Levant and has clear objectives: to gain additional military space in the confrontation with Israel to compensate for the strategic loss of the Golan Heights in 1967; to try to bring the Lebanese card into the game of its regional policy; and to control the Palestinian resistance. While Syria prevents any *federate* action from its territory, it channels them into Lebanon.[8] " But after initially facilitating the extension of Palestinian power in Lebanon in the early 1970s, Syrian troops entered Lebanon in 1976 to put an end to it. By forging an alliance of circumstance with the Christians, it also removed what had historically been the main obstacle to its ambitions for the country: the latter's irreducible opposition. The signing of the separate Egyptian-Israeli peace agreement, however, led it to turn against the Christians and to reconcile with the PLO. But despite this tactical rapprochement, the mistrust between the two parties remained. Hence the promotion by Damascus in Lebanon of Muslim forces competing with those close to the PLO. The latter was popular with Sunnis who were sensitive to the common confessional affiliation that unites them with the majority of Palestinians. Against the PLO and its Sunni allies, Syria therefore encouraged the affirmation of the Shiite community by playing on the kinship between the Alawites, whose home is Syria, and the Shiites, whom it helped to form their own armed militia. Before, during and after the war, the Syrian secret services spared no means to destabilize Lebanon. The Syrian game consists, on the one hand, in instrumentalizing the antagonisms between the different Lebanese communities and, on the other, in supporting a foreign presence on Lebanese territory in order to be able to present itself as an arbiter on the local scene and in the eyes of the international community. Thus, after having favored the establishment of Palestinians in Lebanon, Damascus favored in 1982 that of the Iranian pasdaran to counter the Israeli attempt to satellite the country with the blessing of the United States. This manoeuvre enabled Syria to regain its influence in Lebanon and to appear as the only recourse in the face of the chaos that was taking hold. The bombing of Ashraf in 1978, the siege of Zahle in 1981 and the ruthless war it is waging to break the Lebanese-Israeli treaty and the Phalangist domination over Lebanon are all part of this perspective. To achieve its ends, the criminal regime in Damascus does not hesitate to systematically practice state terrorism: one-off assassinations, mass murders, summary executions, car bombs, sponsoring terrorist groups. A limitless violence that will be exercised not only against the unfortunate Lebanese, but also against France and the United States who will eventually capitulate to the blackmail of the Syrian dictator. His Machiavellianism allowed Syria to demonstrate a remarkable capacity for reversal. Crushed in Lebanon in 1982, it returned in force in 1987. Pushed out in 2005, it regained its influence there. And the symbiosis between the Syrian Alawite regime and the Lebanese Shiite movement was to have a wider strategic scope. It will materialize in the consolidation of the Syrian-Iranian alliance that allows Syria to break the isolation in which the Camp David peace had almost locked it and to play a key role on the regional geopolitical chessboard. Better still, despite this alliance and all the grievances they have against it, the United States, like Israel, continues to consider the Syrian regime as the best bulwark against fundamentalism.

The game of other regional and international players

Throughout the war, Israel's main objective in Lebanon was to fight and, if possible, annihilate the Palestinian armed resistance. It was with this in mind that it turned a blind eye in 1976 to the Syrian intervention aimed at bringing the PLO to heel. However, the Israeli-Egyptian peace led to a change in Israeli policy, which had a freer hand against the Palestinians and felt it had less need to spare Syria in Lebanon. This resulted in Operation Litani in 1978. Then came the Israeli invasion of Lebanon in 1982, with the dual aim of annihilating the PLO and satelliteizing Lebanon. But following the assassination of President Béchir Gemayel and the refusal of President Amine Gemayel to promulgate the peace treaty that he had tried to impose on the Lebanese government, Israel dropped the Christians and worked to encourage the creation of sectarian ghettos. In the end, the operation was a total failure that led to the fall of the Begin government. In spite of American support for Israel, Washington was sometimes obliged to spare the moderate Arab countries, and so had to slow down Tel Aviv's initiatives. This was the case during the Israeli invasion of Lebanon in 1978, and during the siege of Beirut in 1982. The fact remains that, except when the Lebanese crisis is likely to have negative repercussions on its regional policy, the United States only takes a very secondary interest in the fate of Lebanon, which has never been considered vital to its strategic interests. During Henry Kissinger's tenure as Foreign Minister, Lebanon bore the brunt of the strong coordination between Damascus and Washington. After his policy of small steps had succeeded in obtaining military disengagements between Israel and its Egyptian and Syrian adversaries, he was determined to solve the problem of the Palestinian presence in Lebanon. For him, the Palestinian presence in Lebanon had become the main obstacle to any progress in his mediation efforts to advance the regional peace process. Not to mention the fact that Palestinian organizations were using the Lebanese scene as a base for their terrorist actions around the world. Having noted the impotence of the Lebanese state to control them, Washington endorsed during the first phase of the war the Syrian armed intervention in Lebanon in order to bring the PLO into line. But, from the Carter mandate onwards, the American-Syrian honeymoon came to an end. The election of Ronald Reagan marked a hardening of American policy towards the "axis of evil". In 1982, Washington gave the green light to the Israeli invasion of Lebanon and only intervened to try to find a solution to the Lebanese problem when Sharon went too far and laid siege to Beirut.

The main cause of the war in Lebanon was undoubtedly the Palestinian armed presence. By supporting the Muslims in their attempt to control power, they exacerbated the confessional aspect of the conflict. And by serving as a Trojan horse for the Syrian dictator's designs on Lebanon, they paved the way for Syria's occupation of the country and for their own demise. Alongside the PLO, there were two Syrian-based organizations: the Saïka and the ALP, which was only a branch of the Syrian army and which fought the Christians and the other Palestinian groups in turn as Damascus changed its alliances. Turning against them, the Syrians were to complete the Israeli work that had uprooted them from southern Lebanon to Beirut by expelling Yasser Arafat from Tripoli, and then by entrusting the Shiite militia Amal with the task of wiping out the last rebels in the Palestinian camps in the capital. The Iraqi Baathist regime, which has always been at loggerheads with the Syrian Baathist regime, has constantly supported Syria's adversaries in Lebanon, arming in turn the PLO, the Christian militias, and then the troops of General Aoun, when the latter declared the war of liberation against the Syrian occupation. From the time of the seizure of power in Iran by Ayatollah Khomeini, to whom President Giscard d'Estaing had unwisely granted political asylum in France, the mullahs' regime made a dramatic entrance into the Lebanese arena. On the one hand, by settling its accounts with France, described as the "little Satan" (the term "great Satan" being reserved for the United States). And on the other hand by sponsoring the creation of Hezbollah, which was to become both the spearhead of the resistance against Israel and a state within a state in Lebanon. Heir to the Persian Empire, the Iranian Shiite theocracy used the Palestinian cause and its support for its Lebanese Shiite co-religionists to serve its regional hegemonic ambitions. As for the USSR, it is naturally through the prism of the Cold War that it sees the situation in Lebanon. Its action is primarily aimed at combating American influence there through support for the left-wing movements and the PLO. It also wanted to prevent Syria from falling into the arms of Washington, especially after Sadat's reversal of the alliance; following the October 1973 war, he expelled all Soviet advisers from Egypt. In response to the separate Egyptian-Israeli Camp David treaty, a Syrian-Soviet friendship treaty was signed in 1980. Moscow will provide massive aid to Syria to compensate for the losses inflicted on its army and air force by Tsahal in 1982. And it will support it in its fight against the Western forces that came to Beirut in the wake of the Israeli invasion.

The situation from 1990 to 2004

Concluded thanks to a Syrian-Saudi-American arrangement, the Taif Agreement enshrines the pacification of Lebanon under Syrian-Saudi condominium. It provides for the redeployment of Syrian troops, but not their total withdrawal from Lebanon, which legalizes the presence of these troops. It reduced the powers of the President of the Maronite Republic to the benefit of the Council of Ministers and thus of its Sunni President, who, from 1992, was also the protégé of the Saudi-American couple, who are dominant in the region. The power of the Shiite community was somewhat strengthened by the expansion of the powers of the Shiite president of the Chamber of Deputies, which, from 1992, went to Nabih Berri, the influential leader of Amal, considered a moderate, compared to the other major Shiite force that emerged from the war, Hezbollah. Lebanon is also linked to Syria through a series of bilateral agreements that establish the "privileged" relationship announced in the Taif Agreement. However, Saudi influence, especially economic, is increasing considerably, in parallel with that of Iran, which supports Hezbollah, in concert with Syria. The United States and France, as well as the other European states, found nothing wrong with Lebanon's status. This situation did not fail to provoke a feeling of deep despondency among the Christians of Lebanon who were in the grip of an identity and existential crisis. For the first time in their history they found themselves alone and had lost all political weight in the eyes of the West. After the neutralization of France following the Syrian military intervention, the Holy See is their last Western resort. Aware of the primordial role of the Christians of Lebanon as a bastion of Eastern Christianity, which was rapidly diminishing, John Paul II worked to restore their confidence. A new phase in the power struggle between the communities, which was now mainly between the Shiites and the Sunnis, began. As for the Christian party, now politically marginalized, it has a foothold both in the coalition dominated by the Shiite parties and in that dominated by the Sunnis of the Future Movement founded by Rafik Hariri.

"The period 1990-2005 saw the establishment of a Syrian stranglehold on Lebanon with the consent of the West. The head of the Syrian intelligence services, Ghazi Kenaan, was in charge, with the President of the Republic playing only a role as an extra. Assassinations, arbitrary arrests, torture and all sorts of human rights abuses are commonplace[9] . A new page was turned with the appointment of Rafik Hariri as Prime Minister in November 1992. The regime that took over was based on the "troika" of the three presidents of the Republic, the Council and the House. Their frequent disagreements forced them to seek arbitration from Damascus. This dependence reflects the political weakness of the Lebanese government, which has no real popular base. The banning of the Lebanese Forces and the sentencing of Samir Geagea to life imprisonment increased the Christians' feeling of alienation. At the end of Elias Hraoui's second presidential term, Damascus nominated General Lahoud as its candidate, whom the Parliament obediently elected as president on 15 October 1998. On June 10, 2000, when Hafez el-Assad died, his son Bashar succeeded him. The Syrian hold on Lebanon is not loosening. Under the protection and with the participation of Syrian officers, mafia networks are engaged in a real racket on several private and public financial resources.

Operation "Grapes of Wrath" and the Israeli withdrawal from Lebanon.

Hezbollah strengthened its alliance with Syria and continued its guerrilla war against Israel. In retaliation for these attacks, the Israeli air force bombed many Lebanese sites in July 1993. The operation forced 300,000 inhabitants of the south to flee to the north. Then, between April 15 and 30, 1996, Israel launched the "Grapes of Wrath" operation against Lebanon with the approval of the United States. 98 civilians who had taken refuge in the UN camp of Qana in southern Lebanon were killed by Israeli bombing, a tragedy that caused enormous emotion in Lebanon and throughout the world. The bombardment by Tsahal of the Lebanese infrastructure just recovered from the civil war, indignant Jacques Chirac. Without waiting for the end of the operation, he sent the French Minister of Foreign Affairs, Hervé de Charrette, on a mediation mission in Lebanon. France's mediation contributed to the cessation of the fighting and allowed the establishment of a ceasefire monitoring committee. In the first half of 1999, Hezbollah intensified its fight against the Israeli occupation of southern Lebanon, targeting in particular the positions of the South Lebanon Army (SLA). In response, the Netanyahu government bombed civilian installations in January 2000. Faced with effective resistance from Hezbollah, armed and financed by Iran, the new Israeli Prime Minister, Ehud Barak, announced his intention to withdraw Israeli troops from southern Lebanon. Fearing that it would be abandoned, the SLA broke out, provoking a hasty withdrawal of Israeli troops (May 2000). Hezbollah gained immense prestige from this victory. However, despite the end of the occupation, it announced its intention to keep its weapons "until the liberation of the last inch of Lebanese territory". The pretext is that the Israelis continue to occupy a tiny territory of 25 square kilometers between Lebanon and the Golan Heights called "Shebaa Farms".

Franco-Lebanese relations until 2004

The last years of François Mitterrand's second term in office were marked by a cooling of relations between the French government and the new pro-Syrian regime in Lebanon. In 1991 the French president insisted on the redeployment of the Syrian army in accordance with the Taif agreement, and denounced the fact that this agreement had not been fulfilled on this point. Then, in an eternal balancing act of French policy, Roland Dumas visited Damascus in February 1992 where he recognized "the positive role of Syria in safeguarding the unity of Lebanon[10] ". This position can be explained by two considerations: on the one hand, the need for France to build relations with the forces that had recently come to power in Lebanon; and on the other hand, the mutual interest that Damascus and Paris have in a rapprochement. Syria has long sought to establish good relations with European states that have a more balanced position on the Arab-Israeli conflict than the United States, whose bias towards Israel is blatant. For its part, France sought to break the American monopoly in the settlement of the Middle East crisis, which the disappearance of the USSR and the lack of balance on the international scene had further accentuated. The arrival to power of Jacques Chirac marks a strengthening of the Franco-Lebanese cooperation. Rafik Hariri's friendship with Jacques Chirac will make these relations take a personal turn during the latter's two presidential terms (1995-2007). In April 1996, Chirac became the first French head of state to make an official visit to

Lebanon since its independence in 1943. At the initiative of France, international conferences on support for Lebanon were held (Paris I and Paris II). At the same time, the new tenant of the Elysee Palace maintained good relations with the Syrian regime, whose protectorate over the country of the cedars he accepted until 2004. For his part, Hafez el-Assad used the privileged links between President Chirac and the Lebanese Prime Minister to develop direct contacts with the Élysée Palace. Hariri is one of the main architects of the visit of

Hafez el-Assad in Paris, July 16, 1996. But Chirac, who put all his weight behind the success of the Paris III conference aimed at granting three billion dollars in aid to Lebanon, came up against the obstructionism of President Lahoud and his Syrian sponsors. As early as April 2003, French diplomacy raised its tone towards Syria. And by taking the initiative, in agreement with the United States, to have the UN Security Council vote on resolution 1559 demanding the Syrian withdrawal, it played a key role in the restoration of Lebanese sovereignty,

The Cedar Revolution and the end of the Syrian occupation.

In the wake of its invasion of Iraq in 2003, the United States decided to increase the pressure on Damascus in order to force it to abandon any policy hostile to its interests. With the occupation of Iraq, its troops were on the doorstep of Syria, which became one of the main targets of the American policy aimed at reshaping the "New Middle East" according to the vision of the neoconservatives. Syria's support for Hamas and Hezbollah has led to it being designated, along with Iran, as a sponsor of "international" (in fact anti-Israeli) terrorism. Accused of supporting the Iraqi Baathists, Syria became a scapegoat for American difficulties in Iraq. Finally, as part of the American crusade for the establishment of democracy in the Middle East, its authoritarian regime was singled out, while Washington turned a blind eye to the case of its Egyptian and Saudi allies. The Bush administration decided to submit to Congress a draft resolution entitled: "*Syria Accountability and Lebanese Sovereignty Restoration Act*" which served as an instrument of pressure on Damascus. Accused, like Iraq in its time, of developing weapons of mass destruction and of supporting international terrorism, Syria was ordered to withdraw from Lebanon. This pressure received the support of France, which in the meantime had made a radical turnaround in its policy towards Syria. Indeed, President Chirac, who has not spared his support for Bashar al-Assad, considers that he "is not being paid in return[11] ". Not to mention that the status quo in Lebanon is felt as an affront by the Élysée, which had succeeded in obtaining international financial aid to finance a program of reform there. Finally, President Chirac's unfailing friendship with a Hariri who was mistreated by the Syrians explains the reconciliation between France and the United States, which had been at odds since the invasion of Iraq, at the expense of Syria. In fact, Washington and Paris each have their own agenda: "the Franco-American alliance on Syria and Lebanon is unnatural. The Americans sought to destabilize Syria. We were trying to ensure the independence of Lebanon, which they have nothing to do with," laments a French diplomat[12] . Be that as it may, Paris was, along with Washington, one of the two main architects of UN Security Council Resolution 1559, which was adopted on 20 September 2004. The resolution "Reaffirms its strong support for the territorial integrity, sovereignty and political independence of Lebanon within its internationally recognized borders. Emphasizing the importance of presidential elections being held in accordance with Lebanese constitutional rules devised without foreign interference... Noting Lebanon's determination to ensure the withdrawal of all non-Lebanese forces from its territory... Urges all remaining foreign forces to withdraw from Lebanon. [... and demands that all Lebanese and non-Lebanese militias be disarmed[13] . While Syria is not mentioned by name in order to spare it, Hezbollah is clearly targeted by this resolution.

Not measuring his isolation, Bahar el-Assad decided to force the hand of the Lebanese Parliament, which was ordered to unconstitutionally renew the presidential mandate of his ally, Emile Lahoud. Rafik Hariri, who was seen as a rallying point for the opposition, was assassinated in a car bombing on 14 February 2005 in Beirut. The opposition immediately accused Syria and its Lebanese vassals. Washington and Paris demanded an international investigation. A demonstration on 8 March in support of Syria by supporters of Hezbollah and Amal was followed on 14 March by a counter-demonstration by the opposition, which brought together a veritable human tide of around one million people. Forced to withdraw its army to the border, the Syrian regime resorted to attacks targeting Christian neighbourhoods in order to destabilize the country. Eternal victim of regional stakes, Lebanon is becoming the field of a battle between two radically opposed camps. On the one hand, the moderate Sunni Arab regimes, which are in favour of a peace agreement with Israel and allied with the United States. And on the other, the front of resistance to the "American-Israeli axis" led by Syria and Iran. The assassination of Rafik Hariri and the forced withdrawal of the Syrian army from Lebanon, following international pressure and the "Cedar Revolution", led to a political polarization between two camps: on the one hand, the "March 14" alliance (referring to the giant demonstration after Hariri's death) of parties advocating a sovereignist line and supported by Riyadh, Paris and Washington: mainly the Future Current and the Lebanese Forces; and on the other hand, the "March 8" alliance allied with Syria and grouping Hezbollah, Amal, and the Free Patriotic Movement (a Christian party led by General Aoun).

Following the parliamentary elections in the spring of 2005, the March 14 forces controlled the Assembly and a close associate of the Hariri family, Fouad Siniora, became Prime Minister. But President Lahoud refuses to ratify government decisions contrary to Syrian interests, becoming a major source of deadlock. And Hezbollah is spearheading the counter-revolution aimed at undermining the foundations of the "Cedar Revolution". This has had the effect of both undermining the early beginnings of the cross-community sovereignty current and inducing a radicalization of sectarian reflexes. This counter-revolution initiated by Hezbollah is part of the logic of a transnational project anchored, on a doctrinal and religious basis, to the geopolitical designs of the mullahs in Tehran. A new period of violence began, during which several leaders of March 14 were victims of terrorist attacks. The legitimacy of an international tribunal for Lebanon (TSL) created to judge the perpetrators of the attack on Rafik Hariri and his companions was challenged by Hezbollah.

From the Israeli offensive of 2006 to the election of Michel Aoun

On July 12, 2006, following the kidnapping of two of its soldiers, Israel, determined to finish with Hezbollah, launched a major offensive in the south and then on Beirut. Its air force carried out devastating raids, causing enormous destruction to civilian infrastructure throughout the country. But on the ground, the Israeli army was unable to defeat the militia of the "Party of God" which rained thousands of missiles on Israel. Describing its resistance as a "divine victory", Israel emerged politically stronger from the confrontation. The UN Security Council finally adopted Resolution 1701 authorizing the reinforcement of UNIFIL and the Lebanese authorities announced their intention to deploy soldiers of the national army in the South. But this did not prevent Hezbollah from strengthening its arsenal. Hezbollah ignored its commitment not to use its weapons on the domestic scene on May 6, 2008, by invading central and western Beirut and besieging, with its allies, the Presidency of the Council. At the same time, he attacked the Chouf where violent fighting opposed him to the Druze forces. This coup de force caused deep resentment within the Sunni community. A political crisis ensued, which led to the election of General Michel Sleiman as President of the Republic, following an agreement reached in Doha. The election in 2007 of Nicolas Sarkozy as President of the French Republic led to a Franco-Syrian rapprochement. But France's attempts to use its influence to reduce the Syrian hold on Lebanon have no effect.

Following the June 2009 parliamentary elections won by the March 14 coalition, Saad Hariri, who had succeeded his father as head of the Future Movement, formed a national unity government in which Syria's allies had a blocking minority. Since the Doha agreement, Lebanon has enjoyed a certain stability until the outbreak of the Syrian insurrection. This opened a new phase in the opposition between the local allies of the Syrian-Iranian axis and the sovereignist camp supported by the West and the "moderate" Arab countries. In 2011, exercising armed blackmail on the Druze leader Walid Jumblatt, Hezbollah forced the fall of the coalition government headed by Saad Hariri. Negib Mikati was appointed President of the Council by the "March 8" coalition, which had become the majority. It was only after two months of negotiations that the government could be formed. The same day, the indictment against four members of Hezbollah in the case of the assassination of Rafik Hariri was issued by the prosecutor of the SLT. But Hassan Nasrallah said that there was no question of handing them over. As of May 25, 2014, the end of Michel Sleiman's presidential term, Lebanon is without a president. Boycotting the parliamentary sessions intended to elect a president, the "March 8" MPs prevented the holding of elections for two and a half years. Finally Michel Aoun was elected president on October 31, 2016. His election marks a real breakthrough for Hezbollah, which supported his candidacy and concretizes its political and military supremacy. Aoun appointed Saad Hariri as president of the Council, even though Hariri has been his political opponent since the second half of the 2000s.

The impact of the war in Syria

Since 2012, Lebanon has practically been living at the pace of the Syrian conflict, politically, socially, economically and in terms of security. Not to mention the burden, and even the threat to its fragile community balance, represented by the influx of more than one and a half million Syrian refugees on its soil. Despite the government's policy of distancing itself from the latter, Hezbollah has provided military support to the Damascus regime. This armed intervention fanned sunni resentment against the regime and reawakened the demon of "fitna" (discord) between the two communities, sunni and shia. A series of attacks against Shiite areas took place. These incidents could have had serious consequences had it not been for the awareness of all political parties of the need to avoid a repetition of the civil war that tore the country apart. In addition to these internal risks of destabilization, there was the security threat of jihadist groups occupying a region straddling the Syrian-Lebanese border. But in September 2017, the Lebanese army drove out the jihadists who occupied part of the mountainous region north of the Syrian-Lebanese border. This victory raised the prestige of the army and proved its ability to defend the country.

The issue of Lebanese-Syrian relations has come back to the forefront with the debate on the return of Syrian refugees in Lebanon to safe areas in Syria. One part of the Lebanese is in favor of a dialogue on this issue with the Syrian government and the other is categorically opposed. The former believe that it is unrealistic to expect their return without entering into negotiations with Damascus and they doubt the ability of the UN to ensure it, especially since the priority of the international community is to stem the flow of migrants to Europe. While the sovereignist camp fears that this will once again open the door to its interference in Lebanese internal affairs. Mistrust of Syria's hegemonic agenda was rekindled by the threatening statement of a Syrian opposition spokesman that "Lebanon is 'a geographical mistake' and the Lebanese should not forget that it only takes 10% of Syrian refugees to take up arms to set their country on fire[14] ". The bitterness of the controversy is also explained by the confessional factor, as Christians see the presence of Syrian refugees as an existential threat. This controversy and Hezbollah's military intervention alongside the Syrian regime show how closely Lebanon's fate is linked to Syria. If history has separated the two peoples, this separation is largely fictitious since the influx of one and a half million Syrian refugees into Lebanon, a significant number of whom have blended into the local population. That said, the fact that the Syrian authorities have officially shelved the dream of a Greater Syria has not prevented relations between the two countries from being conflictual most of the time. But the Lebanese have never made an amalgam between the regime and the Syrian people. And while European countries are obsessed with the influx of a minimal number of migrants relative to their populations and resources, Lebanon has generously hosted the world's highest proportion of Syrian refugees relative to its population and size.

A new twist in the Lebanese crisis

A new crisis arose on November 5, 2017, when the Head of Government, Saad Hariri, summoned to Riyadh by King Salman, announced his resignation, pointing his finger in virulent terms at the "destructive role of Iran and its military arm (Hezbollah) in the region and in Lebanon." By forcing his hand, Saudi Arabia risked putting Lebanon in front of an impossible choice: either confrontation with Hezbollah or confrontation with Saudi Arabia and its allies. While Hariri was probably being held hostage in Riyadh, President Macron "exfiltrated" him to Paris and then returned to Beirut, where he agreed to reconsider his resignation and adopted a more conciliatory tone toward Hezbollah. The unanimous rejection of the Saudi diktat, as well as international pressure, ultimately backfired on Mohammed bin Salman's untimely initiative. He probably sought to compensate for the failure of Saudi policy in Syria on the Lebanese scene, but he lost his bet. By welcoming Saad Hariri to Paris after having obtained his departure from Saudi Arabia, Emmanuel Macron achieved a great diplomatic success. In the aftermath, the French president took the initiative to convene on December 8, 2017, at the Quai d'Orsay the International Support Group for Lebanon (ISGL), which had been created in 2013 to help Lebanon bear the burden of Syrian refugees. The latter reaffirmed its support for Lebanon's stability. A support that depends, however, on the level of official commitment to the policy of distancing itself from the conflicts in the region.

Community relations

Hariri's triumphant return to the country masks the reality: his personal weakening and, more generally, that of Lebanese political sunnism in the face of the Shiite camp. This weakening is part of a heavy historical trend that has seen four communities successively dominate Lebanese political life: the Druze until the middle of the 19th century; the Christians - in particular the Maronites - between the creation of "Greater Lebanon" (in 1920) and 1975; the Sunnis, for a brief period between the Taif Accords in 1990 and the assassination of Rafik Hariri in 2005; and finally the Shiites since then. It is impossible at this stage to predict the impact of the Syrian conflict on Lebanon. However, we can already observe some significant changes in the relationship between Lebanese communities and in their perceptions of their respective identities. Since the end of the Lebanese civil war in 1990, four major trends, both centripetal and centrifugal, have emerged within society. First, an "Arabization" of the majority of Christians, despite their feeling of having a specific identity in relation to their Arab-Muslim environment. This is matched by a "Lebanization" of

Muslims, especially Sunnis who were once seduced by dreams of Arab unity. Thirdly, and more recently, the birth of a Sunni-Shiite divide. Finally, the progression of communitarianism, a worldwide phenomenon.

The events in Syria and in the region have given rise to new developments in mentalities. Some Lebanese Christians feel a growing distrust of Islam, especially Sunni Islam, which is perceived as less open and less tolerant than Shi'ism. Their concern can only be rekindled by the fate of their co-religionists in Iraq and the fate of those in Syria. This concern is fuelled by the awareness of the rise of a radical Sunni fundamentalism considered more dangerous than Shiite fundamentalism and the presumed impotence of the moderate Sunni majority to counter it. It is not the spectacle of bearded Islamists in Tripoli, nor the presence of two million Syrian and Palestinian refugees on the national territory, and even less the "takfirist" surge in Syria that is likely to allay their fears. Hence a lesser animosity towards Hezbollah on the part of its most fierce opponents. This observation reflects neither an adherence to the thesis of the alliance of minorities nor a plea for a community withdrawal, but a fact. As for Lebanese Muslims, the conflict in Syria has strengthened their attachment to the Lebanese entity and completed the umbilical link between them and the latter. The temptation for Christians to withdraw and the solidarity of Shiites and Sunnis with their co-religionists in neighbouring countries are, however, less strong than the cohesion factors. The attachment of the three major communities to living together should ward off the spectre of the country's integrity being called into question. On the other hand, the dream of deconfessionalization and secularism that some people still harbour appears to be as utopian as ever.

A certain resilience in the face of turmoil

Lebanon has always found it difficult to fully live its independence, because of its history, because of its neighbors, because of the diversity of the communities that make it up, especially religious communities, in a region where religion is political. Its political leaders often act as willing relays for foreign powers and interests in order to consolidate their own power, and have instituted clientelism as a political program. The result is a dependent nation and a paralyzed if not failed state. Despite this, the country has escaped the tragic fate of its Syrian and Iraqi neighbors. Its system of communal power-sharing has ultimately proved more resilient than their authoritarian regimes. And the much-maligned weakness of the Lebanese state has proven more resilient than the dictatorships in Baghdad and Damascus. This resilience is all the more remarkable given that the fate of the country has always depended as much on the internal political game as on the divisions and contradictions of the region of which it is the eternal hostage. Representing an important stake in the balance of power on the regional geopolitical chessboard, it has often paid the price. Today this balance has been modified by the turn of events in favor of the Syrian regime and its allies in the Syrian conflict, which is playing into the hands of the Tehran-Damascus axis and its extension to Lebanon, through Hezbollah. As a democratic and multicommunity country surrounded by mainly Muslim and authoritarian powers, Lebanon is an Arab exception. But its identity is still a problem. Although they share the same language, the Lebanese have never formed a nation and Lebanon is in fact a federation of non-territorial religious communities. And while these communities now share the same desire to live together, they share less of the same morals since the spread of Iranian theocratic values by Hezbollah within the Shiite community and the emergence of a minority fundamentalist current within the Sunni community. These cultural differences and the fifteen-year war almost put a cross on Lebanon. But against all odds, it is still standing. It is true that the country's face and political orientation have changed profoundly since the end of Christian preponderance. But this is as much a thing of the past as Muslim irredentism. Both sunnis and shiites are now all the more attached to the country's independence as they now share (or compete for) most of the power. As for the Christians, they have recovered from their illusions about the West's willingness to come to their rescue. Their political parties are divided between the two main coalitions dominated by the Shiites and the Sunnis, which partially compensates for their lesser political weight by placing them in a sort of arbitration position. In addition, many Muslims see the Christian presence as a valuable asset in the face of the fundamentalist threat to their way of life. However, in the longer term, the inexorable demographic decline of Christians risks making them suffer the same fate of second-class citizens as their co-religionists in the Arab-Muslim world, whose numbers are shrinking like a stone. Despite its shortcomings, including recurrent paralysis, the Lebanese system of power sharing among its different religious components has indeed proved more resilient than the authoritarian regimes in Syria and Iraq, whose formal secularism has not prevented communal power grabbing and the breakup of these two countries. But Lebanon is at the heart of a regional and international tug of war. The Trump administration in Washington and the new crown prince of Saudi Arabia have stepped up their campaign against Hezbollah. And the country is not immune to new external threats. The possibility of a devastating war for Lebanon between Israel and Hezbollah is increasingly raised by some analysts. According to them, the arsenal accumulated by Hezbollah, far from having a dissuasive effect represents on the contrary a "casus belli". They believe that this arsenal represents an intolerable threat to Israel, which will not need a provocation to launch a preventive attack against Lebanon. The question is not if, but when. If it does happen, it will be infinitely more destructive than the one in 2006 and will spare no region and, with Hezbollah in government, no Lebanese institution, including the army, which is obliged to defend the country. On the eve of the parliamentary elections to be held in May 2018, the social crises associated with the administrative negligence, the abysmal and successive deficit of the budgets, the weight of the debt and its service are making Lebanon one of the most politically and financially vulnerable countries in the world. The mismanagement of public services, notably water, electricity and health, the dilapidation of infrastructure, the calamitous management of household and industrial waste collection and its consequences on public health, reinforce in the eyes of public opinion the reputation of the political class as prebendous and corrupt. Lebanon, which has survived wars, could succumb to state failure. This prospect is no longer a hypothetical one. International meetings on Lebanon are more than ever aimed at postponing financial deadlines that the persistent economic stagnation, the failure of economic recovery policies, the burden of the presence of Syrian refugees on infrastructure and employment, as well as political insecurity can no longer hide.

1 *Histoire du Liban des origines au XXe siècle,* Boutros Dib (direction) Philippe Rey éditions 2006

2 *Le Liban et la Syrie au miroir français,* (1946-1991) Marie-Thérèse Oliver-Saïdi, l'Harmattan 1993, p.300

3 *La déchirure libanaise*, Nadine Picaudou, éditions Complexe 1989, p. 107

4 *Une guerre pour les autres*, Ghassan Tuéni, preface by Dominique Chevalier, J.-C. Lattès éditions, 1983 p. 5.

5 *Liban, l'instruction d'un crime*, Roger Azam, Ed. Cheminement 2005, p.70

6 *Geopolitics of the Lebanese conflict*, Georges Corm, Ed. La Découverte 1986, p. 224

7 ibid

8 *Lebanon the investigation of a crime.* Roger Azam Ed. Cheminements 2005, p.355

9 La déchirure libanaise, Nadine Picaudou, Ed. Complexe, 1989

10 *La France au Liban et au Proche-Orient,* Ibrahim Tabet, Éditions de la Revue Phénicienne, p.138.

11 *Une proie entre deux fauves, le Liban entre le lion de Juda et le lion de Syrie*, Annie Laurent and Antoine Basbous, Beirut al Daïra editions 1987

12 *The Syrian exception, between modernization and resistance*, Caroline Donati, La Découverte

13 . *L'Orient-le jour* of February 10, 1992.

14 *France in Lebanon and the Middle East,* op.cit

15 *Chirac* of Arabia, Eric Aeschimann, Christophe Boltanski. Grasset, 2006, p.395

16 UN Resolution 1559

17 *L'Orient-le jour*, June 20, 2017.

Chapter 10. Iraq and the first two Gulf Wars.

Saddam Hussein or "the Republic of Fear".

In 1974, despite a certain autonomy that had been granted to them, the Kurds rose up again with the support of Iran. Saddam Hussein, then Vice-President, aware of the danger, decided to negotiate directly with imperial Iran. The 1975 Algiers agreement was a success for the Shah's government. Iraq abandoned its claims to both banks of the Shatt al-Arab and recognized the delimitation of the border passing through the middle of the mouth of the Euphrates and Tigris rivers. In return, Iran refuses all aid to the Kurds. Deprived of all support, the Kurdish rebellion collapsed. Jalal Talabani took advantage of this to create the PUK, a rival to Mustapha Barazani's KDP. The regime's policy towards the Shiites alternated between brutal repression of extremist Shiite groups and openness to the Shiite population in general. 300 members of the Shiite organization Al Da'wa were executed between 1982 and 1984. But at the same time, a more important role was given to Shiite representation at the various levels of power. In order to avoid too great a dependence on Moscow, and as there was no question of relying on American support, France was seen as an essential Western partner, which took concrete form in 1975 with the signing of a contract for the sale of two nuclear reactors and the construction of the Osirak nuclear power station near Baghdad. Oil revenues and the opening up of certain European countries, in particular France, reinforced Iraq's desire to dominate the Arab scene. But it had to face up to Shiite discontent within the country, and then to the Islamic Republic of Iran. Thanks to the considerable increase in oil revenues, the government was able to embark on ambitious development projects and raise living standards.

On July 16, 1979, having "resigned" from office, Hassan el-Bakr, the vice-president, Saddam Hussein, took over as head of state, ushering in twenty-five years of bloody dictatorship, described by Samir el Khalil as the "Republic of Fear"[1] . He combined the functions of President and Prime Minister, appointed his cousin, Ali Hassan Al-Majid, to the strategic position of head of the intelligence services and confirmed his half-brother Barzan Ibrahim al-Takriti as head of the secret police. He elevated his friend Tarek Aziz to the rank of Deputy Prime Minister and entrusted him with the Ministry of Foreign Affairs, with the main task of ensuring the regime's good image with the West. With their support, on 29 July 1979, he called all the important members of the Ba'ath party to an impromptu conference. After claiming to have discovered a fifth column within the party, he gave the floor to the Secretary General of the Revolutionary Command Council, Abdel Hussein Machhadi. The latter, who had obviously been tortured, "revealed" that he had hatched a plot with the help of the Syrian branch of the party and some of the people present at the meeting with the aim of overthrowing the command. During this pseudo-confession, Saddam Hussein, casually smoking a large cigar, said almost nothing. When

Machhadi began to name his accomplices, they were taken in turn out of the room by guards under the terrified eyes of their colleagues. 68 leaders were arrested, a third of whom were summarily executed. The purge was filmed and video cassettes were distributed throughout the country. The message was clear: Saddam Hussein was now the master of the country.

Putting an end to the attempt at rapprochement with Syria begun by his predecessor, he closed his embassy, imitated by Damascus. In the following weeks, hundreds of other Baath members were arrested. Most were tortured and then executed. Only a few were released to set an example. Between 1981 and 1982, Saddam Hussein had more than 3,000 Iraqis executed for various reasons, even creating a climate of terror within his own entourage. Intimidation became daily, cruelty commonplace and the cult of personality omnipresent. When he punishes an opponent or a traitor, he also punishes his family and close friends. If the repression is particularly aimed at the Shiites, on the other hand, there was no hostility towards the Christians, nor any restriction on their freedom of worship under Saddam Hussein's regime. He wants to make his country an example of modernity in the Arab world. He uses the oil revenues to develop the country's infrastructure, industry, agriculture, a civilian nuclear program and health care. He is also improving social services and the education system.

Following the outbreak of the Iranian Revolution, Saudi Arabia and Iraq concluded a security agreement in April 1979. Saddam Hussein undertook to defend the Saudi kingdom in the event of a threat from revolutionary Iran. This initiative marked his desire to become Nasser's successor at the head of the Arab nation. This ambition naturally met with opposition from Syria. In April 1982, Syria closed its border with Iraq. Ties between the two governments were officially broken until the fall of Saddam Hussein in 2003. The hostility between the two countries manifested itself once again in 1989 when Iraq supported the "war of liberation" against the Syrian occupation of Lebanon led by General Michel Aoun with massive deliveries of arms.

The Iraq-Iran war (1980-1988).

The first two Gulf Wars, the one between Iran and Iraq, and the one between the latter and the coalition led by the United States, are two inseparable parts of the same crisis. Following the Iranian Revolution, Saddam Hussein unleashed a war against Iran in September 1980, which would be the longest of the 20th century[e] . There were several reasons for his decision. First, there was the fear of the influence of the Iranian revolution on the Iraqi Shiite community. Barely a month after the start of the revolution, Iranian provocations took place at the border, while in Iran demonstrations called for the overthrow of the Baathist regime. And on 15 March 1980, Ayatollah Khomeini appealed to Iraqi public opinion in these terms: "O Iraqi people, beware of your leaders and make the revolution until victory[2] ". Saddam Hussein also hoped, by bringing down the Khomeini regime, whose military capabilities he underestimated, to set himself up as the gendarme of the Gulf and the protector of the Arab monarchies against

Persian expansionism. Finally, there is the issue of the border demarcation agreement in the middle of the Shatt el-Arab, which Iraq was forced to accept and which it wants to move to the eastern bank of the estuary. Although Iran is four times larger and three times more populous than Iraq, the Iraqi president believes the Islamic Republic is weakened by its internal dissensions. He was convinced that the disorganization of the Iranian army, weakened by the purges, would ensure him a rapid victory, whereas in fact he was going to provoke a nationalist upsurge around Khomeini.

When the conflict began, Iraq could count on the support of the USSR, France and the Western powers. The Arabs were divided. The Arab countries of the Gulf Cooperation Council, worried by the Iranian threat, as well as Jordan, supported Iraq out of Arab solidarity; while Hafez el-Assad's Syria and Muammar Gaddafi's Libya, who wanted the Iraqi regime to fall, took sides with Iran. In Egypt, Sadat, while hating the Iranian Islamic regime, was not ready to help Saddam Hussein. It was only after Hosni Mubarak came to power that Cairo gave him substantial material support. The United States remained neutral at first, and then supported Iraq when the balance tipped in favor of Iran. But members of the Reagan administration secretly and illegally sold arms to Iran to finance the "contras", a Nicaraguan counter-revolutionary movement. The operation was also intended to allow the release of American hostages held by Iran. This is the scandal known as Irangate. The American duplicity does not give way in any way to the Israeli Machiavellianism which, in order to weaken the Iraqi enemy, supports the war effort of the mullahs' regime, even though it is the mortal enemy of the Hebrew state. While on paper the Iranian army appears more powerful than the Iraqi army, the real balance of power is in favor of the latter and will be more so in the last two years of the war. This was due to the supply of military equipment to Iraq during the conflict, which was far greater than that received by Iran. Some thirty countries sold arms to Iraq: first of all the USSR and France (75% of deliveries between them), followed by China, Italy and Egypt. Iran's suppliers will be China, North Korea and Israel. Iraq's arms purchases will be largely financed by advances from the Gulf Arab monarchies. Iran, on the other hand, will receive no foreign financial aid and will have to rely solely on its oil exports to finance its arms purchases.

The war had four phases: a phase of advances by Iraqi forces into Iranian territory, mainly in Khuzistan, from 20 September to 10 December 1980. A phase of Iranian counter-offensives, ending on 20 June 1982 with the withdrawal of Iraqi forces to the international border. A succession of Iranian offensives on Iraqi territory which ceased on 30 April 1987 and turned into a war of attrition. Finally, a fourth phase which lasted until the end of the conflict in August 1988. Taking the form of an all-out war, it opened with a tanker war which led to a Western and Soviet naval intervention in the Gulf of Oman and saw a reversal of the situation in favour of Iraq. Throughout the war, the Iraqi Minister of Defence was Adnan Khairallah, Saddam Hussein's first cousin. On the Iranian side, the President of the Parliament, Akbar Hashemi Rafsanjani, was appointed commander of the armed forces in 1981.

The beginning of the hostilities.

On 20 September 1980, the Iraqi air force launched hostilities with a surprise attack on Iranian airfields and other targets. But the results of the raids were disappointing and the Iraqi aircraft quickly came up against the Iranian fighters, who were lining up more efficient American aircraft. Ground operations began two days later. They were conducted by three Iraqi army corps totalling 250,000 men. The first was deployed in the north, facing Iranian Kurdistan, and the second in the center between Qasr-e-Shirin and Dezfoul. The main effort, entrusted to the III[e] army corps, was directed towards the south, towards the predominantly Arabic-speaking and oil-rich province of Khuzistan, in order to capture the cities of Ahwaz, Kermanshah and Khorramshahr, isolating the oil complex of Abadan. After hard fighting, the III[e] corps captured Khorramchahr, which fell in November, but it failed to take the other cities. On the whole front, territorial gains were very limited, due to a series of Iranian counter-attacks. The destruction of the Abadan refinery by Iraqi artillery nevertheless reduced Iran's fuel production by half. In response, Iran, whose navy far surpassed the Iraqi naval forces, mounted a joint operation to neutralize the oil terminals through which two-thirds of Iraq's oil exports pass, in order to suffocate the Iraqi economy. The air raids on the cities and strategic objectives of the two belligerents carried out by their respective air forces and the firing of ballistic missiles gained in intensity. After the phase of the Iraqi offensives, which were far from having achieved their objectives, the Iraqis switched to defensive mode and the conflict quickly became bogged down. The military confrontation was coupled with a war of symbols. The Iraqi offensive of 1980 was named Kadisiyya, in reference to the conquest of Iran by the Arabs in the 7th century[e] . The Iranian counter-offensives were named Kerbala 1, 2, etc., evoking the Shiite struggle against the Sunni power. On the Iranian side, mass recruitment, including of very young boys, is accompanied by an exaltation of martyrs. The Iranian regime has no qualms about sacrificing tens of thousands of child soldiers in offensives designed to wear down the Iraqi army. It has happened that indoctrinated young volunteers rush to the minefields. The civilian population is heavily involved, to compensate for the serious deficiencies due to the Khomeini purges of the regular army. In fact, the strongest resistance to the advance of the Iraqi troops came mainly from the Revolutionary Guards Corps, made up of the *Pasdaran* and the *Bassidjis.* At the beginning, these troops constituted only one-sixth of the Iranian ground forces, but this ratio increased rapidly because the revolutionary government intended to give preference to this corps, which was totally devoted to it, unlike the regular army, which it distrusted. In the last year of the war, in 1988, the Revolutionary Guards' strength reached 600,000 men, compared with 250,000 for the regular army.

The initiative changes sides

At the beginning of 1981, the initiative changed sides. The year opened with the failure of a first Iranian counter-offensive. On 15 January, the Iraqi army, opening a new front, penetrated into Iranian Kurdistan where a popular insurrection supported by Baghdad broke out in April. On June 7, the Israeli air force destroyed the Iraqi nuclear power plant Osirak. In September, an Iranian offensive forced the Iraqi army to lift the siege of Abadan and withdraw to the west bank of the Karoun River. In November-December, new Iranian offensives allowed the liberation of the territories conquered by the Iraqis in the central sector of the front. On 15 December Saddam Hussein proposed a "peace of the braves" which was rejected by Iran.

The year 1982 saw the Iranian armed forces once again break the stalemate at the front. In March they won their first major victory against the Iraqis in the central sector. Three skilfully coordinated operations enabled the Iranians to retake Khorramchahr in April and to liberate the province of Khûzistân. The Iraqi forces had to withdraw to the international border under the assaults of the regular Iranian army and the fanatical pasdaran. On 8 April Syria closed the Kirkuk-Baniyas oil pipeline and its border with Iraq. Baghdad and Ankara agreed to double the capacity of the Kirkuk-Dortyol pipeline. In June 1982, Saddam Hussein tried again to end the war, but Imam Khomeini wanted the fall of the Iraqi president and the establishment of an Islamic Republic of Iraq.

The battle of Iraq began in the summer of 1982. However, the Iranian offensives came up against a stubborn defence by the Iraqi army, which was considerably helped by the delivery of Soviet and French weapons. In addition to the delivery of Mirage F1 fighter-bombers, France went so far as to rent Super-Etendards equipped with Exocet missiles to its ally. The countries of the Gulf Cooperation Council (GCC) allocated $80 billion in aid to Baghdad, enabling it to acquire the firepower needed to contain the Iranian onslaught. The United States began a rapprochement with Baghdad, which also received firmer support from the USSR. For its part, Iran acquired arms from China, which now openly supported it, as well as from North Korea. The forces were balanced in bloody land confrontations. The war changed in nature with the intensification of strategic bombing on both sides, notably on the Iranian oil terminal on the island of Kharg. Iraq intended to ban Iranian crude oil exports. In August Saddam Hussein decreed an oil blockade of Iran and established a maritime exclusion zone around the island of Kharg. Tehran responded by establishing its own maritime exclusion zone in the Gulf.

At the beginning of 1983, Tarek Aziz negotiated the purchase of new French arms and reached an agreement with Paris on the rescheduling of the Iraqi debt. In April, Iran launched a vast operation against the Peshmerga in Iranian Kurdistan, followed in July by an offensive towards Iraqi Kurdistan. In November the Iraqi army used chemical weapons for the first time. In January 1984, the Iraqi army was everywhere on the defensive on a front of 1200 kilometers. Iran launched a series of offensives called "Dawn 1, 2, 3, 4 etc." on several sectors of the country. In February, Iranian forces seized the oil fields of the Majnoun Islands in a region of lakes and marshes north of Basra. Iraq retaliated by launching the war of the cities. On 27 March, a first attack by Iraqi Super-Stendars against Iranian oil traffic triggered the tanker war. On June 3, Saudi Arabia shot down an Iranian Phantom and set up an air and naval exclusion zone. The United States announced the dispatch of a naval air group to the Gulf of Oman. In October the Kurdish guerrillas rose up against the Iraqi regime. In March 1985, the Iranian Badr offensive was broken by the Iraqis, thanks to the intensive use of chemical weapons. New Iranian offensives on various sectors of the front were repulsed, while the Iraqi air force began a four-month bombing campaign against the oil terminal on Kharg Island and oil terminals located further south. In early 1986 Iraqi forces retook part of the Majnoun Islands.

In February the Iranian army succeeded, at the cost of heavy losses, in taking the Fao peninsula at the mouth of the Shatt el-Arab, blocking Iraq's access to the sea (Aurora 8). In January 1987, the Iranian army launched two major offensives: Kerbala 5 on Basra, the third largest city in Iraq, and Kerbala 6, north of Baghdad, in the direction of the great dams of the Euphrates. Rafsanjani called the assault on Basra "the mother of all battles" and Khomeini gave a speech in which he compared the war underway to a holy war that must continue until the final victory and the departure of the tyrant from Baghdad. Despite a deluge of fire, the Iranian forces succeeded in crossing the Shatt el-Arab and breaking through the first lines of defence of Basra, which had been transformed into a fortress, causing a crisis in the Iraqi general staff. The losses were enormous on both sides, but despite the fury of the Revolutionary Guards, the Iranian forces were finally blocked. The Iraqis responded to the Iranian offensives with devastating air raids on Iranian economic facilities.

Four new Iranian offensives followed one another between February and April 1987. While in March Turkey made an incursion into Iraqi Kurdistan where the PKK had taken refuge. The PKK agreed with Barzani's PDK and Talabani's UPK to unify the Kurdish rebellion against the Iraqi regime. A final assault on Basra (Kerbala 8) broke down against Iraqi defences (6-11 April 1987). An offensive in the Qasr-e-Shirin area (Kerbala 9) was no more successful. Finally Kerbala 10 (against Iraqi Kurdistan) closed this phase of the war. Iran then changed its strategy. Putting an end to the offensives of human waves, it now favours the war of attrition. Iraq and the USSR renewed their treaty of friendship and cooperation.

The intervention of the fleets of the great powers.

A UN Security Council resolution of 20 July 1987, number 598, imposed a ceasefire along the international borders, which suited Iraq. But Khomeini was wrong not to accept it, because the balance of power would shift in favour of Baghdad, which enjoyed the decisive support of its allies. In July 1987, Iran undertook to control maritime navigation in the Gulf and intensified the tanker war to force the petro-monarchies to interrupt their financial support to Baghdad. The tankers were fired upon by anti-ship missiles and harassed by speedboats, and were exposed to the danger of mines laid in the Strait of Hormuz. The Iraqi Super Etendards fired hundreds of Exocet missiles against the oil tankers supplying Iran and its oil installations. Washington then launched a naval escort operation for its ships. 11 Kuwaiti oil tankers were also placed under the US flag and 3 under the Soviet flag.

The threat to maritime traffic, which affected their vital interests, led to the intervention of the major powers, which deployed the largest naval air operation since the end of the Second World War in the Gulf and the Strait of Hormuz. It totalled 100 warships, including 54 American vessels, 2 of which were nuclear aircraft carriers; 14 French vessels, including 1 aircraft carrier; 11 Soviet vessels; 9 British vessels; 7 Italian vessels and some 15 vessels belonging to other countries[3] . Despite this deterrent presence, a total of 430 foreign merchant ships were attacked (252 by Iraq and 178 by Iran) and 72 sunk by the two belligerents, causing the death of 430 civilian sailors[4] . Numerous incidents took place between the Iranian air and naval forces and the US Navy, which sank several Iranian ships and destroyed three offshore platforms. And on 3 July 1988, an American cruiser mistakenly shot down an Iranian Airbus. Tehran accused Washington of war crimes, but, unable to afford to fight Iraq and the United States at the same time, refrained from retaliating.

The Iraqi counter-offensive and the end of the war

On the Iran-Iraq front, the Iraqi army had almost as many men as Iran at the beginning of 1988 (800,000 men against 850,000) and now had a clear material superiority (3,400 tanks against 1,100, 2,500 artillery pieces against 900, 360 fighter planes against 60 operational ones and 140 attack helicopters against 40).[5] The year began with a war of capitals, marked by the firing of salvos of ballistic missiles on Teheran and Baghdad. The Iraqi army, reinvigorated, liberated Fao, which had fallen two years earlier, on 18 April 1988 (Operation Blessed Ramadan). In May, it drove out the last Iranian troops in the Basra area. Then, after regaining the ground lost in Kurdistan and recovering the oil fields of the Majnoun islands, it penetrated again into Iranian territory. Thousands of prisoners were taken. The People's Mujahideen also launched an attack on Iranian territory, but were turned back. On July 18, 1988, Ayatollah Khomeini was forced to accept the terms of Resolution 598, a decision he publicly confessed was more painful than taking poison. Since the mullahs were procrastinating, Saddam Hussein went on the offensive again on 23 July on the central and southern fronts to increase the pressure on Tehran. It was a stampede in the Iranian ranks. The Iraqis, who had committed twelve divisions, 2,000 armoured vehicles and the entire Republican Guard, penetrated some fifty kilometers into Iranian territory and captured 8,000 prisoners. The ceasefire was finally accepted unconditionally by Iran and came into effect on 20 August, monitored by a UN force. Saddam Hussein claimed victory.

The human and material cost of the war is catastrophic for both countries: about 180,000 dead and missing on the Iraqi side, 500,000 on the Iranian side. Plus:

about 500,000 wounded and mutilated Iraqis and 1,300,000 Iranians. About 115,000 fighters were taken prisoner (70,000 Iraqis and 45,000 Iranians[6] . To these losses must be added on the Iraqi side the victims of the Kurdish uprising, ruthlessly repressed by the Iraqi army, which used chemical weapons against them in Halabja in March 1988. Before this attack, Ali Hassan Al-Majid, known as "Ali the Chemical", did not hesitate to boast: "I'm going to kill them all with chemical weapons! Who will say anything? The international community? Fuck them[7] !" As for the financial cost of the war, it is about 452 billion dollars for Iraq and 645 billion dollars for Iran, including the loss of oil revenues for both countries.

The Iraqi invasion of Kuwait

In 1988 Iraq emerged as the main military power in the Gulf. Saddam Hussein therefore felt invulnerable, believing he had conquered regional leadership. The Gulf petro-monarchies concluded that they had to accept the Western presence on their territory to protect themselves from Iraqi appetite. After the devastating war against Iran, which cost tens of billions of dollars borrowed from the Gulf monarchies, Saddam Hussein blackmailed them more and more aggressively. He is now demanding compensation for the damage inflicted on Iraq's infrastructure, claiming that it was destroyed to stem Iranian expansion throughout the region, and thus protect the petro-monarchies. Turning against Kuwait, he asks the emirate, which he considers an integral part of Iraq, and accuses it of drilling on the Iraqi side of the common border to reduce its oil production, which would allow him to return to his costs. Kuwait refuses. It demands the immediate repayment of the debt contracted by Iraq and, exploiting the Rumaila field which extends over both territories, increases its oil production beyond the quota established by OPEC.

Washington let Baghdad believe that it wanted to stay out of the dispute. On 25 July 1990, while Pentagon satellites showed that the invasion was now imminent, the US ambassador to Baghdad, April Glaspie, assured Saddam Hussein that his country wanted to have the best relations with Iraq and did not intend to interfere in inter-Arab conflicts. Saddam Hussein fell into the trap: a week later, on August 1, 1990, Iraqi forces invaded Kuwait. In addition to being a violation of the law, this occupation and Iraq's control of Kuwaiti oil production posed an intolerable threat to the stability of the region and, by extension, to the world. By invading and annexing Kuwait, Iraq is violating one of the fundamental principles of international politics: respect for borders and the existence of states, and is setting a dangerous precedent. In the face of this challenge, the U.S. government succeeded in conducting a public opinion campaign that led to a worldwide conviction of the moral rightness of the fight for the liberation of the emirate. The Arab world, however, is deeply divided. The masses are sensitive to Saddam Hussein's anti-imperialist and anti-Zionist rhetoric and his declared intention to put an end to the unequal sharing of oil wealth in favour of a minority. A wave of support for the Iraqi dictator, who has been compared to Saladin, is shaking a large segment of Arab public opinion.

King Hussein of Jordan and Yasser Arafat were forced to follow the mobilization of their people for fear of the Jordanian Muslim Brotherhood and Hamas. On the other hand, Egypt and Syria see the Gulf crisis as an opportunity to reassert their key role in regional politics and to curry favour with Washington. Assad also hopes that a fatal blow will be dealt to the despised Iraqi regime and that his participation in the coalition will enable him to complete his takeover of Lebanon. He will reap the benefits of his participation in the operation in Lebanon by invading the Christian country and imposing his control over it. "With Saddam Hussein's troops on the kingdom's borders, Saudi Arabia was threatened and clearly unable to defend itself, despite the billions of dollars it had spent over the years buying ultra-sophisticated weapons and equipment from the Americans. Overnight, the oil wealth of the Saudis and their role as protector of Islam's homeland and its holy places no longer counted for anything[9] . So when Saudi Arabia appealed for American help to defend the kingdom against the Iraqi threat, Egyptian and Syrian contingents joined the armies assembled on its territory in preparation for the liberation of Kuwait. The American media gave wide coverage to the Arab consent to the "Desert Shield" operation. In Arabia itself, the shock of the use of "infidel" troops was immense.

From the beginning of the crisis, the United Nations decided on an economic boycott of Iraq. With the approval of the UN, a military coalition under American command, made up of troops from some thirty countries, was formed at the initiative of President George H. Bush. It has 750,000 men, 70% of whom are Americans. France, which participates in the coalition, expresses its reservations about a selective interpretation of UN decisions, which would apply neither to Lebanon nor to Israel. While condemning the aggression against Iraq, Paris and Moscow believe that the defense of international law must also concern the other problems of the Middle East. For its part, the American administration was convinced of the need to work on the settlement of the Arab-Israeli conflict in order to consolidate the support of the Arab countries for the coalition united under the U.S. banner. The need for an international settlement including negotiations between Israel and the Palestinian people was the subject of a statement by the five members of the Security Council on 28 September 1990. And on October 12, the Council passed resolution 672, which reaffirmed this principle.

Operation Desert Storm

On January 15, 1991, coalition forces under the command of General Norman Schwarzkopf launched Operation Desert Storm. It began with an air bombing campaign targeting the army, airfields and strategic targets in Iraq. For 43 days, the US and allied air forces carried out more than 110,000 sorties with 2,800 aircraft, dropping 250,000 bombs. Cruise missiles were also fired by the American fleet present in the Gulf. Saddam Hussein tried to create a diversion by firing Scud missiles at Israel. Washington forbade any reaction from Israel so as not to jeopardize Arab participation in the coalition. On 22 February Iraq agreed to a ceasefire under pressure from the USSR, but the coalition rejected its proposal. The ground offensive was launched on 24 February. It was conducted on two fronts: one towards Kuwait City, from the southern and eastern borders of the emirate; and the other, mobilizing the bulk of the armored forces, consisting of a vast turning movement aimed at destroying the Republican Guard divisions positioned in southern Iraq. It took only five days for Kuwait to be liberated. Crushed under the bombs, the Iraqi army, supposedly the fourth largest in the world, suffered appalling losses, estimated at more than 100,000 dead, while the American and allied forces suffered only 200 deaths in all, some of them victims of friendly fire. Faced with the enormous air and ground machine amassed against them, the Iraqis did not really fight. "In reality, like any dictatorial regime, the important thing was to retain power, not to enter a war against a coalition of more than 40 countries. With its elite troops in reserve, the regime had the means to survive and to suppress the rebellions that the United States was trying to stir up in the country[10] . Iraqi troops withdrawing from Kuwait applied a scorched earth policy and set fire to Kuwaiti oil wells. The occupation lasted seven months, at the end of which Iraq accepted all UN resolutions. The Emir of Kuwait, Jaber al-Ahmad al-Sabah, returned home after spending more than 7 months in exile. Although the road to Baghdad was open, President George H. Bush wisely decided to stick to the initial objective of liberating Kuwait, without trying to complete the destruction of the Iraqi army. This will not be the case in 2003, when the decision of his son, George W. Bush, to bring down the Iraqi regime will have catastrophic consequences for the entire region.

The consequences of the war

The consequences of the Gulf War are terrible. In 1991, the insurgency in Iraq itself began to grow, but only lasted a few weeks. The military debacle of Saddam's forces in Kuwait pushed the Kurds and the Shiites to rise up against his power. Ba'ath party cadres were massacred and the regime lost control of much of the country. But the insurgents were no match for them. Showing their usual cynicism, the United States, which had pushed the Iraqi people to rise up, left them at the mercy of the regime's vengeance The repression of the Shiite insurrection was terrible. Tens of thousands of people were killed. The Kurds fear a new gas attack, like the one perpetrated in Halabja in March 1988. But the Kurdish region was relatively spared thanks to the imposition of a no-fly zone north of the 36^{e} parallel by the United States and Great Britain. This led to de facto autonomy of the Kurdish provinces from Baghdad. At the beginning of September 1992 a new no-fly zone was created, covering the south in the name of protecting the Shiite population. Unable to overthrow Saddam Hussein's regime and replace it with one that was compliant with their interests, the United States decided to maintain a policy of strict embargo aimed at disarming Iraq and isolating it from the Arab world so that it would not be able to challenge their hegemony. In addition to the victims of the regime's repression, there are also those of the economic embargo that the 20 million Iraqis had to endure until 2003. It is responsible for the death of tens of thousands of children and old people, according to some specialized UN agencies and humanitarian organizations, despite the "oil for food" program. This embargo was decided and maintained in good conscience by the Western powers under the cover of international legality[11] . The sanctions imposed by the UN on Iraq, however, consolidate the regime by encouraging, because of the rationing instituted, an even tighter control of the repressive apparatus over the population. A UN inspection commission was charged with ensuring the destruction of the weapons of mass destruction held by Iraq. As Iraq refused access to certain sites, the United States and Great Britain increased the number of air raids against its military installations and a number of civilian infrastructures in the early months of 1999. While the Ba'ath party, in power since 1963, claimed to be a secular ideology, aware of the mobilizing power of Islam, Saddam Hussein had the inscription "Allahu Akbar" (God is great) added to the Iraqi flag. Advised by two Iraqi political opponents living in the United States, Ahmad Chalabi and Iyad Allawi, the CIA tried in vain to foment a coup d'état to overthrow him.

The "new regional order" and the revival of the peace process

The aftermath of the war is also affecting Kuwait. The emirate has suffered Iraqi depredations and looting. The oil wells are in flames. The financial reserves are largely committed by the subsidies promised to the coalition countries and the population has suffered a moral trauma. In addition, there is a power struggle between the bourgeoisie and the ruling family, which leads to the re-establishment of a parliament with limited powers[10] . A manhunt was launched to liquidate the supposed collaborators of the Iraqis. And most Palestinians were expelled to Jordan. They were replaced by more docile Asian workers.

The second Gulf War increased American hegemony in the region. The main objective of the United States is to secure access to oil resources at a relatively low price and to have a market for its goods and services. It is also vital to its economy and its status as the world's only superpower that oil be priced in dollars. (One of the reasons for the invasion of Iraq in 2003 was Saddam Hussein's threat to sell his oil in euros).) In order to maintain a regional order in line with their interests, they are more than ever called upon to play the role of policeman, through the strengthening of their military apparatus and their involvement, often forced by circumstances, in the settlement of crises. Thus, in the wake of the second Gulf War, when they succeeded in including several Arab countries in the coalition, they set about reviving the Arab-Israeli peace process. "Strategically, the Gulf War had made it clear that Israel was not, in the context of military control of oil-producing areas, the asset that its supporters insisted on. It had been more of a burden, and it had been necessary to multiply concessions to prevent it from intervening in the war after the Iraqi Scud attacks[12] . On the other hand, on the Palestinian side, the PLO was considerably weakened by its support for Saddam Hussein. The Gulf States cut off all financial support. Syria, no longer having a Soviet protector, will have to be more flexible. Finally, the intervention of the United States to liberate Kuwait had given them immense prestige. These favourable circumstances favoured the resumption of the peace process under American auspices. Secretary of State James Baker made every effort to achieve this. "To each of his interlocutors he made it clear that this was the opportunity of the last chance. It is up to the Palestinians to recover what has not been colonized by the Israelis, to the Israelis to obtain a final settlement, and to the Syrians to find their place in the new Middle East[13] . His efforts were crowned by the opening of the Madrid peace conference on October 30, 1991[14] .

1 *Orientales III*, Henry Laurens, CNRS éditions 2004, p. 298

2 *The Iran-Iraq war, first Gulf war*, Pierre Razoux, Perrin, 2013, p. 16

3 ibid. p. 563: The estimated value of military supplies during the war was $80 billion for Iraq, compared to $24 billion for Iran.

4 ibid. p. 565

5 ibid p. 570

6 ibid. p.572

7 *Ces quinze hommes qui ont changé la face du Proche-Orient,* op.cit.

8 *The new question of the East*, Georges Corm, La Découverte, 2017, p.31

9 *Osama*, Jonathan Randal, Albin Michel, 2004, p. 126

10 *Le Proche-Orient éclaté II*, Georges Corm, La Découverte 1997, p. 157

11 *L'Orient arabe à l'heure américaine*, Henry Laurens, Hachette, Pluriel, 2005, p.12

12 ibid. p. 15

13 ibid. p.16

14 see chapter 8 on the Arab-Israeli conflict

Chapter 11. The Iranian Revolution

The reign of Mohammed Reza shah Pahlavi

Mohammad Reza Pahlavi succeeded his father in September 1941 in a difficult context. Iran was partly occupied by the Anglo-Soviet armies and his powers were severely limited by the British. Under the impetus of the Prime Minister, Mohammad Ali Foroughi, the young shah allowed a more democratic regime to be established, breaking with the fifteen years of authoritarian power of Reza shah and granting the Allied forces permission to dispose of the territory. In exchange, a treaty signed on 26 January 1942 guaranteed territorial integrity and the departure of the occupying armies six months after the end of the war. In October 1945, the British and Americans left the country. But the Soviets remained in the north where they militarily supported separatist movements: the Republic of Mahabad, created in January 1946 in Kurdistan, and a People's Government in Iranian Azerbaijan. However, Iran obtained through negotiation that the USSR cease to support the two separatist regions, which were reconquered after the withdrawal of the Red Army. Mohammad Reza Pahlavi drew closer to the United States. Despite the prestige that the recapture of Azerbaijan earned him, his power was still insecure. He faced opposition from the mullahs, the bazaar merchants and the Iranian Communist Party (Toudeh). On February 4, 1949, he was the object of an assassination attempt by a communist militant. After the attack, he used the emotion generated and his renewed popularity to strengthen his power. At the dawn of the 1950s, the energy issue and the Cold War placed Iran at the center of the geostrategic concerns of Great Britain, the Soviet Union and the United States. London was determined to maintain its control of the Persian Gulf and its hold on the oil fields, through *the Anglo Iranian Oil Company* (AIOC). Moscow covets the natural resources of the Caspian Sea and relies on the Tudeh party to influence the course of events. As for Washington, it intends to supplant the traditional colonial powers and to establish a lasting American presence in the Middle East on the economic, political and ideological levels. For its part, Iran, which has been a vassal of the great powers, aspires to regain its full sovereignty. It possesses considerable oil resources which must belong to it. The animosity of the population towards *the Anglo-Iranian Oil Company* is exacerbated by the fact that the country receives only 8% of the profits generated by oil production. And this, while in Saudi Arabia a treaty, concluded in 1950, established a 50/50 distribution between the companies of the American cartel ARAMCO and the country. On 25 April 1951, a riot brought Mohammed Mossadegh to power. His first act as Prime Minister was to nationalize the AIOC, which made him the idol of the Iranian people. The street was unleashed against the Shah as Mossadegh's popularity grew. The British decreed an embargo on Iranian oil. Months passed and Iranian oil was still not sold, the internal situation continued to worsen, riots by all factions continued. On 24 February the Shah agreed to leave the country discreetly, to avoid confrontations. In the Majlis, the majority of deputies turned against Mossadegh. On 13 August 1953, the shah dismissed Mossadegh, provoking a popular uprising which forced him to leave for Rome. Following a plot orchestrated by the British and American secret services, Operation Ajax, Mossadegh was overthrown by the army led by General Zahedi who became Prime Minister. The Shah, who returned to the country, had Mossadegh arrested. He was sentenced to death, then saw his sentence commuted to three years in prison. Mossadegh's deposition allowed the Americans to enter the country's great oil game. The crisis ended in 1954 with the creation of an international consortium composed mainly of British and American companies and secondarily of French and Dutch companies, to manage Iran's oil production. It preserves the interests of foreign companies while ensuring 50% of the oil revenues to Iran.

Faced with his return to the throne in a coup d'état fomented by the CIA and MI6, the shah tried to legitimize himself by emphasizing the link between the greatness of Iran before Islam and the monarchy. After Zahedi's resignation in April 1955, he set up an autocratic regime based on American support. Considered by the Western bloc as an island of stability in the Middle East and as a bulwark against the USSR, Iran received active military and technological support from its Western allies. In 1955, it joined the Baghdad Pact and was then in the American camp during the Cold War. It then signed a military pact with the United States in 1959. The government set up a secret police, the terrible Savak, to quell any opposition. The shah implemented a policy of modernization and westernization from above. He modernized industry and society with the help of very large oil revenues and a program of economic and social reforms called the "white revolution. In addition to land reform, laws were passed that overturned traditional Iranian society. He wants to make his country the fifth world power by the year 2000. Between 1960 and 1974, Iran experienced rapid economic development. In January 1965, the Shah appointed Amir Abbas Hoveida as Prime Minister, and he remained so for 12 years. He launched the Iranian nuclear program with the help of the United States and Europe. He signed the Nuclear Non-Proliferation Treaty (NPT) in 1970. But Iran's desire to master the fuel cycle and to reach a level that would allow it, if circumstances required, to develop a nuclear weapon in a relatively short time could not be doubted.

Measures such as the ban on women's veils and the reform of the education and judicial systems, which deprived the mullahs of their powers, made the religious institution aware of the need to organize to defend its status. However, it remained legalistic until the early 1960s, when the authoritarian policies of the shah, particularly the land reform that threatened its properties, triggered the opposition of the clergy. The spokesman of the religious opposition, Ayatollah Ruhollah Khomeini, called for demonstrations against the shah's absolutism and Westernization, which shook the whole country. He was very critical of the ayatollahs who had agreed to support the shah. He acquired the title of "marja' e-taqlid" in 1961, meaning "model of inspiration", the highest rank granted to an ayatollah. Relying on this legitimacy, he sought to extend his sphere of influence in the country and very quickly established himself as one of the main figures of the opposition, both before and after his exile. Khomeini was exiled to Iraq in 1963 and was forced to leave for France following a rapprochement between Iran and Iraq.

On October 26, 1967 the "king of kings" crowned himself emperor at the Golestan Palace. In 1968, Great Britain announced its intention to withdraw from the Gulf by 1971. Iran immediately claimed Bahrain and claimed to want to play the role of protector of the Gulf after the departure of the British. These Iranian ambitions created new tensions between Iran and the Arab countries. "In October 1971, the shah organized a lavish celebration of the 2500[e] anniversary of the founding of the Persian Empire in Persepolis, a veritable outrageous display of wealth that outraged the poorest bangs of the population as well as the bourgeoisie of the "bazaar[1] ". Opposition to the shah's authoritarian and pro-Western policies and his reform program was growing. For the time has come for revenge for his many detractors, who want to do away with the monarchy in the name of Allah, anti-Americanism and social justice. The popular classes, but also the middle classes, the left-wing intellectuals, the communists and some liberals no longer hide their hostility to the shah. In the ruling circles, they feared chaos. Some believed that only a democratization of the regime could save it, but the shah, who did not seem to see the wind changing, refused to do so.

The Iranian Revolution

From 1975, strikes paralyzed the country and riots multiplied. Mainly led by supporters of the clergy, they were brutally repressed by the secret police: the Savak. In 1977, following pressure from President Carter, political prisoners were released, censorship was relaxed, and the justice system was reformed. American support for the Shah began to wane, however. They knew that he was seriously ill and, fearing a communist takeover in Iran, they did not see it as a bad idea to turn to a cleric, who was by definition anti-communist, which Ayatollah Khomeini actually was, to recover the popular opposition movement to the throne. "The latter, an old opponent of the regime, had left his exile in Iraq a year earlier to settle freely in France at Neaufle-le-Château, near Paris, without being bound by the French authorities to the obligation of reserve, as is generally the case for political opponents who find refuge in a third country[2] . The Western media then relayed daily his speeches and sermons against the Shah, whose regime was still recognized by all states. Recorded on audio cassettes, they are widely distributed in Iran. The Ayatollah, who directed the masses from a distance, launched an appeal on 18 June to bring down this "atheist" regime. On September 8, 1978, a massive demonstration in Tehran of several million people led to the intervention of the army, which caused hundreds of deaths among the demonstrators. The economy was paralyzed and oil exports stopped. In December, more than two million people marched in the streets of Tehran. Thinking to calm the street, the Shah appointed Shapour

Bakhtiar as Prime Minister. The latter asked him to leave Iran for an indefinite period. He was replaced by a royal council. Abandoned by the United States, the sovereign resigned himself to leave Iran, with tears in his eyes, in the middle of popular jubilation, on January 16, 1979. He was never to return. Welcomed by Sadat in Egypt, he planned to go to the United States, but President Carter informed him that his presence was no longer desired. Disgraced, betrayed, defeated and seriously ill, he ended his life in Egypt on July 2, 1980. On February 1er 1979, Ayatollah Khomeini, who had not stopped calling since his exile for the overthrow of the monarchy, arrived in Tehran where he was triumphantly welcomed by a jubilant crowd. His return from France, where he had found asylum in Neaufle-le-Château, was favored by the French government, which feared a takeover by the Communists. A similar situation had occurred when the CIA had incited the Iranian clergy against the Prime Minister, Mossadegh, when the latter had decided to nationalize Iranian oil. Ten days after his arrival in Tehran a bloody insurrection overthrew the Imperial Council still in place. Believing that the government of Shapour Bakhtiar was not legitimate, Khomeini appointed Mehdi Bazargan as Prime Minister. The army refused to take sides and Bakhtiar was forced to flee to France, and Ayatollah Khomeini, who proclaimed himself "Supreme Guide of the Revolution", finally came to power. The army, the administration and the oil industry fell into chaos. The prospect of the collapse of Iranian oil production, combined with fears of destabilization in the region, caused a second oil shock. In a few months the price of oil increased by 65%, its highest increase since the first oil shock in 1973.

The establishment of an oppressive and obscurantist system

From the outset, Khomeini presented a vision of the country that was very different from the one he had previously defended. The one who declared himself in favor of freedom of expression, "of an Islamic democracy" makes a 180 degree turn. "Let's not listen to those who speak of democracy, they are against Islam and want to take the country away from its mission. We will break the poisonous feathers of those who speak of nationalism, democracy and such things," he declared on March 13, 1979, at a conference with teachers and students in Qom[3] . The Islamic Republic was proclaimed on 1er April 1979. But there were dozens of revolutionary groups, each with its own vision of the future of Iran. The anti-Western purge took an increasingly violent turn. Several regionalist factions, including Kurds, Azeris, Arabs and Baluchis, began to dissent. In June 1979, the Islamic Republic was given a draft constitution. Anyone who opposes the regime is subject to the Ayatollah's wrath. "We must warn these intellectuals that they will be crushed if they do not stop their interference. We have been treating you leniently until now, in the hope that you will stop your mischief [...] These pro-Americans must know that we could exterminate them whenever we want in a very short time" he threatened on August 8, 1979 in a declaration to the Iranian people[4] . The Marxist and liberal factions were eliminated by the Revolutionary Guards. They also took control of the courts that tried former security and military officials of the shah's regime. Several dozen officers and senior officials were summarily executed. State administrations were purged of elements deemed "non-revolutionary" and replaced by Khomeini loyalists. These purges specifically affected the army, whose strength fell from 500,000 to 290,000 men in the space of a year. The executions of those who violate the principles of Islam in the eyes of the regime multiplied. An Amnesty International report in 1990 exposed the massacres perpetrated against political opponents in Iranian prisons in 1988, which resulted in over 33,000 deaths. Many laws were repealed, including those protecting the status of women. Women had to wear the chador, music was banned from radio and television and any criticism of religion was severely repressed. These restrictions on individual freedoms led to massive emigration among the wealthier segments of the population.

The Islamic Republic is based on a political system that includes elected and non-elected institutions, formal institutions provided for in the constitution and informal institutions, all of which are linked to clerical elites (religious associations and foundations, paramilitary organizations). The relative stability of the regime, but also its flaws, stem from this system and its functioning. Stability, insofar as it controls the economic and repressive apparatuses; and flaws that stem from its inability to reform itself and to bridge the gap that separates it from the aspirations of the population. Beyond the formal distribution of powers conferred by the constitution, the regime relies on a multiplicity of actors. The country has two, sometimes competing, governments. A secular government headed by a democratically elected President of the Republic, and a hierarchy of conservative clerics headed by a Supreme Leader. Appointed for life and head of the army, he also has bodies under his authority that enable him to ensure his hold on society, such as the *Bassijis*, a particularly brutal shock militia responsible for enforcing Islamic morality, and the Revolutionary Guards (*Pasdaran*). The latter form a full-fledged army alongside the regular army and control entire sectors of the economy. Within them there are cells specialized in intelligence operations and clandestine actions abroad, such as the "Al-Quds" groups. In fact, it is the Leader and not the president who holds the real power through the jurisprudence of the doctor of Islamic law, *velâyat e faquih.* There are also other centers of power, such as the revolutionary foundations whose enormous financial power allows them to have a real influence on foreign Shiite communities, particularly in Lebanon, Iraq and Pakistan. "Contrary to popular belief, the Islamic revolution is not the heir to the traditions and cultural specificities of Iran, but a pure product of modernity. Since the Shiite religion was established as the country's official religion, the clergy has never ruled. On the contrary, Iran's entry into the modern era had resulted in a secularization movement that weakened the prerogatives of the clergy. The outcome of the revolution was the establishment of a totalitarian Islamic regime, infinitely more repressive than the monarchy that Khomeini had just overthrown with the support of the left-wing movements that he then ruthlessly eliminated .[5]

In April 1979 Iran denounced the nuclear cooperation agreement with France and demanded the repayment of the loan granted by the Shah. This was the beginning of the Eurodif affair which was to poison Franco-Iranian relations for a decade. On 7 November the secular government of Mehdi Bazargan, set up after the departure of the Shah, resigned. It was clear that his liberal views and resistance to the clergy had already convinced him that he could not carry out any of the democratic improvements he had in mind. Khomeini appointed Mohammad Ali Rajai, an academic close to the clergy and Islamic radicals, in his place. While the shah had been admitted to the United States for medical treatment, hundreds of Iranian students gathered on November 4, 1979, in front of the U.S. Embassy in Tehran to demand his extradition to cries of "death to America!" Diplomatic personnel were taken hostage. Khomeini publicly gave them his support. American President Jimmy Carter refused extradition, imposed an economic embargo on the Islamic Republic and froze official Iranian assets in American banks. On April 24, 1980, an American helicopter operation (*Operation Eagle Claw*) decided by Carter to rescue the hostages failed miserably. After 444 days of captivity, the 52 hostages were finally released on January 20, 1981, the same day that the new American president, Ronald Reagan, was sworn in. In exchange for this release, Washington gave back the eight billion dollars of American assets blocked in the United States and undertook to deliver to Tehran 480 million dollars worth of spare parts for its tanks and planes, despite the embargo imposed by Congress. In January 1980, Abolhassan Bani Sadr, a representative of the left, was elected President of the Republic by a very large majority. But he was constantly under attack from the clergy, who wanted to establish a theocracy in Iran. A struggle began between progressives and the Islamic party for effective control of power.

The years of war with Iraq (1980-1988)

During the winter of 1979-1980 relations between Iran and Iraq deteriorated sharply. Khomeini openly called for the overthrow of the Ba'athist regime. Clashes increased on the ground at the border between the two countries. Saddam Hussein then decided to attack Iran. The war with Iraq which began on 22 September 1980 provoked a new radicalization and the mass mobilization of volunteers who, in human waves, were to contain and then push back the Iraqi invader beyond its own borders. On June 20, 1981, Bani Sadr was deposed by Khomeini with the support of the Revolutionary Guards. He fled a month later to France with Massoud Rajavi, head of the People's Mojahedin Organization of Iran (PMOI). On June 28, the leadership of the Iranian Islamic party was decapitated by an attack attributed to the People's Mojahedin. The clergy reacted by taking power. A violent repression hit the moderate opposition and the PMOI. This left-wing movement, which had actively participated in the 1979 revolution, then engaged in an armed struggle against the clerical dictatorship. It is a member of the National Council of Resistance of Iran (NCRI), which states that it wants to establish a secular and democratic regime in Iran. The PMOI also developed its struggle from Iraq in 1986 where it created the National Liberation Army of Iran (NLAI). During the Iran-Iraq war its forces regularly attacked Iranian troops along the border and made several incursions into Iran. The PMOI was for a time listed as a terrorist organization by the United States and the European Union. At the end of the war thousands of political prisoners, including many members of the People's Mojahedin, were executed. On July 28, 1981, Mohamed Ali Rajai was elected President of the Republic. He was killed a month later in an attack with his Prime Minister. Ayatollah Khomeini considered it an opportune moment to entrust all power to the clergy. Akbar Hashemi Rafsanjani, who retained the head of parliament and control of finances, was appointed as the new commander of the armed forces. And Ali Khamenei was elected President of the Republic. These senior clerics share power. They agreed to appoint Mir Hossein Mousavi as Prime Minister. In April 1982, Sadek Ghotzbadeh, former Minister of Foreign Affairs, was arrested and tortured and denounced a plot by officers, which provoked new purges in the regular army. Khamenei was re-elected president in August 1985.

The Iran-Iraq war resulted in the radicalization of the Iranian regime and the revival of its nuclear program. It served as a pretext for a power struggle that continues to rage today. It allowed the most radical members of the clergy to gradually get rid of the secular revolutionary fringe (Bazargan, Bani Sadr), the idealistic religious movement (Ayatollah Montazeri), the radical opposition (People's Mujahedin and the Communist Party) and the Kurdish, Azeri and Baluch separatist movements. And since then, the pasdaran have formed a powerful pressure group that wields significant political and economic power.

After the Iranian revolution, the Iranian nuclear program was halted in part under American pressure. And the Iraqi air strikes against its reactors have further compromised it. The United States has not returned to Tehran the billions of dollars it had already received in payment for the nuclear fuel it was supposed to deliver. France also refuses to deliver enriched uranium. This was despite a payment of one billion dollars made by the Shah to the Eurodif factory in order to have the right to buy 10% of its production. This refusal created a serious dispute between France and Iran, which did not hesitate to resort to terrorism to recover its rights and to punish France for its military aid to Iraq. This blackmail was expressed by the taking of French hostages in Lebanon. The delivery to Iraq in 1983 of five Super Étendards equipped with Exocet missiles was considered by Iran as France crossing a red line. Rafsanjani delivered a violent indictment against Paris. On 31 July 1984, the Pasdaran took an Air France Airbus hostage. A series of attacks sponsored by Iran took place in France in 1985-1986. In February 1987 Wahid Gorgi, identified as the organizer of these attacks, took refuge in the Iranian embassy, provoking an "embassy war" between Paris and Tehran which lasted four months. France then sent a naval air group off the Iranian coast. Its mission was twofold: on the one hand to put pressure on Iran and on the other to protect French maritime traffic in the Gulf. Direct negotiations between France and Iran then began. These negotiations focused on the Eurodif affair, the expulsion of Massoud Rajavi who found refuge in Iraq, and the stopping of French arms sales to Iraq. In May 1986, France declared itself ready to reimburse the Eurodif debt to Iran. Finally, the balance of the loan was settled in December 1991. "It is probable that the aggression to which the country was subjected led the Iranian authorities to the conclusion that only nuclear weapons would dissuade a new aggressor and guarantee the continuity of the regime. In any case, as early as 1987, a uranium enrichment program was secretly started. Using nationalism as an instrument, as had been done previously with Shiism, the leaders of the Islamic Republic tried to use the nuclear issue in their legitimization strategy and to forge a consensus in the country around the acquisition of nuclear technology, making it the new emblem of Iranian nationalism[6] . The same approach guided the development of ballistic missiles, which were supposed to protect the national territory.

The will to export the revolution.

"The new revolutionary power, far from being conservative, took up the torch of modernization by adapting it to its own ideological register. And, in seeking to export its revolution, it demonstrated in foreign policy an even more aggressive will to power than that of the imperial regime.

He has effectively taken the themes of anti-imperialism and anti-Zionism and given them a new vigour with a religious vocabulary and the millenarianism of Shi'ism[7] . The Islamic Republic's support for Iraqi Shiites and Lebanese Hezbollah has led to much talk of a Shiite crescent stretching from Iran to Lebanon, through Iraq and Syria. This prospect worries the Gulf monarchies, where Shiite minorities live, and explains their support for Iraq during the Iraq-Iran war. The Iranian Islamic revolution has never defined itself as Shiite and has wanted to embrace the entire "ummah". "We want to found an Islamic state that unites Arabs, Persians, Turks and other nationalities under the banner of Islam[8] ," declared Ayatollah Khomeini in April 1980. But the Iranian revolution failed to export itself in a sustainable way because it could not overcome the opposition between Shiism and Sunnism, Persians and Arabs. While the Shiite/Sunni opposition seemed to be fading, from 1980 onwards it led to an increase in sectarian tensions between the two communities and to a politicization of religious affiliation in the Muslim world. Saudi Arabia, Kuwait and Bahrain succeeded in containing the attempts, albeit limited, of the Shiites in the oil-rich areas of the Gulf to rise up. In Iraq, Saddam Hussein unleashed an intense crackdown on the Shiites. And before his fall and replacement by a shia-dominated regime in Baghdad, the only country where the themes of the revolution found a lasting echo was Lebanon. This was thanks to Hezbollah, the only shiite mass movement to have integrated itself into a game of alliances with local parties by combining Lebanese nationalism, pan-Islamism and shiite identity.

"Iran has had two channels for extending its influence among non-Iranian Shiites: the traditional clerical networks and the radical Shiite movements, often launched by younger mullahs. But many traditional clerics, in particular some of the great quietist ayatollahs, do not adhere to the principle of "velâyat e faqih" (absolute authority of the supreme guide in politico-religious matters), which is at odds with the Shiite tradition[9] . On the domestic scene, the best known case is that of Ayatollah Shariat Madari, who had supported Khomeini when he spoke out against the shah, but who, from the day after the revolution, was critical of the new regime's policies, denouncing in particular the exactions of the revolutionaries. At the regional level, behind this reticence, the rivalry between the two great religious schools of Najaf in Iraq and Qom in Iran is apparent. And not all radical Shiite movements have the same allegiance to Tehran as the Lebanese Hezbollah. In 1989, the Iranian Revolution showed the extent of its moral influence in the Islamic world by launching its murderous anathema, followed by large-scale demonstrations around the world, against the writer Salman Rushdie, author of a book deemed blasphemous about Muhammad. While the policy of radicalizing shiite movements was relatively successful and saw the establishment of shiite political-military movements, it did increase the isolation of shiites and the weight of wahhabis and saadists among sunni radicals. So much so that at the end of the 1980s, Tehran not only lost all hope of reaching the Sunnis, but saw the emergence of an anti-Shiite Sunni movement

The Islamic Republic since 1988

Iran came out of the war against Iraq exhausted in 1988. The death of Ayatollah Khomeini on 3 June 1989 marked the end of the expansion of the revolution. Khomeini's successor, Ali Khamenei, who did not have the same religious legitimacy, took the title of "Guide of the Islamic Republic" and no longer "Guide of the Islamic Revolution. A struggle for power between fundamentalists and pragmatists then began, which was won by the election of Akbar Hashemi Rafsanjani as president of the republic in July 1989. The new president began a more pragmatic and less sectarian policy. He was re-elected until 1997 on a program of openness and reform. Then he was appointed to head the assembly of experts. A strong rivalry opposed him to Khamenei, who was promoted to Ayatollah. His policy was continued by President Khatami, elected in 1997. He had to manage the country while taking into account the demands of a society calling for reforms and a very conservative clergy that wanted to keep a hold on power. This discrepancy reached its peak in July 1999, when protests against the government took place in Tehran. Khatami was re-elected in June 2001, but immediately conservative elements in the Iranian government worked to destabilize the reform movement, banning liberal newspapers and disqualifying candidates for parliamentary and presidential elections. "September 11, 2001, changed all that. Through their military interventions in Afghanistan and Iraq, the Americans rid Iran of its two Sunni enemies (Saddam Hussein and the Taliban), and very quickly alienated Sunni public opinion, while weakening the conservative Arab regimes[10] . Following the American invasion in 2003, Iran supported and used the Iraqi Shiite opposition against the United States. The strategy paid off, as Iran appeared better able to take advantage of the situation than the United States itself. This is the great failure of the Bush administration. Much of the Iranian program was thus realized and Iran could resume its dream of the beginning of the revolution: to put the Shiite axis at the service of the "refusal front" and to present itself as the champion of anti-imperialism and anti-Zionism in order to become the great power of the Middle East. Its regional ambitions have been reinforced by the arrival in power in Baghdad of a government dominated by Shiites. The election of Mahmoud Ahmadinejad in 2005 brought a revolutionary backlash. President Ahmadinejad took up, with even greater determination, the main thrust of Iran's foreign policy: absolute hostility to the United States and Israel, which he did not hesitate to threaten with destruction; Tehran's support for anti-Israeli resistance movements: Palestinian Hamas and Hezbollah, Iran's armed wing and spearhead of Shi'ism in Lebanon; and finally, its alliance with Syria, the only Arab country opposed to American-Israeli collusion. In 2006, Ahmadinejad stated that the Iranian nation would not give up its right to enrich uranium. In 2009 his disputed re-election led to mass opposition protests, probably the largest since the 1979 Revolution. These peaceful demonstrations were violently repressed by the Islamic authorities. They are caused by the social and economic bankruptcy of the regime, as well as the divorce between the state and civil society. There is a Westernized and educated youth that is increasingly resentful of the Islamic yoke and the prohibitions of religious fundamentalism.

In 2013, a new turning point occurred in Iranian politics with the election of a moderate candidate, Hassan Rohani, as President of the Republic. He has long been a militant for the opening of Iran to the outside world. He is nonetheless a product of the clerical system that shaped him and to which he belongs, and he does not hesitate to practice double standards. In order to obtain the lifting of sanctions imposed by Western countries which penalize the economy, he is entering into negotiations with them to find an agreement on the Iranian nuclear program. If Tehran seeks to sign a nuclear treaty, it is for internal reasons. It trembled in 2009 under the pressure of social discontent. Hence the urgency of ending international sanctions, even if it means temporarily abandoning the race to the bomb. For their part, the United States and its European partners aim to prevent Iran from acquiring nuclear weapons, which would encourage other regional powers to follow suit. Their bet is also that by encouraging the moderate camp represented by Rohani, Tehran would adopt a less aggressive foreign policy. After several extensions Iran and the 5+1 countries (the United States, Russia, China, France, the United Kingdom and Germany, as well as the European Union) finally reached an agreement on July 14, 2015 in Vienna to guarantee the peaceful and civilian nature of Iran's nuclear program in exchange for a progressive lifting of sanctions. Benefiting from the agreement, at least tacit, of the guide of the Islamic Republic, Ali Khamenei, this historic agreement maintained a certain climate of optimism. At the time, some analysts even believed that the thaw between Iran and the Obama administration could see them cooperating on the hot spots in the Middle East. Admitting that there was still too much rancor for the two enemies to rebuild a relationship of trust overnight, they pointed out that the conflicts in Afghanistan, Syria or Iraq and the proclamation by a Sunni terrorist group of an "Islamic State" harbored common interests that could push the two powers to find a certain modus vivendi. Both the United States and Iran do not want the Taliban back in power in Kabul, and are alarmed by the rise of al-Qaeda and Sunni extremism in Syria and Iraq. But the fundamental differences in interests between Tehran and Washington ultimately won out. And the election of Donald Trump to the White House has completely changed the game.

Iran has an obvious expansionist policy in the region. After taking advantage of the U.S. wars against Iraq a decade later, Tehran is taking advantage of the Syrian conflict to expand its direct influence with ground troops in that country. There is a territorial expansion of the Iranian presence and a junction with Hezbollah in Lebanon, closely linked to the Islamic Republic. The United States has tried in vain to prevent the formation of the so-called "Shiite crescent" in the Middle East, by cutting off the corridor linking Iran to Lebanon via Iraq and Syria. But the victories of the Syrian regime, allied with Iran, whose forces have joined forces with the Iraqi army on the border between the two countries, have prevented this. The conflict in Yemen is also part of the Iranians' strategic game and the Tehran-Damascus-Beirut axis is now a reality. Tehran has become a key player on the Iraqi, Syrian, Lebanese and Yemeni scenes, not to mention its relationship with Hamas, and today appears to be the big winner in the reconfiguration of the balance of power in the region. The Iranians do not hide this fact. They even have an increasing tendency to boast about it: their power in this area is unprecedented in Iran's contemporary history. But this is what worries Israel, Saudi Arabia and a good part of the American Congress. The desire of a Persian and Shiite power to dominate a predominantly Arab and Sunni region is difficult to accept, especially with its great rival, Saudi Arabia. And the nuclear agreement has not, despite the hopes it raised, led to any change in Tehran's expansionist ambitions. Claiming that Barack Obama had made a big mistake in betting on the Islamic Republic's moderation, President Donald Trump is threatening to denounce the agreement, "the worst ever" in his words.

And, as of the end of 2017, many sanctions have not yet been effectively lifted, which is a major obstacle to the country's recovery. That said, confronting Iran's power cannot be done lightly. Its power of nuisance is very real. In the past, it has not hesitated to resort to asymmetrical warfare by practicing kidnapping and attacks by proxy militias, and during the war with Iraq it attacked oil infrastructures, planted mines and fired missiles in the Gulf. It is not excluded that he will do the same today or tomorrow if he considers it in his interest or if he is forced to do so. Finally, the war has shown that the Iranian government only gives in when it is convinced that its adversary is about to hurt it very badly, both militarily and economically. "Before engaging in a process of confrontation with the Iranian regime, whether in Syria, Iraq, Lebanon, Iran or elsewhere, experience shows that it is necessary to analyze very carefully the scope of its actions. This does not mean that one should not act. It does mean that any action must be part of a strategy to achieve truly crucial goals[11] .

While the Arab-Israeli conflict was the main destabilizing factor in the Middle East, it has been marginalized by the cold war between Tehran and Riyadh. If the stakes of this confrontation are more political than religious considerations, it is clear that the narratives of the actors are full of religious references aimed at legitimizing the fight against the other. From December 28, 2017, popular demonstrations of discontent that target President Rohani's disappointing economic record spread across the country. The Iranian president must also face the conservatives headed by Ayatollah Khamenei who hold large parts of the Iranian state apparatus. The Iranian president therefore has limited room for maneuver in responding to the protests. The slogans chanted to criticize the socio-economic crisis are mixed with cries of anger against the regime's military interventions in the region. The gradual lifting of international sanctions after the nuclear deal has yet to bear fruit, as promised by the Iranian president, while the cost of Iran's proxy wars in the region has continued to rise. Iranians feel that the regime is more interested in protecting Iranian power and maintaining an image of power than in caring for the people. But the protests have not, by any means, reached the scale of the great movement of 2009. And the regime quickly regained control of the situation. Faced with the revolt in the streets, Hassan Rohani is trying to play both sides of the fence. This tendency of the regime's notables to support each other beyond their rivalries explains why the Islamic Republic has survived in relative stability until today.

The rebellion has nevertheless revealed certain potentially destabilizing parameters: a muted struggle for power, more precisely for the succession of the Supreme Guide, between the so-called "moderate" camp and that of the pasdaran and the radical wing; an acute economic crisis (due to the need to export the revolution); a high rate of unemployment (nearly 30% among young people); resentment provoked by the corruption of part of the political class; and the emergence of a youth thirsty for openness.

1 *Ces quinze hommes qui ont changé la face du Proche-Orient, Reza Pahlavi, le dernier empereur de Perse,* Caroline Hayek, L'Orient-le Jour, special issue of November 2, 2017

2 *The new question of the East,* Georges Corm, La Découverte, 2017, p.35

3 https://www.lorientlejour.com/.../14-khomeyni-la-revolution-et-lobscurantisme.html

4 ibid.

5 *The Shiite Worlds and Iran*, edited by Sabrina Mervin, Karthala-Ifpo 2007

6 *Iranian nuclear power, an international hypocrisy,* Yves Bonnet, Michel Lafon, 2008

7 *Le monothéisme le pouvoir et la guerre*, Ibrahim Tabet, l'Harmattan, 2013, p.253

8 *The Iran-Iraq war, first Gulf war*, Pierre Razoux, Perrin 2013, p. 18

9 *Les mondes chiites et l'Iran, op.cit.* p. 40

10 ibid.p. p. 41

11 *The Iran-Iraq war,* op.cit. p. 498

Chapter 12. Post-Kemalist Turkey

"Turkey today is a country with an ambivalent identity. The traumatic memory of the dismemberment of the Ottoman Empire reinforced the ultranationalist reflexes of the nascent Republic. Hence the repeated coups d'état each time the army, custodian of the Kemalist legacy, felt that the country was in danger. It wanted to consider any expression of non-Turkish identity as a fatal pathology, denying the existence of its Kurdish and Alevi communities very late. In order to secure the deed of ownership of a land wrested from foreign aims, it proceeded to rewrite its history. The search for a Kemalist identity has led to the construction of a culture that privileges its ethno-linguistic and pre-Islamic origins. The mode of construction of the new Turk excluded any affinity with Islam. Turkey has been a champion of secularism for more than half a century. However, it is currently under a predominantly Islamist government and the army, a bastion of Kemalism, has been stripped of its political powers. Already largely Islamized, it could become even more so[1] . The divisions in Turkey are also economic and geographic. There are two Turquias: one in the west, prosperous and westernized; the other in the east, re-Islamized, backward and underdeveloped. This divide overlaps with the one between the so-called "white" Turks and the "black Turks". The "whites" are the educated elites who share Atatürk's views. They are urban and in the minority. While the "blacks" advocate a greater respect for the values of Islam. The democratic game means that they are the ones who have seized - by winning the elections - the levers of power.

The distancing from the Kemalist model

After the Second World War, the USSR put pressure on Ankara to change the status of the Straits, and the Turkish government asked for the support of the United States. In response, the Truman Doctrine, formalized in July 1947, ensured Turkey's protection against the Soviet bloc. Putting an end to Mustapha Kemal's isolationist policy, Turkey sent troops to Korea and allowed the installation on its soil of American rockets aimed at the USSR, becoming one of the pillars of NATO in the face of the Soviet threat. It was also the centerpiece of Western strategic arrangements in a Middle East shaken by successive crises. By recognizing the State of Israel from the outset, it has chosen its side. "Posing as a direct adversary of the revolutionary Arab nationalism embodied by Nasser, it took the initiative with Hashemite Iraq to form the Baghdad Pact sponsored by London and joined CENTO, the Middle Eastern equivalent of NATO, which included Iran and Pakistan[2] . The 1958 military coup in Iraq sounded the death knell for this pact. Ismet Inonü put an end to the regime of the national leader and the single party. The country experienced a brief democratic interlude between 1950 and 1960, marked by greater religious tolerance. The radical anti-Islamism of Mustapha Kemal gave way to a recognition of Islam as a cultural, moral, historical and social fact, which still permeates daily life. The 1950 elections saw the victory of the Democratic Party of Adnan Menderes and Celal Bayar at the expense of the Republican People's Party (CHP), the historical representative of Kemalism. These elections also saw the emergence of the first party claiming to be based on political Islam: the Nation Party (*Millet partisi*), which obtained 3% of the vote. Its program refers to the "moral order", a key concept of political Islam that will mark all Islamist parties. And he was the first to resort to duplicity and to come forward masked, announcing the Islamist parties to come. As soon as it came to power in 1950, the new government took symbolic measures that had the effect of eroding the secular component of Kemalism and reintroducing Islam into civil society.[3] " Thus, for example, the call to prayer in Arabic is restored. The schools of preaching imams (*imam hatip*) reopened. In 1956, religious education (only Islamic) in middle schools became compulsory; then in 1967, optional religious courses were reintroduced in high schools, and the same year a law re-established certain provisions of Islamic law. At the same time, a faculty of theology was created in Ankara. It was also in the 1950s that religious leaders proclaimed more openly their hostility to secularism and demanded a dismantling of the secularist provisions enacted in the previous years. This tolerance brought out of hiding the religious brotherhoods that had been banned by the 1924 constitution and that would become unavoidable at the end of the century. This is the case of the *Nurcus* ("partisans of the Light"), founded by the Sufi sheikh Saïd Nursi, who advocated the reconciliation of religion with science. Imprisoned several times and released in 1952, he was considered a saint by his followers after his death in 1960. For their part, the traditional Sufi brotherhoods, with *Nakchibendiye* at the forefront, were opposed to secularism and the religious reformism of the Kemalists.

The policy of re-Islamization hardened the opposition to the government of the Kemalist elite and the army, which considered itself invested with a historic mission to safeguard the Kemalist heritage. Throughout the 1960s, several military committees opposed to the democratic government were formed. The latest was the National Unity Committee, which set itself the mission of "saving the Republic of Atatürk". The army overthrew the civilian government on 27 May 1960. This first military coup was followed by three others in 1971, 1980 and 1997, all of which were directed against the resurgence of Islamism. Islamic parties were dissolved for "activities contrary to the principle of secularism" and their leaders imprisoned. The deposed Prime Minister, Menderes, and two of his ministers were sentenced to death. However, the coup did not lead to authoritarian rule. Members of the junta opposed to parliamentary democracy, such as Colonel Alparslan Tiirkeş, a supporter of pantouranism, were removed. The military had a constitution passed in July 1961 that was paradoxically more liberal than the previous one. It was they who then authorized the elections, while reserving the presidency for General Gürsel, who was considered "the guarantor of the May 27 revolution." The elections of 15 October 1961 saw the return to power of Inonü's CHP, which formed a coalition with the Justice Party

(*Adalet Partisi*). In 1962, the Cuban missile crisis placed Turkey at the heart of the Cold War. In return for the withdrawal of Soviet missiles from Cuba, the United States dismantled the Jupiter missiles installed in Turkey and pointed at the USSR. Three years later, the Justice Party led by Süleyman Demirel won a clear victory. Demirel put Turkey back on the rails of religious conservatism. The year 1969 saw the foundation of an extreme right-wing party, the MHP, which was in the tradition of pantouranism. Partisan of a homogeneous Turkish state - armed nation led by its commander-in-chief - it is supported by part of the army, and the police against the left, and acquires a militia, the "Gis Wolves" led by Tiirkeş. On the opposite side emerges a radical left. The third pole is constituted by the Islamists. Sunnis from Anatolia for the most part, they represent the traditional countryside in conflict with the modern, secular and Westernized city. Led by a charismatic leader, Necmettin Erbakan, they founded the National Order Party in 1969. It advocates social justice, national and spiritual values, and rejects Westernization. For their part, the Kurds gradually formed their own organizations. At the turn of the 1970s, Turkey became the scene of multiple radicalisms and violent confrontations that the government was unable to put an end to. On March 11, 1971, Süleyman Demirel, leader of the Justice Party, which had been in power since 1965 and was judged to be too favourable to a "return to Islam," was forced to resign by the army, which, with the approval of the President of the Republic, Cevdet Sunay, who had come from its ranks, instituted a military regime for two years. A "white terror" fell mainly on the radical left. About 5000 people were arrested. Three leftist leaders were executed, dozens of others were shot or tortured to death. The regime authorized elections to be held in October 1973. They were won by the CHP led by Bülent Ecevit, who had replaced Inonü as head of the Kemalist party and represented its left wing. In July 1974, a coup d'état carried out by the EOKA (National Organization of Greek Cypriot Fighters, supporters of the attachment of Cyprus to Greece), pushed the Ecevit government to intervene militarily. The Turkish army occupied the northern part of Cyprus, which became an independent state in 1983. Recognized by Turkey alone, it was protected by thirty thousand soldiers and separated from the rest of the island by a demarcation line, the "green line".

From the 1980 to the 1997 coup d'état

Between 1975 and 1980, the country experienced a veritable descent into hell. The violence, suspended for a time by the 1971 coup d'état, resumed with renewed vigour and took on a communal dimension. From the 1977 elections, which confirmed its victory, the radical right opted for the worst strategy. Pogroms against the Alevis, committed by the "Grey Wolves", followed one another, several left-wing intellectuals were assassinated and the Kurds were subjected to fierce repression. Faced with the deteriorating political, economic and security situation, the National Security Council, headed by the Chief of the Joint Chiefs of Staff, Kenan Evren, seized power in September 1980. It took strong action against politicians and intellectuals, accusing them of allowing the country to slide into crisis and violence. Most politicians, among them Ecevit, Demirel Erbakan, and Tiirkeş are arrested. Martial law is declared. The National Assembly is dissolved and the junta assumes executive, legislative and even judicial powers through military courts. Most unions and associations were banned. Violent repression was unleashed on "individuals and organizations deemed dangerous. More than four hundred leftists were shot, tortured to death or disappeared. Nearly eighty-five thousand people were imprisoned. "The military decreed that any ideological affiliation other than Kemalism, any ethnicity other than Turkish, any religious affiliation other than Sunni was a "perversion"[4] The spoken use of Kurdish was banned and the mountains of Kurdistan were once again decorated with Atatürk's motto "Happy is he who calls himself a Turk. However, although it was an enemy of political Islamism, the military junta, which emerged from the 1980 coup d'état, considered that a moderate Islam was the best bulwark against religious radicalism, communism and Kurdish separatism. Anxious to strengthen national cohesion, it adopted as its doctrine the synthesis of Turkish nationalism and Islam. This turnaround took place in the context of the Cold War: the United States had linked up with global Islamism to encircle the Soviet Union. In 1982, it passed a new constitution establishing an authoritarian regime in which the National Security Council (MGK) saw its powers strengthened. The MGK is made up of the President of the Republic, the Prime Minister, the Ministers of Defence, the Ministry of Foreign Affairs and the Ministry of Foreign Affairs.

The so-called "Islamist-Western tuque" synthesis developed by a conservative intellectual group was confirmed with the 1983 election victory of the ANAP, Turgut Ô's Motherland Party. The so-called "Islamist-Western tuque" synthesis developed by a conservative intellectual center was confirmed by the electoral victory of Turgut Ôzal's ANAP, Motherland Party, in 1983. Prime Minister, then President of the Republic, he had to share power with the military until his election as President in 1989. A supporter of the "moral order" and the Islamic-Turkish synthesis, his party, which governed from 1983 to 1991, was conservative, liberal, democratic, pro-European and nostalgic for the Ottoman Empire. Described as an "economic wizard" for having put an end to inflation, Ôzal adopted a centrist position and claimed to be the defender of the middle classes. He played a key role in accelerating the liberalization of political life and opening up Turkey culturally and politically to the world. The radical options in society are giving way to a more peaceful climate. The Islamist political formations managed to get through the 1980s, changing their names every time the authorities decided to ban them.

Thanks to the "islamo-liberalism" implemented by ANAP, the country is emerging from the economic slump. A decree law authorized the opening of Islamic banks. The government had to take into account the religious aspirations of the population by financing the construction of mosques, subsidizing Islamic schools and introducing compulsory religious instruction in public schools. The article of the penal code prohibiting political parties claiming to be religious was abolished. And in 1986, a law was passed punishing "insults to religion, Allah and the Prophet" with six months to two years in prison. Tolerance of the wearing of the veil, initially outside public establishments, developed. Although still officially proscribed, Sufi brotherhoods finally emerged from the shadows; this was the case for the most fundamentalist and most opposed to secularism: the Suleymanciya and the Naqshibendiye, which alone had two million members. The communities (*cemaat*) are becoming more and more influential. Combining religious puritanism and the pursuit of profit, their Islam has a similarity with the Protestant work ethic. The most powerful of these is led by the preacher Fethullah Gülen, who has claimed that "Islam is the cement of national unity" and, at the head of a financial, media and educational empire, is working to infiltrate the machinery of the state. The year 1984 saw the beginning of the guerrilla war led by Abdullah Ôcalan's PKK against government forces. The ensuing clashes left more than 42,000 people dead until 2010 and many more displaced. Unlike the Kurds, the

The Alevi community, which represents about 20% of the population, has never had any political pretensions.

Since the beginning of the 1980s, the foreign policy priority of Turkey's pro-Western elites has been to ensure Turkey's accession to the European Union. In 1987, the Ôzal government made an official request for membership. But this accession is constantly postponed by European officials under various pretexts. The real reason for the Tucs being that Turkey is a Muslim country and that the European countries consider the Union to be a "Christian club". In reaction to this rejection, President Ôzal and his successors have endeavoured, since the break-up of the Soviet Union, to create links with the Turkic and Muslim countries of the Caucasus and Central Asia. This redeployment of Turkey to these regions is driven not only by the dream of becoming the leader of a Turkish community of nations, but also by the desire to counter the temptation of Iran and Saudi Arabia to extend their influence and promote Islamic fundamentalism there. They believe that their Turkish model of a secular, democratic Muslim state and a market economy represents an alternative to radical Islam. In addition, Turkey hopes to contain the resurgence of Russian influence. Most significantly, Turkey has intensified its relations with Arab and other Muslim countries. Until now, these were characterized by a policy of mutual ignorance. This orientation is partly caused by a rise in religious feelings among the population. These were manifested all the more vigorously because, as in the Soviet Union, any expression of religious convictions, considered to be an enemy of progress, had long been violently repressed. This period marks the beginning of the proliferation of Islamic-style beards and veils for women. Mosques attract more and more worshippers. Bookstores were full of books, newspapers, tapes and videos extolling Islamic precepts and lifestyles, and glorifying the Ottoman Empire. After the implosion of the USSR in 1991, there was at first a feeling that Turkey, because of the disappearance of the logic of the blocks, would lose its geostrategic value. On the contrary, the dismemberment opened up the former Soviet Turkic and Muslim republics of the Caucasus and Central Asia. The first Gulf crisis, following the invasion of Kuwait by Iraq in August 1990, also gave Turkey the opportunity to legitimize its place in NATO. Without sending troops to the theater of operations, it authorized the Americans to use NATO installations on its soil, notably the Incirlik base, to bomb Iraq. In April 1991, hundreds of thousands of Kurds took refuge in Turkey after their revolt in Iraq was crushed.

The 1991 elections could have given rise to a stable Turkey, capable of resolving the Kurdish question and integrating its different political sensibilities. However, the 1990s were to see constant crises, accentuating the political fragmentation of the early 1980s. The right-left division of the 1970s was followed by a series of conflicts between Kemalists and Islamists, Kurds and Turks, Alevis and Sunnis. It explains the rapid (almost annual) changeover of incoherent governments during this period. The 1991 elections led to the formation of a coalition government led by Demirel, relegating the ANAP, led by Mesut Ilmaz since Ôzal's presidency, to the opposition. When Ôzal died in 1993, Demirel was elected President of the Republic. He left the leadership of the party and the government to his protégée, Tansu Çiller, a fervent supporter of Kemalism and secularism and projecting the image of an open and pro-European Turkey. The re-Islamization of society led to the victory of the Islamist Refah (Prosperity Party), led by Necmettin Erbakan in the 1994 municipal elections. This is how Recep Tayyip Erdogan became mayor of Istanbul. The Kemalist press spoke of an earthquake and the newspaper *Cumhuriyet* wondered with contempt whether the "peasants" would now govern the cities[5] . However, it soon became clear that the Islamist mayors were offering their constituents better services than their predecessors. In the parliamentary elections of December 1995, Refah became the country's largest political party. And in June 1996, for the first time in the history of the Turkish Republic, the leader of a religious party became Prime Minister. Erbakan's arrival in power provoked jubilant scenes in religious circles and marked the rise of another Turkey, that of the traditions and the countryside. The Kemalist and left-wing press, on the other hand, went wild against him, while the military was on the alert. Erbakan multiplied the number of imam high schools and adopted a resolutely pro-Arab foreign policy. Parallel to the rise of Refah, the main phenomenon was the emergence of Fethullh Gülen's Hizmet movement, which established itself as the most powerful *cemaat.* Its empire finances more than two hundred schools, seven universities, a television channel, two radio stations and several newspapers.

The "postmodern" coup of February 2017

On February 28, 1997, frightened by the consequences of the policy of Islamo-nationalist synthesis, which it had at first looked on favorably, the army forced the Erbakan government to resign. This coup de force is described as a "postmodern coup d'état" insofar as it required only a simple injunction from the military command. His party was banned, and a series of eighteen measures aimed at eradicating all Islamist manifestations and activities in Turkey were enacted. Through the National Security Council, whose permanent structures are composed solely of military personnel, the army becomes the real organ of power in Turkey. It became the sole authority on crises and the responses to them. The eighteen measures imposed on the government have gradually become a kind of "surveillance code" by which all the speeches and actions of the Islamist parties, brotherhoods and *cemaat* are judged.

February 1997 represents in a way a return to the great principles of the Republic, in particular secularism. After the forced resignation of the Erbakan government, the Democratic Left Party led by Bülent Ecevit formed a coalition government supported by the military with the Nationalist Action Party (MHP, radical right). The coalition governments followed one another until 2002. In 1998, Turkey threatened Syria, which was sheltering Abdullah Ôcalan, with war if it did not expel him. Kidnapped in Kenya where he had taken refuge, he was imprisoned and sentenced to death. But the sentence was not carried out. On August 3, 2000, Ôcalan proclaimed the end of the armed struggle, despite some dissenting voices. The European summit of Helsinki in December 1999 pronounced itself for the granting to Turkey of the status of candidate to the membership of the European Union. However, Ankara did not make enough effort to meet the conditions necessary for this membership. Constitutional amendments were passed in order to adapt the existing system to the Copenhagen criteria, but the reforms undertaken were a cover-up and presented as a concession to Europe, which was described as an adversary in thinly veiled terms. Any demonstration demanding the right to teach the Kurdish language is harshly repressed. And human rights violations remain massive. Political Islam is struggling to recover from its electoral defeat. In 2001 the Virtue Party was banned. Torn between a conservative wing and a renovationist wing, its supporters split in two and gave birth to new formations. The Party of Bliss, loyal to its old leader, Erbakan, and the Justice and Development Party (AKP). The latter, led by the young and dynamic mayor of Istanbul, Recep Tayyip Erdogan, is less in the continuity of traditional Islamist parties than in that of ANAP, which was an alliance of Islamist and Western nationalist tendencies. Corruption and the economic crisis - the Turkish lira lost half its value in a few days - finally discredited the Ecevit government. In July 2002, seven of his ministers announced their resignation, forcing him to accept to organize early elections.

The arrival in power of the AKP

The November 2002 elections were won by the AKP. The AKP won the elections in November 2002, beating the CHP, the only other party to enter Parliament, by a wide margin. It has 363 deputies out of 550 and can therefore govern the country alone. The AKP's accession to power is a major turning point in Turkey's history, a victory for democracy and a setback for the army. It represents a vote of confidence by the people against the other political parties, which have been disavowed by repeated political and financial scandals.

Presenting itself as "Muslim-democratic" like the European Christian Democrats, the AKP declares itself in favour of secularism in Turkey, openness to Europe and economic liberalism. A former mayor of Istanbul, Erdogan had declared "mosques are our barracks, domes our helmets, minarets our bayonets and believers our soldiers[6] ", which had earned him prison. Deprived of his civil rights, he could not run for parliament. It was therefore his loyal lieutenant Abdullah Gül who initially assumed the post of Prime Minister. But Parliament passed a law allowing Erdogan to be elected as a member of parliament and he became Prime Minister in March 2003, while Gül took over the Foreign Ministry. The policy of the Erdogan government seems to disavow its former hardline Islamic positions and it adopts a more open, albeit conservative, political line on social issues. But it is not without ambiguity. On the one hand, the Prime Minister is speeding up the implementation of liberal and progressive reforms to bring Turkish legislation into line with European Union criteria. On the other, a virtuoso of double talk, he is flattering his Islamist electorate. Turkey has twice hosted the Organization of the Islamic Conference, in 2002 and 2004 in Istanbul. And it was the Turkish Ekmelettin Ihsanoglü who was elected secretary general of this organization in 2004. At the same time, Ankara is continuing negotiations on Turkey's application to join the European Union, which was finally accepted in principle in October 2005. The AKP government is working to bring the army to heel and is achieving remarkable economic success. But, under the guise of defending religious freedom, it is gradually changing its policy, multiplying measures in favour of the re-Islamization of society and giving the impression of going back on the gains of Kemalism. Thus, despite secular opposition in Parliament, the wearing of the Islamic headscarf was liberalized in the civil service and in education. Created in 1924 to control the Muslim religion, the Diyanet, the directorate of religious affairs, has become, over the years, a veritable instrument of social engineering in the hands of the Islamo-conservative government, which is determined to shape "a pious generation. He set out to dismantle the "deep state" composed of CHP members, Republican leftists, officers and judges opposed to the policies of his Islamo-Conservative party. The 2007 presidential elections provoked a crisis with the army, which, denouncing "the danger that Islamic fanaticism poses to the principles of the Republic founded by Atatürk," spoke out against the candidacy of Abdullah Gül. However, the AKP succeeded in having him elected president following the legislative elections of July 2007. These elections consolidated its majority, but saw the entry into Parliament of the far-right MHP party, which came third behind the Kemalist CHP and 24 Kurdish deputies who ran as "independents" to comply with the law banning parties with ethnic or religious names. From 2007, following the Ergenekon affair, which designated a network suspected of wanting to overthrow the government, the Erdogan government began a fight against the military institution and the secular elites. At the same time, measures against freedom of expression are becoming more frequent and several opposition newspapers are being banned. Some secular Turks, generally of the centre-left and loyal to the legacy of Atatürk, see the

Ergenekon trial as the final act in the long-running feud between pro-secular leftists and Islamo-conservatives. However, many of the defendants belonged to the extreme nationalist right.

Foreign policy

The coming to power of the AKP accentuates the redeployment of Turkish foreign policy towards the Arab and Muslim world. The new Turkish leaders consider that Turkey's posture, which until then had been too exclusively focused on Europe and turning its back on its neighbors to the east and south, did not take geography and history into account. They believe that Turkey's European anchorage and its membership in NATO and the OECD are not incompatible with its membership in the Islamic world and a greater involvement in Middle Eastern affairs. For them, Turkey is the only power, along with Iran, that can claim to play the role of a leading state in the Muslim world and a counterweight to Russia in the Caucasus and Central Asia. No other Muslim country has all the assets it enjoys: its geographic position as a strategic pivot between the Mediterranean and the Black Sea, Asia and Europe; its population of 74 million; its economic weight; its military power; its influence among Turkish-speaking peoples; its membership in the majority Sunni faith in the Muslim world; and finally its moderate Islam and democracy, which serve as an antidote to Islamic fundamentalism and as a counter-model to Iranian theocracy. The Middle East has historically been dominated by two powers: Turkey and Iran. But while Iran's influence rightly worries the countries of the region and the "international community," the same should not be said of Turkey, which should be seen as a factor of stability in the Middle East. One of the manifestations of this role of regional pivot was the inauguration in July 2006, with the American blessing and the presence of an Israeli delegation, of the Baku-Tiblisi-Ceyhan oil pipeline, intended to bring oil from the Caspian Sea to the Mediterranean and from there, later, to the port of Ashkelon. Bypassing Russian territory, the pipeline passes through Azerbaijan and Georgia, which, like Turkey, are allies of Washington, and is part of the United States' key strategic objective of controlling the region's hydrocarbons. The revision of Turkish diplomacy was further affirmed with the stumbling of negotiations with Brussels at the end of 2005. The arrival of Ahmed Davitoglü at the Ministry of Foreign Affairs allowed him to put into practice a doctrine theorized in his book *Strategic Depth: Turkey's International Positioning,* published in 2001[7]. Although he did not question its membership in NATO, he wanted Turkey to use its geographical position and its Ottoman past to diversify its alliances. He is the sponsor of the "zero problems" policy with Turkey's neighbors. Pursuing a diplomacy based on "conciliation, peace", Ankara wants to be on good terms with all, including Syria, which the Turkish president has declared to be "Turkey's gateway to the Middle East". Despite or because of its good relations with Tehran, the "moderate" Arab countries consider that only Turkey can counterbalance Iran's hegemonic aims in the region. In general, until the 2011 uprisings, Turkish diplomacy in the Arab world was as much commercial as political. Ministerial visits were accompanied by delegations of businessmen who sometimes received direct support from members of the government. This new perspective on the Arab and Muslim world does not prevent Turkey's accession to the European Union from remaining its strategic priority. In October 2010, it amended its constitution to meet the political criteria set by the European Union. But this amendment, which abolishes the political role of the army, has the perverse effect of favouring currents favourable to the re-Islamization of Turkey. Turkey remains a privileged ally of the United States, as confirmed by President Obama's visit to Ankara, where he advocated its accession to the European Union. And it is beginning a historic process of reconciliation with Armenia. One can certainly consider this all-out opening as contradictory and it is not surprising that the "pro-Arab" policy of the AKP does not please either Israel or certain American neo-conservative circles. However, while it is true that the AKP government has an Islamic religious sensibility, its policy choices are above all dictated by a realistic and rational analysis of the country's interests. Economically, they have contributed to the growth of its exports to Muslim countries and Russia, of which it has become the leading trading partner. At the geopolitical level, occupying a strategic pivotal position between the Mediterranean and the Black Sea, Asia and Europe, Turkey's natural vocation is to rely on all its circles of belonging in order to be a bridge between the West and the East. Two events illustrate a radical change of course with previous governments: the Turkish refusal to accede to Washington's request to use its territory to open a second front against Iraq in 2002. And Turkey's stance on the Iranian nuclear issue in 2009 is beginning to worry Western nations about the true intentions of the Islamo-conservative government. Despite these frictions, Turkey maintains a privileged relationship with Washington. Turkish-American cooperation remains very close on the military front. The United States has an air base in Incirlik. The government is seeking to project its economic success onto the political terrain in the former territories of the Ottoman Empire by multiplying its partnerships with Arab and Turkish-speaking countries. This new policy is described as neo-Ottoman. The Islamic reorientation of the AKP's foreign policy was clearly evident in the Israeli-Palestinian conflict. While Turkey used to cooperate closely with Israel, including on the military level, it has violently condemned the bombing and blockade of Gaza by the Jewish state. And the dispatch of a Turkish ferry in 2010 to break the blockade made Prime Minister Erdogan immensely popular among his own people and in the Muslim world, which was probably the intention. But the cooperation that had broken down following the Israeli navy's assault on the Turkish ferry was re-established in 2014; including a gas pipeline project to bring Israeli gas from the Leviathan field to Europe via Turkey. As part of the good neighbor policy, Turkey is moving closer to Syria. The spectacular rapprochement between Turkey and Syria after years of animosity is one of the manifestations of the redeployment of Turkish foreign policy. Political scientists and Western media are concerned about it. "Wondering whether Turkey is not tilting towards the Muslim world at the expense of its attachment to Europe and the Western camp, they ask the question: "Are we losing Turkey?[8] ? But the outbreak of the Arab Spring and President Assad's refusal of any form of concession to the Syrian opposition will lead Ankara to turn against the Damascus regime and bury its policy of "zero-problems" with its neighbors. Since the beginning of the wave of uprisings that swept through Arab countries from 2011, Turkey has supported the Tunisian, Egyptian and Syrian Muslim Brotherhood. A policy that has only met with setbacks with the electoral setback of the Tunisian Muslim Brotherhood and their Egyptian rout. Its territory has served as a rear base for jihadists fighting in Syria. And it has refrained from joining the coalition of Western and Arab countries assembled by Washington to fight the terrorists of the "Islamic State" (Daech).

The turn to absolute power

On the domestic front, resentments are building up between the AKP and Fethullah Gülen's Hizmet movement, with which it has been allied since 2002. The latter has taken advantage of this to infiltrate the workings of the state. In early 2011, Hizmet, at the height of its power, demanded a third of the AKP deputies (about 100 seats). Erdogan played on the rivalries of the Gülen movement with the traditionalist brotherhoods to marginalize it and set about purging the administration of its members. In 2013, the rupture between the two former allies was consummated. Four decades of Hizmet's patient work of entryism vanished. In the spring of 2013, a protest movement against the authoritarianism of the Erdogan government, *which* started in Taksim Square in Istanbul, gathered millions of people across the country. Erdogan was elected president of the Republic of Turkey on August 10, 2014, after the first election of the head of state by universal suffrage. He displays his ambition to strengthen the powers of the presidential office by amending the Constitution. And he is becoming increasingly megalomaniacal, having a 1,000-room presidential palace built in Ankara, earning him the label of the new sultan. On July 15, 2016 a small group of military tries to overthrow the power. The coup plotters claim to want to "restore democracy" through their operation. Clashes took place in Ankara and Istanbul on the night of Friday to Saturday, July 16, between mutineers, loyalist soldiers and supporters of the president, leaving several hundred dead. F16 fighter-bombers from the Incirlik air base (which also serves as an American base) tried in vain to intercept President Erdogan's plane between Ankara and Marmaris where he had taken refuge. It seems that it was the Russians who warned him of the coup attempt. This one is quickly put in failure.

The failure of the putsch strengthens Erdogan's power. Described as a "gift from Allah" by the president, it allowed him to carry out the purges he had long dreamed of, particularly in the army, and to further harden his regime. He accuses Gülen who resides in the United States of being the instigator of the plot. Since July 15, 2016 the renewal of the quarterly state of exception has become the rule. The country is governed by government decrees under the total control of the president. A very important repression follows. Around 150,000 civil servants were dismissed, 50,000 were arrested. 11 opposition MPs, 63 mayors, the overwhelming majority of whom are Kurdish, 172 journalists and 10 human rights activists have been arrested, often without being tried; and 50 new prisons are being built, 19 universities and a total of 2,099 schools have been closed. 187 media outlets were closed and banned, 560 foundations, 54 hospitals, 1,125 associations, and 19 trade unions were closed. Around 550 private companies were nationalized, their assets and property looted. With the end of the european contract the regime felt it had wings to transform not only the political system but also the society. On April 16, 2017, a constitutional referendum transformed the parliamentary system into a presidential one by abolishing the post of prime minister and instituting instead a post of vice president. The referendum constitutionalized the total power given to the president of the republic. However, the yes vote obtained only 51.4 per cent of the votes, indicating that a large proportion of citizens remain opposed to the president's ambitions. To ensure his re-election in 2019, he has formed an alliance with the right-wing nationalist party MHP. "There is now no power capable of counterbalancing the regime's omnipotence. Today, the country's educational, military, judicial, economic, administrative and diplomatic systems function on the basis of loyalty to the Islamist regime, in stark contrast to what the country has experienced since the end of 1999, when the European process began. All in all, there is a direct link between the collective co-opted failure of Turkey's European process and the regime's authoritarian and anti-Western radicalization[9] .

The Kurdish question and foreign relations

Following measures adopted by the authorities in 2005 and 2012 in their favour, the conflict with the Kurds had experienced a period of calm. But the PKK, considered a terrorist organization by Ankara, has reopened hostilities, raising fears that the Kurds of Turkey will be contaminated by the separatism of their Syrian and Iraqi brothers. Real urban insurrections are taking place in the south-east of the country, triggering major population displacements. The country has been the target, since 2015, of a series of terrorist attacks perpetrated by the PKK and the Islamic State group and is suffering the negative fallout of the Syrian conflict on its soil. On the regional scene, the rout of the Muslim Brotherhood in Egypt, of which Ankara had been one of the most fervent supporters, and the maintenance in power of Bashar al-Assad, whose head Erdogan never stopped calling for, constitute serious failures, shattering his dreams of neo-Ottoman grandeur. The Russian intervention in Syria in September 2015, which thwarted Turkish designs, seriously soured Russian-Turkish relations. But Ankara's foreign policy missteps and the failed coup of July 2016 are paving the way for a reconciliation with the Kremlin. The rapprochement is reflected in an understanding between Moscow and Ankara on the ground in Syria. The two leaders are making concessions to each other. Erdogan is becoming less intransigent on the departure of Bashar al-Assad, Russia is bending its support for the Syrian Kurds, Ankara's bête noire. Turkey and Iran have ambivalent relations. After a period of marked improvement in the second half of the 2000s, these have deteriorated since 2011 with the "Arab springs" which saw the respective protégés of the two powers clash, and the authorization given by Turkey to the deployment on its soil of NATO's anti-missile shield, perceived as a threat by Tehran. The Astana talks initiated in 2017 under the aegis of Russia and Turkey testify to a cooperation if not a convergence of interest between the three powers on the Syrian issue. They were followed in November 2017, by the Sochi summit between Presidents Putin, Erdogan and Rohani devoted to the search for a political solution to the Syrian conflict. Donald Trump's decision to recognize Jerusalem as the capital of the Jewish state provided an opportunity for the Turkish president to pose as a leader of the Muslim world. "This decision plunges the region into a ring of fire and risks encouraging terrorism," Recep Tayyip Erdogan said on December 6, 2017[10] , who is working to mobilize the Muslim world. He also invited the leaders of the 57 member countries of the Organization of Islamic Cooperation (OIC) for a summit in Istanbul on December 13 focused on the issue of Jerusalem. In the race for control of the Red Sea, Ankara is actively projecting its military and economic presence in Sudan and Somalia. On the other hand, the Turkish president's authoritarian drift, his arrogant attitude, the regime's human rights violations and the Islamization of Turkey make its membership in the European Union, with which it has increasingly tense relations, even more unlikely.

Turkey, somewhat schizophrenic and completely dependent on the moods of its leader, has changed its face in 2016. Weakened by terrorist attacks committed by the Islamic State or the Kurdistan Workers' Party (PKK), divided by the autocratic drift of its president Recep Tayyip Erdogan, it is experiencing a strong period of instability, illustrated in particular by that crazy night of July 15, 2016, when the "sultan" almost lost everything. From that night, the Turkish president emerged stronger, more popular, more determined to assume his political positions both internally and internationally, despite criticism from his allies. But the country itself has been weakened by the policy of purges carried out by the current government, which, in the name of the fight against terrorism, seeks to silence all dissenting voices. The country is now hostage to the strategic reversals of President Erdogan, who has decided to fuel anti-Westernism and to draw closer to Vladimir Putin's Russia, while militarily and economically, Turkey remains closely linked to the West. The regime is in open conflict with two major allies, Germany and the United States. The new U.S. administration has refused to extradite Fethullah Gülen, considered to be the main culprit behind the coup attempt. Washington, to Ankara's great despair, has also refused to comply and has continued to provide arms and protection to Kurdish militias in Syria in their war against Daesh. But the defeat of the Islamic State group could see the Americans cut the Kurds loose. The regime's intention to buy SS-400 anti-aircraft missiles from Russia has angered Washington and NATO HQ. Relations with the European Union have been stalled for a long time and have no chance of restarting.

1 *La Turquie moderne et l'islam*, Thierry Zarcone, Flamarion 2004, p. 255

2 *History of Turkey from Altai to Europe*, Ibrahim Tabet, L'Archipel, 2007, p. 331

3 ibid. p. 338

4 *Histoire de la Turquie contemporaine*, Hamit Bozarslan, La Découverte 2004, p. 60

5 *History of Turkey from Altai to Europe*, op. cit. p. 361

6 *History of contemporary Turkey*, op. cit. p.66

7 *Turkey, the authoritarian turn, Is Turkey still a regional power* Jean-Baptiste le Moulec. Middle East N° : from January-March 2018, p. 65

8 *History of Turkey from Altai to Europe*, op. cit. p. 366

9 .https://lecourrierdumaghrebetdelorient.info/turkey/turquie-premier-bilan-dune-quete-du power-absolute/ Gengiz Akhtar

10 ttps://www.lexpress.fr/.../monde/erdogan-la-decision-de-trump-sur-jerus alem.

Chapter 13. Political Islam and Jihadism

Modern Islamism is a generic term that encompasses all ideological currents that aim to establish a state based on the principles of Islam, whether at the level of a country or of the entire Muslim community. It is thus possible to distinguish between nationalist Islamists, who are in the majority, and the transnational Islamism represented by al-Qaeda. These heterogeneous and often rival movements were born out of the resentment of the populations towards Western hegemony and the failure of Muslim states. While most of these states had restricted the application of sharia law to family law and adopted modern laws for the rest, the movements claiming to be militant Islam have set themselves the goal of abolishing the Western-inspired secular reforms and mores of the past 100 years. Some of them intend to achieve this goal through the ballot box, while others, the most radical, have chosen violence. Thus, several Islamist movements have engaged in bloody battles against the regimes in place, also targeting the secular opposition. The birth of modern political Islam can be dated to the founding of the Muslim Brotherhood by Hassan al-Banna in 1928, and its radical version by Sayed Qotb in 1964. Another very influential fundamentalist theologian was the Pakistani Sayed Maududi. He was the founder of the Pakistani Jamaat-e-Islami party in 1941 and advocated the creation of a unified Islamic state based on the strict application of sharia law. He was the first Islamist of the 20th century to promote a return to jihad. Long crushed by the existing Arab regimes, Islamism only began to assert itself as a dominant ideology in the 1970s. "The pan-Islamism that re-emerged in the 1970s is quite different from its reformist ancestor. Unlike it, it is culturally closed to the ideas of European modernity.[1] "

The contradictory nature of certain verses of the Koran means that Islam has been described as either a tolerant or a warlike religion. Its opponents do not fail to favor the second interpretation. For moderate Muslims, however, the actions of jihadists are a betrayal of authentic Islam. The rise of Islamism and the reaffirmation of the identity of Islam are part of the reversal of the trend towards the "exit from religion" and the "disenchantment of the world" that began in the Enlightenment. This "return of the religious", described by Gilles Kepel as the "revenge of God", takes on different forms and intensities depending on the society. In Europe, it is less a question of stopping dechristianization than of reacting to the materialism of a satiated consumer society and to the "crisis of culture". After having defeated the secular ideologies, Nazism and Communism, the post-Christian West is struggling to redefine its ethical and political values. The reaffirmation of its "Judeo-Christian" values may seem like an antidote to the supposed internal and external challenge of Islam, in a global context of identity-based tensions. In the Muslim world, on the other hand, this return often expresses a feeling of frustration, humiliation and failure, as well as a revolt against situations of injustice, exclusion and poverty. Hence the rise of a political Islamism that wants to put a stop to the secularization initiated by the

Nahda and often takes on a radical and violent aspect. Reflecting the crisis that the Muslim world is going through, it is within it that the irruption of the religious into the political sphere is most evident with the rise of competing Islamist movements, both Sunni and Shiite. "Sunni Islamism and revolutionary Shi'ism are not only, as they claim, the embodiment of Islamic authenticity in the face of ideas and political forms imported from the Western world [...] Because of their totalitarian and authoritarian vision and their constitution as an ideology, both are at odds with the tradition of classical Islam[2] . Their competition was sharpened by the Iranian revolution of 1979 and the deposition of Saddam Hussein's regime in 2003, which caused a radical shift in the balance of power in the Middle East in favour of what has been called the "Shiite arc. The revival of Islam has several faces. On the one hand, there is violence and terrorism: most of the conflicts between states or civil wars that have occurred in the world over the past twenty years have involved Muslim countries or countries with Muslim populations: from Bosnia to the Philippines, including Chechnya, sub-Saharan Africa and Afghanistan. Not to mention attacks against Western targets. On the other hand, it is a quest for identity, meaning and dignity. And finally, that of a response to the ills from which Muslim countries suffer. This hope is symbolized by the slogan of the Sunni Islamist parties: "Islam is the solution", which turned out to be far from being the case. While they have succeeded in "Islamizing society from below," as Gilles Kepel puts it, by making up for the state's shortcomings in social services, their political failure is obvious. Apart from the electoral victory of Hamas in the Gaza Strip, which provoked a fratricidal struggle and a split within the Palestinian Resistance, no Arab party had succeeded until 2011 in gaining power through the ballot box. Nor, moreover, to overthrow it by force, whether in Saudi Arabia, Algeria, Egypt or Syria. Only the Khomeinist revolution in Iran in 1979 succeeded, and that was in the Shiite world. This violence and these failures led Gilles Kepel to consider in 2000, in his book *Jihad* 3, the radicalization of political Islam as a sign of decline rather than a rise in power. This thesis seems to have been reinforced by the bitter failure of the Tunisian and Egyptian Islamists, who came to power through the ballot box in the wake of the so-called "Arab Spring" and who have not succeeded in keeping it. As a specialist in Islam, Olivier Roy had foreseen this failure, as he had analyzed, as early as 2005, the foreseeable causes of the Arab Spring, warning against the errors of analysis made by Western governments in their support for Arab autocratic regimes, for fear of Islamist drifts. Commenting in 2011 on the popular uprisings in Tunisia and Egypt, he had to declare "Yes: in the outbreak of all these revolutions, Islamists have been absent. This does not mean that they will not return. Islamism is finished, as a political solution and as an ideology. But the Islamists are there[4] .

In the XX[e] century, few ideologies were as mobilizing as communism and nazism. The former conceived of history as a class struggle and the latter as a struggle between races. The emergence of radical Islamism has many similarities with these two ideologies. It has the same totalitarian nature and the same power of mobilization, all the more so as it plays on the religious fibre. It sees history as a struggle against the despised Western civilization, and between believers and unbelievers, of which, for the Sunni "takfirists" who are followers of Ibn Taymiyah, the Alawites are considered the worst apostates. This movement is fed by the incendiary propaganda of religious preachers whose deleterious influence fuels the worst excesses. Representing in the eyes of sincere Muslims a true blasphemy of the interpretation of the Koran, the nihilistic suicide attacks committed in the name of Allah are the paroxysmal expression of it. These manifestations of fanaticism also take much less horrific but pernicious forms. Like the anathema pronounced against any work critical of Islam, such as that of Salman Rushdie, which earned him death threats. Or the immense wave of indignation in a hypersensitive Muslim world when Pope Benedict XVI evoked, in September 2006, the controversy which had opposed Basilus Manuel II to an Iranian cleric in 1391. Many explanations have been put forward to explain these disturbing trends. Some emphasize the totalitarian nature of Islam, which would constitute an obstacle to democracy and social progress. Others point to the feeling of alienation and humiliation of the Muslim masses in the face of the failure of the regimes in place and Western hegemony, as well as poverty and ignorance. Any analysis of political Islamism and jihadism must first distinguish between three different things: the religious message, constituted religions and the political instrumentalization of religion. It is true that Islam does not distinguish between religion and the state and that the Koran contains verses that clearly call for war. That said, modern jihad is less about this or that verse of the Koran serving as an alibi than about a conjunction of socio-political and secular cultural causes. This applies even to the "Islamic State" (IS), which represents the height of Islamic fanaticism and violence and whose emergence is largely due to political causes: the American occupation of Iraq and the marginalization of Sunnis by the Baghdad regime.

Sunni Islamism

Sunni political Islamism is characterized by a wide range of currents, from the most moderate to the most extremist. The most moderate is the Tunisian party Ennahda, and the most fanatical is the Islamic State group (Daesh by its Arabic acronym). Apart from the Tunisian case, and unlike the Turkish AKP which, until the regime's authoritarian drift, compared itself to European Christian democrats, Sunni Arab political Islamism is overwhelmingly anti-democratic, if not outright totalitarian and anti-Western. Although the main targets of its imprecations are Western imperialism, Zionism, the Jews, the "new crusaders" or atheistic communism, it considers local secular reformers, right or left, as adversaries to be fought. Repressed, sometimes ferociously, by the military regimes of Algeria, Egypt and Syria, it is on the contrary actively promoted by the conservative regimes of the region: Pakistan, Saudi Arabia and Qatar. It has been a curse for the Arab countries that the most backward of them, Saudi Arabia, has benefited from the most important oil revenue. Wealth that it uses to promote Wahhabism, the most rigorous version of Islam. However, while vilifying secularism and the loose morals of the West, it is careful not to criticize the international policy of the United States. For their part, the latter have always considered it a privileged ally in the region because of its anti-communism and its oil wealth. They also have a rather favourable policy towards the Muslim Brotherhood, which is considered more "friendly" than the radical Islamists. The main Sunni Islamist currents, the Muslim Brotherhood and the Salafists, have in theory the same fundamentalist approach. However, the ideology of the Muslim Brotherhood is less religiously literalist and more politically oriented. Combining moral conservatism and a desire for modernization, while opposing Westernization, they have a dual face, one of non-violence and social action that has appealed to many Muslims, and one that, on the contrary, calls for violence. For Hassan al-Turabi, leader and theorist of the

Sudanese Muslim Brotherhood: power emanates from God, does not know the notion of a sovereign people. He declares himself to be against the separation of religion and politics, against democracy, "a fundamentally Western concept, alien to Islam," and against nationalism, which contradicts the ideal of the community of believers (*ummah*).[5.] In 1991, he created the Arab Islamic and Popular Conference (AIPC) to counterbalance the Organization of the Islamic Conference (OIC) and to federate the Islamist movements.

The Muslim Brotherhood

The association was founded in Egypt in 1928 by Hassan al-Banna. Determined to fight against "the Western secular hold and the blind imitation of the European model", his movement quickly gave itself a political goal, that of establishing an Islamic state based on the application of the sharia. While advocating a pure and hard Islam, Hassan al-Banna did not call for violence or *Takfir* (removing one's membership in the Muslim world). However, his successor, Sayed Qotb, became the theorist of armed jihad. In 1945, an armed branch of the movement was created with the objective of fighting the Zionists in Palestine. In 1949, following the assassination by this branch of the Egyptian Prime Minister, the organization was banned and Hassan el-Banna assassinated by government agents. The latter, in its fight against terrorism, decreed the death penalty for the perpetrators of political crimes and attacks. Illegal possession of arms and ammunition was punished with extremely severe sentences, including life imprisonment with hard labor. However, he was unable to control the underground cells of the movement. In 1954, President Abdel Nasser, who feared for his person, decided again to ban the organization. Nearly 20,000 militants were imprisoned. Then, in 1966, Sayed Qotb was sentenced to death. His reference book, (*Ma'alim fil Tarik*), will become the bedside book of many jihadists. He accuses today's Muslim society of being "*jahiliya*", that is, in a state of ignorance similar to that which prevailed before the birth of Islam. The true Muslim must break with this situation, struggle to destroy it and finally build the Islamic state on its ruins. For him "the Western age, its domination of the world, is coming to an end, not because Western civilization is materially bankrupt or has lost its economic and military power, but because the Western order no longer possesses that set of values which gave it its pre-eminence. The turn of Islam, the only one capable of offering hope to the world, has come[6] ", In order to promote this Islamic resurrection, Allah has singled out a vanguard to whom he entrusts the mission of imposing this state. The jihad will only end with the conversion of the whole world to Islam. The Other is inferior to the Muslim, who must wage war against him or subdue him. Peace is excluded before conversion or submission to Islam. In the 1970s, President Sadat used the Muslim Brotherhood as a counterweight to the extreme left and promised them the future integration of Sharia into Egyptian law. In 1984, the Egyptian government recognized the Brotherhood as a religious organization, but refused to allow its participation in political life. In the late 1990s, the Brotherhood made an ideological shift, proclaiming its respect for democracy and minority rights, and stating its willingness to adhere to Egypt's secular constitution, while advocating for a society governed by sharia law. In order to gain power and not scare Egyptians, she says she takes the Moroccan and Turkish Islamist movements, known for their pragmatism, as her models. Economically, it is liberal, which suits the bourgeoisie. The logo of the brotherhood, which consisted of two crossed swords, has been temporarily abandoned in favor of a less aggressive logo: two hands joined around a lump of earth where a green shoot is taking root.

In Saudi Arabia, the attack against the Great Mosque of Mecca in November 1979 ended in failure. During the Iraqi invasion of Kuwait in 1991, the Muslim Brotherhood tried to adopt a median position, torn as they were between their pro-Saddam base and their Gulf sponsors. The Brotherhood condemned both the annexation of Kuwait by Iraq and the Saudi use of American troops. Saudi Arabia sanctions them by expelling them from the kingdom. They were replaced in educational institutions by salafists, followers of a literalist interpretation, therefore strictly apolitical, of sacred texts. In Palestine, the Palestinian branch of the Muslim Brotherhood became active again from the mid-1960s in the occupied territories. The movement refrained from violence until the mid-1980s and devoted itself to social works and the construction of mosques in the West Bank and Gaza Strip. The Israeli occupation forces had supported them in the belief that they were a counterweight to the PLO. But the fact that the PLO had achieved nothing in twenty years of struggle, the humiliation of the occupation and the extension of colonization led the Brotherhood to become more radical. "Under the leadership of Sheikh Yassin, they moved from socio-educational activity to political-military activism[7] The year 1987 marked the birth of the Hamas movement, whose charter included as an objective, until its amendment, the establishment of an Islamic state on all the land of the former Mandate Palestine. And it was not long before Hamas and the even more radical Islamic Jihad resorted to bombings and suicide attacks. In Algeria, from 1991 to 2002, a deadly conflict pitted the national army against the armed Islamic group (GIA) and other Islamist militias. It began when the Algerian government cancelled the elections after the first round of results, predicting a victory for the Islamic Salvation Front (FIS), which it accused of wanting to establish an Islamic Republic. During this period, known as the "black decade" or "the years of fire," the conflict claimed the lives of more than 80,000 people, not to mention thousands of missing persons, one million displaced persons and tens of thousands of exiles. During the conflict, the Algerian military manipulated Islamist violence by clandestinely creating armed Islamist groups controlled by the secret services, which pushed them to commit atrocities in order to justify the repression. The leading political force in Algeria after the establishment of a multiparty system in the early 1990s, the islamists lost ground after the failure of islamism in the countries of the "Arab Spring" and, for the first time, did not present a candidate in the presidential election of April 2014. In Syria, the Brotherhood plays a big role. It is the main opposition force to the Baathist regime. The movement was founded in the 1930s by Syrian students, former members of the Egyptian Muslim Brotherhood. They do not consider themselves to be a political party, because for them all political parties are gatherings of atheists. The movement is mainly present in Homs and Hamah and among the working classes. In the late 1970s, it launched an armed struggle against the regime of President Hafez al-Assad, carrying out attacks on Alawites. In July 1980, law no.° 49, which is still in force, stipulates that "anyone who is affiliated with the Muslim Brotherhood is considered a criminal and will be punished by death". From then on, it was the object of a fierce repression. This was particularly the case during the uprising in Hamah in 1982, when the death toll from this repression reached more than 20,000. In Sudan, the Khartoum government's decision to introduce Sharia law in 1983 led to an upsurge in rebellion by Christians and animists in the south. This rebellion had begun when the country gained independence in 1958. Representing approximately 30% of the country's population, the latter became victims of a veritable genocide that resulted in more than one and a half million deaths, without this tragedy arousing much emotion in the world. South Sudan will eventually proclaim its independence. Tunisia appears to be an exception in the world of Arab political Islamism and proves that it is possible to be a religious fundamentalist and accept democracy. In Tunisia, Ennahda is now a government party, which accepts a coalition with other parties. For Olivier Roy, "In its case, we can speak of 'post-Islamism' in the sense that it is not the ideology and revolutionary action of these Islamists that has brought them to power; they have accepted democratization (which they do not condemn, although it was not in their program 30 years ago) and now occupy the center-right of the political space. It is a conservative party in social, cultural and religious terms. They are rather liberal in economic terms and legalistic in political terms. In this sense they have lost their revolutionary dimension, just as the social democratic and communist parties in Europe have lost it .[8]

Salafism and Wahhabism

Salafists (from the word *salaf,* ancestor) aim to regenerate the faith and reislamize society. Salafism advocates a return to the Islam of the origins through the imitation of the life of the Prophet and his companions, and the blind respect of the *Sunna.* It condemns all theological interpretation, in particular the use of human reason, accused of distancing the faithful from the divine message, and all Western influences, such as the way of life and the consumer society, but also democracy and secularism. It originates from the Hanbali school, the most rigorous of the four Islamic legal schools, which later inspired Wahhabism. It is divided into two main currents: the quietist salafists, who are apolitical and only concerned with living in symbiosis with the Koranic prescriptions; and the jihadist salafists, who have a revolutionary vision of Islam that legitimizes the use of violence for a "just" cause: the establishment of an Islamic caliphate. Within the salafist movement, there are many associations for the propagation of Muslim fundamentalism. One of the most important is the *Tabligh* (which means preaching). Founded in 1927 in India, this non-political movement has since developed its activity worldwide through decentralized branches using missionaries of different nationalities. It aims to revive the faith of Muslims within the framework of a literalist interpretation of it and to bring back to a strict practice of Islam those Muslims who have gone astray. It is particularly influential among young Muslims of the second generation of immigration to Europe. Some of these young people are easy to recruit because they feel alienated, considered as second-class citizens in the countries where they were born, and at the same time cut off from their roots to the point of ignoring the mother tongue of their own parents. Islam then becomes for them a way to assert their difference and establish their identity in European countries where they have difficulties to integrate. Although the Tabligh does not get involved in politics, this did not prevent it from being accused (in the 1980s) of more or less voluntarily recruiting candidates for jihad by inciting young European Muslims to go to Pakistan or Afghanistan to receive religious instruction, knowing that once in these countries they were taken in hand by radical groups, often involved in terrorism. Wahhabism, for its part, takes its name from its founder, Mohammed ibn Abd al-Wahab (1703-1792), who is linked to the house of Saud. This thinker believes that Islam must return to its sources and to a stricter application of the sharia. He refused any attempt to interpret the religious text by human thought. He based himself on the teachings of Ibn Hanbal (died around 855), whose fatwas were adopted by the Saudi judiciary as current legislation, and on those of Ibn Taymiyah, known for his literalist interpretation of the Qur'an, particularly with regard to the relationship between political power and the people. Thus inspired, the Wahhabi ideology condemns thought, humor, theater, cinema, works of art, emancipation of women, etc. It also condemns any intellectual innovation (e.g., the use of the word "religion"). It also condemns any intellectual innovation (*Bidaa*) in relation to the original teaching. It advocates the segregation of men and women and the limitation of women's rights. Until recently, the status of women in Saudi Arabia had not changed much and they were subject to many prohibitions, such as the right to drive a car. However, a timid evolution is emerging since September 11, 2001. King Abdullah has begun to control the Wahhabi establishment. And in 2017, Crown Prince Mohammed bin Salmane initiated a package of societal reforms, particularly in favor of women. Outside of Saudi Arabia, the only other country whose population adheres to the Wahhabi belief is Qatar. For the past 40 years Saudi Arabia has been working to export Wahhabism and actively supports fundamentalist movements that are spreading throughout the world. Wahhabi associations offer a monthly subsidy to all women who cover themselves with the Islamic cloak and veil.

Sunni jihadists

Inspired by Sayyed Qotb, jihadism is a synthesis of salafism and the Muslim Brotherhood's strategy of taking power. It found fertile ground during the Mujahideen war against the Soviets in Afghanistan, during which links were forged between would-be Islamist terrorists from various Muslim countries. From that point on, the Salafi jihadists have been committed to armed struggle to liberate Muslim countries from foreign occupation and from Muslim regimes that are considered ungodly. They are represented by two tendencies: those who favour fighting within a national framework, and that of al-Qaeda, which intends to take the fight against the infidels to a global scale. One gets the impression that they want to make the West pay for the few centuries during which it has ruled the planet. To bring down the despised Western civilization, democracy, what they call neo-colonialism, gender equality, secularism, human rights and progress. And they have a paranoid vision of history, perceived as a vast Judeo-Christian conspiracy against the Muslim world. While terrorist attacks have been committed in Europe by jihadists, it is mainly the Middle East and Africa that are the scene of their fanaticism. In Syria, jihadist fighters ritually slit the throats of their Alawite and other prisoners while shouting "*Allhahou akbar*". In Iraq, they slaughter Shiites. In Egypt they attack Copts and burn their churches. And the Libyan revolution has led to an influx of jihadists into sub-Saharan Africa with disastrous consequences for the region, as events in Mali show. Their warrior jihad often takes on a terrorist dimension bordering on nihilism and can go as far as the supreme sacrifice, in other words, martyrdom (*shahid),* which is embodied in the figure of the kamikaze. "This figure has no real antecedent in Arab-Muslim culture other than the Assassin sect. In the contemporary era, we have to wait for the Iranian revolution to see it at work. At first, it was Shiite and was seen on the front lines of the war between Iraq and Iran, where waves of people rushed to attack the Iraqi defense lines. It was then seen in Lebanon, but in a more individual way, in the form of suicide vehicles used against Western interests or in the fight against the Israeli occupation[9] . Since then, however, indiscriminate suicide attacks have been carried out mainly by Sunni jihadists, like those targeting Shiites since the beginning of the civil war in Iraq. For Jacques Beauchard: "The martyrdom of the *shahid* has developed a sacrificial society, the idea of a salvation that inevitably passes through death is now imposed. [...] A millenarian ethos is taking hold, which favors the expectation of a theocracy and the recruitment of God's mercenaries[10] ".

The terrorist dimension of international jihad, which took off in the second half of the 1990s, culminated in the attacks of September 11, 2001, Bali (2002), Madrid (2004) and London (2005). However, its actions have been undermined since then, notably by NATO's intervention in Afghanistan and a counter-terrorism campaign combining intelligence with actions targeting its sources of funding and support bases, with the cooperation of Muslim states themselves. As a result, between 2011 and 2013, there was a decline in international anti-Western terrorism. For example, no terrorist attack has hit the United States since 2001. On the other hand, a new wave of attacks has hit Europe since 2013 with the emergence of new terrorist groups such as Al Nosra, the Islamic State (Daech) and Al Qaeda in the Arabian Peninsula (AQPA), which, although they are fighting in a local context, constitute a breeding ground for potential anti-Western terrorist. The elimination of Osama bin Laden, who has been replaced by Ayman al Zawahiri, and the dismantling of his Afghan base have not eradicated the threat of al-Qaeda, which has been transformed into a nebula of more or less autonomous groups claiming to follow its ideology and label. This new reality is facilitated by the new communication technologies that favor networked organizations resembling franchises. While the first generation of fighters was recruited from among veterans of the Afghan war, the network today recruits mainly young people seduced by the call to jihad. Al Qaeda and Daech are increasingly seeking to recruit European Muslims, mostly of North African origin, and Western converts to Islam (a growing phenomenon) because they attract less attention in Europe, which makes the network less vulnerable. A number of bookstores, mosques and cities in Western Europe are known to be recruitment bases for radical Islamists among these new converts and second-generation Muslims born in these countries. A new danger for Europe is that of the thousands of young jihadists who have left to fight in Syria, where they are indoctrinated and trained in the use of weapons, and who, once they return to their country of origin, are likely to carry out attacks there. This is the case of Mohammed Merah who committed attacks in France in March 2012, the authors of the attack perpetrated in Brussels against a Jewish museum in May 2014, and those perpetrated in January 2015 by French Muslims against a kosher supermarket and the satirical magazine Charlie Hebdo which had caricatured the Prophet. The latter were claimed by the AQPA branch in Yemen. But many of the perpetrators are not former jihadists, such as the one committed in Nice in 1916 by a Moroccan who drove a truck into a crowd, killing some 30 people and injuring dozens. This new type of vehicle attack is committed by lone individuals with no link to Daech or al-Qaeda and is becoming increasingly common. This new wave of attacks is in part linked to the war being waged against Daech by an international coalition of Western and Muslim countries.

Daech is quick to claim responsibility for them, although it is not clear that the organization sponsored them all, let alone organized them. The more states organize themselves to fight this phenomenon together, the more young Muslims and radical Islamist groups are tempted to join the jihad led by the new self-proclaimed caliphate. And it is especially Muslim countries that are the target of its most frequent and deadly attacks.

The threat posed by jihadists to Arab regimes has led to a reversal in Saudi policy. In March 2014, Saudi Arabia labeled the Muslim Brotherhood and jihadist groups as terrorist organizations and issued an ultimatum, ordering its nationals fighting abroad to return home. The Saudi government also issued a list of banned organizations and groups, including al-Qaeda and its branches in Yemen, Iraq and Syria (the al-Nosra Front). It also cites the Muslim Brotherhood, Daech, Hezbollah and the Yemeni Houthi rebels. These decisions constitute a major escalation against the Muslim Brotherhood, as Riyadh is one of the main supporters of the military in Egypt that overthrew it. They reflect the kingdom's growing fears of a return to the country of seasoned Saudis fighting in the ranks of jihadist organizations in Syria. The policy of fighting Islamist extremism was reinforced in 2017 by the new crown prince, Mohammed bin Salman. His stated intention to promote a tolerant Islam would, if realized, constitute a real break from Wahhabi dogma and practices. Arab regimes' fear of Islamist jihadists has also led them to join the military coalition grouped around the United States to fight Daech. And some Arab countries are participating in the aerial bombing campaign targeting the organization's positions. An uncomfortable position that now forces them to fight both a double enemy: the latter and the Syrian regime.

Rise and fall of the self-proclaimed "caliphate".

It was in the early summer of 2014 that a jihadist military-political organization suddenly appeared, calling itself the "Islamic State in Iraq and the Levant" ("Daech" in Arabic). Having conquered parts of Syria and Iraq, it was to change its name to "Islamic State" (IS) to mark its universal ambitions. And on June 29, the leader of this terrorist organization, who took the name Abu Bakr al-Baghdadi, proclaimed the establishment of a caliphate in the territories under its control. Combining the mobilizing power of this old-fashioned notion with the most modern communication techniques, it has succeeded in rallying thousands of jihadists around the world, breaking down centuries-old borders and resisting one of the most formidable military coalitions of all time for three years. The so-called restoration of the caliphate raises the question of its symbolic significance. This is underlined by the choice of the name of Abu Bakr, the first caliph and companion of the Prophet, to whom he thus affirms his filiation, as well as by the messianic and millenarian dimension of the notion of caliphate, which is far from the notion of Islamic state. The suppression of the caliphate in 1920 gave way to numerous debates about the relevance of this concept in the XXe century. It was then that the term Islamic State appeared for the first time. It is a state organized according to the precepts of the Koran and the Sunna.

However, this modern concept does not correspond to any historical reference. Classical Islam does not in principle recognize state borders, which was the case of the ancient caliphate. This universalism, which makes the concept of caliphate theoretically superior, explains why Daech claimed it and why thousands of young jihadists in search of meaning and recognition were ready to die to build what they thought was an ideal society. Reflecting an ambition that exceeds that of all jihadist groups prior to the EI, this organization poses as a rival to Shiite Iran and a unifier of Sunnis. It wants to be recognized as the only power capable of defending their interests. It posed a much more serious threat to the security and stability of the region and the world than al-Qaeda, which never formed a state and had a territorial base and structure. This strength and the power of attraction of its project has enabled it to recruit thousands of fighters from all over the world, and several jihadist movements have pledged allegiance to it. These include Boko Haram, the Egyptian group Ansar Beit el Makdis and the Libyan group that slit the throats of 21 Egyptian Copts. And it has supplanted al-Qaeda at the forefront of the international jihadist movement. That threat led the United Nations to pass a binding resolution calling for measures to fight Daech, which President Obama has called a cancer. The United States, joined by France and several Arab countries, then launched a campaign of aerial bombardments targeting its positions in Iraq and Syria. The participation of the oil monarchies in this campaign is all the more significant as they were among the main financial supporters of Islamism. Because the so-called Islamic State scares everyone. It uses this fear as a psychological weapon. The more its enemies refer to it as a monstrosity, the more it behaves like one. The more his beheadings are viewed and shared on social networks, the more he is encouraged to do it again, as shown by the defiant gesture represented by those of Western citizens and Muslims. It has demonstrated a barbarity surpassing all other jihadist movements. Its conquest of the province and city of Mosul has been accompanied, in the words of its denunciation by the Vatican, by "unspeakable criminal actions: the massacre of people for the sole reason of their religious affiliation. The execrable practice of beheading, crucifixion and hanging of corpses in public places. The forced choice between conversion to Islam, payment of tribute *(jizya)* or exodus. The forced expulsion of children, sick people, pregnant women and old people. The abduction of young girls and women, especially Christians, as spoils of war. The imposition of the barbaric practice of infibulation. The destruction or desecration" of places of worship. The removal of crucifixes and other Christian religious symbols". The destruction of Christian heritage to force them to surrender or flee[11] . These barbaric practices have also been denounced as contrary to authentic Islam by several Muslim religious leaders. And when a Jordanian pilot whose plane was shot down in Syria was burned alive by Daech, outraged by this crime, the Grand Imam of Al-Azhar, the highest Sunni religious body and one of the most influential in the world, strongly condemned this crime which, according to him, "requires the punishment provided in the Koran for these corrupt aggressors who fight against God and his Prophet: death, crucifixion or the amputation of their feet or hands. This is tantamount to curing evil with evil, even as the retrograde nature of the Wahhabi doctrine that inspires Daech is denounced.

Once the conquest is accomplished, the new administration of the proto-state is immediately put in place. It encouraged the population to hunt down and hand over "miscreants" and "apostates". The police and the religious judiciary brutally enforce the strict application of Sharia law. Women's brigades are specifically tasked with ensuring that women comply in every way with the requirements of Islamic propriety. The sexual slavery of Yezidi women, considered polytheistic, is not only permitted but openly promoted by the iE, and strictly codified. The EI anchors its actions in the framework of Islam. It lists the main crimes that are punishable and the respective penalties that are incurred. Blasphemy against Allah: death; blasphemy against the Prophet Muhammad: death, even if the accused repents; blasphemy against Islam: death; adultery: stoning to death if the perpetrators are married, 100 lashes and exile if he or she is single; sodomy (homosexuality): death for the person committing the act as well as for the person receiving it; theft: hands cut off; drinking alcohol: 80 lashes, spying on behalf of the disbelievers: death; apostasy: death; theft in a banditry setting: right hand and left leg cut off. This list is far from exhaustive, but it does at least indicate the type of punishment to which those who dare to contravene the order set by the EI are exposed. In the field of education, the IR stipulates the definitive abolition of several subjects: history, philosophy, social sciences, psychology, music education, art education, sports, archaeology, commerce, tourism. In parallel with the total overhaul of the education system, the EI has opened military camps for minors. To fill them the sheikhs in the mosques urge young people to fight "the infidels and enemies of Allah. At the same time, money, food or clothes are offered to parents to let their children go. The soldiers who fall into the hands of the jihadists are used for their propaganda: beheaded with knives or explosives, drowned, burned alive, skinned, crucified, they will provide the Daech film crews with multiple filmed sequences that will be the subject of professional editing. One of these films shows the beheading of the American Peter Kassig and eighteen Syrian pilots.

A rapid advance on the ground initially allowed the Islamic State to conquer a vast territory straddling Iraq and Syria. But starting in 2016, the combined onslaught of its enemies and the massive military resources mobilized to take it down gradually pushed it back, and it was ousted in late 2017 from the last areas it controlled. Tens of thousands of jihadists were killed in Iraq and Syria during the recapture of Mosul and Raqqa, mainly by coalition bombing. But their elimination and the military defeat of this terrorist organization will not eradicate the terrorist threat it poses to neighboring countries and the West. Daech cells remain in the Levant and Islamist groups claiming to be Daech are still active in North and sub-Saharan Africa. Several political scientists refer to the Thirty Years' War that ravaged Germany from 1618 to 1648 in connection with the probable duration of the wars raging in these regions and the fight led by the "international coalition" against Islamist terrorism. Without denying the effectiveness of this fight and of the anti-terrorist measures, only a treatment that attacks the political roots of the evil could possibly defeat it. This is an extremely difficult task, given the depth of its roots, as evidenced by the multiple avatars of the jihadist hydra that have arisen over the past two decades. The military victory against Daech will not solve the problem of fanaticism and Islamist terrorism. The fight against this scourge is not so much on the battlefield as on the ideological and social level. This is a long term undertaking that begins at school.

Islamization from below

While the political record of Islamism is largely negative, the manifestations of its efforts to Islamize society are spectacular. Although religion has never ceased to be omnipresent, children in families are often more religious than their parents. The questioning of the revolution of the unveiling of women in the XXe century in countries such as Egypt or Turkey is probably the most visible example of this regression. At the socio-political level, whereas previously the trend was towards secularization, a new trend aimed at restoring a sacred foundation to the organization of society has emerged. At the individual level, in response to a quest for meaning and identity, the influence of Islamist preaching is reflected in a surge of religiosity among people who were previously detached from religion, although this often rarely reflects a spiritual and moral quest, and manifests itself in ostentatious expressions of religious belonging. The practice of the dietary prohibitions and the young Ramadan is much more widespread than before and its non-observance leads to a social reprobation that many non-practitioners are reluctant to face. The many NGOs and pious foundations created for this purpose benefit from both official and private funding, from many wealthy Gulf princes and businessmen, as well as from Islamic banks. A video from the 1950s shows the changes in Arab society largely due to the activism of Islamists. Widely circulated on the internet after the election of Mohamed Morsi as president in Egypt, it shows Gamal Abdel Nasser joking about the Muslim Brotherhood's requirement to wear the veil. In this video, the former Egyptian president, hilarious, returns to the discussions he had with the Muslim Brotherhood in 1953. We really wanted to work honestly with the Muslim Brotherhood so that they would move in the right direction," he says, sitting at a podium in front of a large audience. But the negotiations between the two parties soon came up against ideological differences. The raïs explains in the tone of a good joke that a leader of the Muslim Brotherhood asked him to impose "that every woman wears the veil when going out in the street". The public gathered for this speech bursts out laughing. One man even shouted in the room: "Let him wear it himself! Delighted with his effect, Nasser smiles and continues to joke about this episode: "I told him that it was going back to the time when religion ruled and when women were only allowed to go out at nightfall. He even mocks, with a certain pleasure, the contradictions of his political opponent: "I answered him: 'Sir, you have a daughter in the faculty of medicine and she does not wear the veil. Why don't you force her to wear it?

And he added: "If you can't get one girl to wear the veil, and she is your daughter, how can I get 10 million Egyptian women to wear it? [12]

Shiism and politics in the Middle East

Unlike Sunni political Islamism, revolutionary Shi'ism has succeeded not only in forming a coherent institutional model, but in gaining and retaining political power in Iran. The Iranian Islamic Revolution, the emergence of the Lebanese Hezbollah, and the coming to power of the Shiite majority in Iraq highlighted the revival of militant Shi'ism that had begun to emerge in the early 20th century . [ee]"From the second half of the 19th century, the *hawza* (religious school) of Najaf (Iraq) became the seat of the *marja'iyya* (religious authority) which provided Shi'ism with a religious leadership in the person of a great cleric, the *marja'a,* and an institution organizing both the clerical hierarchy and the relations of the believers with the top of this hierarchy. [e]At the beginning of the 20th century, Najaf experienced not only doctrinal but also political effervescence, first with the Iranian constitutionalist movement (1906-1911), championed by the great Persian clerics who resided in the holy city. Then, its ulama played a decisive role in the struggle against the British mandate in Iraq. But the political defeat they suffered weakened them, and some of them were exiled to Iran, where they participated in the re-foundation of the Qom school in the 1920s. Thus began the competition between the two centers of Qom and Najaf, which they still engage in today[13] . The establishment of the Iranian Islamic Republic strengthened Qom at the expense of Najaf and the other Iraqi holy cities which had already been weakened by the repression of the Ba'athist regime of Saddam Hussein. Like Najaf, it is today the center of a transnational clerical network spread throughout the Shiite world.

Unlike Sunni political Islam, which was initially built in opposition to the traditional religious establishment, most of the Shi'a Islamist movements active today were founded by, or include among their cadres, clerics trained in the *hawzas* of Najaf, Qom and, to a lesser extent, Karbala (Iraq). In addition, the political influence of the great Shiite religious leaders was and is far greater than that enjoyed by their Sunni counterparts. In this respect, it is worth mentioning the Ayatollahs Mohamed Baker al-Sadr, assassinated in 1980, and co-founder in 1957 of the first Iraqi Shiite party, Al Da'wa, who played a central role in the politicization of the clergy; Ali Sistani, head of the religious school of Najaf since 1992, who, although representing the quietist current, played a leading political role after the fall of Saddam Hussein; Hassan al-Shirazi, forced into exile from Iraq, founded the Sayida Zaynab school in Syria after having directed the one in Karbala; and finally Mohammed al-Shirazi, whose transnational network contributed to exporting the Iranian revolution, while challenging the status of Ayatollah Khomeini's supreme spiritual guide and, even more so, that of his successor, Ali Khamenei In Lebanon, two prominent Shiite religious figures, Mohamed Mahdi Shams-al-Din and Mohammed Hussein Fadlallah, are from the Najaf school and have been close to Al Da'wa. The latter, although the spiritual guide of Hezbollah, has not, like Shirazi, recognized the religious leadership of Ali Khamenei and the doctrine of *velayet e faquih*. These clerics (*faquih*) are both interpreters of the Law (*mujtahid*) and sources of inspiration for believers (*marja' taklid*). They often come from ancient lines of clerics who, like the Sadrs, are related. This is the case of Mohamed Baker al-Sadr, Mohamed Sadiq al-Sadr, and his son Muqtada al-Sadr, who became a key player on the Iraqi political scene after the fall of Saddam Hussein. As well as Musa al-Sadr who played a key role in the revival of the Lebanese Shiite community. The latter was born in Qom and comes from a prestigious family of clerics from Jabal Amel in southern Lebanon who had settled in Najaf in the 18th century[e] at the time of the persecution of Shiites by the local Ottoman governor. His action was decisive on several levels. "On the one hand, he upset the political balance within the Lebanese Shiite community by denouncing the power of the notables and by creating in 1973 the movement of the disinherited which will become the Amal militia at the time of the outbreak of the civil war in 1975. On the other hand, he strongly contributed to reinforce the status of the Lebanese Shiite community[14] . His disappearance in 1978 during a trip to Libya, probably assassinated by Gaddafi's regime, did not fail to fuel Shiite millenarianism

Al-Da'wa and Iraqi Shiite militias

In Iraq, the ideology of the Iranian revolution spread through the political-religious networks set up by Mohammed al Shirazi and al Da'wa (preaching). At first, al Da'wa gave unambiguous support to the Islamic Republic. But the Iraq-Iran war put it in a difficult position that led to a split within it between clerical and secular cadres. The former perceiving politics through a religious prism. And the latter are increasingly reluctant to the idea of an alignment with Iran. The latter then created a new Islamist organization called "Cadres d'al Da'wa". The front of shiite formations of which it is the main party came to power in 2005 with the support of Ayatollah Ali al-Sistani. In its vision, the policy of the Iraqi government must certainly be in accordance with Islamic law, but must not be subject to the approval of the clergy. The Prime Minister from its ranks, Nouri al-Maliki, distances himself more from Tehran. While the Sadrists (supporters of Muktada al-Sadr), whose militia ("Mahdi Army") had spearheaded the insurrection against the American occupation forces, denounce both the Iranians, Sistani, and the government! They fought not only the Americans, but also the pro-Iranian Badr militia and even tried to take control of Najaf, but were defeated militarily. Politically, the Sadrist factions won more seats in parliament than the other Shiite movements. Later, Sadr made a rapprochement with Tehran. At the same time, the nature of the violence in Iraq gradually changed. Initially directed primarily against coalition forces, it turned into a confrontation between Sunni and Shiite community militias that degenerated into civil war. This has taken on an existential aspect since the lightning victories of Daech and the inability of the regular army to oppose it without the support of Shiite militias. Their intervention can only widen the gap between Shiites and Sunnis. After the fall of Mosul at the hands of Daech, the Shiite militias supported by Iran grouped within the coalition called Hachd al-

Shaabi ("Popular Mobilization Units") will support, with the blessing of Ayatollah Ali Al-Sistani, the reconstituted Iraqi army in the reconquest of the territory that has fallen to the terrorist organization. In 2018, after the defeat of the Islamic State, the Hashd al-Shaabi aspire to play a political role in Iraq.

Hezbollah

Hezbollah is the centerpiece of Khomeini's imperial project, which relies on both anti-imperialist rhetoric and Shiite messianism, an ideology that is even more mobilizing than communism and more effective than Sunni Salafism, to achieve its ends. The emergence of the movement originated in the split in the Amal party between secular and religious leaders after the death of Musa al-Sadr. Challenging the line initiated by its new leader: Nabih Berri, the latter created "Islamic Amal" under the leadership of Hussein Mousawi. Taking in 1982, following the Israeli invasion of Lebanon, the name of Hezbollah (Party of God), this faction will become in a few years the best known and most formidable Shiite Islamo-nationalist group sponsored by Iran abroad. It has never hidden this allegiance, proclaiming loudly its adherence to the doctrine of *velayet e faquih* recognizing the authority of the Supreme Guide of the Islamic Republic of Iran. Transforming itself into a political-military party, it quickly became the main actor of the resistance against the Israeli occupation, even setting as its ultimate goal the destruction of the Jewish state. Both by the mass demonstrations of its supporters and by the methods it uses against its political opponents, it shows clear fascist tendencies. As a symbol of his warlike ideology, the name of Allah is written with an "L" in the form of a vengeful arm brandishing a Kalashnikov on his flag. Supported by both the Syrian regime and the Iranian pasdaran, its objectives, at the time of its formation, were the expulsion of the Western multinational force from Lebanon, and the liberation of the country from Israeli occupation. The end of the Lebanese civil war in 1989 and the total Israeli withdrawal from Lebanon in 2000 prompted it to adapt its strategy and action to the new situation. Driven by its pragmatic leader, Hassan Nasrallah, its integration into the national political system made it one of the main political forces in the country. In parallel to its "resistance against the Zionist enemy", Hezbollah has set itself the mission of defending the interests of the Shiite community and has become the spokesperson for those it describes as "disinherited". Very active in the social field through hospitals, schools and orphanages, it acquires a great popularity. "Whether it is health, education, information, social action, including care for the families of the "martyrs" and the reintegration of wounded fighters, Hezbollah has built over the years a network of institutions allowing not only the Shiite civilian population to bear the human and material cost of the Israeli attacks, but also to broaden the social base of the Islamic resistance[15] . Believing that the communal sharing of power enshrined in the founding national pact of the Lebanese state between the Sunnis and the Maronites had given the Shiites a political weight that no longer corresponded to their demographic weight, it naturally aims, like the other Shiite party, Amal, to correct this imbalance. Or even to impose, as its opponents accuse it, its hegemony over the country. While its charter called for the creation of an Islamic state, it claims to have renounced this claim, which is inapplicable in a multi-faith country like Lebanon. But it does not hesitate to wave the scarecrow of its military arsenal to intimidate its opponents. Exercises constant intellectual terrorism on them. He has often used the street to impose his will on them. And is suspected of having committed most of the terrorist attacks that have targeted their leaders. This is the particular case of the assassination of Prime Minister Rafik Hariri in 2005, which he is suspected of having perpetrated on the instructions of the Syrian regime. Ultimately, the very existence of Hezbollah is incompatible with the building of a state governed by the rule of law, which is supposed to enjoy a monopoly on armed force. Its weapons represent a sword of Damocles hanging over the heads of its political opponents. Its Islamo-fascist warrior ideology is the antithesis of Lebanon's pacifist and liberal vocation. And its strategy serves the hegemonic designs of a foreign power. Hezbollah's involvement in the war in Syria marks a major turning point in the life of the party and of Lebanon. By siding with the Syrian regime in its battle against the opposition, Hezbollah has placed its actions in the broader regional context and subordinated its conduct and objectives to a framework defined by the regional balance of power and the central position of Iran in it. It has become an important player in the conflicts that are ravaging the Middle East. In addition to Syria, this powerful armed movement has sent advisers to Iraq to support the Shiite militias of the Hachd al-Shaabi in their fight against the EI. It is also accused by Sunni Saudi Arabia, a great rival of Shiite Iran, of training the Yemeni Houthi rebels in ballistic fire. It is considered a terrorist organization by the United States and the European Union (regarding only its military wing) and, since its intervention in the Syrian civil war in 2013, by the Gulf Arab monarchies.

Europe and the Islamist challenge

The threat of Islamist terrorism and the influx of Muslim migrants are fuelling the feeling that Europe is now facing one of the greatest challenges in its history: the cultural, demographic and security challenge posed by Islam. Some political leaders even claim that Europe is now in a state of war against radical Islam. We are also witnessing a revival of Islamophobia in the West. After the end of the colonial era, the calls for a "dialogue of civilizations and religions" and the politically correct discourse of the main European political parties, with the exception of the extreme right, the negative view of Islam is now being revived. The atrocities committed in the name of Islam by terrorist organizations, the absence of democracy, the lack of respect for human rights and the inferior status of women, which are common in Muslim countries, give Islam a deplorable image. Essentialist analyses of Islam abound in the media and in political debates. And the Internet is full of messages stigmatizing Muslims. For Raphaël Logier "Islam has become the negative of European identity[16] ". In France, the dechristianization does not prevent most of the French people "of origin" from feeling culturally attacked by the ostentatious manifestations of religious belonging on the part of certain Muslims, such as the wearing of the veil by women. Combined with the perception of a supposed threat to European civilization from Muslim immigration, the link between immigration and delinquency, and the terrorist attacks perpetrated by French jihadists, this feeling explains the rise of Islamophobia. Although the majority of Muslims adhere to the French model of secularism and seek only to integrate, many French people believe that any Muslim, even a moderate one, is unassimilable. Believing that Islam is a warlike religion, they conflate Islam and violence. Playing back on their propensity to scare themselves, Michel Houelbeck describes in his novel "*Submission*" a France governed peacefully and without real opposition by a Muslim party in 2022 (although the Muslims of France have never had the will to create a party or even a Muslim lobby). And in "*Le Suicide Français*[17] ", Eric Zeymour, analyzes the loss of values which, according to him, characterizes France since May 68, and denounces the communitarianism and the corrosive action of Muslim immigration on the model of republican secularism. Feeding the theses of the National Front, this antagonism towards Islam is quite widespread among European countries. For example, Germany is the scene of anti-Muslim demonstrations by extreme right-wing racist groups such as Pegida (Patriotic Europeans against the Islamization of the West), which bring back bad memories and are denounced by the majority of the public. The integration of a growing Muslim population appears to be one of the main challenges that Europe will have to face. Anglo-Saxon communitarianism and French secularism are having just as much difficulty managing it. Although the majority of Muslims seek only to integrate into their adopted country, others are reluctant to adopt their morals and values. The ban on the veil in public institutions (perceived by those concerned as an infringement of their freedom when it is an instrument of submission), cannot stop their propensity to ostensibly claim their identity. More effective are measures aimed at ensuring the emergence of a European Islam, such as the training of imams, the prohibition of the financing of Muslim places of worship by foreign institutions or the fight against Islamist propaganda on social networks. The difficult integration of Europe's Muslims requires dealing with the factors at the root of their feelings of frustration, humiliation and exclusion, especially among young people hard hit by unemployment. And if the fight against Islamist terrorism requires a reinforcement of security measures, the challenge is to find, on the domestic scene, a balance between freedom and security. Finally, the defeat of Daech will not eliminate the ideology that gave rise to this criminal organization, nor the other jihadist movements that have an inexplicable hatred of the West.

Countering radical Islam

The task of countering the rise of radical Islam is first and foremost the responsibility of Muslims themselves, for it threatens not so much the West as the Muslim world, which is doomed to a desert journey of sectarian wars and obscurantism. This rise is due to deep-rooted political and socio-economic as well as religious causes. It cannot be explained solely by the incompatibility between Islam and human rights, and the verses of the Koran preaching violence against "infidels". However, these verses do exist. Even if there were a hierarchy and a supreme religious authority within Islam, it could not abrogate them. As for the Muslim exegetes who try to promote a reading of the Koran compatible with modernity and liberalism, they can only have a limited influence. Should we hope for the emergence of a Muslim Luther who would initiate a rupture, such as the one that Christianity experienced with the birth of Protestantism? This would be to provoke a new intra-Muslim religious war such as the one raging between Sunnis and Shiites. What is needed instead is a progressive and liberal movement such as Baha'i. Emerging from a Shiite background, the Baha'i faith calls for gender equality, the compatibility of science and religion, the relativity of truth (including religious truth) and the absolute oneness of humankind. By making the status of women one of the main axes of its religion, Baha'i has signaled its willingness to break the framework of Islamic fundamentalism. Criticizing all established religions, it asserts that religion should be understood neither as a belief nor as an ideology, but as an authentic relationship between God and man on the one hand, and between all human beings on the other. On a more global level, it is especially important, in order to disprove the prediction of the clash of civilizations, to promote living together around the Mediterranean area, which could be inspired by Lebanon, the ultimate refuge of Mediterranean cosmopolitanism and living together between Europe and the Arab world, Islam and Christianity, Sunnism and Shiism.

1 *Pour une lecture profane des conflits*, Georges Corm La Découverte, 2012, p. 140

2 *The great game, Arab East and international rivalries*. Henri Laurens, Armand Colin, 1991.

3 *Jihad. Expansion and Decline of Islamism,* Gilles Kepel, Gallimard, 2000.

4 Olivier Roy : Interview in the *Nouvel Observateur* of February 20, 2011.

5 *Islam, future of the world*, Hassan Al Tourabi, interviews with Alain Chevaliers, JC Lattès, p.83

6 *Histoire des peuples arabes*, Albert Hourani, Seuil, Point Histoire, 1993, p. 583

7 *Victimes, histoire revisitée du conflit arabo-sioniste*, Benny Morris, éditions Complexe, 2003, p.625

8 *Le Monde des religions*, number 67 of 6 /12/2011.

9 *Considerations on Arab unhappiness*, Samir Kassir, Actes Sud.

10 *The genius of terrorism and political identity*. Jacques Beauchard. L'Harmattan, 2003.

11 *Le Figaro*, August 13, 2014.

12 *Le monothéisme le pouvoir et la guerre*, Ibrahim Tabet, l'Harmattan2015, p. 289

13 *The Shiite worlds and Iran,* edited by Sabrina Mervin, Karthala-Ifpo, p. 14.

14 *Shiism and politics in the Middle East,* Laurence Louer, Perrin, collection Tempus, 2008.

15 *Le Hezbollah, un mouvement islamo-nationaliste*, Walid Chrara, Fréderic Domond,

Fayard, 2004.

16 *Geopolitics of Christianity*, Raphaël Logier, Ellipse 2001

17 *Le suicide français*, Eric Zeymour, Albin Michel 2014.

Chapter 14. The bursting of the powder keg

A clash of civilizations?

The endemic violence on the Arab and Muslim scene has finally spilled over into the United States and European countries. The powder keg in the Middle East, which the West had helped to ignite, exploded in its face in the form of terrorism, whose internationalization was spectacularly marked by the attacks of September 11, 2001. More than any other event, this event contributed to the thesis of the "clash of civilizations". For its author, Samucl Huntington, since the end of the Cold War, the major distinctions between peoples are not ideological, political or economic. They are cultural. According to him, "religion is increasingly intruding into international affairs [...] And in today's world, it is cultural identity that determines above all the associations and antagonisms between countries[1] ". He cites, among other examples, the clear refusal of the European Union to admit Turkey into its fold and the break-up of Yugoslavia (the civil wars in Iraq and Syria had not broken out when he wrote his book). Starting from the observation that of all the elements that define a civilization, the most important in general is religion, Huntington attributes to the religio-cultural factor a determining role in the explanation of the conflicts and civil wars that have broken out since the end of the Cold War, or are called to do so. According to him, the Islamic civilization would be the only one to be in conflict with so many others at the same time: the West, the Slavic-Orthodox world and Hinduism. He admits however that if Islam generates a common identity consciousness, it has on the other hand, since the end of the Ottoman sultanate, no political cohesion. Organized militarily around NATO, the West has only a heterogeneous group of Muslim countries in front of it, among which it has several allies. Turkey is also a member of NATO. The thesis of the clash of civilizations obscures the fact that today the most horrible massacres are taking place within the same "civilization". It is refuted by Georges Corm who, in his book *Pour une lecture profane des conflits, Sur le retour du religieux dans les conflits contemporains du Moyen-Orient (For a profane reading of conflicts, On the return of the religious in contemporary conflicts in the Middle East)*[2] , denounces the simplistic analysis that tends to privilege ethnic-religious or cultural causes in their triggering, whereas these are mainly explained by "profane", geopolitical, economic, demographic or historical issues. In *Un mythe contemporain : le dialogue des civilisations,* Régis Debray also denounces the tendency to "dress up conflicts of geo-economic interests as 'civilizational' confrontations, and to impute to radical religion this or that popular insurrection against a foreign invasion, without asking what can radicalize the Islamic religion and what is the cause of the void for which the omnipresent community withdrawal serves as a substitute[3] ".

While Muslim jihadists had been considered "freedom fighters" who had contributed to the withdrawal of the Soviet army from Afghanistan, with these attacks they dealt the United States one of the most terrible blows in their history, with catastrophic consequences for the Middle East and the world. Al-Qaeda, which had become a global terrorist organization, continued its campaign of anti-Western attacks with the Bali (2002), Madrid (2004) and London (2005) bombings. And it gave birth to the "Islamic State" which in turn gave birth to branches in several Muslim countries such as Al Qaeda in the Islamic Maghreb (AQIM), Al Qaeda in the Arabian Peninsula (AQPA) or Ansar Beit El-Maqdis in Egypt. Taking over from Al Qaeda, the Islamic State will commit a series of attacks in Europe, among the most deadly of which are those in Brussels (March 2016), Nice (July 2016) and London (June 2007). The terrorist threat is provoking new Western military interventions in the Middle East and negatively affecting the Western perception of Islam. The Arab-Muslim world, plagued by the rise of radical Islamism and the exacerbation of religious and identity-based tensions, will be the scene of new civil wars or wars between states in the region. Their oppressive regimes lead to the "Arab Springs" of 2011, which constitute a new major turning point in the history of the Middle East and provoke the overthrow of several dictators who had been in power for decades. The many causes of these popular uprisings: the existence of corrupt dictatorships, socio-demographic changes, economic crisis, unemployment will be discussed in the chapter dedicated to these events.

Although Arab animosity toward the United States predates it, two events were directly responsible for the September 11 attacks: the war in Afghanistan and the presence of American troops in Saudi Arabia during Operation Desert Storm. "U.S. support for the mujahideen helped give the Afghan resistance against the Soviet invasion a more Muslim than national dimension[4] . The repercussions of this intervention were particularly disastrous. It favoured the takeover of power by the Taliban, as well as the appearance of Osama Ben-Laden and the birth of al-Qaeda. This organization and its jihadist emulators have an inexplicable hatred of "crusaders and Jews" and their goal is to bring war to the West. Then came the first Gulf War following Iraq's invasion of Kuwait, which led to a massive American military presence in Saudi Arabia. Bin Laden and his followers considered it the worst kind of sacrilege that armed "infidels" should set foot on the sacred soil of the kingdom where the holy places of Islam are located. It facilitated the recruitment and indoctrination of terrorists ready to sacrifice their lives for their cause. This was the case during the attacks of September 11, 2001, of which, significantly, fifteen of the nineteen perpetrators were Saudis. "These events had an enormous symbolic impact, imposing on Western opinion the image of a struggle between democracy and terrorism, civilization and barbarism, and even between Islam and the Christian West[5] . It is true that Western leaders, led by the American president, have repeated in chorus that Islam has nothing to do with the horrible crimes committed in its name. But Italian Prime Minister Silvio Berlusconi caused consternation when he declared that human rights and fundamental freedoms were the fruit of a Christian tradition that was clearly superior to

Islam, thus breaking with the practice of political correctness and saying out loud what many in the West were probably thinking in silence. These attacks marked a radical turn in American policy, justifying all the liberticidal measures, both internal and international, taken in defiance of the rule of law and international law to confront this global danger. For example, under the *US Patriot Act,* hundreds of suspected terrorists were detained for years without trial at the US base in Guantanamo Bay, Cuba. In response to these attacks, the Bush administration declared a "global war on terrorism" targeting Al Qaeda and the Taliban, defined as part of the "axis of evil. The American president obtained international support for his expedition in Afghanistan. However, the Western intervention in Afghanistan did not succeed in eliminating the Taliban. Leaving the Afghan mission unfinished, the Bush administration shifted its focus from 2002 on to regime change in Iraq, against which it diverted resources from its war on terror. In George Bush's State of the Union address in January 2002, Saddam Hussein's regime was suddenly resurrected as part of the "axis of evil" with Iran and North Korea. This was no longer the war on terror that America's allies had joined in mid-September[6] . The invasion of Iraq in 2003 had even more catastrophic consequences than the first Gulf War for that country, which has been plagued by increasing sectarian violence ever since. And, by destroying Iran's worst enemy, it opened a boulevard for the extension of its regional influence. "Faced with the repeated failures of American actions in the region, the United States administration will develop with its Arab allies the thesis of the existence of a subversive "Shiite" triangle, a successor to the axis of evil dear to George W. Bush, comprising Iran, Syria and Hezbollah, which would sabotage American efforts to reorganize the Middle East .[7]

Ambiguous positions on terrorism

The lack of real pressure on U.S. Muslim allies, particularly Saudi Arabia, to curb their support for the Islamist proselytizing that inspires jihadists raises many questions. Even more serious was the revelation of the perverse effect of U.S. policy in the development of Islamist terrorism by then Secretary of State Hilary Clinton. In a congressional hearing on April 23, 2009, she claimed that the United States, with the help of Pakistani special services, created the Taliban organization and encouraged Saudi Arabia to train the "mujahideen. "We funded the same people we are fighting today," she said. She said that this policy has paid off for the United States, as the war in Afghanistan hastened the fall of the USSR, but that we are now reaping the rewards. "Let's be careful what we sow, because we are reaping the fruits". More recently, an article in the British daily *The Independent*, dated October 14, 2016, based on emails revealed by WikiLeaks, denounces the cynical policy of the White House and its Saudi and Qatari allies who have supported Daech and al-Qaeda type terrorist organizations[8] ." Washington and Riyadh have shown the same cynicism by funding and supporting terrorists fighting the Syrian regime who are considered "moderate Islamists." On the other hand, Hezbollah, which is fighting these terrorists, is considered by them as a terrorist organization. But it is above all the qualification as "terrorist" of the attacks carried out by the Palestinian resistance against the Israeli occupation that raises the question of the definition of this term, showing to what extent it can give rise to opposing points of view and political instrumentalization. There are "good" and "bad" terrorists, "moderate terrorists" and "radical terrorists", freedom fighters or resistance fighters for some and terrorists for others. This difference in treatment also applies to the coverage of terrorist attacks by the Western media. Those that take place in Muslim countries are hardly mentioned, while those that target Western countries are strongly condemned, sometimes even with large mobilization campaigns. One of the most important was the one that followed the attack on the satirical magazine "Charlie Hebdo" in January 2105. Many foreign heads of state and government joined François Hollande at the head of the protest demonstration against this attack and brandished the slogan: "I am

Charlie". Not to mention the fact that terrorism claims far more victims in Muslim countries than in the West.

The Soviet invasion of Afghanistan and the creation of Al Qaeda

The war in Afghanistan, which began in December 1979 with the Soviet invasion, had enormous repercussions not only regionally but also internationally. Washington, which wanted to take revenge for the affront inflicted by the communists in Vietnam and to get Moscow stuck in a long-lasting conflict, did not hesitate to support the Afghan Islamist mujahideen fighting against the Red Army without measuring the consequences of this commitment. National security advisor to President Jimmy Carter, Zbigniew Brzezinski, who conceived the clandestine military operations intended to push the Soviets a little further into the Afghan quagmire, declared in 1998 to the *New Observer*: "What is more important in terms of world history? The Taliban or the fall of the Soviet empire? A few excited Islamists or the liberation of Central Europe and the end of the Cold War[9] ? "Jihadists of all nationalities who go to fight in Afghanistan against Soviet troops are then seen as "freedom fighters" and not at all as a future threat to the freedom of Muslim societies or a potential source of future transnational terrorism[10] ". Saudi Arabia also sees the benefit it can gain from this proxy war. By supporting the Afghan resistance, it becomes the spearhead of a Sunni mobilization against atheistic communism. Egypt also saw an opportunity to break its isolation in the Arab world by embracing this "Islamic" cause. American, Saudi and Egyptian secret services and advisors financed and armed Afghan fighters on a massive scale from Pakistan. With the agreement and support of the head of the Saudi secret service, Prince Turki bin Faysal, Osama bin Laden worked to recruit an army of Arab volunteers in Afghanistan, which had become the new "land of jihad. In 1984, he and the Palestinian dissident of the Muslim Brotherhood, Abdallah Azzam, set up a real organization in Peshawar, in western Pakistan, via a "Service Bureau", which provided military and ideological training for fighters as well as arms supplies.

After the withdrawal of the Soviet army, Bin Laden returned in 1989 to Saudi Arabia where he was considered a hero. He organized conferences in mosques, schools and universities on his "jihad" against the Soviets. In 1991, shortly after the invasion of Kuwait by Saddam Hussein's army, Bin Laden had a stormy meeting with the Saudi Minister of Defense, Prince Soltan, who refused his proposal to use his "veterans" from Afghanistan to defend the kingdom. At odds with the Saudi regime's decision to use "infidel" troops, Bin Laden became increasingly critical of the royal family. He was deported to Pakistan in May 1991 and stripped of his nationality in 1994. He finally settled in Sudan where a military junta with Islamist pretensions welcomed the outcasts of international terrorism. When Azzam was assassinated, he patiently wove the web of his own secret organization, called "the Base", in Arabic, Al-Qaeda, from Khartoum from December 1991 to May 1996. He finances the most radical Islamist mujahideen who have returned to their country of origin after the war in Afghanistan (they are nicknamed "the Afghans" there). He was joined by the Egyptian jihadist Ayman Zawahiri, who theorized the distinction between the "distant enemy" - the United States - and the "near enemy" - the falsely Muslim regimes - priority targets of al-Qaeda[11] . The overthrow of the Saud became an obsession for Bin Laden. His representative in Great Britain, Khaled Fawaz, ensures the dissemination of al-Qaeda's theses from the heart of "Londonistan". In February 1993, an attack attributed to Al-Qaeda at the World Trade Center in New York killed six people and injured hundreds. And Zawahiri attempted to assassinate Mubarak during an African summit in Ethiopia in June 1995. But his attempt was foiled by the head of Egyptian intelligence. The Sudanese regime, which had already delivered the terrorist Carlos to France, offered the United States to hand over Bin Laden. But the CIA underestimated the extent of al-Qaeda's international network and the Clinton administration feared that the detention of a terrorist would lead to other attacks to obtain his release. Thus, Bin Laden left Sudan freely and returned to eastern Afghanistan, from where he proclaimed, in August 1996, a jihad against the United States, accused of occupying the sacred land of Arabia.

The attacks of September 11, 2001

By the time bin Laden returned to Pakistan in 1996, the Pakistani secret service (ISI) was busy supporting the armed advance of the Taliban in Afghanistan. This Islamist militia - whose name means "students" (in theology) - defeated one by one the warlords who had divided the country after the withdrawal of the Soviet army. The establishment of their power was accompanied by the imposition of a medieval moral order. Their leader, Mullah Omar, took Bin Laden under his protection, because he found in him an unexpected Arab support for his project. However, the relationship between the two men was reversed, and Bin Laden acquired a growing hold on Mullah Omar. He also received discreet support from the ISI, despite the denials of the Pakistani government. In August 1998, al-Qaeda carried out two simultaneous suicide attacks on the U.S. embassies in Kenya and Tanzania, killing 224 people, including 12 Americans. The Clinton administration retaliated with cruise missile strikes on suspected al Qaeda hideouts in Afghanistan. Bin Laden emerged unscathed from this onslaught of American technology, which increased his prestige. As for Mullah Omar, he denounced the U.S. aggression and claimed to be hosting al-Qaeda. After the FBI's decision to put a $5 million price on Bin Laden's head in June 1999, Al Jazeera broadcast a report entitled "One man against an empire. "Stateless jihadism, adorned with the title of "public enemy number one" acquires a global icon status[12-] . Jihadists of all nationalities flock to al-Qaeda training camps in eastern and southern Afghanistan with their superficial memorization of the Koran as their main intellectual baggage. In October 2000, a boat bombing nearly destroyed the American destroyer Cole in the port of Aden.

Bin Laden and Zawahiri then decided to strike the American territory in order to trigger an intervention by the "distant enemy" in retaliation, which would destabilize the "near enemy" in the Middle East. These were the attacks of September 11, 2001. On the morning of Tuesday, nineteen Arab terrorists hijacked four planes from American domestic routes. Two planes hit the twin towers of the World Trade Center in New York and a third the Pentagon in Washington DC, killing everyone on board and many others working in those buildings. Both towers collapse less than two hours later. A fourth plane crashed in Pennsylvania before reaching its target (possibly the Capitol or the White House) after passengers and crew tried to regain control. The bombing killed 2977 people and gave rise to multiple conspiracy theories. Khalid Cheilh Mohammed was later arrested and identified as the main organizer of the attacks. He admitted the facts during the preliminary interrogations for his trial. The television footage of the planes hitting the World Trade Center towers and their collapse caused shock throughout the world. Bin Laden did not claim responsibility for the attack, in order to present the American response as an aggression. On the other hand, foreseeing the inevitable response of the United States, he recorded a speech for Al Jazeera to be broadcast at the beginning of the American strikes on Afghanistan. He posed as a resister against American imperialism and "Israeli oppression in Palestine" which he had never cared about. This is another form of the great detour of the Arab struggles, but it can only work if the United States gives credence to this fable. And the manipulation will succeed beyond Bin Laden's wildest expectations.

The American military intervention in Afghanistan

In response to the attack on the United States, the first on its territory, the neoconservative government of George W. Bush launched a "global war on terror" in the fall of 2001. This terror is, of course, Islamic, although it is not named as such. He then assigned as goals to the war the "defense of freedom and democracy" and their imposition in the Middle East, which gave it an ideological and moral scope beyond its retaliatory character. The American public, shocked by this aggression that has left nearly 3000 dead, naively wonders about the motives that have earned so much hatred in the United States.

For their part, "the Arab dictators quickly grasped the interest they had in joining the 'global war' against terrorism by eliminating their own most dangerous jihadists and offering the Americans the services of their police forces to track down the terrorists[11] . Khadafi recalls that his country issued an international arrest warrant for Bin Laden as early as 1998. Mubarak offers to subcontract, including on Egyptian territory, the "interrogations" (in fact the torture sessions) of jihadist suspects rounded up by the United States throughout the world. George W. Bush found an unconditional ally in the person of the British Prime Minister, Tony Blair, who committed British troops alongside the American army in Afghanistan and Iraq.

The "crusade" against "the enemies of America and freedom" began with an armed intervention against Afghanistan in December 2001, with the military contribution of other Western nations, especially the United Kingdom, as well as the Northern Alliance (an Afghan armed group fighting against the Taliban, whose emblematic figure was Commander Massoud before his assassination). The goal of the operation, according to the United States and its allies, was to capture Osama bin Laden, destroy the bases of al-Qaeda and overthrow the Taliban, under the guise of finding Osama bin Laden. Another objective was to create a government in Afghanistan that could serve as an example for other Islamic countries. Crushed by bombs, the Taliban had to evacuate Kabul and the major cities and retreat to their mountainous retreats. The Americans did not want to risk committing ground troops to track down and eliminate Bin Laden and Zawahiri, so they managed to flee to Pakistan. A pro-Western government presided over by Hamid Karzai was set up in Kabul, despite the majority leaning towards the restoration of the monarchy around Zaher Shah. Convinced that the Taliban were finished, Washington turned its attention to Iraq in 2002. But the Afghan government of Hamid Karzai, which had little legitimacy, was powerless to counter the Taliban's return in force and, in 2006, it only controlled the Kabul sector. A massive intervention of international troops under NATO command in Afghanistan was met with increasingly effective guerrilla warfare by the Taliban. And in 2009, the Taliban are active in an estimated 70 percent of the country, despite the presence of some 113,000 foreign troops, including 71,000 American troops in the country. These figures do not include the troops of private military companies, such as Blackwater. Armed groups are also operating from the tribal regions of northwestern Pakistan.

The invasion of Iraq

In order to justify the Bush administration's military action plans, American propaganda is unleashed against Saddam Hussein, denounced as a criminal dictator. Washington accuses him of sponsoring terrorism by giving refuge to Abu Musab Zarqawi, a Jordanian jihadist who has taken refuge in northern Iraq. President Bush claims that his intelligence services know that Iraq is developing weapons of mass destruction that threaten the West. The Secretary of State, Colin Powell, went so far as to brandish before the United Nations Security Council pictures showing rocket launch pads that turned out to be fakes. Despite the weakness of the official pretexts, the impossibility of finding weapons of mass destruction, and the fact that Iraq accepted UN experts to carry out controls on its soil, the United States was determined to invade the country. Turkey rejects the American request to use its territory to invade Iraq. The European Union is deeply divided on the issue. Britain, Italy, Spain and Poland agreed to join the military coalition that the United States was putting together. Germany and France are categorically opposed. "Jacques Chirac had some scathing words for the leaders of the Eastern European countries who supported the American plans, and his foreign minister, Dominique de Villepin, announced that France would veto any American resolution on military intervention in Iraq at the UN Security Council[13] . Washington decided to bypass the UN framework by availing itself of a doctrine of pre-emption: the possibility for the United States to declare war on any adversary, alone or with allies of its choice, without referring to the UN.

The United States set an ultimatum for Baghdad on 19 March, which they knew would be impossible to achieve. On March 20, 2003, war was formally declared by Washington and the bombing began immediately, as did the offensive against Iraqi territory by American and British ground troops from Kuwait. The Anglo-Saxon media spoke of "surgical strikes", supposed to destroy strategic military targets, but civilians were dying every day. The Iraqi army, exhausted by twelve years of sanctions and war of attrition, is rapidly collapsing. The United States is claiming victory. On 1[er] May 2003, President George W. Bush triumphantly declared the end of the fighting on board an American aircraft carrier under the banner "Mission accomplished".

As soon as Baghdad was taken, the American army hunted down senior Baathist officials. The American administrator in Iraq, Paul Bremer, decided to disband the Iraqi army. The soldiers who could have served the "new Iraq" were sent back to their homes. The Iraqi administration was purged of its Baathist officials. This meant in practice the dismantling of the Iraqi state, since membership of the Ba'ath was necessary to be part of it. A puppet government was set up. The ignorance of the local context, the inability of the American occupation forces, ill-prepared for this task, to manage the situation created by the collapse of the Iraqi regime, and the numerous errors of the provisional administration they had set up, plunged the country into chaos. The looting is massive and does not spare the museum of Baghdad. The cultural disaster is immense. The Americans proved incapable of getting the country back on track quickly. The clerics regained their influence over a large part of the Shiite population. They are divided between radicals, such as Moqtada Sadr, and moderates such as Ayatollahs Ali Sistani and Mohamed Baker el-Hakim. All of them welcome the fall of the regime, but demand the rapid departure of the occupying forces. They expect a devolution of power to them, since Shiites represent 60% of the population. The officers loyal to Saddam Hussein, who have distributed arms caches throughout the country, are already secretly preparing the resistance. On August 19, 2003, a truck bomb destroyed the UN headquarters in Baghdad. This attack, attributed to al-Qaeda, marked the beginning of a cycle of continued violence in the country. Saddam Hussein was captured on December 13, 2003, after a nine-month long hunt. He is weakened, shaggy, dirty. He has nothing left to do with the imperious head of state he was in his heyday. His trial, marred by irregularities before an Iraqi court, lasted two years, at the end of which he was sentenced to death for crimes against humanity. "The trial and then the swift execution of the Iraqi dictator had a whiff of revenge about it. His request to be shot - "for honor" - was refused. He was hanged like a common prisoner in the Kazimiya district, named after Moussa el-Kazim, the seventh Shiite imam .[14]

The Americans did not discover any "weapons of mass destruction". Guerrilla warfare and attacks were to hit their troops constantly, who were seen more as occupying troops than as liberating forces. The insurgency, which at first was exclusively Sunni, was suppressed by collective punishment and imprisonment. The vast majority of the detainees were Sunni Arabs. In order to minimize the national character of the insurrection, American propaganda exaggerated the role of the Jordanian Zarqawi, which attracted fighters from all sides, including former Iraqi officers. In response to this rise in power, Bin Laden appointed Zarqawi as head of the Iraqi branch of al-Qaeda. "Zarqawi describes the US intervention in the heart of the Middle East as "divine grace"[15] . From then on, the anti-American jihad in Iraq attracted recruits from all over the world. Bashar al-Assad, anxious to bog down the United States in Iraq, favored the transit of volunteers through Syria.

The invasion of Iraq, whose official justifications have rarely seemed so implausible, has aroused much resistance. In Europe, the United States and elsewhere, many anti-war demonstrations took place. Many young people became politicized on this occasion, discovering in a raw way what an imperialist war means. The fallacy of the arguments used by the George W. Bush administration to justify the invasion of Iraq: the so-called presence of weapons of mass destruction, the fight against Islamist terrorism and the establishment of democracy in the Middle East, is no longer in doubt. Moreover, other elements raise doubts about the motives of the intervention, such as the links between the neoconservatives (including Vice President Dick Cheney and Under Secretary of Defense Paul Wolfowitz), the Israeli right wing and oil companies and the army. Journalist Ari Shavit wrote in the Israeli newspaper *Haaretz* on April 3, 2003, "The Iraq war was engineered by twenty-five neoconservatives, most of them Jewish, who are urging President Bush to change the course of history[16] ." The pretext of establishing democracy, moreover, was only invoked after no "weapons of mass destruction" had been discovered. Thus, to justify their "global war on terror", the American neoconservatives placed it within a general framework of reforms of the Arab regimes called the "New Middle East". It is clear that in reality their aim was to consolidate, through military control of the Middle East and its hydrocarbons, the supremacy of the United States over its Russian, Chinese, Japanese and

European rivals, and to strengthen the position of Israel. But by crushing Iraq, the Bush administration has created a power vacuum into which Iran, a far greater threat to Israel and American interests, has stepped. And while the pretext for its aggression against Iraq was to continue its "war on terror" there, which began in Afghanistan, where it was really at home, it has instead created an upsurge in terrorism and an unprecedented wave of anti-American sentiment in the region and around the world.

The breakup of Iraq

The American failure had far more catastrophic consequences for Iraq. Dictatorial but secular, Saddam Hussein's regime at least maintained the unity of the country and, after the first Gulf War and the "international" embargo, was no longer a threat to its neighbors, let alone to the United States. After the Shiites, it was the turn of the Sunnis to be marginalized. First by the Americans who, by deciding to dismantle the Iraqi army and hunt down the cadres of the deposed Baathist regime, provoked their revolt and sowed the seeds of an ethnic and religious conflict. Then by the Shiite-dominated government. While the Kurds took advantage of this to conquer their autonomy. Thus the fall of Saddam Hussein's dictatorship did not put an end to the violence, far from it. And the American project to establish democracy by force in the country is a clear failure. The inability of the occupation troops to assume the task of pacification, their ignorance of the local culture and their racist behaviour, illustrated by the scandal of the abuses committed by their soldiers in the Abu Ghreib prison, have alienated the population.

At first, the American soldiers were the main target of a Sunni guerrilla war led mainly by Baathists and Islamists, the majority of whom joined the local branch of al-Qaeda. While the Sunni areas were plunged into daily horror, the Shiite areas in the south were rather calm. On the one hand, because the British troops were able to manage the post-war period better, but above all because the Shiites, who had been subjected to ruthless repression by Saddam Hussein's regime, saw in his fall an opportunity to finally gain power and considered the occupying troops as objective allies. Several Shiite militias were nevertheless formed, the main one being the Mahdi Army of the young radical sheikh Moktada el-Sadr. It controls the vast Shiite suburbs of Baghdad and is firmly established in the Shiite holy cities. But its revolt, stirred up by Iran, was crushed by American troops in the summer of 2004, with the tacit support of Ayatollah Ali Sistani. Representing the voice of moderation, the latter is the supreme authority of Iraqi Shiites and comes from the school of the holy city of Najaf, which has never accepted the thesis of the vilayet e-faqih embraced by Khomeini. By securing the evacuation of Najaf by Moktada Sadr's militia and its transformation into a political movement, he has imposed his authority on both the provisional government and the shia militant factions.

As the majority Shiite community asserted its desire to dominate the institutions of the new "free and democratic" Iraq that the Americans wanted, attacks on the occupying troops were relegated to the background, while intercommunal unrest and its attendant killings and bloody reprisals, mostly targeting civilians of both communities, intensified. The Sunnis, who had always dominated Iraq, found their new situation very hard to bear. First there was the establishment in 2003 of an Interim Governing Council whose composition reflected the new sectarian and identity-based balances to the detriment of the sense of national belonging. Then, the January 2005 elections, which saw the victory of the Kurdish-Shiite alliance, followed by the adoption in October 2005 of a new constitution of a communitarian nature, completed the alienation of the Sunni community. This feeling of alienation is all the greater because government commando units do not hesitate to carry out reprisals against sunnis themselves. Finally, the Sunnis fear that the federal nature of the new institutions will deprive them of the financial benefits of Iraq's oil resources. Indeed, their community is mainly concentrated in the center of the country, where there is no oil, while the Shiite-majority south and the north, where the Kurds have formed a largely autonomous province, are full of oil. The new institutions were supposed to ensure equitable representation of ethnic and religious communities. Thus, in a Lebanese-style formula, the new Iraqi government is formed on the basis of strict confessional and ethnic representation. It is composed of thirteen Shiite, five Sunni, five Kurdish, one Christian and one Turkoman minister. The presidency of the Republic is given to a Kurd, that of the Parliament to a Sunni, and that of the Council of Ministers to a Shiite. But it is as if the Iraqis were unable to find an acceptable power-sharing compromise. The brutal dictatorship and Sunni domination of the Baathist regime has been replaced by a Shiite domination that is probably less brutal, but just as unbearable. The sectarian and exclusionary policies of Prime Minister Nouri al-Maliki, an ally of Iran, have fuelled tensions between Arabs and Kurds, and between Shia and Sunni.

The emergence of the Islamic State in Iraq and the Levant

Within the sunni community, frustration at being marginalized provided fertile ground for terrorists affiliated with al-Qaeda to carry out attacks against shiites. In February 2006, an attack was carried out against the Shiite mosque in Samara, a major pilgrimage site that has been venerated for 1,200 years and which houses the tombs of the tenth and eleventh Imams. Despite calls for calm from religious leaders of both communities, it was followed by retaliation against Sunni mosques that triggered a civil war between Sunnis and Shiites that killed tens of thousands. After the death of Zarqawi in June 2006, the local branch of al-Qaeda became the Islamic State in Iraq and the Levant (ISIL). This was supported by the Nakhsibendye brotherhood and was joined by several former Iraqi army officers who brought their military expertise. In 2008, Shiite militias took control of Baghdad and drove most of the Sunni population out of the capital. The Kurdish north formed a de facto quasi-independent state largely spared from violence and enjoying a certain prosperity thanks to the oil windfall. As for the situation of the Christian community, whose numbers are dwindling like a stone, it has become dramatic. The latter are collateral victims of the conflict.

In 2008, the new American president, Barak Obama, decided to withdraw American troops from Iraq. From 2009 onwards, the United States gradually disengaged by financing the Sunni Shahwa militias in order to confront the Islamic State. The Shiite militias gradually came to power and a relative lull settled over the country temporarily. The withdrawal of American troops was completed in December 2011. After their withdrawal, violence between Sunnis and Shiites continued throughout the country. And the Kurds, who have formed an autonomous Kurdistan Regional Government, are increasingly at odds with the central Iraqi government.

The fate of Christians in Iraq and the East

The tragic fate of the Christians of Iraq is reminiscent of that of the Christians of the East, which, from Egypt to Iraq, passing through Palestine and Syria, has worsened considerably since the mid-1970s. While the demographic and political weight of the Christians in Lebanon is clearly declining. If the civil wars that broke out in Lebanon, Iraq and Syria are the main cause, they are not the only one. Faced with insurmountable economic difficulties and the insecurity caused by these conflicts and the absence of peace at the regional level, many Christians have chosen to leave the country and their numbers are dwindling. Moreover, with the exception of the Lebanese case, they are faced with the prospect of a political project carried by the Islamists which would no longer leave them any space or specific role. Some fear that, in the long term, if this phenomenon is not contained, Christians will be reduced to such a small portion that they will count for nothing in the region where Christianity was born. The Arab world would become for the first time in its history almost exclusively Muslim, something that many Muslims themselves fear. Unfortunately, Western governments are not very concerned about the fate of the Christians of the East. Somewhat out of a guilty conscience and fear of being blamed for their colonial past. In any case, any intervention by the West to protect them against the threats of discrimination that weigh on them, assuming that it has the intention to do so, would be counterproductive. Only Vatican diplomacy and the Russian Orthodox Church are trying to use their influence in this direction.

In Lebanon, it was estimated that in 1975 the proportion of Christians was 50%. In 1990, as a result of the war, this proportion had fallen to 36.5%. Although the Christians of Lebanon continue to be the only ones in the region to play a political role, even if it is a diminished one, in the longer term their inexorable demographic decline risks minimizing this role, if not causing them to suffer the same fate of second-class citizens as their co-religionists in the Arab-Muslim world. This trend can only accelerate since their massive exodus from Iraq, the aggressions they are subjected to in Egypt and the civil war in Syria. In Syria, there were about 1.9 million Christians, or about 10% of the population before the civil war, half of them in Damascus and Aleppo. Since the beginning of the conflict, the Christian community, considered a supporter of Bashar al-Assad's power, has felt threatened by the rebellion. Although they have stayed away from the clashes, they are seen as allies of Assad. In Palestine, as long as the Palestinians' ideal was the creation of a secular state, Christians were fully committed to the Palestinian cause. But since the Islamist movement has gained momentum, the attitude of Muslims has become increasingly fundamentalist and sectarian in their demands. The Christians of the Holy Land, of the occupied territories, feel trapped, refused by both the Muslims and the Israelis. In addition to this, there are economic reasons. 60% of Palestinians live below the poverty line.

The most tragic fate is that of the Christians in Iraq. The two American interventions in Iraq have been fatal for them. While there were about a million Christians in 1980, the majority of whom were Chaldeans, there are now only about 300,000. Since the fall of Saddam Hussein's regime, Christians have been particularly targeted by certain armed extremist groups and have been the victims of various forms of violence: kidnapping and demands for exorbitant ransoms, assassination of priests and nuns, obligation for women to wear the veil, Christians forced to convert or to go into exile under threat of death, terrorist attacks against churches, etc. Those Christians who have not fled abroad have migrated for the most part to the north of the country to the autonomous region of Kurdistan, where they enjoy the protection of the Kurdish authorities. Since the establishment, in the summer of 2014, of an Islamic State over part of Iraq, their situation has taken a catastrophic turn. Driven out of their historical cradles of Mosul and then Karakoch, they risk disappearing forever from the history of a country with which they have been inseparable for nearly twenty centuries. This would be an immeasurable loss for Iraq, for the Middle East, for Christianity and for humanity. Their fate has troubled Western public opinion. However, although commendable, the statements made by the French government in particular are problematic. Paris quickly declared itself ready to welcome on its territory Christian refugees from Iraq who would request it. This decision, motivated by confessional solidarity, contributed to the idea that the existence of a Christian population in Iraq constituted an anomaly and that the place of these populations was not in their country of origin but in Europe or in the West, among their own people.

After the Christians in Iraq, the Islamic State did the same to the Assyrian Christians in Syria who were expelled from their villages in the north of the country. But the height of horror was the horrific scene broadcast on the web in March 2015 by the terrorists of the Libyan branch of the Islamic State where they filmed themselves slitting the throats of 21 Egyptian Copts raised an immense indignation throughout the world. Christians can only worry about the fate of their co-religionists. This concern is fuelled by the awareness of the rise of a radical Sunni fundamentalism considered more dangerous and much more intolerant than Shiite fundamentalism, and the presumed powerlessness of the moderate Sunni majority to counter it. Faced with this rise in Sunni Islamism and its refusal to accept pluralism, they are swayed between the temptation to emigrate and to turn inward. This trend was recently demonstrated in Lebanon by the rallying of part of Christian opinion behind a draft electoral law providing for the election by each religious community of its own deputies. Although it was not adopted, it would have reinforced political confessionalism, making the establishment of a secular citizenry in Lebanon more illusory than ever. Nevertheless, it reflects the view that a political system that allows for strict representation of the different communities is better suited to multi-ethnic or multi-confessional states than political systems based on a democracy of numbers. Moreover, the misfortunes of Iraq and Syria seem to demonstrate that in the East, the formal secularity of political institutions is not synonymous with democracy and does not prevent sectarian seizure of power. And it is not impossible that, in the hypothetical case that a political solution should emerge in Syria, it would be inspired either by the Lebanese model of a de facto federation of communities on a non-territorial basis, or by a confederal model. These are probably the only solutions capable of avoiding its dismemberment, bloody reprisals or ethnic cleansing.

The repercussions of September 11 in Saudi Arabia

The expulsion of al-Qaeda from its Afghan hideout and the elimination of three-quarters of its leaders did not prevent it from continuing its operations. Bin Laden decided to strike Saudi Arabia. A first terrorist attack, on May 12, 2003, killed 35 people, including 9 Americans, and a second one, on November 9, killed 18. After 13 years of presence, the U.S. Army decided to withdraw from the PrinceSoltan base that it kept on Saudi soil. The Saudi government hoped that its departure would invalidate bin Laden's major argument against the regime, namely that infidel soldiers were defiling the land of the two holy mosques. But this did not diminish the anti-Americanism of the majority of Saudis. For their part, the Saudis were enraged at the "friendly" country that had produced 15 of the 19 suicide bombers of September 11. The old criticisms of the West about the deplorable human rights situation in the kingdom resurfaced. On the domestic scene, radical preachers propagated a rhetoric similar to that of bin Laden. After September 11, Crown Prince Abdullah deemed reforms necessary to improve the kingdom's external image, which included removing intolerant passages from school textbooks and modernizing the curriculum. In contrast, Prince Nayef, Minister of the Interior, was banking on the Saud's traditional alliance with wahhabi fundamentalists. The Al Qaeda attacks of May 2003 had the effect of both temporarily interrupting the reforms initiated by Prince Abdullah and Prince Nayef's complacency towards radical Islamists. Al Qaeda cells in the country were hunted down relentlessly.

1 *The Clash of Civilizations,* Samuel Huntington, ed, Odile Jacob, 1997, p. 135

2 *Pour une lecture profane des conflits, Sur le retour du religieux dans les conflits contemporains du Moyen-Orient,* Georges Corm, La Découverte, 2012

3 *A contemporary myth: the dialogue of civilizations.* Régis Debray, CNRS Éditions, p.6 .

4 *Pour une lecture profane des conflits*, op. cit. p. 68

5 ibid.

6 *Osama*, Jonhatan Randal. Albin Michel, 2004, p. 43.

7 *The New Question of the East,* Georges Corm, La Découverte 2017 p. 169

8 *Le Nouvel Observateur*, 15-21 January 1998. Interview quoted in *Oussama*, op. ct. p.95r

9 *The new question of the East,* op. cit. p. 79

10 *Les Arabes, leur destin et le nôtre, histoire d'une libération*, Jean-Pierre Filiu, La Découverte 2015, p.186

11 ibid. p.190

12 ibid. p.192

13 *France in Lebanon and the Near East*, Ibrahim Tabet, Ed. de la Revue phénicienne, 2011, p. 271

14 *These fifteen men who changed the face of the Middle East, Saddam and Gomorrah*, Samia Medawar, L'Orient-le Jour, special issue of November 2, 2017

15 *The Arabs, their fate and ours,* op.cit

16 https://www.haaretz.eom/1.4764706 *White man's burden,* Haaretz, April 3, 2003

Chapter 15. From the Arab Spring to 2018

The failure of the Arab Spring

Starting in December 2010, a wave of popular protests successively swept through six Arab countries: Tunisia, Libya, Egypt, Syria, Yemen and Bahrain. Never before had the region as a whole experienced such a popular groundswell. Contrary to the military pronunciamientos customary in the region, it reflects deep demographic, socio-economic and cultural changes, amplified by the new means of communication, including social networks. One speaks then, with a premature optimism, of "Arab Spring", in reference to the "spring of the people" of 1848 in Europe (which was crushed by reactionary forces). Indeed, these revolutions do not lead, except in Tunisia, to democratic regimes and are either repressed in blood as in Syria, or are the object of counter-revolutions as in Egypt. And in the phase of violence that follows the revolts, foreign interventions in the internal affairs of Syria, Libya and Yemen will only sow bloody chaos in these countries and provoke their implosion[1] .

The libertarian movement began with the revolution in Tunisia. On December 17, 2010, a street vendor, Mohammed Bouazizi, whose cart had just been seized by the police, killed himself out of desperation in front of the prefecture of Sidi Bouzid in the south of the country. This gesture will upset the Arab crowds that rise against the regimes in place and chant everywhere the same slogans: "the people want the fall of the regime" and to the address of the dictators: "get out! Political, economic and social demands fuel the revolts. As everywhere in the world, these are more caused by inequality and injustice than by poverty. On January 14, 2011, President Zine el-Abidine Ben Ali, whom the army refused to support, was forced to leave power and flee to Saudi Arabia. Arab satellite channels and social networks helped spread the protest movement throughout the Arab world. By a domino effect, other peoples in turn took up the same slogans. In Egypt, the revolution led to the departure of Hosni Mubarak. In Libya, the insurrection provoked violent fighting between forces loyal to the Gaddafi regime and the insurgents. Supported by a NATO military intervention, the insurgents eventually won and Gaddafi was assassinated. In Yemen, the dictator Ali Abdallah Saleh, who was suppressing the revolt, was eventually forced to resign. While in Tunisia, Libya and Egypt it was only a matter of bringing down a man, the case of Syria is different in that, beyond the person of Bashar al-Assad, the Alawite community and other minorities felt threatened by the uprising against his regime. Apart from the fact that he has no desire to suffer the fate of Ben Ali, Mubarak and even less Gaddafi, this factor explains why he remains in power despite the forces arrayed against him. Because of its sectarian character, the Syrian uprising soon turned into a bloody civil war. Unlike the Egyptian and Tunisian cases, where the clashes involved only insurgents and regime forces, the Syrian conflict saw the military intervention of several foreign powers, giving it a regional and international dimension. This specificity has led some analysts to draw a parallel between the Syrian conflict and the Thirty Years' War that ravaged Germany in the early 17th century. As in Syria, it began with a local politico-religious confrontation, in this case between Protestants and Catholics. And, just as in Syria the Sunni countries intervened alongside their co-religionists, the Thirty Years' War involved the intervention of several foreign states: Spain alongside the Habsburgs of Austria, the armed wing of the Catholic Counter-Reformation, Lutheran Denmark and Sweden alongside the German Protestant princes, supported also, for considerations of realpolitik, by Catholic France[2] . No one can predict whether the war in Syria, which is entering its eighth year, will last much longer, but the antagonism between Sunnis and Alawites, which is not new, and the foreign interventions can only prolong it.

In Bahrain, Saudi Arabia and the United Arab Emirates helped the sunni monarchy to suppress a shia uprising. For his part, King Abdullah of Arabia announced a $93 billion social program to buy social peace and nip in the bud any hint of an uprising. Like other Western countries, France was caught off guard by the sudden outbreak of the "Jasmine Revolution" in Tunisia in February 2011. Not measuring the extent of the popular protest, it seemed at first to lean towards the established order. Certainly, it had even closer relations with the Ben Ali regime than the other Western countries. But they are not enough to explain its reluctance towards a popular uprising against an old dictator who has been in power for more than thirty years. Alain Juppé's gesture of meeting with the students in Cairo was a first step towards a shift in French foreign policy in favor of the rights of the Arab peoples, breaking with a Western tradition of complacency towards authoritarian regimes[3] .

"The process initiated in 2011 came up against two poles: the regimes in place and the Islamist movement (Muslim Brotherhood, Salafists). These fundamentalist groups were able to prosper in relation to the other progressive and nationalist forces, which were caught in a vice and gradually phagocytosed due to the lack of support shown to them. Consequently, the counter-revolution took the form of a violent opposition between these two dominant poles, dictatorial regimes and fundamentalist groups[3-] . The dominant feature of this revolutionary wave is the Islamist turn it soon took. Absent at the time of its outbreak, the Islamists did not take long to confiscate for their own benefit the revolutions initiated by the liberals. They are the only ones to have an organization, ideas, leaders and a social base, unlike the secular and left-wing parties. Moreover, they have the active support of Turkey, Qatar and Saudi Arabia. While all three have a sunni Islamist project for the Middle East, each has its respective clienteles: the Muslim Brotherhood for Ankara and Doha, the Salafists for Riyadh. The Erdogan government has especially targeted the Syrian regime. It is from Turkey that the bulk of the reinforcements and weapons intended for the Islamist militias determined to overthrow it have left. Qatar's financial support contributed to the rise to power of the Muslim Brotherhood in Tunisia and Egypt.

Originally, from Tunis to Damascus to Cairo, the crowds took to the streets, not in the name of sharia or Islam, but for freedom, dignity and social justice, and against the corruption of the regimes in place. This is not to say that all the demonstrators were secular, but simply that they did not see Islam as a political ideology capable of creating a better order. But, disunited and lacking organization, they were supplanted by the Islamists. The rise to power of political Islamist parties in Egypt, Tunisia and Libya, and the entry of radical jihadists in Syria, has led analysts and the media to talk about the transformation of the "Arab Spring" into an "Islamist winter. Certainly, in Tunisia, Ennahda rejects radical Islamism and claims to be close to Turkish Prime Minister Erdogan's Justice and Development Party and to the Turkish, Malaysian and Indonesian models that combine Islam and modernity. And the statements of the Egyptian Muslim Brotherhood were along the same lines. But despite their declarations in favour of women's rights and equal civil rights for men and women, attacks on women in the streets and in drinking establishments by bearded Salafists were commonplace. Above all, they disappointed the aspirations for democratization raised by the overthrow of the regimes in place, and showed authoritarianism, corruption and total incompetence. Apart from the economic and social crisis that they were unable to resolve, their ideology could only augur a long desert journey of obscurantism, cultural regression, restrictions on individual freedoms and attacks on the status of women. The only glimmer of hope in this bleak picture was the liberal and secular opposition that Ennahda faced in Tunisia, which forced it to relinquish its hold on power. This opposition led to a victory for democracy with the accession to power of a coalition government between Islamists and moderate secularists. It led to the adoption of a constitution that gives a smaller place to Islam and also introduces, for the first time in the Arab world, a goal of parity between men and women in elected assemblies. It also led to the election of a President of the Republic from a secular party.

The same cannot be said of the turn of events in Egypt, where the brutal repression of the Islamists and the military takeover seem to lend credence to the thesis that in many Arab countries the choice is between a military dictatorship and the Islamists. But, apart from a few protests, the army's power grab did not raise the outcry one might expect in the West. This relative complacency can be explained by the counter-revolutionary reversal of Western opinion and leaders who had initially welcomed the Arab Spring. Although these at least show that the Arab peoples are no longer willing to passively support despotism, they have disappointed, except in Tunisia, the hopes of democratic transition. And despite the dismal failure of the Islamists, which discredited their ideology, the secular and democratic forces did not succeed in winning.

Egypt: from one dictatorship to another

In 2010 the unpopularity of Hosni Mubarak reached new heights. Nevertheless, he was surprised by large demonstrations against his power that broke out in Cairo on January 25, 2011. They took place shortly after the Tunisian revolution had brought down the "wall of fear", which prevented Egyptians from demonstrating for fear of the police. Like the Tunisian revolution, it was sparked in response to abuses by the Egyptian police force, corruption, and the permanent state of emergency and its expeditious procedures. Structural demographic factors, unemployment, lack of housing, rising prices of basic goods and lack of freedom of expression, as well as the deteriorating urban living conditions for the working classes are also important causes of the protests. The primary objective of the demonstrators was to obtain an end to the police state, the departure of President Mubarak, who has been in power since 1981, the dissolution of the National Democratic Party (NDP) and a fairer distribution of wealth. Bringing together demonstrators from diverse socio-economic backgrounds, it is the largest popular movement in the country's history. Western governments are calling for more freedom and economic, political and social reforms to improve the welfare of the people.

On January 28, Mubarak dismissed the government and appointed Omar Suleiman, head of the intelligence services, as first vice president. On February 1er , he announced that the constitution should be amended to limit the number of presidential terms, while affirming that he would serve out his fifth term, which expires in September 2011, nearly 30 years at the head of Egypt. But the protests continue. The attack on the occupants of Tahrir Square provoked new demonstrations demanding the indictment of those responsible for the hundreds of protesters killed by the police and the release of political prisoners. Strikes became widespread, leading the generals to force the president to resign. In a final speech on February 10, 2011, he announced his intention to remain in office until free elections were held, as well as the transfer of his powers to the vice-president, provoking the fury of the demonstrators, who then planned to take control of the official buildings and march on the presidency of the Republic. The military forced his hand, and the new vice president announced the resignation of Hosni Mubarak, who left Cairo to settle in Sharm el-Sheikh. Demonstrations continued to demand his indictment. On April 10, two investigations were opened against him, one concerning his responsibility for the civilians killed during the Egyptian revolution, and the other for corruption. During an interrogation, he suffered a heart attack and had to be hospitalized. His trial opened on August 3, 2011. He was sentenced, in the first instance, to life imprisonment, but appealed this sentence. And on March 2, 2017 he is acquitted and released on the 24th.

During the uprising that led to the removal of President Mubarak in 2011, the Muslim Brotherhood, which founded the Freedom and Justice Party, remained relatively backward. Better organized than other opposition groups, they opted for an alliance with the military of the Supreme Council of the Armed Forces (SCFA) against the protesting youth and threw all their forces into the electoral battle. The parliamentary elections of January 2012 marked the defeat of the secular parties. The Muslim Brotherhood won 37% of the vote. The more rigorous Salafists, who have their own party, Al-Nour ("the Light"), came in second, ahead of the secular candidates. However, the CSFA continues to dominate political power, with the government accountable only to it, not to parliament. The struggle for power between the Muslim Brotherhood, which holds Parliament, and the Supreme Council of the Armed Forces, which runs the country, has been going on for months. the Muslim Brotherhood candidate, Mohammed Morsi, and General Ahmed Shafiq, Mubarak's last Prime Minister, qualified for the first round of voting. The election, far from calming tensions, polarized Egyptians and aroused the anger of those who refused to choose between Islamists and the military and who felt that their revolution had been stolen. As for Morsi, his statements are contradictory to say the least. On the one hand he said he did not want to impose the wearing of the hijab on women. And, in order to rally the supporters of the liberal current as well as the Copts, he described the latter as "brothers and partners with full rights like Muslims". And on the other hand, he said that Egypt will be Islamic and that Christians will have to pay the jizya or emigrate[5] . In June, the Muslim Brotherhood's candidate, Mohammed Morsi, was narrowly elected president of the Republic with 52 per cent of the vote. He thought he would subdue the CSFA by decapitating it. But the promotion of Abdelfattah Sissi as Minister of Defence and new head of the CSFA marked the advent of a new generation of generals. The extraordinary powers granted to the president, the drafting of a constitution largely inspired by sharia law, the questioning of equality between men and women and, above all, the economic crisis, made him unpopular. The obvious failure of the Muslim Brotherhood and Morsi's clumsy attempts to monopolize power led to violent clashes between the secular opposition and the Islamists, resulting in numerous victims. These disturbances led to the forceful intervention of the army. Sissi capitalized on Morsi's narrowly partisan politics and opened channels with activists who launched the Tamarrod movement (rebellion, different from "revolution," a term not favored by Sissi) in April 2013. Monster demonstrations, gathering millions of people framed by the army follow one another throughout the country against Morsi.

The return of the army to power

Egypt's first democratically elected president was finally overthrown on July 3, 2013, by a military coup and thrown into prison along with thousands of his supporters and the Muslim Brotherhood's supreme leader. Riyadh welcomed the Egyptian army's coup, while the United States denounced it, even though it had not particularly spoken out against the Muslim Brotherhood's liberticidal practices. They were imitated by Turkey, Qatar and many European countries, which expressed their disagreement with the removal of the president. A ruthless crackdown then fell on the Islamists. Hundreds of them, including the president, were sentenced to death (the sentence had not been carried out at the time of writing). The hunt for Islamists became so intense that, according to a newspaper article, wearing a beard or a nikab could become dangerous in Egypt. Then, in December, the Egyptian government, dominated by the military, officially declared their movement a "terrorist organization." Finally, in May

2014, as if the revolutionary years had changed nothing, the former army chief general, Abdel Fattah al-Sissi, meanwhile promoted to field marshal, won a landslide victory with 96% of the vote in the presidential elections, after having literally eliminated all opposition, Islamist, then liberal and secular, from the political spectrum. "However, Sissi does not hesitate to appeal to the religious feelings of Egyptians, the vast majority of whom are Sunni Muslims. The man described by his entourage as pious, who says he makes a point of performing his five daily prayers and whose wife wears a veil, also wrote a memoir in 2006 entitled "Democracy in the Middle East" in which he insisted on the role of Islam in legislation[6] . After his election, he said it would be unrealistic to expect democracy in Egypt for another 25 years. Pragmatically, the U.S. government, which initially saw Mohamed Morsi's election as a victory for democracy and denounced the coup, says it is "eager to work with the new president." He can count on the financial support of Arabia and the Emirates, who are satisfied with the sidelining of the Muslim Brotherhood and whose aid to Egypt amounts to thirty billion dollars in the eighteen months following the overthrow of Morsi. But the army's crackdown was bound to provoke further violence. Terrorist actions against the army increased. On August 14, 2013, while supporters of Mohammad Morsi, were organizing sit-ins in Cairo to demand his return, the security forces perpetrated a real massacre. A thousand people are killed or missing. This was the beginning of a manhunt that lasted five days.

The attempt to eradicate the Muslim Brotherhood has only radicalized them, and strengthened the incomparably more threatening jihadists. The latter have taken control of a large part of Sinai, from where they wage a veritable guerrilla war against the regular forces and carry out attacks in Cairo and other cities. Their movement called Ansar Beit al-Makdis (the Partisans of Jerusalem) has pledged allegiance to Daech. On November 26, 2017, they carried out the worst terrorist attack in Egypt's history, which killed 305 worshippers, not including the injured, attending Friday prayers at a mosque near El-Arich. Other jihadist groups are also active in several regions of the country. While the crackdown on the Muslim Brotherhood has not been as dramatic since 2013, a total of 900,000 members and two million supporters have been subjected to an unprecedented campaign of coercion. And human rights organizations agree that the number of political detainees in Egypt exceeds 60,000, the vast majority of whom are Muslim Brothers. "The hyper-presidential and authoritarian nature of the regime was revealed during the filing of candidacies for the March 2018 presidential election. Five of the six candidates in the running were forced to withdraw guaranteeing in advance the "democratic" re-election of Marshal-President Sissi[7] ". Unsurprisingly he was elected with 97% of the vote!

Foreign policy

Under the presidency of Hosni Mubarak, Egyptian diplomacy was particularly conditioned by the alliance between Cairo and Washington. The arrival of the Muslim Brotherhood to power in 2012 with the presidency of Mohammad Morsi, and then that of Abdel Fattah al-Sissi in 2014, allowed for the diversification of Egyptian diplomatic activity. From the beginning of his term, Morsi had announced that he wanted to pursue a "balanced foreign policy" declaring "international relations between all countries open". If at first Sissi launched a foreign policy influenced by his hostility to the Muslim Brotherhood, he returned to a policy more in line with the national interests of the country. In the front line on the Libyan and Palestinian issues, alongside Saudi Arabia in its open conflicts with Yemen, Qatar and Iran, Egypt is redoubling its efforts to once again become a key player on the Middle Eastern diplomatic scene. Cairo wants to present itself as the sponsor of Palestinian reconciliation. Egypt, which sought to distance itself from Saudi Arabia on the Syrian issue by moving closer to the Damascus-Tehran-Moscow axis in 2016, is playing a balancing act through its alliances with the various regional powers. On the Libyan issue, Cairo supports Marshal Haftar by multiplying meetings with Tunisia and Algeria for a peaceful solution to the conflict so as to contain the implantation of members of the Islamic State organization in Libya.

The repression of the Shiite spring in Bahrain

In the wake of the fall of Mubarak, Shiite opponents of the Sunni monarchy in Bahrain proclaimed a "day of rage. On February 14, 2011, they occupied Pearl Square in the center of Manama. They demanded a democratic constitution, without questioning the reigning Khalifa dynasty. (Shiites represent 70% of the population). Saudi Arabia and the Emirates intervened militarily to save the Khalifas. At their request, a thousand Saudi soldiers and 500 Emirati policemen entered Bahrain with dozens of tanks. Even if they do not participate directly in the repression, these troops allow the local security forces to reoccupy the Pearl Square. It is a counter-revolution of the classical type. This was the second time, after the Kuwait war, that the Gulf Cooperation Council's mutual protection agreement, known as the Desert Shield, was put into action.

The Libyan chaos

Provoked by the outbreak of the uprising against Muammar Gaddafi, the Western military intervention has plunged Libya into chaos. Following the outbreak of clashes on February 17, 2011, in Benghazi, between rebels and regime forces, Nicolas Sarkozy, alerted by the sulphurous Bernard-Henri Levy, recognized on March 10, the Libyan Transitional Council set up by the rebels. The French president led the diplomatic offensive to convince his European partners of the need for military intervention on their behalf. With the support of British Prime Minister David Cameron, he almost had to force their hand in Brussels to obtain their approval, despite Muammar Gaddafi's terrorist past and his threats to drown the rebellion in blood. The hesitations of the Arab League and the United States had to be overcome in order to obtain a UN Security Council resolution. Security Council Resolution 1970 of 26 February 1971 put in place an embargo on arms to Libya and froze the regime's assets. Resolution 1973 established a no-fly zone over the country's territory and allowed for "all measures deemed necessary to protect the civilian population. Unwilling to engage in a new war against another Muslim country, the United States held back from France and Great Britain. Even if, afterwards, it was decided to coordinate military operations through NATO structures. Saudi Arabia, which had an old score to settle with Gaddafi, the United Arab Emirates and Qatar joined the coalition. All operations are conducted within the framework of Operation *Unified Protector.* Although UN Resolution 1973, which established a no-fly zone, was intended solely to protect the civilian population, the French and British air forces provided decisive support to the rebels. On August 20, the rebels launched an uprising in Tripoli, which fell on September 15. The way in which France and the United Kingdom, supported by the United States, violated the UN resolution aroused the disapproval of Russia and China, which systematically vetoed any draft Security Council resolution allowing the establishment of a no-fly zone in Syria. A month later the Libyan dictator, who was courted by all European governments, was ignominiously assassinated in Sirte. The National Transitional Council (NTC), which was recognized by Paris, is not representative and has no authority over the insurgents. And the first statement of its president, Mustapha Abdeljalil, was in favor of the establishment of sharia law.

The collapse of the regime has led to a division of the country into the provinces of Benghazi, Tripoli and Fezzan. It has led to tribal clashes and the proliferation of Islamist militias that spread terror and assassinated the American ambassador. It has also increased the threat of destabilization to the countries of the Sahel, particularly with the influx of arms from Libya that has benefited AQIM (Al Qaeda in the Islamic Maghreb). Libya's chaos is also affecting its Egyptian and Tunisian neighbors. And while Libya was a dam preventing the influx of refugees from sub-Saharan Africa and other countries into Europe, it has grown almost beyond control. Not to mention the tragedy of thousands of deaths in makeshift boats crossing the Mediterranean. These developments have led Western leaders to question the validity of their intervention in Libya. This is particularly true of France, which had to come to the aid of the Malian government threatened by a rebellion supported by AQIM. But, as if they had not learned the lessons of the past, Western countries will work, from 2012, to bring down the Syrian regime with even more devastating effects in terms of export of terrorism and refugee flows. After the July 7, 2012 elections, Libya is governed by the General National Congress (GNC), which replaces the National Transitional Council. Dominated by Islamists, it decided to implement sharia law in the country in December 2013 and to extend its mandate beyond its scheduled term (January 2014). In February 2014, General Khalifa Haftar, commander of the Libyan army, ordered the dissolution of the nGC and called for the formation of an interim government committee to oversee new elections. The NGC ignored his demands and denounced an attempted coup. It was unable to regain control of the oil installations that had fallen into the hands of armed Salafist groups. General Haftar then began to reconquer the areas that had fallen into the hands of these groups in Bengazhi and Sirte. The country was then divided and a second Libyan civil war broke out between two rival governments and several jihadist groups. In Tripolitania an Islamist government controlled the capital from 2014 to 2016. Dominated by the Muslim Brotherhood, it is supported by Qatar and Turkey. But to the east of Tripoli, the Islamist militias of Misrata control the port cities. The parliament then took refuge in Tobruk under the protection of General Haftar. The Tobruk government is supported by Egypt and the United Arab Emirates. The country was also the scene of clashes involving jihadist groups linked or close to al-Qaeda and the Libyan branch of the Islamic State, which controlled the Sirte region until it was taken over by General Haftar's forces. In 2016, a Government of National Accord (GNA) was created at the initiative of the international community to reconcile the two sides of Libya. But the country has not managed to regain political stability and is deeply divided, with Cyrenia controlled by General Haftar and the Tobruk parliament, and Tripoli and the west by the internationally recognized Government of National Unity (GNA), led by Fayez el-Sarraj. All efforts led by Libya's neighbors to reunite Tripoli's Prime Minister Fayez el-Sarraj and Khalifa Haftar, who has become Field Marshal, have failed. However, at a meeting on July 25, 2017, hosted by President Macron in La Celle-Saint- Cloud, they adopted a joint declaration for a way out of the crisis that has yet to be implemented. And the release of Saif al-Islam, Khahafi's son, in June 2017, chosen as the representative of the confederation of tribes that remained loyal to his clan, has complicated the situation.

Conquest and defeat of the "Islamic State" in Iraq

A Sunni stronghold, El Anbar province in western Iraq was, in early 2014, the scene of an insurgency mixing anti-government Sunni tribal forces and jihadists, belonging to EIIL (Islamic State in Iraq and the Levant). Then, on June 10, 2014, EIIL jihadists, backed by former Sunni officers from Saddam Hussein's army, members of the Nakchibandis brotherhood and Baath supporters captured Mosul, abandoned by the routed government forces, and other areas in the north of the country including Nineveh province. In a few days, more than 500,000 civilians fled the city of Mosul, while another part of the population, Sunni, fed up with the exactions committed by the Iraqi army, welcomed the jihadists as liberators. By taking Mosul, they got their hands on brand new American military equipment and

500 million in gold and foreign currency from the central bank. After the fall of the city, the jihadists and Sunni insurgents continued their offensive towards southern Iraq and attacked the provinces of Salah ad-Din, Diyala and Kirkuk. Their advance was only halted at Samarra. On June 12, the Iraqi army abandoned Kirkuk, and the peshmerga of the Kurdistan Regional Government immediately intervened to take control. Dozens of Shiite soldiers were brutally executed during this advance. During the capture of Tikrit at the end of June 2014, the men of Daech had to execute 1700 young Iraqi recruits in waves with Kalashnikovs and point weapons. It took them several hours to slaughter everyone and summarily bury the mass of corpses. Showing the same

iconoclastic obscurantism as the Taliban, the jihadis destroyed several places of worship and religious monuments in the areas under their control. Then, after symbolically abolishing the border between Iraq and Syria, they proclaimed the establishment of a caliphate in the territory they had conquered, announcing that they were changing the name of their group to "Islamic State" *without* any geographical reference. Islamic State (IS) leader Abu Bakr Al-Baghdadi, who had assumed the title of "caliph" and commander of the believers on July 3, 2014, then appeared in a video posted on jihadist websites, calling on all Muslims to "obey" him. This proclamation was followed by the expulsion of Christians from Mosul. Summoned either to convert to Islam, or to submit to the condition of dhimmi and pay the jiziya, or to perish by the sword, they had to leave the city in a hurry without taking anything with them. Leaving all their belongings behind, most of them took refuge in the areas controlled by the Kurds.

These dramatic events can only exacerbate communal hatred, raising fears that the country could be plunged into a new and even bloodier civil war. Responding to the call of the central government and Grand Ayatollah Ali al-Sistani, Iraq's highest Shiite religious authority, thousands of Shiites have volunteered to take up arms against Daech and defend the Shiite holy sites. But they seem to be powerless against their trained and fanatical fighters. As for the United States, although it is determined to counter the terrorist threat posed by the iE, it has criticized the policy of exclusion pursued by Nouri el-Maliki and has made its support for the Iraqi government conditional on the formation of a government of national unity. For their part, the Kurds, taking advantage of the rout of the regime's forces, seized Kirkuk and its oil fields. Expanding their territory by 40%, they seemed to be the big winners in this new episode of the Iraqi civil war, thanks to the weapons provided by Washington and its allies. On August 2, 2014, EI forces began an offensive against Iraqi Kurdistan and seized the Sinjar region, which the Yazidi minority had been forced to flee en masse in the face of the threat of genocide hanging over them because of their belief, with Muslims accusing them of worshipping a deity associated with the Devil. After watching the establishment of the Islamic State with relative passivity, the international community suddenly woke up. The United States, France and Britain undertook a humanitarian operation to rescue the Yazidis. However, their intervention came too late to prevent the EI from seizing Karakosh, Iraq's largest Christian city, causing a new exodus. France has offered to take in Iraqi Christians who request it. And the European Union has decided to arm the Kurdish forces.

Elected in 2008 on a promise to withdraw U.S. troops from Iraq, Barak Obama in August 2014 authorized his military to conduct airstrikes, three years after withdrawing from the country, to stem the advance of the Islamic State in Kurdistan. France and other countries followed suit. On the other hand, Turkey, which has facilitated the supply of weapons, has not condemned the terrorism of the iE, unlike the king of Saudi Arabia, for whom the proclamation of a caliphate represents a challenge. Yielding to pressure, Prime Minister Nouri el-Maliki finally agreed to give way in September 2014 to a national unity government led by Haidar el-Abadi. And a broad international coalition with the objective of fighting the Islamic State was formed under the aegis of Washington. Iran, an ally of Iraq but not a member of the coalition, is also deploying troops in Iraq. On Sept. 21, Iran announced that elite Al-Quds Force soldiers were being deployed to Iraq to help the government fight the Islamic State's advance into its territory. The fighting is indecisive between the fall of 2014 and the spring of 2015, but starting in the summer of 2015 Iraqi forces supported by the coalition begin to regain the advantage. In July 2015 the Iraqi army, supported by the Shiite militias of Al Hachd al Chaabi and the strikes of the international coalition go on the offensive to retake the province of Al Anbar from the EI, whose reconquest is completed in June 2016. Meanwhile, in November 2015 Sinjar was retaken by the Kurds and. in March 2016, the Iraqi army launched an offensive to regain a foothold in Nineveh province. In October, the Battle of Mosul begins. About 80,000 men were deployed around the city: soldiers of the Iraqi army, peshmerga, Hachd al-Shaabi supported by Iran, coalition troops and various Kurdish and Sunni Arab militias, facing the 5,000 to 9,000 fighters of the Islamic State, whose last pocket of resistance did not fall until 16 July 2017. The battle ended in the blood of Sunni civilians, of whom the Iraqi army, which is overwhelmingly Shiite, paid little attention, preferring to crush the western part of the city under the bombs. Moreover, both the army and the Shiite militias have engaged in acts of revenge against the inhabitants, who are accused of having supported the Islamic State, which is largely true. The Sunni population of Mosul thus perceives the Iraqi army's capture of the city as a Shiite "reoccupation" of Sunni territory. After the recapture of Mosul, the last pockets of resistance of the EI began to fall one by one. The fall (or liberation) of Mosul, depending on one's point of view, does not necessarily mean the end of Daech and of violence in Iraq. The absence of inclusive democracy, as in all Arab-Muslim countries, has led to the alienation of marginalized or oppressed communities. From the Abbasid caliphate to the dictatorship of Saddam Hussein, this was the case for the Shiites. Now it is the case of the Sunnis, whose resentment can only increase after the defeat of the iE and the multiple bullying and abuses they suffered at the hands of the shiite militias and the Iraqi army during the latter's reconquest of their strongholds

The reunification of Iraq

In Iraq, the elimination of the Islamic State, to which they believe they contributed, is pushing the Kurds to want to wrest their independence. Despite, the opposition of the Iraqi government, Turkey, Iran and the international community, a referendum in favor of the independence of Kurdistan collected on September 25, 2017, the approval of 92% of votes in this region. Baghdad and Ankara immediately announced an economic blockade of Kurdistan. As much as Turkey accepts the autonomy of Iraqi Kurdistan because ultimately it controls it, because the entire Kurdish economy depends on the opening or closing of the Turkish border, it would not tolerate its independence. The Iraqi government has threatened to use force to retake Kirkuk and its region, which it says is illegally occupied by the Kurds. And the Iraqi army seized it within 48 hours. This advance was facilitated by inter-Kurdish divisions between the Patriotic Union of Kurdistan (PUK), which had asked the peshmerga to withdraw, and the Kurdistan Democratic Party (KDP) of President Massoud Barzani, which had taken the initiative for the independence referendum. Armed by Israel during the rebellion against Saddam Hussein, exploited by the Western powers in the fight against Daech, are the Kurds doomed to the status of eternal losers? After the capture of Kirkuk, the government in Baghdad regained control of the whole of Iraqi Kurdistan, putting an end to the chimera of Kurdish independence[8] . By taking back from the jihadists almost all the territory they had conquered, and from the Kurds the disputed regions, Iraqi Prime Minister Haidar al-Abadi appears to be the man who has reunified Iraq. But in the run-up to the parliamentary elections to be held in May 2018, he has to contend with the Hachd al Chaabi militias (a coalition of mainly Shiite and pro-Iranian paramilitary forces), the ambitions of his predecessor, Nouri el-Maliki, who wants to take over the leadership of the Daawa party, and the very popular Shiite anti-Iranian cleric Moqtada Sadr, who poses as the representative of Iraqi nationalism in the face of Iranian interference.

The new war in Yemen

In Yemen, Ali Abdullah Saleh, ruler of the unified country since 1990, has long-standing ties to the jihadist networks that assisted him in the struggle against the Marxist south. Saleh has managed to insert himself into the U.S.-led global war on terror, while diverting U.S. aid to his praetorian guard. Despite receiving counterterrorism funding, the regime did little to combat the reconstitution of al-Qaeda in the Arabian Peninsula (AQAP) on its soil in January 2009. On March 18, 2011, government forces slaughtered protesters in Sana'a. This bloodshed caused dissension within the army, a division of which joined the revolutionary camp. In May, President Ali Abdullah Saleh ordered his troops to abandon the city of Zinjibar to the jihadists, making it the capital of an "Islamic emirate" in southern Yemen. Saudi Arabia, worried about the worsening crisis in Yemen, took advantage of the hospitalization of President Saleh, who was wounded in an attack in June 2011, to impose a transitional solution under which power was transferred to Vice President Abd Rabbo Mansour Hadi. Saleh's departure did not end the violence, and the government is facing both al-Qaeda in the south and the Shiite Houthi rebels of Ansarallah ("the followers of Allah") in the north. President Hadi denounced the collusion between Saleh and AQPA. A national dialogue concluded in January 2014 with a pact involving all political forces, according to which the country would be transformed into a federation. But this solution was rejected by the Houthis. Saleh, who saw that his gamble on the jihadists had failed, turned to his former opponents in Ansarallah. He hopes to win by playing both sides. The Houthis seized the capital, Sana'a, in September 2014, much to the dismay of Saudi Arabia. Riyadh indeed fears being threatened with encirclement by an Iraq dominated by Shiites in the north, and the Houthis on its southern border. Hadi managed to flee in February 2015 and set up his government in Aden. Arabia supported him, while Iran supported the Houthis. The changing situation in Yemen led, in March 2015, the Sunni countries of the region to stand together against the Shiite arc despite their differences. Split between the Houthi-controlled north and the south, controlled by Sunni forces loyal to the legitimate president and the local branch of al-Qaeda, Yemen has become, after Iraq and Syria, the new arena of confrontation between Shi'iteism and Sunnism and between Riyadh and Tehran. Ansarallah, openly allied with Saleh's loyalists, carried out a blitzkrieg offensive on Taez in March 2015 and came dangerously close to Aden. President Hadi then took refuge in Saudi Arabia. The threat posed by the Houthis to Aden prompted Saudi Arabia to intervene directly in the conflict by launching an aerial bombing campaign on Yemen in March 2015. These raids cause enormous destruction and a large number of casualties among the civilian population. Ali Abdullah Saleh, posing as a recourse, concluded a power-sharing pact with the Houthis in 2016 and established a parallel government, while having preserved his links with the jihadists. Saudi Arabia's military intervention, the first in the kingdom's history, shows that, for Riyadh, the fight against Shiism and Persian expansionism is more important than the fight against jihadist organizations. To counter this expansionism, all the Sunni powers in the region (Egypt, Jordan and the Gulf monarchies) have joined the military campaign led by Riyadh, which has also received the support of Washington, Pakistan and Turkey. Faced with this unprecedented Sunni coalition, Tehran is likely to limit itself to diplomatic and financial support for the Houthis. A direct intervention on its part would risk triggering a regional war, at a time when negotiations on its nuclear program are about to be concluded. Despite this, it is doubtful that the Saudi intervention, sending troops on the ground being out of the question, will be successful. The Yemeni adventure is now a quagmire and the military coalition led by Riyadh is regularly accused of mistakes. While the outcome of the conflict, which is very costly for the kingdom, is still uncertain, there are already divergences among the countries in the coalition. Operation "Decisive Storm" has been anything but decisive. It has highlighted the limits of Saudi military power. Despite the deployment of tens of thousands of troops on its border, Saudi Arabia has had to evacuate a strip of territory 200 kilometers long and 20 to 30 kilometres wide; residents have been forced to leave their villages for fear of Houthi incursions, and the Houthis continue to fire missiles against cities in southern Saudi Arabia. And to add insult to injury, the Houthis have fired ballistic missiles at Riyadh. The Saudi government is therefore seeking to extricate itself from this quagmire. But getting out of the war is, as always, more difficult than getting in. Not only must Arabia take into account its Iranian enemy, but its allies, particularly the UAE, are developing their own strategy. Finally, the destruction by the Saudi air force has provoked strong international emotion. Saudi Arabia and the United Arab Emirates are destroying a very poor country. The blockade of ports, airports and road access in Yemen has caused a famine that could claim hundreds of thousands of victims. And the health situation is catastrophic with a cholera epidemic that is spreading rapidly due to the lack of means to stop it. Riyadh claims to be defending the legitimate government, but bombed day and night, the population of Yemen is starving because of the blockade. Of the country's 27 million inhabitants, 10 million, according to the UN, require emergency humanitarian aid, 7 million are threatened by famine and one million are prey to a cholera epidemic. This is not a war against combatants, but an enterprise of demoralization of the population, of total destruction. The combined action of air strikes and blockade (air and sea) aims to bring an entire population to its knees. A new turn in the Yemeni crisis that does not help the Riyadh-led military coalition wanting to get out of the Yemeni quagmire occurs in early November 2017. Former President Ali Abdullah Saleh having turned his back on his Houthi allies, was killed by them. Since his death no settlement of the conflict, which is entering its fourth year, is in sight, while a certain rivalry is emerging between Arabia, which supports President Hadi, and the United Arab Emirates, which supports the Southern Transitional Council (STC), which favors the autonomy of South Yemen.

The evolution of Saudi Arabia

In 2005, Abdullah bin Abdel Aziz, regent of the kingdom since 1996, succeeded his half-brother, Fahd, at the age of 82 and reigned until 2015. During his reign, he promoted interreligious dialogue and on November 6, 2007, he was received by Pope Benedict XVI at the Vatican. During the wave of protests and revolutions of the "Arab Spring", he supported President Mubarak before his resignation, and granted political asylum to Tunisian President Zine El Abidine Ben Ali. When the Muslim Brotherhood and its emulators won the first democratic elections in Tunisia and Egypt, this only added to the mistrust of the Saudi authorities, especially since Saudi Islamists openly displayed their support for their comrades. In Arabia, Islamist figures took the opportunity to call for reforms; various petitions to that effect circulated during 2011. While calls for protests were made in the kingdom, the king took social measures to the tune of $36 billion. In September 2011, he grants women the right to vote and stand for election in municipal elections, the only type of election in the country. The kingdom supported the coup against President Mohamed Morsi, and then provided considerable financial support to President Sissi after the overthrow of the Muslim Brotherhood regime in Egypt. In the aftermath the Muslim Brotherhood and all related groups are declared terrorists. The first arrests took place in 2013 and 2014, and again in 2016, but they involved a small number of second-tier figures, until the much more massive arrests in September 2017. Saudi Arabia is distancing itself from its U.S. ally in response to Washington's military non-intervention during the Syrian war and the Iranian-U.S. rapprochement that follows the election of Hassan Rohani as president of the Islamic Republic. Although hostile to the Arab Spring revolutions, Saudi Arabia began to support the rebels in Syria a few months after the start of the war in order to counter Iran's influence. When King Abdullah died, the King Salman who succeeded him was already old and ill when he took the throne. Once he came to power, the new king ousted the relatives of his predecessor. Appointed by his father as the kingdom's vice crown prince in January 2015, Mohammad bin Salman led operations against the Houthi militias in Yemen (supported by Iran). In April 2016, he launched a vast plan of socio-economic reforms called Vision 2030, aimed at profoundly transforming the Saudi economy, shaken by the decline in oil prices. He came to prominence in June 2017 when he dismissed and replaced Mohammad bin Nayef as crown prince. To justify what looks like a real palace revolution, Mohammed bin Salman (MBS) argues the need to put the state and society in battle order to, on the one hand, address local and regional challenges, including "Iranian expansionism." The crackdown has intensified against dissenting voices. MBS is believed to be behind the banning of Qatar by its Gulf neighbors, who blame Doha for its support of the Muslim Brotherhood and an alleged "complacency" toward Iran. On June 5, 2017, the Saudi government broke off diplomatic relations with Qatar and closed its border with the emirate. Its allies, the United Arab Emirates, Bahrain, Yemen and Egypt will follow suit. Considered the strongman of Saudi Arabia, the young crown prince (31) advocates a more open policy with decrees that move towards greater tolerance and a fight against religious extremism. The morality police have been curtailed, and he is considered to be the inspiration behind the decision to lift the ban on women driving. Entertainment, once severely restricted, is also increasing, a move that can only satisfy the youth, who make up 70% of the population. He said he wanted to "return to a moderate, tolerant Islam that is open to the world and all religions.[9] Marking his determination to break with the policy of complacency, or even support for Islamist movements, he brought together in Riyadh an anti-terrorist coalition of 40 Muslim countries. At the same time, he has worked to strengthen his political grip on power, including a wave of arrests of dissidents, including influential clerics and intellectuals. And on November 6, 2017, in preparation for his ascension to the throne, he carried out what amounted to a full-blown coup. On the one hand, by arresting some thirty Saudi princes and businessmen under the guise of fighting corruption, and on the other hand, by forcing the Lebanese Prime Minister Saad Hariri to resign and make a statement violently denouncing the stranglehold of Iran and Hezbollah on Lebanon. These arrests call into question the foundations of the Saudi system, which embodied a traditional patrimonial state. In such a system, co-optation, fuelled by oil revenues, was the preferred method of managing political conflicts, with repression seen as a last resort that was best avoided. The main members of the royal family shared power, each having a fiefdom, often a ministerial one, that allowed him to maintain his clientele. By liquidating any political opposition within the royal family itself. By attacking what had been the heart of the kingdom's political tradition: the principle of compromise and the balance of power. Between the royal family and the Wahhabi clergy. Between the different clans within the royal family. It is this whole system that is brought down with the power grab of Mohammed Ben Salman. The thunderclap that has just erupted is also in the wake of two changes on the regional political-religious chessboard: the Trump administration's decision to counter Iran's expansionism. And the victories of the Syrian regime, an ally of Iran, which constitute a serious setback for the United States and Saudi Arabia. It is a "new kingdom" that the Saudi prince promises. A kingdom that is undoubtedly more liberal, socially more efficient, but more despotic than ever. By demonstrating his desire to exercise undivided power, MBS wants to embody the awakening of Arab Sunnism in the face of the triumphalism of Shia Persia. And by advocating a more open Islam, it will no longer be possible to send Wahhabi obscurantism and the theocratic dictatorship of the mullahs back to back. Combined with the rout of Daech, this could mean the twilight of sunni extremism and play into the hands of moderate sunnism, which represents a more acceptable and effective counterweight to Iranian influence. Unless Arabia's bogging down in Yemen and the failure of its policy of isolating Qatar jeopardizes its ambitions to play the role of a flagship state in the Muslim world. The religious dimension of the rivalry between Saudi Arabia and Iran is less important than its political dimension. The main cause is the hegemonic ambitions and subversive activities of the Islamic Republic, illustrated by its support for Hezbollah, which is its armed wing in Lebanon and beyond. Saudi policy should also be seen in the context of its relationship with the United States. "America needs Riyadh not only to provide it with cheap oil in exchange for the Kingdom's security, but also to sell it arms and, above all, to overplay its rivalry with Tehran to Israel's advantage. For the new Saudi government, the risk linked to this American "abandonment" is very important. It needs to rebalance its alliances by getting closer to Moscow, to make itself indispensable to America again (by linking up with Israel) and by concluding huge military and commercial contracts for its benefit as a form of reassurance, and above all to catch Tehran off guard in terms of social reform. This is undoubtedly the origin of the Crown Prince's recent and spectacular desire to break with the Kingdom's strained traditionalism in order to advance Saudi society .[10]

Quarantining Qatar

With its partners in the Gulf Cooperation Council, Qatar's relations are on the rocks. Saudi Arabia, the United Arab Emirates, and Bahrain recalled their ambassadors to Doha on March 5, 2014, blaming Qatar for supporting Islamists in the Arab world and seeking to destabilize neighboring countries. Qatar had indeed openly sided with the Muslim Brotherhood, which was repressed in Egypt after being ousted from power, while the other three countries provided massive support, both political and financial, to the power installed by the army in Cairo. Subsequently, Riyadh and the other Gulf Cooperation Council countries reconciled with Doha to form a common front against Tehran's hegemonic designs. But an even more serious crisis erupted in September 2017. Saudi Arabia, the United Arab Emirates, Bahrain and Egypt accused Qatar of supporting terrorism and being complacent towards Iran. They suspend all land, air and sea links with the emirate, ask Qatari citizens to leave their territories and close the offices of the Qatari news channel Al-Jazeera in their countries.

They send the emirate a list of thirteen demands to which it is summoned to submit to obtain the lifting of the blockade. The main ones being the drastic reduction of its relations with Iran, the closure of a Turkish base and the expulsion of all opponents considered as terrorists by these four countries. While rejecting these conditions, Qatar has declared itself open to negotiation. But the mediations intended to find a compromise have failed and the impasse remains total. However, this seems to affect Riyadh more than Qatar, which is holding out thanks to its considerable financial resources and the support it enjoys, particularly from the United States, Turkey and Iran. This Turkish support deeply irritates Riyadh. In an interview granted to the newspaper al-

Chorouk during his visit to Egypt in March 2018, Mohammed bin-Salman considered Turkey to be part of the "triangle of evil," along with Iran and Islamist groups. A qualifier that shows that the gap between the two aspirants to leadership in the Sunni world continues to grow, while Riyadh, Abu Dhabi and Cairo are opposed on many regional issues to the axis Ankara- Doha[11] .

United Arab Emirates

In 2011 the UAE was not affected by the wave of protests of the Arab Spring, but the government took a series of measures to buy social peace and repressive measures in prevention. The confederation is currently one of the most stable countries in the entire Middle East region. Almost a miracle. Wars, conflicts, terrorism, revolts, community tensions, political instability: nothing seems to affect this small country of 9 million inhabitants, the majority of whom are expatriates (only one million are nationals). Despite the fall in oil prices, the UAE is holding up well thanks to its economy, which it has been able to diversify. This is characterized by investments abroad and the development of the tourism sector (opening of luxury hotels, creation of the Palm Islands), cultural (opening of the Louvre Museum in Abu Dhabi), scientific (branch of the Sorbonne and the Yale University Art Institute in Abu Dhabi) and financial (Dubai World Financial Center). From 2015, the UAE intervenes alongside Saudi Arabia against the Houthis in Yemen and will participate in the isolation of Qatar in 2017. In June 2107 the Emir of Abu Dhabi and President of the UAE, Khalifa bin Zayed Al Nayhan agreed with the Crown Prince of Saudi Arabia, Mohammed bin Salman, to divide the unfortunate Yemen into zones of influence. Control of the north fell to Saudi Arabia, while the Emirates took military leadership in the east to fight Al Qaeda in the Arabian Peninsula (AQAP) in cooperation with the loyalist army and local tribes. The central part of the country, rich in oil infrastructure, was the subject of a "condominium" between the two countries. Considered to be the strongman of the country, his brother, Crown Prince Mohammed bin Zayed, leads operations in Yemen. However, while Riyadh supports President Abd Rabbo Mansour Hadi, Abu Dhabi reproaches the latter for his proximity to the Muslim Brotherhood, from which he originates. This policy has caused some gnashing of teeth. Criticism of the Emirates has been voiced: military intervention in Yemen; construction of military bases in Africa (Eritrea and Somaliland); participation in the anti-Is coalition led by the United States; interference in the internal affairs of certain countries to combat the influence of the Muslim Brotherhood (Egypt, Tunisia, Libya); aggressive policy against Qatar and Iran; subordination to the United States and complacency towards Israel.

1 *The New Question of the East,* Georges Corm, La Découverte 2017, p. 139

2 *Monotheism, power and war*, Ibrahim Tabet, l'Harmattan 2015, p. 97

3 *France in Lebanon and the Near East,* Ibrahim Tabet, ed. of the Phoenician Review, 2012, p. 279

4 *Les Arabes, leur destin et le nôtre*, Jean-Pierre Filiu, La Découverte, 2015, p. 238

5.https://www.lorientlejour.com/article/.../Printemps_arabe_ou_hiver_islamique_.html

6 *Les Arabes, leur destin et le nôtre*, op. cit.

7 *L'Orient-Le Jour* of January 38, 2018

8.https://www.lexpress.fr/.../kurdistan-d-irak-les-chimères-de-lindependance_19845086,

9.https://www.la-croix.com/Religion/Islam/Le-prince-heritier-dArabie-saoudite-veut-ret.

10.http://galacteros.over-blog .com/2018/01/lcdr-iran-the-diabolization-in-motion .html.

11https://www.lorientlejour.com/.../rien-ne-va-plus-entre-larabie-saoudite-et-la-turquie.

Chapter 16. The war in Syria, its actors and its stakes

When President Hafez el-Assad died on June 10, 2000, he left his son Bashar an economy in ruins and a dilapidated production system. His son succeeded him smoothly. Parliament amended the Constitution to lower the minimum age for presidential candidacy from 40 to 34. He was elected President of the Republic in July 2000. The regime became timidly liberalized. Political prisoners were released and forums bringing together intellectuals to discuss the democratization of Syria were created. But Bashar al-Assad had to deal with the members of the old guard of the party set up by his father, who were still thinking of an armed conflict with Israel. In less than two years, he managed to remove three quarters of the former regime's leaders. But there is no question that he will tolerate the questioning of the hegemony of the three pillars of power: the Baath party, the army and the Alawite clan to which he belongs. However, in recent years, the Ba'ath has been in decline in favour of the National Progressive Front (NPF). An open monopartism has been instituted: several parties have had their bans lifted and can express themselves, but only within the NPF. This change is due, among other things, to the gradual abandonment of the baathist socialist doctrine, even though pan-Arab nationalism remains in the discourse and propaganda, particularly in favour of the Palestinians. "But Bashar al-Assad has never sought to pose as a defender of the liberal democracy described here as Western. One could say that his ideal would rather be an efficient state and economy, framing a deeply depoliticized society[1] . He thus carried out economic reforms in favour of the private sector, in particular by liberalizing the banking sector. He was inspired by the Chinese model, proclaiming that "economic reforms come before political reforms. These reforms benefited the business community of the Sunni upper class. But economic growth is widening the gap in wealth. Corruption is becoming endemic and the biggest beneficiaries of the liberalization of the economy are the clique close to the regime and the family of the head of state: the fortune of Rami Makhlouf, his cousin, is estimated in billions of dollars. The state remains locked in and, with the rise of anti-Syrian demands in Lebanon, Bashar al-Assad hardened his position and put an end to the liberal movement in 2003. He showed much less skill than his father in foreign policy. In April 2002, the head of the US State Department, Colin Powell, told him, during a brief visit to Damascus, that Syria should change its policy on the regional scene and stop supporting Hezbollah. He did not comply, and in 2003 the United States began to impose economic sanctions on Syrian officials. His control over Lebanon and his mistreatment of Lebanese Prime Minister Rafie Hariri earned him the enmity of President Chirac. While Syria's assistance to Islamist insurgents fighting American troops in Iraq put it in the crosshairs of the United States. The combined pressure of Paris and Washington, the assassination of Hariri and the Cedar Revolution led to the humiliating departure of Syrian occupation troops from Lebanon in 2005. A wave of political attacks and assassinations, most likely fomented by the Syrian regime, hit Lebanon. Bashar al-Assad was re-elected to the presidency of the Republic by 97.62% of the votes cast in a presidential referendum on 27 May 2007. However, he will return to grace with the successor of Jacques Chirac, Nicolas Sarkozy, who will invite him to attend the military parade of July 14, 2008 to encourage Syria to participate in the Union for the Mediterranean project. He had also initiated indirect negotiations to conclude peace with Israel, "negotiations that will not succeed, but whose mere holding had opened wide the doors of the Élysée Palace to the Syrian head of state[2] . But Bashar al-Assad will be demonized again from the outbreak in January 2012 of the war in Syria.

The outbreak of the uprising

In his book "*Sectarianism in Syria's civil war*[3] ", Fabrice Balanche explains that the outbreak of the uprising in Syria was due less to the oppressive character of the regime than to its sectarian character, which reflects that of the Syrian population. (Composed of five ethnic or religious communities: Sunni, Alawite, Christian, Ismaili and Kurdish). He adds that this sectarian dimension, absent from the Tunisian and Egyptian uprisings, and which was exacerbated by the war, also explains its duration and the fact that Bashar al-Assad has remained in power; he has benefited from the support of minorities and part of the Sunni population. One of the causes of the uprising was the marginalization of rural areas and the terrible drought that the country experienced between 2006 and 2010. The four years of devastating drought deprived 800,000 farmers of their livelihoods, forcing them to abandon their villages for the cities in search of almost non-existent jobs. The UN has estimated that between 2 and 3 million of the 10 million rural people have been reduced to extreme poverty.

The spark that ignited the war was the clumsy repression, on 15 March 2011, of a demonstration in Deraa, a city particularly affected by the economic crisis and where socio-political frustrations had long been building up. Emboldened by the example of the Arab Spring, some young people brandished the slogan of the crowds that had taken to the streets of Tunis and Cairo: "the people want the fall of the regime". Spontaneous or manipulated, this small peaceful demonstration and the brutality of the repression exercised by the security services, were exploited by the internal and external enemies of the regime to try to reverse it. Washington and Paris do not have words harsh enough to condemn the repression and demand the departure of Bashar al-Assad, while Qatar and Saudi Arabia seize the opportunity to settle their accounts with him. It seems that the destabilization of Syria has been planned for at least two years, as evidenced by the fact that, shortly after the Deraa demonstration, which was on a scale not comparable to the mass uprisings in Tunisia and Egypt, thousands of well-armed and well-equipped foreign fighters suddenly poured into Syria. Spreading like wildfire to the most disadvantaged areas of the country, the protests turned into an armed revolution, largely supported by the regime's enemies. The regime refused to accede, even partially, to the demands of the opposition, as advised by Turkish President Erdogan. While at the beginning of their revolt, the opponents demanded more democratization and social justice, the conflict soon took a sectarian turn. Support for the regime or the opposition was conditioned by the interests of the clan and the community: freedom, democracy and human rights became empty slogans. On the other hand, mobilization in the name of Islam against a godless regime progressed among the Sunni working classes. Symptomatically, the battle cry of most Sunni fighters on the ground is "*Allahu Akbar*. The involvement of shia militias, particularly Hezbollah, in the fighting alongside Assad's forces also played a large part in giving the conflict a sectarian and confessional twist. There was certainly resentment in Syria against the Alawite hold on power. But as long as the Assad family's dictatorship was accompanied by a certain redistribution of national wealth in favour of the poorest regions and classes, the sunni majority was content with it. As for the criticism levelled at the regime for its alliance with Iran, it should be remembered that this choice, initiated by Hafez al-Assad, was not motivated by the kinship between Shiites and Alawites, but by considerations of realpolitik: the existence of a common enemy, in this case Saddam Hussein's Iraq, and the desire to break the isolation in which Syria had found itself after the Camp David agreement. While it had managed to make Syria a major player, it has become, as Lebanon was not long ago, the arena where the main geopolitical issues on the regional scene are settled. The war has thus largely turned into a proxy conflict between powers motivated by their own interests, hardly coinciding with those of the Syrian people, despite the formation of a group of "friends of Syria" at the initiative of France. The conflict pitted the regime and its allies (Russia, Iran and Hezbollah) against its regional opponents (Saudi Arabia, Qatar and Turkey), and its Western adversaries (mainly the United States and France, whose government made the fall of the Syrian dictator a high moral obligation). For Russia, scalded by NATO's intervention in Libya and its attempts at encirclement, there is no question of abandoning Syria, which is its main ally in the region, to Western interests alone. Not to mention that the growth of jihadist groups threatens its own national security. While the regime's allies share the same objective, namely to keep it in place, this is not the case with its opponents, whose only real common denominator is the desire to break the Damascus-Tehran axis. The Muslim countries aimed to substitute a Sunni domination for the Alawite hold on power. While the United States and European countries claimed to want to replace it with a democratic regime. But they were torn between their desire to destroy it and their fear of the installation of a radical Islamist power in Damascus. Moreover, the interrupted flow of Syrian refugees from Turkey to Europe since 2015 has probably cooled down somewhat the ardor of some European countries that are desperate to change the political regime in Syria. This flow has been facilitated by Ankara, which has benefited in its relations with the European Union.

Another factor explaining the impasse in which they found themselves was the illusion that Bashar al-Assad would agree through negotiation to voluntarily relinquish power, and even a parcel of power, within the framework of a transitional government. Since a political solution proved impossible, the only solution left open was a military one, which they did not have the means to provide. In addition to the ideological and political motivations of Syria's adversaries, oil issues were also at stake in their destabilization efforts. In November 2010, Saudi Arabia and Qatar asked Bashar al-Assad to open oil and gas export pipelines to the eastern Mediterranean. Syria refused, with the support of Russia. In February 2011, the first unrest encouraged by Qatar and Saudi Arabia broke out in Syria. On July 25, 2011, Iran signed agreements to transport its gas through Syria and Iraq. "Because of its position between the Gulf production fields and the eastern Mediterranean, it is clear that if a political change favorable to the West, the Turks, the Saudis and the Qataris were to occur in Syria, and Syria were to cut itself off from Russia, the entire oil and gas geopolitics of the region would be turned upside down to their advantage. This fact explains in part why Syria is attacked by the Turks, the West and the Gulf monarchies, and conversely why it is not let go, either by the Russians or by the Iranians[4] .

The evolution of the conflict until 2015.

Since the outbreak of the civil war in Syria, the Muslim Brotherhood has enjoyed the support of Turkey and Qatar, while Saudi Arabia, which considers them to be rivals, finances and arms the Salafist movements. As a protector of the Brotherhood since Saudi Arabia repudiated it in the early 1990s, Qatar is convinced that the Islamo-conservatism of the Brotherhood corresponds to the deep aspirations of the Arab peoples. As an instrument of the Qatari government, the satellite channel Al-Jazeera has opened its airwaves to scenes of massacres from Syria. In his flagship program, "Sharia and Life," Sheikh Qadrawi vilifies the Assad clan and its Iranian and Lebanese Hezbollah allies, with increasingly sectarian overtones. As in Libya, where it had supported the National Transitional Council, the political showcase of the rebellion, Qatar has sponsored the Syrian National Council (SNC), which is supposed to be the opposition, but where the Muslim Brotherhood is in the majority. Created in 2011, in Istanbul, on the initiative of the Turkish Islamist party, the AKP, with Qatari funding, it will be sunk by Washington, which considered that it was not representative enough, and instead created the "National Coalition of Opposition Forces and Revolution". Like the NSC, it was weakened by the lack of international recognition and was unable to impose itself on the fighters on the ground. All attempts to form a credible political opposition have proved futile. Faced with this failure, Turkey, Saudi Arabia and Qatar decided to silence their rivalries and join forces to increase the military pressure on the regime. It is mainly the Al-Nosra Front, the Syrian branch of Al-Qaeda, and other Islamist groups that have benefited from their largesse. Thanks to their support, they launched several offensives on the regime's forces, which were losing ground on several fronts. Withdrawing from the countryside and small towns, its troops concentrated on the major cities and main roads. The violence of the regime is matched by that of the Al Nosra Front, which carries out suicide attacks, condemned by the Free Syrian Army (FSA), which is made up of secular opposition fighters.

The escalation of violence prompted the Arab League to propose a peace plan in January 2012 that called for the devolution of power to the vice president, Farouk Charaa, and the opening of a dialogue between the regime and the opposition with a view to forming a national unity government. The plan was endorsed by the UN, but the idea of a devolution of power was buried. A mission of 300 UN observers failed to secure a cease-fire and the fighting resumed. The United States and European countries closed their embassies in Damascus, but no Western state broke off diplomatic relations with Syria. In July 2012, armed opposition groups, believing in a military solution, launched a simultaneous offensive in Damascus, Aleppo and other parts of the country, including Ghouta, and Deraa province. But the regime is firmly holding the capital despite the establishment of opponents in some suburban areas. And the front is stabilizing in Aleppo, between an eastern part held by the regime and a western part held by the opposition.

Alongside the predominantly Arab opposition militias, the Kurds have created their own militia: the Kurdish People's Protection Units (YPD), the military wing of the PYD, the Syrian Kurdish Democratic Party. With American support and the relative passivity of the regime, they have taken control of the northeast of the country and want to make it an autonomous region adjacent to the Kurdish regions of Turkey and Iraq. This objective naturally clashes with Turkey's interests, especially since the PYD is allied with the Turkish PKK, considered a terrorist organization by Ankara. In order to prevent the Kurdish cantons of Jazira and Kobane in the northeast from joining the canton of Afrin in northwestern Syria, Turkey has had an army-backed force occupy an area between that canton and Kobane. President Obama warned Bashar al-Assad in August 2012 against crossing the red line of using chemical weapons. But this warning excludes other weapons used by the regime, which does not deprive itself of them. In particular, the regime has used its air force to drop barrels of TNT on opposition-held areas, causing hundreds of civilian casualties and enormous destruction. After declaring Damascus' use of chemical weapons against civilians a red line, Obama refrained from carrying out his threat of air strikes when, on August 21, 2013, the regime's bombardment of an opposition-held Damascus suburb with chemical shells left 1,400 dead. This retreat embarrassed François Hollande, who had made the same threat. It was Vladimir Putin who cleverly embarrassed Washington by proposing the transfer of Syria's chemical arsenal out of the country, under UN control. This initiative has greatly contributed to strengthening his influence on the Syrian issue.

After the uprising began, many foreign observers thought the regime would collapse quickly, unaware of its internal cohesion and the strength of the bond between its Alawite hard core and the existential threat to the community. But the regime's astonishing resilience and, above all, the Islamist drift of the opposition have changed the situation. While Russian and Iranian support for

Damascus remains unwavering, Western support, led by the United States, for the opposition has begun to wane. In fact, they have no coherent policy on Syria. On the one hand, the Americans want the Assad regime to fall, and on the other hand they have no control over the Islamist opposition, which can only worry them. Unable to accept that the Islamists take power in Syria, the fall of the regime was no longer a priority. From that moment on, Washington gave priority to finding a political solution to the crisis. However, the conference convened in Geneva in February 2014 was a failure, despite the joint American-Russian desire to bring the views of the regime and the political opposition closer together. Divided, its representatives proved their inability to present a viable alternative after forty years of power by the Assad dynasty. Their intransigence, inversely proportional to their influence on the ground, has naturally played into the hands of the regime, which is determined not to make any real concessions. This impasse could only prolong the conflict.

As a result of the West's abandonment, the balance of power has shifted in two directions: in favour of the regime's army, supported by Russia, Hezbollah and the Iranian Revolutionary Guards; and within the opposition groups on the ground. These can be classified into three categories: groups described as "moderate" that fight for a democratic Syria, represented on the ground by the increasingly marginalized Free Syrian Army (FSA). The multiple Islamist factions composed of non-jihadist fundamentalist fighters. This is particularly true of the Muslim Brotherhood and the Salafists, several of whose "brigades", each fighting on its own behalf, have joined forces within the Islamic Salvation Front. Finally, there are the jihadists linked to al-Qaeda, represented by the al-Nosra Front and the Islamic State (Daech according to its Arabic acronym), which first appeared in Syria in late spring 2013. The latter group has a large number of foreign fighters in its ranks who kidnap, indiscriminately execute and subjugate the population to the most obscurantist version of Islam, and even European Muslims who have come to assist their Sunni brethren. The Islamic State's (IS) goal of establishing a caliphate over parts of Iraq and Syria that would mean the partition of those two countries is obviously incompatible with that of the Syrian opposition factions fighting for control of the whole of Syria, and Al- Nosra. While Daech, the most radical rebel group in Syria, and al-Nosra both originated from al-Qaeda's branch in Iraq, their relationship has deteriorated and fighting has raged between them. After unsuccessfully calling on Daech to confine its fight to Iraq, Ayman al-Zawahari, the head of al-Qaeda, disavowed him and declared the al-Nosra Front to be the only movement recognized by al-Qaeda in Syria. From the winter of 2013-2014, the latter finally drove Daech out of the provinces of Aleppo and Idlib. But with its victories in Iraq, Daech took control of the entire Euphrates Valley in Syria in June 2014. Having become by far the most powerful Islamist group, it has won several victories against the regular army, capturing and executing hundreds of soldiers and officers, in a strategy of terror designed to demonstrate both its strength, its resolve and its impunity. Aiming to impose its hegemony over all opposition forces, it represented, along with Al-Nosra, the most serious threat to the regime. In May 2015, it conquered Palmyra, a city of both archaeological and strategic importance in the center of the country. The destruction of part of the ancient site, including the destruction of the Temple of Baal, caused enormous outrage around the world. For their part, the Al-Nosra Front and its allies seized the northwestern governorate of Idlib in March and April 2015. In July 2016, the Al-Nosra Front changed its name to Fath el-Sham and superficially broke its allegiance to al-Qaeda at the request of its Arab sponsors, who made it a condition of their continued support. And in January 2017 the groups associated with Fath al-Sham merged under its leadership into a formation called Hayat Tahrir al-Sham. The balance of power between these three components is completely unbalanced. The democratic and secular current represented by the ASL does not receive substantial aid, while the Islamists have benefited from aid provided by Saudi Arabia and Qatar, as well as by private and occult networks. In addition, they have taken control of the oil resources in the northeast of the country, especially in Deir ez-Zor, which provides them with substantial funding by selling the oil. As a result, the Islamist currents have grown stronger and have taken over the field from the democratic opponents, even seizing the weapons delivered to them by the CIA and other secret services.

Damascus cleverly manipulates Sunni extremism to frighten the West and divide the opposition. It has deliberately fueled Syrian Sunni jihadism, both by facilitating its intervention in Iraq during the American occupation, and by releasing its militants from Syrian prisons in 2011, at the same time that the regime was brutally repressing and arresting thousands of democrats in the Syrian uprising. The Islamization of the opposition and the terror wrought by the Islamic State play into the hands of Bashar al-Assad's regime, which has been at liberty to proclaim, "Look what awaits Syria if the Islamists win!" Consecrating the fiasco of Western policy towards Syria, his presidential mandate has been renewed. But he appears increasingly subservient to Moscow and Tehran. Until the victories of the EI and the coalition between Al-Nosra and its Islamist allies, around 50% of the population was still in the regions controlled by the regime. The rest was divided between contested areas (including the city of Aleppo) and areas controlled by Daech (in the northeast and east), Al-Nosra (in the northwest) and the Kurds[5] . While the population of regime-controlled areas is multi-communal, the population of opposition-controlled areas is exclusively Sunni, as minorities have been forced to flee. In May 2015, the regime appeared to be forced to withdraw to "useful Syria" from Damascus to the coast, passing through Homs and Hama. Or, at worst, to the Alawite reduction on the coast.

The reversal of the balance of power

Russia's intervention in September 2015 completely changed the situation. It put the regime back in the saddle and pushed the rebellion into its entrenchments. After fierce fighting against the militias occupying certain localities surrounding Damascus, which were also besieged by its troops, the regime managed to force them to evacuate. Benefiting from the decisive air support of the Russian air force, its forces and their allies reconquered in December 2016 the part of Aleppo held by the opposition; a victory that constitutes a turning point in the war. Then, between June and November 2017, they recaptured Palmyra and Deir ez-Zor besieged by the jihadists. For their part, the mostly Kurdish Syrian Democratic Forces (SDF), supported by the United States, dislodged the so-called Islamic State from Raqqa and its province in October. But the city was almost completely leveled by U.S. bombing. The geostrategic stakes in this dual advance are control of the land corridor linking Iran to Syria through Iraq, with the regime wanting to secure it and the Americans trying to prevent it. The Russian air force bombed the SDF east of Deir ez-Zor in September 2017 to prevent them from advancing further south. The aim is to block the advance of pro-American forces to Bou Kamal on the Syrian-Iraqi border, after the latter occupied the al-Tanf border crossing further south in June 2017. In early October 2017, the SDF seized the country's largest oil field, located in Deir ez-Zor province on the border with Iraq. But regime forces and their allies scored a decisive point by seizing Bou Kamal, the last town held by the EI, in late October, reaching the Iraqi border and joining forces with the Iraqis. Significantly, General Kassem Souleymani, head of the Iranian pasdaran announced that this victory marked the end of the Islamic State group.

The former Al Nosra Front, which dominates Hayat Tahrir el Cham, has taken advantage of the collapse of the EI to reposition itself as the leader of all jihadist groups fighting in Syria. Desertions within the EI to Hayat Tahrir al-Sham have multiplied. The victory over the various terrorist groups, including Daech, in Syria does not mean the end of radical Islamist ideology, nor does it mean the end of these organizations. On the contrary, their defeat on the ground could lead to an increase in their attacks on Syrian territory and transnational terrorism. "The rout of the EI on the Syrian-Iraqi front and the lost gamble of Abu Bakr al-Baghdadi offer a new terrain of conquest, or rather reconquest, for al-Qaeda. Its leader, Ayman Al-Zawahri, is reportedly actively working on this. He and Osama bin Laden's son, Hamza, who appears to be the rising star of the organization, are calling on all jihadists around the world to join his fight[6] . In a recording released on September 14, the now 29-year-old calls for the mobilization of his "Muslim brothers from Indonesia to the Maghreb to join the jihad" in Syria against the regime and the coalition countries.

The unavoidable role of Russia

The Syrian conflict has produced two winners: Russia and Iran, and two losers: the West and the Arab petro-monarchies. Turkey, a Sunni power neighbouring Syria, could also be among the winners if it manages to extend its zone of influence to northern Syria. Two years after the start of its military intervention, Russia has established itself as a key player in Syria and the Middle East. While the Americans, for whom Syria represents a relatively secondary interest, are handicapped by their hesitations and contradictory objectives, Vladimir Putin has a clear strategy and objectives: to prevent the fall of the main regime allied to Moscow in the region. To have a naval base in the eastern Mediterranean. To ensure control of the potentially oil-rich Syrian coast. Remove the jihadist threat which weighs much more on the Russian Federation than on the United States. Finally, to consolidate its status as a great power in a context of resumption of the Cold War since the Ukrainian crisis. Since the fall of Aleppo East, the Russians have tried to turn their military success into a political victory by organizing negotiations in Astana, the capital of Kazakhstan, on May 4, 2017. They resulted in an agreement between Russians, Turks and Iranians, providing for the creation of four de-escalation zones: in the provinces of Idlib and Homs, in the Eastern Ghouta region, as well as in southern Syria. This role was previously played by the UN, the United States and the Europeans. In addition to being able to rely on its military commitment in Syria, Russian diplomacy is the only one that can now boast of speaking to all the players in the region, whether it be the Syrian regime, Turkey, Iran, Israel, the Kurds or Saudi Arabia. It has taken Russia less than two years to become a strategic competitor of the West in the Middle East. But it is struggling to turn military victory into political success. Russia's peace efforts face two obstacles: the intransigence of the insurgency, which, although it has become a very small minority, has boycotted the Astana talks and still refuses to consider the future of Syria with Bashar al-Assad, and the obstruction of the United States. What comes next is likely to be complicated. Russia has achieved success in Syria. But it will be difficult to win the peace. Even if it manages to get everyone to agree, it will not have the means to finance the reconstruction of the country.

The global power imbalance between Russia and the United States in favour of the latter has not prevented Vladimir Putin from re-establishing his country's influence in the Middle East to the detriment of the West. The latter is preponderant in Syria, where Russia has been relatively consistent in its stance since 2011. "It is probably the state that has been the clearest over time and does not prejudge the political action itself. Russia has a position that says: I support the Syrian army, more than the Syrian political regime; and I support the integrity of the state in Syria[7] ." Putin is undoubtedly aware that Bashar al-Assad's continued rule mortgages the stabilization of his protectorate, but he cannot afford to let him go. And he has to deal with the interests of Iran and Turkey, two powers without which a solution to the conflict is impossible. Having military bases in Syria, Russia controls the Mediterranean coastline, which is potentially rich in hydrocarbons; a situation which Qatar has taken note of by signing an important agreement with Moscow which could eventually lead to the delivery of its gas through a pipeline leading to the Syrian coast (although this issue was one of the reasons for the outbreak of the war!) But the most spectacular manifestation of Russia's growing influence is the about-face of a Turkey, weakened by its internal difficulties and the spectre of the creation of a Kurdish entity in Syria, which has engaged in increased military and economic cooperation with Russia. As a sign of Russia's preponderant influence in Syria, Vladimir Potin received, on November 20, 2017, Bashar el- Assad, showing by this, on the one hand, that the latter is destined to remain in place. Then, on the 22nd, he organized a summit in Sochi between himself, and the Turkish president, Erdogan and Iranian president, Rohani, aimed at finding a political solution to the Syrian conflict. The Kremlin does not only intend to transform the Astana process, which has created military de-escalation zones in Syria, into a political solution. It also hopes to compete with the Geneva negotiations, which are due to resume under the auspices of the UN. The three presidents said they were in favour of holding a congress between the opposition and the regime. But the idea does not please either the opposition or the West, which favours the Geneva framework. Despite these reservations, the Sochi summit illustrates the failure of the heterogeneous coalition bringing together the United States, European nations, Israel, Turkey and the Gulf petro-monarchies.

The position of other powers

The U.S. is both less engaged than Russia in Syria and its policy is less clear. According to the former US ambassador to Syria, Robert Ford, the US has spent at least $12 billion in military and civilian expenditures to bring about regime change in Syria over the four years from 2014 to 2017, in addition to the billions already spent in the previous three years after the war broke out in 2011.8 The US has not been a major enemy in Syria. Barak Obama nevertheless considered that the main enemy was not Bashar al-Assad, who never posed a terrorist threat to the West, but Daech. This position was confirmed by Donald Trump, although in April 2017 he ordered the cruise missile bombing of a Syrian regime military base, after the latter had again used chemical weapons against the civilian population. It was not this one-time bombing that could change the game in Syria. On the one hand, because Washington has once again made it clear that its priority is to defeat Daech and not to overthrow the regime. And on the other hand, because a direct military engagement on its part against the latter entails a risk of confrontation with Russia. Not to mention that strikes, especially limited to missiles, without a commitment - out of the question - of ground troops cannot win the decision. As evidence of the American about-face, the Washington Post had thought it would announce the end of CIA support for the "moderate" rebels. But the United States has announced that it wants to remain in Syria - where it has 2,000 troops - until the EI is completely defeated, but also to counter Iranian influence and use the Syrian card in its dealings with Russia. What seems to prove this is the announcement of the creation of a 30,000-strong border force under US command, composed of the mostly Kurdish Syrian (so-called democratic) forces (SDF). Unveiling the U.S. strategy, Secretary of State Rex Tillerson on January 18, 2018, justified the continued U.S. presence in Syria by the need to "prevent a resurgence of the Islamic State, ensure that the resolution of this conflict does not allow Iran to move closer to its grand goal of control of the region, and lead to the departure of Bashar al Assad." A stable, united and independent Syria, requires, in fine, a post-Assad leadership to come into being he insisted[9] ". Commenting on this announcement, Professor Joshua Landis explained that "the United States wants to keep Syria weak and poor.

According to him, they are occupying the northeast of Syria to prevent it from accessing its oil. They want Syria to become a quagmire for Russia and Iran[10] . Betting on the PYD to put pressure on the regime, Iran and Moscow, however, seems to be a very risky bet, especially since Washington does not give itself the means of its policy; and the control by the Kurds, supported by the Americans, of cities like Raqqa and Mambij arouses strong resentment among their Arab inhabitants[11] . As if they did not have enough enemies in Syria, the Americans have alienated Turkey. Ankara and Damascus, of course, reacted virulently to the American announcement. And on March 25, 2018, U.S. General Joseph Votel, head of Central Command (Centcom), which directs U.S. military operations in Asia and the Middle East, said that the American mission in Syria is "strictly focused on defeating the EI." This statement seems to moderate the objectives stated by former Secretary of State Rex Tillerson and indicates that Washington is aware of the need to allay Turkish fears regarding their support for the Kurds. But it will not be easy for them to balance the two. Finally, in a sign of the wavering of American policy, Donald Trump declared in early April 2018 that American troops in Syria should soon "come home." Whether this is in line with his campaign promise to put "America first, or whether it serves as a means of pressure on Riyadh to extort more resources from it to finance the maintenance of American forces there, does not diminish the impression of confusion of the signal it sends. Taking note, as it were, of the American and Western defeat in Syria, it can only delight Washington's Russian, Iranian and Syrian adversaries and worry its allies: the Arab monarchies of the Gulf, who fear that a possible American withdrawal would offer an unexpected gift to Iran. And above all the Kurds, who risk being left at the mercy of Turkey after having served as auxiliary troops against the Islamic State. "Russia and the United States agree on fighting Islamic terrorism in Syria. But they still differ on how to fight it. Russia says the Bashar al-Assad regime should be retained, although it remains ambiguous about the fate of the Syrian president, because it believes he is the best bulwark against terrorism. The United States believes that President Assad's regime, which has bombed its own population, is responsible, because its functioning and the stubbornness of its leader to cling to power create an open door for terrorism[12] . The conflict of interests between Moscow and Washington is therefore inevitable. Each will try to minimize the role of the other in resolving the crisis.

Turkey initially viewed with extreme mistrust the Russian intervention, which countered its own aims in northern Syria. It expressed this mistrust by shooting down a Russian military plane under the pretext that it had violated Turkish airspace. This serious incident obviously poisoned Russian-Turkish relations. But, American support for the Kurds in Syria led, from the summer of 2016, Turkey to move closer to Moscow and Tehran to the great displeasure of NATO, of which it is a member. After having been the main sponsor of the rebellion against the regime, Turkey withdrew the Islamist militias it supports from the front of Aleppo, the bastion of the rebellion, which allowed the capture of the western part of the city. In return, the Russians acquiesced to the Turkish army's occupation in 2016 of a corridor separating the two Kurdish cantons of Afrin and Kobane. Ankara's reversal was motivated by its desire to counter Kurdish expansion in northern Syria, and by the feeling that it had been betrayed by its American ally, the main supporter of the Syrian Kurds. Despite this calculation, the Turks have sought to take advantage of their support for the rebel forces to gain influence on the Syrian terrain and to settle the Kurdish problem. This now leads them to defend positions that are antagonistic to those of their new allies, concerning Bashar al-Assad and the Kurds. The contradictions of Turkish policy were again highlighted in January 2018 by the intervention of loyalist forces in the province of Idlib, which threatens the heart of Ankara's zone of influence. By dint of having a foot in each camp, Turkey almost lost on all fronts in Syria. But it managed to regain control by driving Kurdish militiamen out of Afrin canton in March 2018. And the fate of Idlib, the last jihadist-dominated province in Syria, will largely be determined by the attitude of Turkey, which is engaged in a consolidation of its sphere of influence in northwestern Syria.

The failure of the West to overthrow the Syrian regime by financing and arming the Islamists, despite the calamitous consequences of its interventions in Iraq and Libya, is obvious. Will he learn from this? Will he put an end to his policy of ostracizing Russia and demonizing Vladimir Putin? Since his election, Emmanuel Macron has adopted a more pragmatic attitude towards Syria than his predecessor. "Bashar is the enemy of the Syrian people, but not of France," he declared. But ruining Paris's chances of having an influence on the Syrian file, the French head of state nevertheless considered that President Assad was a "criminal" and would have to answer for his crimes before international justice, while specifying that it was up to the Syrian people to freely choose their leader[13] .

Russia's ally of circumstance, the other winner of the war in Syria is Iran. But this can only reinforce the hostility of the Gulf states, particularly Saudi Arabia bogged down in Yemen, towards the Islamic Republic, whose Shiite co-religionists have reconquered the Sunni city of Mosul. Moreover, Iranian forces and their Hezbollah clients are now present near or opposite the part of the Golan Heights controlled by Israel and the Quneitra crossing that separates it from the part of the territory controlled by Syria. This situation is intolerable for Israel, which cannot allow the Iranians to make this region an active second front line against the Jewish state, in addition to southern Lebanon, and has conducted several dozen raids since 2012 against bases and arms convoys destined for Hezbollah, or other targets linked to Iran.

For Caroline Galactéros: "The Western powers must now face up to their inconsistency and acknowledge their defeat: Syria has resisted its programmed break-up and the overthrow of its regime. They must also save face while admitting an inescapable reality: the return of Moscow to the Middle East, which upsets all balances and alliances, and that of Iran as a regional power.

And she continues: "The last actor whose intentions remain unclear and whose destabilizing maneuvers are to be feared remains Israel. It must take note of the military victory of the 'axis of resistance' in Syria. But this pragmatism cannot go so far as to allow the much feared "Shiite crescent" to consolidate without a word in the form of a land corridor linking Lebanon, Syria, Iraq and Iran. This red line is sharper than ever for Tel Aviv, whose real fear is to have the Revolutionary Guards on its doorstep and, in the event of war, to face a front running from southern Lebanon to the Golan Heights .[14]

What future for Syria?

It is becoming increasingly clear that, thanks to Russia's decisive intervention, Bashar al-Assad, who already controls the most populous part of the country and all the major cities, will remain in place, even if he finds himself at the head of a country in ruins. The victories against Daech and other jihadist groups raise the question of Syria's future. The collapse of the Islamic State arguably removes the specter of challenging the country's borders. At the beginning of 2018 four parts of the territory still escaped the regime's authority: eastern Ghouta, the regions dominated by the American-backed Kurds and the provinces of Idlib and Deraa. Eastern Ghouta, the last rebel stronghold on the outskirts of Damascus, with a population of around 400,000, was a threat to the security of the capital and a challenge to the regime's authority that it could not tolerate. The Kurds who form the majority of the SDF (which is democratic in name only) are far from being considered liberators by the Arab population of Raqqa, Manbij and Tell Abyad, who do not want to be under their domination, which raises the problem of its governance. Hayat Tahnir el-Sham jihadists and militias affiliated with Turkey still occupy the Idlib governorate. They are not covered by the ceasefire agreed by Russia, Turkey and Iran and accepted by the regime and moderate rebels. They are also excluded from the negotiations to find a political solution. The governorate of Idlib is therefore set to become the next theater of the confrontation that will decide the outcome of the war. The regime cannot afford to leave this region in the hands of Hayat Tahrir el Cham, while Turkey considers it part of its sphere of influence.

With more than 350,000 people dead, 7 million refugees and 6.3 million internally displaced, there is no reason to be optimistic about Syria's future. Sunni resentment at the setbacks suffered by the opposition can only deepen the age-old SunniAlawite divide. The establishment of an inclusive democracy advocated by western states is illusory. Some experts believe that the Syrian government will eventually extend its control over the entire territory. But this does not guarantee peace as long as Bashar al-Assad, who has bombed his own population, remains in power. Nor is it clear how the hatred accumulated by the atrocities perpetrated on both sides and the hundreds of thousands of victims of the war could make national reconciliation possible. The regime's use of terror to silence opposition has claimed more lives than the violence of Daech. The abuse of detainees in Syrian jails has been commonplace. A military police photographer in exile made public in 2015 53,000 photographs of bodies tortured to death. And the number of missing was estimated at 200,000 in 2017. For Farouk Mardam-Bey "None of the conditions required for civil peace and national reconciliation exist in Syria. On the contrary, everything that happens is a portent of new misfortunes in the near or distant future. For Syria, for the Middle East, for the whole world that has witnessed the ordeal of the Syrian people in indifference and often in an unacknowledged complicity with the executioners[15] .

The beginning of the end or the end of the beginning?

After the victory at El Alamcin, which marked the beginning of the turnaround in the fortunes of arms in World War II, Winston Churchill said, "Now this is not the end. It is not even the beginning of the end. But it is, perhaps, the end of the beginning[16] . The same remark could be made about the Syrian conflict. The near elimination of the Islamic State, which had the advantage of uniting everyone against it, has opened a new phase of the war. "As long as the tug of war between Russia and the United States, but also between Iran and Saudi Arabia, continues, there will be no peace in Syria. Everyone is trying to establish their influence in the region via the Syrian theater. It is a global war, by proxy, that is now being played out[17] . The regime and its allies are determined to reconquer the last strongholds held by the jihadists. The Turks cannot tolerate the presence of the Kurdish PYD on their border. Moscow is letting Ankara attack the Kurds to force them to seek protection from Russia via the Syrian regime and to break their alliance with the United States. The possibility of an Israeli intervention, which is multiplying its threats against the presence of Iran and Hezbollah in Syria, cannot be ruled out. As for the United States, its policy is less clear than ever. After having stated that they do not intend to step aside in Syria, they seem to want to withdraw. In any case the chapter of military confrontations is far from closed. The attack in January 2018 on the Russian air base of Hmeimim and the naval base of Tartus by a large dozen armed drones, assumes sophisticated technology that implies a powerful sponsorship. And several offensives led by the regime and Turkey respectively have begun. The regime has tried unsuccessfully to regain a foothold in the oil-rich part of the province of Deir ez-Zor located east of the Euphrates and held by the Kurdish allies of the Americans, attracting a devastating response from the latter.

The Syrian army supported by its Russian and Iranian allies has launched an offensive on the province of Idlib, the last still in the hands of jihadists, where those who were driven out of their other enclaves have retreated. As for Ankara, its response to Rex Tillerson's statement was not long in coming. Fighters from the Free Syrian Army (FSA), with strong support from the Turkish army, dislodged the PYD from the Kurdish "canton" of Afrin with the tacit consent of the Russians, who left the city as soon as the Turkish offensive began (operation "olive branch"). After taking control of Afrin, Turkey is threatening to push its offensive all the way to the Euphrates. The entire border region should serve as a reception area for Syrian refugees settled in Turkey, who would be placed under its protection. According to Fabrice Balanche, a specialist in the countries of the Levant at Stanford University, this eventuality could push the Kurds to turn to Russia and Iran for protection from Ankara, since the Americans refuse to support them[18] . For its part, during a raid against Iranian targets in Syria, an Israeli F16 fighter jet was shot down by Syrian air defence; a clear sign that the war in Syria is far from over and that each of its actors is seeking to mark its territory. This is the opinion of Fabrice Balanche, for whom the year 1918 will not be the year of peace in Syria and the solution will not be political but military. For him: "the Westerners do not want to admit that they have lost the war. They prolong the conflict to show the Russians that they have not abandoned the field. They cry about the humanitarian disaster at the UN, but in any case, they are also responsible for it. Everyone knows the outcome of the conflict .[19]

In February 2018, the Syrian army set out to dislodge the jihadists from Eastern Ghouta. At the cost of deadly bombardments killing hundreds of civilians, it managed to regain control of this area in early April 2018, the fall of which marks one of the worst defeats of the rebels since the beginning of the war. The Afrin and Ghouta fronts have led to one of the worst humanitarian crises since the conflict began in 2011, with tens of thousands of civilians displaced by the fighting. As for the jihadists and their families, they have been evacuated, under Russian protection, to the province of Idilb. The alleged use of chemical weapons by the regime against the town of Douma in Ghouta has led to threats of retaliation from the American and French presidents and British Prime Minister Theresa May. Without the endorsement of the Security Council and without waiting for the outcome of the UN experts' investigation, the United States, France and the United Kingdom decided to carry out these threats, in the name of the "right to protection" (of civilians), despite warnings from Moscow. Limited to Syrian military targets, their strikes, carried out at night on April 14, 2018, will have no effect on the outcome of the war. The three leaders have moreover clarified that the objective of this warning strike, which carefully avoided attacking Russian facilities, was in no way to overthrow the regime or change the balance of power on the ground. Its detractors have described it as illegal and as a gesticulation masking their impotence.

Even if a de jure division of Syria is now excluded, and if the sovereignty of the central power will nominally be exercised over the whole country, it will probably be de facto divided into three zones of Russian-Iranian, Turkish and probably American influence. Unless the United States gives up a military presence in Syria, in accordance with Donald Trump's statement. Most of the territory and population will be under Russian-Iranian influence. Turkey already exerts its influence over part of Idlib province and Afrin canton. And it wants to extend it to the region along its border from Afrin to the western bank of the Euphrates, which can only create more friction between Ankara and Washington; unless the two NATO partners come to an agreement on the back of the Kurds. The possibility of a U.S.-Turkish deal could ruin Kurdish dreams of self-government, as it did in Iraq. The rival countries that are home to

Kurdish minorities all agree on one thing: there is no question of undermining their territorial integrity for the benefit of the Kurds. In the context of the balance of power that is in its favour, thanks to Russian and Iranian support, the regime is called upon to retain power and is probably not ready to make concessions that could lead to a political solution. If such a solution does eventually materialize, representatives of the "moderate" opposition are expected to join the government in Damascus, provided of course that they do not call for President Assad's departure. UN Special Envoy for Syria Staffan de Mistura said the Syrian opposition must accept that it has "not won the war," while urging the government not to claim victory. If the regime agrees to form a government that includes representatives of the opposition, the government should in principle begin to draft a new constitution. Assad is naturally in favour of maintaining a strong central power, while the formulas that are most likely to win the support of the other parties are broad administrative decentralization or even a federal system. But in any case, it is illusory to think that this could lead to the establishment of democracy. As long as Bashar al-Assad remains in power, which is almost certain for the foreseeable future, the Syrian regime will not be recognized by the West and the oil monarchies. And they will not agree to finance the reconstruction of Syria without a change that ensures an effective political transition. Will China, which has the means, take advantage of this to gain a foothold? Another question is that of the demographic consequences of the war in view of the large-scale displacement of populations, sometimes taking the form of ethnical and religious cleansing. There is also the problem of the fate of the seven million refugees outside the country. It is to be feared that the majority of them will not want to or will not be able to return to their homes any time soon, not only because of their destruction and the enormous cost of rebuilding the country, but also because of the regime's probable reluctance to welcome them in the regions from which they were expelled. It has a vested interest in reducing the demographic weight of the sunni population, which is mostly hostile to its power. The government has thus passed, at the end of March 2018, a law requiring all Syrians to register their property titles within 2 months. As this will be impossible for

Most of the refugees will be able to get their hands on their belongings, making their return even less likely. This problem affects not only Syria but also neighboring countries, especially Lebanon, which hosts more than one and a half million refugees on its

1L'Orient arabe a l'heure américaine, Henry Laurens, Hachette Pluriel 2004, p. 115

2 The New Question of the East, Georges Corm, La Découverte 2017, p. 59

3 Sectarianism in Syria's civil war, Fabrice Balanche www.washihingtoninstitute.org

4 https://fr.novopress.info/.../aymeric-chauprade-ou-vont-la-Syrie-et-le-Moyen-Orient/

5 https://www.lorientlejour.com/article/1072078/assad-controle-desormais-plus-de-la-half-land-in-a-country-in-ruin.html

6 https://www.middleeasteye.net/fr/opinions/en-syrie-le-plus-grand-fiasco-de-la-cia-

7.https://arretsurinfo.ch/un-ambassadeur-us-confirme-que-des-milliards-ont-ete-expenditure-to-cause-a-regime-change-in-syria/

8 almashareq.com/en/articles/cnmi_am/features/2017/10/05/feature-01

9 Statement made during a joint press conference with Donald Trump in Paris on September 19, 2017: www.lefigaro.fr

10 http://galacteros.over-blog.com/2017/10/quelle-equation-israelienne-au-moyen-orient.html

11 www.wikistrike.com/.../hamza-le-fils-d-oussama-ben-laden-aurait-pris-les-orders

12 https://www.lorientlejour.com/article/1104936/farouk-mardam-bey-aucune-des-conditions-required-for-civil-peace-in-syria.html

13 https://www.brainyquote.com/quotes/winston_churchill_163144

14 http://www.europe1.fr/international/sept-ans-de-guerre-en-syrie-racontes-en-sept-images-3599495

15 http://www.lemonde.fr/international/article/2018/01/18/face-a-l-ei-l-iran-et-assad-l-armee-americaine-va-rester-en-syrie_5243245_3210.html

16.https://www.al-monitor.com/pulse/originals/2018/02/turkey-olive-branch-syria-slows.html

17. "The United States wants to keep Syria weak and poor" @joshua_landis #F24Debate @France24

18 http://www.france24.com/fr/20180314-syrie-guerre-occidentaux-perdu-russie-assad- poutine-kurdes-entretien-balanche?ref=fb

19 ibid.

Chapter 17. The power game since 2001

United States Policy

The September 11 attacks were used to justify the U.S. "crusades" against Islamic totalitarianism and "rogue states. The military interventionism of the United States reached its peak under the Bush father and son administrations in Afghanistan and Iraq. With the conquest of Iraq in 2003, the Arab East seems more than ever to have come under American hegemony. However, in the summer of 2003, the failure of the roadmap to resolve the Arab-Israeli conflict marked the first major American setback, followed by the gradual realization of the extent of the difficulties in Iraq, which was supposed to be a model for the region. The State Department was concerned about the deterioration of the image of the United States in the Arab and Muslim world. In this context, the Bush administration prepared and announced, in early 2004, the "Greater Middle East Initiative[1] ". For the neo-conservatives who inspired it, the aim was to encourage the emergence of a democratic Middle East by means of various forms of aid or incentives to progress along the path of social and political reform and opening up to the market economy. The American initiative was presented at the G8 meeting in June. However, it aroused strong reservations among the Arab regimes in power, which viewed the desire to involve civil society with suspicion. Since the initiative was not a success, Washington quickly reverted to a carrot-and-stick policy. States that agreed to follow its policies were labelled "moderate", notwithstanding their authoritarian nature and disregard for human rights, while those that opposed them were denounced as "radical". Traditional U.S. support for Israel and the fight against radical Islam cannot alone explain U.S. military interventions in the Middle East. They cannot be understood without taking into account the geostrategic importance of the region's oil and gas resources. Analysts and political scientists are accustomed to attributing to the United States a determining role in the affairs of the region. Their military interventions since the first Gulf War in 1991 have certainly proved them right. But these interventions were probably the culmination of its attempts to reshape the region to suit its interests and those of Israel. Since then, their influence has diminished for several reasons: the disastrous consequences of these interventions; their enormous cost; the fact that they are called upon to be less dependent on oil from the region and to turn more towards the Asia-Pacific zone; and finally the emergence of a multipolar international geopolitical context in which the so-called "BRICS" countries, principally Russia and China, have more and more influence in world affairs, and the common desire to counter the supremacy of the West.

The disastrous effects of the invasion of Iraq under President George W. Bush led to the beginnings of a retreat under President Barak Obama, who was wrongly denounced as pusillanimous, particularly with regard to the conflict in Syria. Despite his realization that the United States could not and should not assume the role of world policeman, as long as this did not jeopardize American interests, his foreign policy cannot be described as isolationist. The "strategic pivot" to Asia that American foreign policy has undergone during his presidency will in no way diminish his involvement in Middle Eastern affairs. Moving away from the policy inspired by the neoconservatives, Obama has tried during his two terms to repair the mistakes of his predecessor. Washington's relative disengagement was evident during his presidency in the military intervention in Libya, where he left the initiative to Britain and France, as well as in his reluctance to support the Syrian opposition militarily. Extremely skeptical, the American president was eventually persuaded to intervene in Libya within the framework of international legality to protect the population against the threats made against it by Muammar Gaddafi. The chaos caused by the fall of the regime will make him regret it. On the other hand, he not only maintained American troops in Afghanistan, but intensified the campaign to eliminate the main terrorist leaders, culminating in the elimination of Osama Bin Laden. Overwhelmed by the magnitude of the 2011 wave of uprisings, the State Department supports the Muslim Brotherhood, believing that the Brotherhood could provide a credible political alternative, not only in Egypt but also in Tunisia and Syria. The American services deployed a lot of resources and energy to help the Brotherhood gain access to vacant powers. It was a short-lived success: Rached Ghannouchi, the leader of Ennahdha, came to power in Tunisia, while Mohamed Morsi, the president of the Freedom and Justice Party, an offshoot of the Brotherhood, took the throne of Mubarak, who had been the Brotherhood's main Arab ally. After a year in power, the coffers were empty, thirty million Egyptians were on the streets and allowed the army to take over. Tunisia also experienced a development that gradually marginalized the Muslim Brotherhood. When the civil war became widespread in Syria from the fall of 2011, risking destabilizing the entire region, the American services were going to rely on the "Free Syrian Army" and the Islamists who supported a "local jihad" against those of Al Qaeda, supporters of the "global jihad. But the latter will end up eliminating their rivals, confirming the failure of American policy in Syria.

The nuclear agreement with Iran, on the other hand, can be considered one of the greatest diplomatic successes of the Obama presidency. Convinced that the diplomatic path is the best way to prevent Iran from becoming a nuclear power, he will make this objective his strategic priority in the region. Even if it means alienating the two traditional allies of the United States, Israel and Saudi Arabia, who will take a very dim view of this consecration of Iran's role as a regional power. The Zionist lobby in Washington is trying in vain to oppose it. The agreement between Iran and the 5+1 (United States, China, Russia, United Kingdom, France, Germany), signed in Vienna on July 14, 2015, is the perfect example of the Obama doctrine. The bet being that Iran will end up being less repressive internally by reintegrating the concert of nations and adopt a less aggressive foreign policy. However, the American president has not succeeded in putting an end to American wars. Far from it. On the contrary, his willingness to disengage from Iraq and Afghanistan has virtually undone hard-won gains. The withdrawal of the U.S. military has allowed the rise of the Taliban in Afghanistan and the birth of the Islamic State (IS) in Iraq and Syria, which are much closer to Europe and the United States than the caves of Afghanistan. While the Iraqi power set up by the US has distanced itself from them. The relative American withdrawal has encouraged Iran to pursue its enterprise of conquering regional hegemony in direct confrontation with the Saudi rival and has left Russia to make a dramatic comeback in the Middle East. The 44e American president has not been able to take advantage of the Arab Spring to support moderate forces in the region. And he waited until the last month of his term to make a strong gesture in favour of the Palestinians, by refraining from vetoing a UN resolution condemning Israeli colonization, after having offered the Jewish state record military aid for the next ten years.

Illustrated by the slogan "America first," Donald Trump's foreign policy in the Middle East seemed at first glance to be in line with the relative disengagement initiated by his predecessor. It should not be forgotten that the latter had even described the United States as an "indispensable nation". But in view of the many reversals of the new White House tenant, nothing is less certain. Should U.S. allies be concerned? Should their adversaries rejoice in the power vacuum that may result? The least we can say is that Donald Trump is blowing hot and cold. After calling NATO "an obsolete organization" he went back on his words. And after having expressed a desire for rapprochement with Russia, he had to backtrack under pressure from Congress. His hostility towards Iran should reassure the Gulf petro-monarchies and Israel. But his intention to call into question the Iran nuclear deal is causing great concern, not to mention the opposition of the European co-signatories to the agreement. It shows that he is determined to counter the Islamic Republic's hegemonic ambitions by all means. The March 2018 replacement of Secretary of State Rex Tillerson with Mike Pompeo, reputed to be a hawk, is a sign of this hardening. Trump's dramatic visit to Riyadh is along the same lines and is also likely aimed at encouraging a Saudi-Israeli rapprochement. Playing on the Saudis' fear of the Iranian threat and of being abandoned by the United States, which is less dependent on their oil, he took advantage of the opportunity to extract hundreds of billions of dollars in arms purchases and contracts from them in exchange for American protection. In the Arab-Israeli conflict, no solution was possible without the Americans. Almost no one in the last few decades could seriously dispute this claim. Even the actors most hostile to American influence had to accept, at some point, that negotiations had to go through Washington, the only superpower in the Middle East since the end of the Cold War. By announcing his decision to recognize Jerusalem as the capital of Israel, Donald Trump broke with decades of American diplomacy, which consisted of avoiding at all costs taking a decision that could jeopardize the future peace process. It is this caution that, despite the strategic alliance between Israel and the United States, has allowed

Washington to present itself as the best possible mediator in the Israeli-Palestinian conflict since the early 1990s. "The Americans have taken themselves totally out of the game. They have disqualified themselves from their position as mediators. To want to play the mediator and at the same time take a decision that is radically contrary to international law is to put an end to their own initiatives," analyzes Jean-Paul Chagnollaud, a researcher at the Institute for Research and Studies of the Mediterranean and the Middle East (Iremmo)[2] . And Mahmoud Abbas has pronounced the Oslo process dead. But Washington does not care and, aware of the impotence of the Arab world, has clearly opted to accentuate its unconditional support for Israel.

Other potentially far-reaching initiatives by the Trump administration concern the Syrian issue. Its initial decision to continue its military support for the predominantly Kurdish "Syrian democratic forces", despite the defeat of Daech, had several objectives: to create a strategic anchor for American influence on the Iranian-Iraqi-Syrian border, to counter that of Russia, and undoubtedly to compromise the reunification of Syria by the Assad regime. But this could only further alienate Turkey, strengthen the Russian-Turkish-Iranian tactical alliance and further distance Ankara from the Western camp. By playing the Kurdish card, the United States risked losing on both counts. Then Donald Trump hinted in early April 2018 that Washington was considering withdrawing its troops from Syria, a few days after the State Department and the Pentagon had said the opposite. This would not be the first American flip-flop, nor would it be the first time the U.S. has dropped its allies. "Keep me from my friends, my enemies I will take care of." This saying could apply to U.S. allies, as opposed to those of Moscow, which is otherwise more reliable towards them. Not to mention that an American withdrawal from Syria would be a gift to Iran and Russia. Donald Trump's headshots and contradictory statements from the White House, the State Department and the Pentagon highlight the current lack of American doctrine regarding the region. It contrasts with the clear vision and mastery of the game of a Vladimir Putin or a Xi Jin Ping on the global geopolitical chessboard. All these maneuvers on the ground are a sign of an even more global struggle. "It is the order of the new world that is taking shape. An order that was believed to be immutable and which has been challenged by the rise of China, the Russian renaissance, the reconfiguration of the balance in the Levant in the wake of the Afghan, Iraqi, Libyan and Syrian fiascos and the failure of the Arab Spring, and finally the spectacular gain of influence of the Moscow-Tehran axis .[3]

Europe

The ambivalent relations between Europe and the countries of the Middle East are determined by factors that create communities of interest and others that generate friction. Among the first are geographical proximity, the fact that Europe imports most of its energy - oil and gas - from the region and that it sells a substantial fraction of its exports there, and the presence in Europe of several million Muslims. But there is no shortage of tensions, such as the memory of colonialism, the Israeli-Palestinian conflict, which has never ceased to fuel the resentment of the Arab states towards the West, the negative image of Islam, the radicalization of a large segment of Europe's Muslim youth, the resurgence of jihadist terrorist attacks and the considerable influx of migrants from the Middle East and North Africa. As a result, these regions tend to be perceived as a source of unwanted migration and terrorism. While many Europeans see Islam as a threat to European civilization and values; some European leaders do not hesitate to declare that Europe is at war with radical Islam. Aware of the gap that had opened up between European countries and the countries of the southern and eastern Mediterranean, the European Union had tried to bridge it. The main Euro-Mediterranean partnership initiative was the Barcelona Process, also known as Euromed, which began in 1995 and aimed to establish a Euro-Mediterranean zone of peace, stability and security. The challenge was to turn the Mediterranean into an economically integrated area beyond its political divisions and its cultural and religious heterogeneity. But the results of this process were very mixed, which gave rise to the politically more ambitious project of the Union for the Mediterranean, launched in 2008 by Nicolas Sarkozy, who initially wanted to call it the "Union of the Mediterranean" and include only the riparian countries. Despite the fact that its initial mission and objectives, notably the creation of a free trade zone between the European Union and the southern and eastern Mediterranean countries, were scaled back, it was more or less put on hold following the "Arab Spring. That said, its failure is also due to the fact that the northern and eastern countries of the European Union, which were associated with it at the insistence of Germany, did not see the same interest as France, which had taken the initiative, Italy or Spain. Despite the awareness of all stakeholders of the magnitude of the crisis, no serious attempt has been made to revive Mediterranean and Euro-Arab cooperation since the "Arab Spring". Although the instability of the Middle East and the rise of radical Islamism affects it more directly, the loss of influence of Washington has not benefited Europe, which is struggling to define a common foreign policy. Or rather, it is largely aligned with that of the United States. It has difficulty finding vectors on which it can intervene outside of humanitarian issues. Although less biased towards Israel, it has too many differences to develop a credible political line that would allow it to have an influence on the Arab-Israeli conflict. Europe is thus content with a role as a banker or patron of the peace process. When Brussels tries to play the role of mediator in the Middle East, it comes up against difficulties due to both the Israeli-American partnership and the strong mistrust of a large part of Israeli opinion. With the exception of Shimon Peres and certain intellectuals, the promoters of a more active European role are rare within the Israeli political class. Nor does the European Union have more influence in the conflicts in Syria and Iraq, despite its participation in the military interventions against the Islamic State group led by the US-led coalition. At the state level, France and Great Britain, for obvious historical reasons, are the countries most politically and militarily involved in the Middle East. But while the latter has long been the dominant power in the region, it is now less active than France and its policy is more aligned with that of the United States. The Brexit can only strengthen its special relationship with Washington and exclude it from any initiatives the EU might take towards the region in the future, while remaining a major pillar of NATO. As for Germany, the fact that it refrains from participating in Western military interventions in the region does not prevent it, on the contrary, from having a strong influence in the region thanks to its economic weight and its humanitarian action.

France

Although French foreign policy is largely framed within a European and Atlantic framework, France is called upon to continue to play its own role in relations between the northern and southern shores of the Mediterranean. As a first-rate Mediterranean power, it is also the European country with the strongest historical and cultural ties with the countries of the Maghreb and the Levant. Its influence also benefits from the fact that it enjoys a less biased image towards Israel than the United States. While American policy in the Middle East is linked to its strategic alliance with Israel, France's is more balanced. But from the second term of François Mitterrand, we witnessed a rapprochement with the United States, which had become the only superpower since the collapse of the USSR. In 1991, France participated in the coalition gathered at the initiative of Washington against the invasion of Kuwait by the Iraqi army. This upheaval reduced to nothing the claim of French diplomacy to play a clean score. It was up to President Chirac, elected to the Élysée Palace in 1995, to revive the Gaullist foreign policy of which he proclaimed himself the heir. With the fall of the Iron Curtain and the implosion of the Soviet Union, the French idea of autonomy in relation to America resurfaced when the Soviet danger no longer existed. France made a strong comeback on the Lebanese scene, especially on the economic level, where it resolutely supported the ambitious reconstruction plan for Lebanon initiated by Prime Minister Rafic Hariri, a personal friend of Jacques Chirac. The second Palestinian intifada provoked a rupture between France and Israel that lasted four years from 2000 to 2004. The French government, which had established close relations with Saddam Hussein's regime before the first Gulf War, contested the continuation of the embargo that penalized the Iraqi people and declared itself hostile to Anglo-American bombing of Iraq. In 2003, he found himself confronted by the United States, which was openly preparing a new war against Baghdad. President Jacques Chirac was one of the only heads of state in the world to have the lucidity and courage to take the measure of the disastrous consequences of the war with which Washington is threatening Iraq. He adopted a Gaullist stance against the United States by refusing to use force against Baghdad before the end of the UN inspectors' mission. For France, it was necessary to avoid at all costs the "war of civilizations" that would pit the Muslim world against the Western world and that would fuel terrorism, and it announced that it was ready to use its veto right in the Security Council to do so. During the meeting of March 7, 2003, the Minister of Foreign Affairs, Dominique de Villepin, made a memorable speech: "France will not allow a resolution to pass that would authorize the automatic use of force [...] What is at stake goes beyond the sole case of Iraq. Let's look at things with lucidity: we are defining a method of crisis resolution. We are choosing the organization of the world in which we want our children to live. This is true in the Middle East: can we still wait while the violence multiplies? The roots of these crises are numerous; they are political, religious and economic. They plunge into the tumult of the centuries. Some may believe that these problems can be solved by force. This is not France's conviction. On the contrary, we believe that the use of force risks stirring up resentment and hatred, fuelling a clash of identities and a clash of cultures [....]. To those who believe that war is the shortest way to disarm Iraq, I say that it would create wounds that would take a long time to heal [...] We do not subscribe to what would be the other objectives of a war. Is it to change the regime in Baghdad? No one is unaware of the cruelty of this dictatorship and the need to do everything possible to promote human rights. This is not the objective of resolution 1441. And force is certainly not the best way to bring democracy. It would encourage dangerous instability here and elsewhere. Is it to fight terrorism? War would only increase it, and we could face a new wave of violence. Let's not play into the hands of those who want a clash of cultures, a clash of religions. Are we finally reshaping the political landscape in the Middle East? Then we run the risk of increasing tensions in a region already marked by great instability. Especially since in Iraq itself the multiplicity of communities and religions is a source of division. We all have the same demands: more security, more democracy. But there is another logic than that of force, another way, other solutions. We understand the deep feeling of insecurity in which the American population lives since the tragedy of September 11, 2001. But there is no indication today that there is a link between the Iraqi regime and Al Qaeda. And will the world be safer after a military intervention in Iraq? I want to tell you my country's conviction: no[4] .

While in 2003 France opposed the American invasion of Iraq, French diplomacy began to move closer to the United States. The opportunity was provided by the Iranian nuclear issue, the fight against the Islamic terrorism of al-Qaeda and the opposition to the rise to power of Hamas in Gaza. And in 2004, the issue of the Syrian occupation of Lebanon provided common ground between the two parties. Paris, along with Washington, was one of the two main architects of UN Security Council Resolution 1559, which demanded the withdrawal of the Syrian army from Lebanon. In foreign policy, Nicolas Sarkozy, putting an end to the policy of independence from Washington initiated by de Gaulle, has proceeded to realign French policy with the United States and in favor of Israel, unlike his predecessor who favored his Arab friendships. It also appears to be one of the countries most in the forefront against the Iranian regime on the nuclear issue. It is in this context that we must situate the decision of Paris to establish a joint arms base in the United Arab Emirates. Intended to contribute, alongside American forces, to the protection of oil transport through the Persian Gulf, it also has the more or less avowed objective of reassuring the Arab oil monarchies that are worried about Tehran's hegemonic ambitions. On the

Lebanese issue, the President of the Republic declared himself ready to defend "with strength the independence, sovereignty and integrity of Lebanon. However, while France had broken off all relations with Damascus following the assassination of Rafik Hariri, a personal friend of Jacques Chirac, he felt that the ostracism of the Syrian regime was counterproductive. Thus, he invited Syrian President Bashar el Assad to the July 14, 2007 celebrations on the occasion of his presence at the Union for the Mediterranean summit in Paris. On the Palestinian issue, since the creation of the so-called "quartet" (United States, European Union, Russia, UN), French diplomacy no longer has the means to play a role that belongs to it, especially since the EU itself is unable to play its own. The most consequential decision of Nicolas Sarkozy's presidency was however the French military intervention in Libya in 2011, promoted by the sulphurous Bernard Henri Levy, a notorious Zionist. Bypassing the UN mandate, and under the pretext of protecting the civilian population, it led to what was probably its real objective: the overthrow of the regime of Muammar Gaddafi. Its repercussions are still being felt today: tribal chaos and the disintegration of Libya. More serious, in terms of French and European interests: the appearance of a den of Islamist terrorists threatening Europe and Sub-Saharan Africa. Finally, an influx of refugees into Europe that the Libyan dictator had at least the advantage of containing. As if the lessons of the catastrophic repercussions of the policy of regime change in Iraq and Libya had not been learned, French policy towards Syria has made the same mistakes. More royalist than the American king, Roland Fabius declared at the beginning of the uprising against Bashar al Assad that he "simply did not deserve to live on earth[5] !" His blatant bias in favor of Israel has led him to outbid the Americans in terms of intransigence in the negotiations that led to the Iranian nuclear deal. This choice was undoubtedly also dictated by the French government's concern to please the rich petro-monarchies of the Gulf, while Wahhabi Saudi Arabia and Qatar generously finance Islamist movements. Had it not been for Barak Obama's decision to refrain from bombing forces loyal to the Syrian regime, François Hollande was ready to do so, which would have opened the gates of Damascus to radical Islamists and emptied Syria of the majority of its Christian inhabitants, as is already the case in Iraq. Since the election of Emmanuel Macron, French foreign policy has become more pragmatic. Recognizing that the regime of Bashar al-Assad is not ready to fall, it no longer makes the departure of the Syrian dictator a prerequisite for the opening of negotiations on the future of Syria. It also seemed that he was initially aware of the need not to ostracize too much Russia, which is a natural ally in the fight against Islamist terrorism and is an essential interlocutor on the Syrian issue. But it has changed its attitude, although several voices are being raised to denounce Washington's instrumentalization of the threat of the Russian bear to justify the maintenance of NATO, whose main raison d'être since the fall of the USSR is, according to them, to keep European countries under its thumb. On the Syrian issue, only a more realistic and less ideological policy will allow France, which has lost all credibility during the presidency of François Hollande, to regain any influence.

That said, we do not see how joining the American strike against Syria in retaliation for the alleged use of chemical weapons by Damascus can contribute to the achievement of this objective.

Regional powers

The main "strong" Sunni Arab countries (Egypt, Saudi Arabia and Iraq) are weakened by two other non-Arab regional powers: Iran and Israel. The big winner in the fragmentation of the Arab world is Israel, which is more powerful than ever and continues its policy of colonizing the occupied territories with impunity. But if no Arab country has long been in a position to threaten it, this is undoubtedly not the case for Iran, especially since the presence in Syria of its forces and those of the militias allied to it, notably Hezbollah. Tel Aviv never ceases to denounce Iranian expansionism, multiplying its bellicose declarations against it. It plays on the fear it inspires in the Gulf monarchies to present itself as their objective ally against the Islamic Republic. The latter, whose influence is already being exerted in Iraq, Syria, Lebanon and Yemen, is the main beneficiary of the errors of American policy. Until 2003, it remained relatively marginalized on the regional scene, with Syria as its only ally. The American invasion of Iraq, followed by the fall of the Baathist regime of Saddam Hussein, was a godsend for Iran. By destroying Iraq, the Americans have strengthened their hegemonic ambitions in the region. The victory of the Iraqi Shiites and that of the Syrian regime is also that of Iran, which benefits from the disunity of the Arab countries and from the impasse in which Saudi Arabia has strayed in Yemen and its policy of ostracism of Qatar. Thanks to its human potential, its independence and its cooperation with Beijing and Moscow, Tehran is reinforcing its status as a regional power and appears to be the last bulwark against a lasting U.S. stranglehold on the entire region. Today, Iran's clout is such that President Rohani has been able to declare that "the importance of the Iranian nation in the region is stronger than at any other time. The war won regionally by Iran with Russian support vividly manifests the triumph of the side that aimed to keep Syrian President Bashar al-Assad in power. The defeat of the Islamic State and the reversal of the situation of Saudi Arabia and the Gulf states, which were forced to let go of the jihadists they were helping under the table, have left the Sunni Arab regional powers without an alternative plan to contain Iran. And the only factor that could curb its expansionist aims is the serious economic crisis it faces.

The other regional heavyweights trying to fill the power vacuum left by the relative disengagement of the United States are Turkey and Saudi Arabia. Already weakened by the Kurdish problem, Turkey was shaken by the failed coup against the president and the massive purges that followed. And it is experiencing a real existential crisis. While it had set itself up as a model of a state combining moderate Islamism and democracy, the regime's authoritarian drift, the internal and external challenge represented by the Kurdish question, the failure of its gamble on the Egyptian and Tunisian Muslim Brotherhoods, and finally the Russian intervention in Syria, seemed to ruin the neo-Ottoman ambitions of Recep Tayyip Erdogan. However, his personal power has never been so strong and he is in the process of regaining control in Syria since his intervention in Afrin. The situation in Saudi Arabia is more worrying with the fall in oil prices and its stalemate in Yemen. Crown Prince Mohammed bin Salman is aware of this and the future of the kingdom will depend on the ambitious train of reforms he has embarked on. With the rout of the "caliphate" and the consolidation of the Iraqi and Syrian regimes, the Middle East has been experiencing a phase of recomposition of political alliances since the fall of 2017. Baghdad has reconciled with Saudi Arabia at a time when Iranian influence in Iraq has never been stronger, while Tehran and Riyadh have been waging a cold war in different theaters for several years. A few weeks earlier, King Salman of Saudi Arabia had visited Russia, for the first time in the kingdom's history, while Moscow is the main ally of its Iranian rival in Syria. In a sign of Russia's growing influence, Saudi Arabia and Turkey, a NATO member, have signed agreements to purchase Russian anti-aircraft missiles. Turkish President Recep Tayyip Erdogan visited Tehran to display a common front against the independence aspirations of Iraqi Kurds, while Ankara has made no secret of its fears about Iranian expansion on its borders. Qatar, which hosts the largest American base in the Middle East, is quarantined by Riyadh, Cairo and Abu Dhabi, the main American allies - with the exception of Israel - in the region. The situation is even more complex when it comes to relations between states and parastatal groups, such as militias. For example, Washington supports the Syrian Kurds against the Islamic State, while its NATO ally Ankara has made it its main enemy in the region. And Turkey, which was the main supporter of the jihadists, has turned against them. But the most important factor that could lead to a recomposition of political alliances in the Middle East is the real paranoia that has gripped Saudi Arabia in the face of Iranian expansionism. It is not impossible that Riyadh, encouraged by Washington, is getting closer to Israel, another bitter enemy of the Islamic Republic. Faced with the regional upheaval, the kingdom is no longer content to use the traditional *soft power* tools of diplomacy and financial aid and is adopting a more aggressive and interventionist foreign policy. This has been the case since the beginning of King Salman's reign in January 2015, and especially since the emergence of Crown Prince Mohammed bin Salman as its architect. .

Russia

It is especially Russia, which has taken the most advantage of the relative American disengagement in the region. Since the time of the Tsars, Moscow has always worked to strengthen its influence in the "warm seas", i.e. the Mediterranean. Pursuing the same objective, Vladimir Putin has succeeded in placing his country at the center of the Middle East game. NATO's intervention in Libya had important consequences on Moscow's strategy in the Middle East, besides signaling in its eyes the end of good faith in international relations. Russia had decided not to prevent Resolution 1973 of 17 March 2011 concerning Libya. The Russians thought that the West would not overstep the limits of their mandate. The policy of changing undesirable regimes by force, which resulted in the lynching of Muammar Gaddafi in October 2011, prompted Vladimir Putin to pursue a more assertive and activist foreign policy. Moscow has learned the lessons of this crisis, which has allowed it to formulate its strategy in the Syrian conflict. In this case, Russia has not hesitated to use its veto power in the Security Council on several occasions. The Kremlin's policy is based in part on a categorical rejection of the policy of regime change from outside and the imposition of democracy by force, which can only lead to chaos and the disintegration of the state, as developments in the region show. "The Russian intervention in Syria marks a break in Moscow's Arab policy, which until now has been based on a clean history of colonization and direct military involvement. Russia's objectives are obviously multiple. To maintain a traditional ally in place, to weaken the *pax americana*, to contain as much as possible a rise in power of Iran, to fight Sunni Islamism and to avoid that it spreads in the Caucasus as in Russia[6] . Moscow was a stakeholder in the negotiations on the agreement on the Iranian nuclear issue and the lifting of sanctions against Tehran. The Kremlin considers Tehran to be an objective partner in Syria for the time being, but at the same time is trying to spare its Israeli ally, which considers Iran to be a threat to its security. Since its military intervention in Syria, Russia has established itself as a key player in the Middle East and has reaffirmed its status as a major power. By securing a base in the eastern Mediterranean, it has succeeded in breaking the encirclement it is subject to from Washington and its NATO allies. Nothing better illustrates Washington's policy of encirclement of Russia than the crisis in Ukraine, partly fuelled by its intelligence services. It is also symptomatic that several European leaders are speaking out against the ostracism practiced against Russia, which is detrimental to Europe's interests; and that, since the Russian intervention in Syria, the question of the "annexation" of Crimea and Russian control of the Donbass has passed into the background of the Atlantic Alliance's concerns. The Russian intervention in Syria is also driven by economic considerations, as Syria is both a necessary passage for pipelines carrying oil from the Gulf to the Mediterranean and a potential offshore gas producer. As a sign of Russia's preponderant influence in Syria, after receiving Bashar el Assad, Vladimir Putin organized a summit between himself and the Turkish and Iranian presidents on November 22, 2017, in Sochi, aimed at finding a political solution to the Syrian conflict, in an attempt to compete with the UN-sponsored Geneva negotiations. Regardless of the success or failure of this initiative, it illustrates the failure of the motley coalition of the United States, European nations, Turkey, and the Gulf petro-monarchies. Another important dimension of this intervention is the defense of the Christian minority, which has earned Russia renewed popularity among Eastern Christians. Embracing the Orthodox faith is for the Kremlin a source of influence abroad. Orthodoxy is an essential part of Vladimir Putin's strategy and his vision of Russia's role in the world. In order to affirm this link, he made a highly symbolic visit to Mount Athos in 2005. By paying homage to one of the most sacred places in the Orthodox world, he posed as a defender of the Orthodox faith. A role that the Tsars had played in the past, and which they had taken advantage of during their wars against the Ottoman Empire and their interventions in favor of the Christians of the Balkans and the Levant. This does not prevent the Kremlin from maintaining excellent relations with Muslims in the Russian Federation, as evidenced by the inauguration in September 2015 of the Great Mosque of Moscow, the largest in Europe. And Vladimir Putin's policy has the support of Muslim religious leaders in Russia[7] . In contrast to the reversals of U.S. policy and its tendency to drop its allies when it no longer needs them, not to mention the disastrous consequences of its interventions, Russia appears to be a reliable ally concerned with the stability of the region in the eyes of its leaders. And the partiality of the United States, which contrasts with its friendly relations with everyone, could offer it an opportunity to play a mediating role in the Israeli-Palestinian conflict. Finally, its return to the Middle East has important economic repercussions. For example, it has concluded agreements for the construction of nuclear reactors with Jordan, Egypt and Saudi Arabia. While the main buyers of Russian arms are Syria, Iraq, Iran and Egypt, precisely the Kremlin's current areas of influence in the Middle East, it has signed major arms supply contracts with several countries, including U.S. allies such as Turkey and Saudi Arabia. However, its ambitions are limited by its economic weakness and demographic decline, which it seeks to compensate for with its main asset: military strength.

1 *L'Orient arabe à l'heure américaine*, Henry Laurens, Hachette littérature 2008, p.359

2 *L'Orient-le Jour* of May 9, 2017

3 https://www.lecourrierderussie.com > News

4 *L'Orient arabe à l'heure américaine*, op.cit. p. 223

5 *The new question of the East*, Georges Corm, La Découverte, 2017, p 57

6 *Middle East*, issue 30, *Russia in the Middle East*, *Putin's Poker Move*, p.21

7 https://www.lecourrierderussie.com > News

Conclusion. Where the Middle East is going

An endless battlefield?

Today, the Middle East is experiencing a chaotic situation that affects not only the countries that make up the region, but also external countries in the East and in the West. Attacks on the integrity and sovereignty of the states in the region are still ongoing and the Middle East remains the epicenter of Islamist terrorism. The toll of the wars that devastate it is particularly heavy. For nearly forty years now, this region has been a battlefield that has claimed several million victims, not to mention the destruction of a considerable real estate and historical heritage. This situation is likely to continue and the prospect of a return to a certain stability and a fortiori peace seems distant. The Arab world continues to live in a serious crisis with many facets. It has never been so torn apart and subject to interference from foreign powers. Since the Arab Spring "Arab regimes are struggling to find a second wind as the drop in oil prices by half between the summer of 2014 and the winter of 2015 threatens the internal balance of despotic systems, which had been able to rely on unparalleled hydrocarbon prices to cushion the shock of the 2011 revolutionary wave[1] . Egypt's economic and security problems prevent it from playing the role it should as an Arab and Muslim heavyweight. The army has failed to muzzle Islamist protest and end the violence. Four years of undivided rule by Marshal-President Sissi has led the country into misery and terror. The dictator's disastrous economic record is reflected, among other things, in an increase in foreign debt from $38 billion to $100 billion and in domestic debt from 130 billion to 350 billion Egyptian pounds[2] . The Palestinian cause has been overshadowed by the wars in Syria and Yemen and by Shiite-Sunni and Arab-Persian antagonism. The fate of the Palestinian people seems more desperate than ever, and the political resolution of the conflict increasingly unlikely. For Israel, this is a "low-intensity conflict" and not a serious threat, comparable to that posed by Iran. Yemen is the victim of a proxy war between Saudi Arabia and the United Arab Emirates and Iran. The coalition led by Riyadh is increasingly being singled out. It is waging a war with no prospect of victory, sinking deeper into the Yemeni quagmire every day. The attempt by Saudi Arabia and the United Arab Emirates to isolate Qatar is also a failure that has broken the cohesion of the member countries of the Gulf Cooperation Council. The Arab League, which should have been a body that brings member countries together, has for several years been nothing more than a space for division and the display of dissension. Libya, in the grip of anarchy, is divided between two governments that are fighting for power. A political solution in Syria, the scene of a real world war between regional and international powers, is not in sight. That said, the latest military developments on the ground and the reunification of Iraq mark the failure of the "plot" - assuming it really existed - to partition these two countries into ethnic and/or confessional entities. The war in Syria is heading towards a victory for the regime and its allies. The country has resisted its programmed dismemberment. But if this scenario has been ruled out, it will undoubtedly be divided into zones of influence: Russian, Iranian, Turkish and American. It is doubtful that Bashar al-Assad, who seems likely to remain in power, will agree to make concessions with a view to the establishment of a transitional regime. Winning the peace will be more difficult than winning the war. The country, which has an appalling number of victims and refugees, both inside and outside its borders, is completely devastated. Countries with the means to finance its reconstruction are unwilling to do so as long as the regime is in place, so its prospects for recovery look bleak. And the Syrian Kurds' dreams of independence are likely to go up in smoke, just like those of their Iraqi cousins. This is the situation as the Syrian conflict enters its eighth year and as two competing, and so far unsuccessful, attempts to find a political solution to the conflict take place. One sponsored by Moscow and its Iranian and Turkish partners. And the other taking place in Geneva under the aegis of the UN. By ricochet, the confessional balance of Lebanon risks being upset by the presence of nearly one and a half million Syrian refugees, the vast majority of them Sunni, on its soil. With parliamentary elections scheduled for May 2018, there is little chance that they will lead to the renewal of a corrupt political class, responsible for the decay of the Lebanese state.

The victory against Daech and the collapse of the Kurdish dream of independence have reunified Iraq. The head of the Iraqi government, who has no blood on his hands, enjoys greater legitimacy than the Syrian dictator. And Baghdad's victory is even clearer than Damascus', because it was largely won by its own forces and the country is not under foreign tutelage. The reunification of territory, however, does not mean the reunification of hearts. While Iraq has been reunited by the Shia-dominated government, there is a deep sense of alienation and frustration among the Sunni and Kurdish communities, which will cause many problems in the future. The recapture of the Islamic State's territory straddling Syria and Iraq has certainly removed the spectre of a challenge to the territorial integrity of both countries. But the quest for an inclusive political system, let alone national reconciliation, is in both cases another matter. And it does not mean the end of this criminal organization, which will go underground like al-Qaeda, nor the eradication of Islamist terrorism. The concentration of efforts on Daech should not make us forget that Al Qaeda remains a major threat, both to the states of the Middle East and to countries outside the area, in Europe and Asia. Only a long-term policy aimed at eliminating the causes that have led to the emergence of terrorism will eventually solve this problem.

In Saudi Arabia, by attacking what has until now constituted the heart of the kingdom's political tradition: the principle of compromise and the balance of power between the different clans within the royal family, and between the latter and the Wahhabi clergy, it is this entire system that has been brought down with Mohammed Ben Salman's coup de force. He even seems to want to start a real cultural revolution by ending the Wahhabi proselytism that has always been one of the main objectives of the kingdom while blaming the outside world: "We have propagated Wahhabism at the request of our American and European allies in order to curb the influence of the Soviet Union in the Muslim countries. This lasted during the Cold War and, since then, the various governments that have succeeded one another have continued along the same path. It is time to rectify this[3] " he indeed declared in an interview with the Wasington Post on March 25, 1918. "MBS embodies the well-known figure in the Arab world of the modernizing autocrat. If the societal reforms and the fight against obscurantism undertaken by the young crown prince are going in the right direction, his authoritarianism in domestic policy and his adventurism, which contrasts with the kingdom's traditionally cautious foreign policy, are not without risks. The kingdom wants to spearhead the sunni and Arab counter-offensive against shia Persia. But despite its financial resources, which have been declining with the fall in the price of oil, and American support, it is no match, either demographically or militarily, for the great regional power that Iran has been throughout history.

A reconfiguration of alliances and the regional balance of power

Favored by the divisions of the Arab countries and the repeated failures of Western interventions, a reconfiguration of alliances and a new balance of power in favor of Russia and Iran on the Middle East chessboard are taking place. The latest regional developments play in favour of Tehran, whose influence is already being exerted in Iraq, Syria, Lebanon and Yemen. The joining of Syrian and Iraqi forces on the border between these two countries, which the United States tried in vain to prevent, has opened up the corridor between the Islamic Republic and southern Lebanon, via Iraq and Syria, to the great displeasure of Israel, which sees its worst enemy strengthening on its doorstep. While Iran's influence has never been so strong, this is not the case for the other great historical Muslim power: Turkey. While it had set itself up as a model of a state combining moderate Islamism and democracy, the authoritarian drift of power, the internal and external challenge represented by the Kurdish question, the failure of its gamble on the Egyptian and Tunisian Muslim Brotherhoods, and finally the Russian intervention in Syria, have ruined the neo-Ottoman ambitions of Recep Tayyip Erdogan. And the country, already weakened by the Kurdish problem, was shaken by the failed coup against the president and the massive purges that followed. However, it remains a key player in the regional power game, particularly in Syria. And Erdogan is determined to counter the formation of a Kurdish entity in Syria, which entails a risk of confrontation with the United States.

The other big winner in the break-up of the Arab world is Israel. Having remained relatively aloof while its neighbors were tearing each other apart, Tel Aviv cannot afford to tolerate the presence of the Revolutionary Guards and Hezbollah in Syria and, in the event of war, to have to deal with a front stretching from southern Lebanon to the Golan Heights. Hence the increasingly insistent rumors of a preventive war waged by the Hebrew state to avert this threat. A war that would unfortunately be even more devastating for Lebanon than that of 2006. There is a similarity between Israel's and Saudi Arabia's reading of Iran's geostrategic role. This similarity can lead to a strategic convergence as evidenced by the words of Shimon Peres in 2010: to the question: "Is the Middle East facing new dangers? Asked by Laurent Zecchini, a journalist from Le Monde, the Israeli statesman replied, "Yes, because we are facing new ambitions. The Persians want to control the Middle East again. Whether it is for religious reasons is not important [...] and concerning the Arab countries, he adds: most Arabs are deeply concerned about it. They are afraid of Iranian aggression, and they don't know what to do. Israel is no longer the main problem for them, it is Iran, which uses the Arab-Israeli conflict as an excuse for its ambitions. They will never say this openly, of course. But today, secret contacts are more important than diplomatic ones[4] .

At the level of international powers, the relative disengagement of the United States during the Obama presidency, as well as the contradictions of American policy, have created a power vacuum into which Russia has rushed. Not to mention the fact that they have thrown Turkey, a NATO member, into Moscow's arms. Although they were made for different reasons, Turkey's rapprochement with Russia and Iran and the unofficial one between Saudi Arabia and Israel, objective allies against Iran, inaugurate a reconfiguration of alliances in the Middle East. These are essentially structured around the problem of the constitution of the famous Shiite triangle whose centrality has replaced that of the Arab-Israeli conflict. The decision taken by Donald Trump on December 5, 2017 to recognize Jerusalem as the capital of the State of Israel and to transfer the American embassy there was certainly criticized by most countries, but ultimately rather softly (including in the Arab world). Even if a majority of the 193 countries making up the United Nations General Assembly voted for a resolution condemning its decision, it is a relative defeat for Washington's opponents. The Saudi and Egyptian reactions to its declaration are almost as timid as those of the European chancelleries. The consequences of this declaration should not be exaggerated. It certainly discredits Washington as the main mediator in the Israeli-Palestinian peace process. And it embarrasses American allies on the regional scene. The issue of Jerusalem is perhaps the only one that can currently unite not only Arab countries, but more generally Muslims around the world, including the Saudis and the Iranians. If Donald Trump had wanted to unleash the wrath of the Arab world and further damage the image of the United States in the region, he certainly would not have done it any differently. But the anger of the Arabs is above all an admission of powerlessness. They simply do not have the means to respond to the American initiative. Burning flags will not change the situation. Calling for armed struggle, launching rockets against Israel, as Hamas is doing, will only strengthen the conviction of the Americans and the Israelis. And given the balance of power between the parties, this will only serve to undermine the Palestinian cause. The Arabs are trapped by their weakness and divisions. Their voice is no longer taken into account because they no longer play a significant role on the international scene. Syria and Iraq are devastated by war. Jordan, Egypt and Saudi Arabia are intimately linked to the Americans and too dependent on them to seriously challenge their decision. But the main effect of the White House's decision is to weaken the position of these same allies, the very ones who had chosen the path of moderation, in favour of the most virulent rhetoric. The Iranians and their allies did not ask for much to make people forget their warlike ventures in the Arab world and to present themselves once again as the best defenders of the Palestinian cause. The most radical Sunni groups will try to benefit from the American decision. It is the whole process of normalization of relations between the Arab countries and the Jewish state that Donald Trump has undermined with his decision. Firstly, because it buries the two-state solution a little more. Secondly, because it puts the Arab countries that have made or are ready to make peace with Israel in an untenable position, while their public opinion remains sensitive to the Palestinian cause. Like Hassan Nasrallah, their detractors are now at liberty to mock their strategic failure to bet everything on the diplomatic path and to trust the Americans. The path of moderation has only reinforced a status quo situation in negotiations, which is accompanied by a continuous deterioration of the Palestinian position. But the main effect of the Arab wars against the Jewish state has been to allow Israel to expand its territory at the expense of the Palestinians. In the same vein, despite their rhetoric of being the only legitimate resistance, Hamas, Hezbollah and Islamic Jihad - all movements that still advocate armed struggle - have not advanced the Palestinian cause one inch in recent decades. If they really want to make a difference, if they want to live up to the Palestinian cause, the Arabs have no choice but to finally speak with one voice, one that can be both firm and moderate. One that can collectively trade peace with Israel for the creation of a Palestinian state, even if it is doubtful that this is still possible. Otherwise, the Palestinian cause will have to be content with remaining a mere outlet for Arab misery.

The American president's decision is in fact the translation of new power relations. These are not only related to the technological, economic and even demographic rise of Israel, but also to the balkanization and catastrophic collapse of the Arab world. Even those Arab states that escape chaos and civil war are being undermined: by falling oil prices (Gulf petro-monarchies), by terrorism (Egyptian Sinai, Iraq), by national geopolitical rivalries (Qatar/Saudi Arabia, United Arab Emirates, Bahrain), or by all three at once. And that's without counting corruption and serious social dissatisfaction that generate instability. As for the war in Syria, it has already caused three times as many deaths and ten times as many refugees in six years as the Israeli-Arab wars have in seventy years, all violence included. In this generalized chaos, the Israeli-Palestinian conflict has been relegated by the great powers and the Arab states to the rank of a simple dispute. At the moment, the main issue in the Near and Middle East is undoubtedly the cold war between the Sunni axis (behind

Riyadh) and the Shiite axis (behind Tehran). The rest is geopolitically secondary.

A negative economic and social balance sheet

The repeated defeats of the Arab states at the hands of Israel and the Arab Spring uprisings are the product of the extent of their maldevelopment. This is reflected in low economic growth, gross inequality, the highest youth unemployment rates in the world, leading to increased poverty and exclusion, and the maintenance of large pockets of illiteracy. While the standard of living in the Arab countries was higher at the threshold of the 1950s than that of the countries of Southeast Asia and China, it is the opposite today. For Georges Corm, the main factor in the technological and scientific backwardness of the Arab states has been the ravages of the oil rent economy that has affected them all[5] . It produced an easy enrichment of the producing countries. From 1974 onwards, the fourfold increase in the price of oil was not accompanied by efforts to create a real local industrial fabric. The enormous revenues generated by the oil windfall discouraged productive investment. As for the fallout from this windfall in other countries, it is mainly made up of remittances from their nationals who work in the Gulf countries, which also has the effect of encouraging, albeit on a smaller scale, a cash economy. One of the most significant indicators of the poor economic performance of the Arab world is its trade balance, which shows a huge deficit, despite oil and gas exports. By comparison, the trade balance of South East Asian countries is not only in surplus but is mainly due to their exports of manufactured goods. The comparison with Israel's scientific and technological development is even more unfavorable. As for the number of industrial patents or intellectual property obtained in the Arab world, it is negligible. All these negative data explain why so many Arabs are seeking to emigrate; whether they are skilled managers or unskilled workers. And the trend is not likely to be reversed as oil prices fall and long-term reserves dry up.

The failure of a world

Return of the military to power in Egypt. Bloodbath in Syria. Sectarian civil wars between Sunnis and Shiites in Iraq and Alawites in Syria. Destruction of Yemen, disintegration of the Gulf Cooperation Council. Genocidal and iconoclastic fanaticism of the former "Islamic State". The terrorist threat that jihadists pose to the region and the world. Ethnic cleansing of the Christian and Yazidi communities in Iraq. These dramatic events are the symptom of two deeper crises that feed each other: the crisis of Islam, and the failure of an Arab world undermined by its divisions, the absence of rule of law and freedoms, and the disastrous economic and social record of authoritarian and corrupt regimes. Unfortunately for them, instead of recognizing this, Arabs are all too prone to conspiracy theories, attributing their misfortunes to the aftermath of Western imperialism and a mythical "American-Zionist conspiracy. That said, there is some truth in this thesis. It is undeniable that Western bias towards Israel has fostered Arab resentment and the rise of radical Islam. And Western interventions in Iraq and Libya have not only destabilized these two countries, but the entire region and beyond. From Libya to Yemen, through Syria and Iraq, the balkanization of the Arab world is a reality, even if the borders of the states in the region have not been modified. The exacerbation of the Sunni-Shiite conflict and the rise of radical Islamism, with its attendant cultural and societal regression, intellectual poverty and democratic deficit, mean that it is not just this or that country that meets the definition of failed states but the Arab-Muslim world in general. There are certainly exceptions to this bleak picture. This is particularly true of the United Arab Emirates, which combines remarkable stability with insolent prosperity, symbolized by the futuristic skyscrapers of Abu-Dhabi and Dubai. But what does their indigenous population weigh against the 90 million Egyptians and the misery endured by the Syrians and Iraqis? In *Consideration on Arab unhappiness* Samir Kassir wrote already in 2004: "It is not good to be an Arab these days. With the exception of sub-Saharan Africa, the Arab world is the region of the planet where today's man has the least chance to flourish. All the more so for women. More than in numbers, Arab unhappiness lies in perceptions and the feeling that the future is blocked. It is also due to the way others look at it and to comparisons with Asia (economic growth) and Latin America (democratic transition). The political powerlessness of Arabs is also at issue. While in the political field the Arabs, particularly Egypt and Algeria, were actors in international relations, this sequence has now closed. The Arab states are all unfit to be subjects of their own history, and the Arab world is the only region in the world where the absence of democracy is combined with such a marked foreign hegemony[6] . This bleak picture seems to support the thesis that Islam is an obstacle to freedom, science and economic development. But if this is the case, how is it that it once shone in these three areas? How is it that a country like Turkey, although devoid of oil, enjoys such economic development? And that Iran has reached an appreciable scientific and technological level. This leads us to question both Arabism and Islam. The question is not only: "What has Islam done to the Arabs, but what have the Arabs done to Islam? Although the violence in the Arab world has spilled over into other regions, notably Europe, this question is primarily a matter for Arabs and Muslims themselves. Fortunately, there are enlightened people among them who are asking this question, especially after the horrors perpetrated by Daech in the name of Islam. And all Arab states, including those that have encouraged radical Islamism, are determined to fight it.

1 Les Arabes, leur destin et le nôte, Jean-Pierre Filiy, La Découverte, 2015, p.247

2,https://lecourrierdumaghrebetdelorient.info/headline/egypte-moise-et-pharaon-la- comedie-noire-des-elections-presidentielles/

3 https://www.valeursactuelles.com/monde/selon-mohamed-ben-salmane-cest-loccident-who-claims-exportation-of-wahhabism-94398

4 *The New Question of the East*, Georges Corm, La Découverte, 2017, p. 231

5 *Le Monde* of March 9, 2010

6 *Considerations on Arab unhappiness.* Samir Kassir, Actes Sud, 2004

Chronology

February 1896, publication of *The State of the Jews*, by Theodore Herzl.

1911, Italian occupation of Libya.

June 1913, Arab congress in Paris, which pronounces itself in favor of the autonomy of the Arab provinces of the Ottoman Empire.

October 1914, Great Britain imposes its protectorate on Egypt.

July 1915-January 1915, Hussein-McMahon correspondence.

January 1916, Sykes-Picot agreements between France and Great Britain.

November 1917, Balfour Declaration concerning the establishment of a national home for the Jewish people in Palestine.

October 1918, the Allies enter Damascus.

August 1920, Treaty of Sevres.

April 20, 1920, San Remo Conference ratifying the British mandate over Palestine, Iraq and Transjordan and the French mandate over Syria.

September 1920, creation of Greater Lebanon and division of Syria by General Gouraud, French High Commissioner to the Levant.

July 1921, Faysal 1er proclaimed king of Iraq.

1921-1922, Turkish war of independence

October 29, 1923, the Turkish Republic is proclaimed by Mustapha Kemal.

March 1924, the Turkish Parliament abolished the caliphate.

July 1925, outbreak of the Druze revolt against the French in Syria.

1925, Abdul Aziz Ibn Saud founded Saudi Arabia.

December 12, 1925, Reza Pahlavi new shah of Iran

1930, Anglo-Iraqi treaty: Iraq is recognized as "independent".

1936, Arab rebellion against the British occupation in Palestine.

August 1936, Anglo-Egyptian treaty recognizing the sovereignty of Egypt.

1938, death of Mustapha Kemal Atatürk, Ismet Inonü succeeds him.

June 1941, the British and the Free French Forces (FFL) dislodged the Vichy army in Lebanon and Syria.

September 1941, Mohammad Reza Pahlavi succeeds his father in Iran

November 22, 1943, proclamation of the independence of Lebanon.

March 1945, creation of the Arab League.

May 29-30, 1945, bombing of Damascus by the French army

November 29, 1947, vote on the partition of Palestine at the UN.

May 14, 1948, the State of Israel is proclaimed by David Ben-Gurion

May 15, 1948, outbreak of the first Arab-Israeli war (1948-1949)

March 1949, Husni Zaïm's coup d'état in Syria, followed by two other military putsches during the year.

July 23, 1952, the Free Officers overthrew the monarchy in Egypt.

August 1953, overthrow of the Iranian Prime Minister Mossadegh at the instigation of the CIA

November 1954, Gamal Abdel Nasser takes power in Egypt.

1955, Baghdad Pact (regional defense treaty initiated by Great Britain)

October-December 1956, Suez crisis: Israeli-French-British attack against Egypt.

1957, Eisenhower doctrine directed against the USSR in the Middle East

1958, proclamation of the United Arab Republic (UAR), dissolved in 1961.

1958, insurrection against president Chamoun and American intervention in Lebanon

July 14, 1958, overthrow of the monarchy in Iraq.

1969, Cairo agreements between the Lebanese state and the Palestinian resistance.

27 May 1960, military coup in Turkey, execution of Prime Minister Adnan Menderes.

1961, Great Britain grants independence to Kuwait.

September 27, 1962, overthrow of the monarchy and proclamation of the Republic in North Yemen.

February 8, 1963, bloody Baathist coup in Iraq

March 8, 1963, a coup d'état brought the Baath to power in Syria.

May 1964, creation of the PLO.

November 1964, Faysal becomes king of Saudi Arabia.

June 5-10, 1967, Arab-Israeli Six Day War.

September 1969, Muammar Gaddafi overthrows the monarchy in Libya

September 29, 1969, creation of the Organization of the Islamic Conference.

September 1970, clashes between PLO and Jordanian forces.

28 September 1970, death of Nasser, Anwar Sadat succeeds him

November 13, 1970, Hafez el-Assad seized power in Syria.

11 March 1971, overthrow of the Demirel government by the Turkish army.

December 1971, formation of the United Arab Emirates.

October 6, 1973, outbreak of the Yom Kippur War.

April 13, 1975, beginning of the Lebanese war

April 1976, the Syrian army enters Lebanon

November 19, 1977, Sadat's visit to Jerusalem.

March 1978, operation Litani of the Israeli army in South Lebanon to push back the Palestinians.

September 17, 1978, signing of the Israeli-Egyptian agreements of Camp David.

January 1979, outbreak of the Iranian revolution, the Shah forced into exile

1er February 1979, Ayatollah Khomeini arrives in Tehran

July 16, 1979, Saddam Hussein, takes over as head of the Iraqi state

September 1980, the army seizes power in Turkey

September 1980, beginning of the Iran-Iraq war (1980-1988).

November 4, 1979, American diplomats taken hostage in Iran

1981, Saudi Arabia, UAE, Bahrain, Qatar and Oman form the Gulf Cooperation Council

October 6, 1981, assassination of Sadat, Hosni Mubarak succeeded him.

1982, crushing of a Muslim Brotherhood uprising in Hamah

June 1982, Israeli invasion of Lebanon (operation "Peace in Galilee")

1984, beginning of the PKK guerrilla war in Turkey

1987, outbreak of the first intifada

July 1988, end of the Iran-Iraq war

June 3, 1989, death of Ayatollah Khomeini, Ali Khamenei succeeded him as Supreme Guide of the Islamic Republic.

October 22, 1989, Taef agreement establishing the second Lebanese Republic

October 13, 1990, Syrian invasion of the Christian area ending the war in Lebanon.

August 1, 1990, Iraqi forces invade Kuwait

1990, merger of North and South Yemen.

January 15, 1991, launch of Operation Desert Storm to drive Iraqi troops out of Kuwait.

September 13, 1993, signing of the Oslo agreements

July 25, 1994 signing of an Israeli-Jordanian peace treaty.

November 4, 1995, assassination of Yitzhak Rabin.

15-30 April 1996, Israeli operation "Grapes of Wrath" against Lebanon.

28 February 1997, the Turkish army forces the Erbakan government to resign.

May 2000, Israeli withdrawal from South Lebanon.

June 10, 2000, death of Hafez el-Assad, his son Bashar succeeded him.

September 2000, outbreak of the second intifada.

September 11, 2001, Al Qaeda terrorist attacks against the United States December 2001, American military intervention in Afghanistan.

November 2002, the AKP led by Recep Tayyip *Erdogan* wins the elections in Turkey.

March 20, 2003, American invasion of Iraq.

October 2004, death of Yasser Arafat, Mahmoud Abbas succeeds him as head of the Palestinian Authority

February 14, 2005, assassination of the Lebanese Prime Minister, Rafic Hariri.

March 2005, end of the Syrian occupation of Lebanon.

September 2005, Israeli withdrawal from the Gaza Strip

February 2006, beginning of the civil war between Shiites and Sunnis in Iraq July 2006, Israeli offensive against Hezbollah in Lebanon

June 2007, Hamas ousts the Palestinian Authority from the Gaza Strip.

January 2009, Israeli operation "Cast Lead" in the Gaza Strip.

January 2011, beginning of the "Arab Spring" uprising in Tunisia

February 11, 2011, forced resignation of Egyptian President Hosni Mubarak following massive demonstrations in Cairo.

February 2011, repression of the Shiite spring in Bahrain

February 2011, Western military intervention in Libya, followed by the assassination of Muammar Gaddafi in September.

March 2011, start of a civil war in Yemen15 March 2011

March 15, 2011, beginning of the uprising against the Syrian regime

November 2012, new operation of the Israeli army against Gaza

July 3, 2013, the Egyptian army overthrows President Morsi.

2013, Hassan Rohani elected president of the Iranian Islamic Republic May 2014, General Abdel Fattah al-Sissi becomes president of Egypt

June 10, 2014, capture of Mosul by Daech, followed by the proclamation of the "caliphate" by Abu Bakr Al-Baghdadi

June 2014, control of the entire Euphrates Valley in Syria by Daech.

July 14, 2015, Iran nuclear deal.

March 2015, Saudi military intervention in Yemen

March-April 2015, capture of the Syrian province of Idlib by the Al-Nosra Front

September 2015, the beginning of the Russian military intervention in Syria.

July 15, 2016, failed coup against President Erdogan

July 16, 2017, recapture of Mosul by the Iraqi army.

October 31, 2016, Michel Aoun president of the Lebanese Republic.

December 2016, Syrian regime seizure of the opposition-held part of Alcppo

June 2017, Mohamed Ben Salman becomes crown prince of Saudi Arabia.

September 2017, blockade of Qatar at the initiative of Riyadh and the UAE.

October 2017, U.S.-backed SDF recapture of Raqqa from the Islamic State.

December 6, 2017, President Trump decides to recognize Jerusalem as the capital of the State of Israel

March 2018, Turkish invasion of the Kurdish canton of Afrin in Syria

April 2018, capture of Eastern Ghouta by the Syrian regime

Bibliography

Alexandre Adler, *Rendez-vous avec l'islam*, Grasset 2005

Roger Azam. *Lebanon, the investigation of a crime.* Cheminements, 2005

Antoine Basbous, *Saudi Arabia at war*, Perrin 2004

Jacques Benoist-Méchin. *Mustapha Kemal or the death of an Empire*. Albin Michel, 1956

Jacques Benoist-Méchin. *Lawrence of Arabia*. Perrin, 2004

Paul Blanc, *Le Liban entre la guerre et l'oubli*, l'Harmattan, 1992

Jean Paul Bled (*dir*), *Le général de Gaulle et le monde arabe* (Proceedings of the colloquium organized by the Paris-Sorbonne University of Abu-Dhabi in Nov. 2008) Edition. Dar el Nahar, 2009

Yves Bonnet, *Iranian nuclear power, an international hypocrisy*, Michel Lafont, 2008

Hamit Bozarslan, *Histoire de la Turquie contemporaine*, La Découverte 2004

Anne-Lucie Chaigne-Oudin. *France in the games of influence in Syria and Lebanon (1940-46).* L'Harmattan, 2009

Walid Charara, Frédéric Domont. *Le Hezbollah*, Fayard 2004

Vincent Cloarec. *France and the question of Syria.* CNRS editions, 2010

Georges Corm. *Le Proche Orient éclaté*. La Découverte, 1983.

Georges Corm. *Geopolitics of the Lebanese conflict.* La Découverte, 1986.

Georges Corm. *L'Europe et l'Orient, de la balkanisation à la libanisation, histoire d'une modernité inaccomplie*. La Découverte, 1989.

Georges Corm, *Pour une lecture profane des conflits*, La Découverte, 2009

Georges Corm, *The New Question of the East*, La Découverte, 2017

Boutros Dib (under the direction of) *Histoire du Liban des origines au XXe siècle.* Philippe Rey editions, 2006

Caroline Donati. *The Syrian exception, between modernization and resistance.* La Découverte, 2009

Pierre Dufour. *France in the Levant.* Pygmalion edition, 2001

Paul Dumont, *Mustapha Kemal invents modern Turkey*, Édition Complexe, 2006

Frédéric Encel, François Tual. *Geopolitics of Israel.* Éditions du Seuil, 2006

Jean-Pierre Filiu, *Les Arabes, leur destin et le nôtre,* La Découverte, 2015

Robert Fisk: *The Great War for Civilization. The West's Conquest of the Middle*

East (1979-2005). La Découverte, 2005.

Daniel le Gac. *The Syria of General Assad.* Éditions Complexe, 1991

Samuel P. Huntington. *The Clash of Civilizations*. Éditions Odile Jacob, 1997

Gérard D. Khoury. *La France et l'Orient arabe, naissance du Liban moderne,* Armand Colin edition, 1993.

Gérard D. Khoury. *A colonial tutelage. The French mandate in Syria and Lebanon, political writings of Robert de Caix*. Belin 2006

Samir Kassir. *La guerre du Liban,* Karthala, Cermoc, Paris 1994

Samir Kassir. *Considerations on Arab unhappiness.* Actes Sud, 2004

Kazem Khalifé. *Lebanon, phoenix to the test of the international geopolitical chessboard.*

Gilles Kepel, *Le Prophète et le Pharaon, les mouvements islamistes dans l'Égypte contemporaine*, La Découverte, 1984

Gilles Kepel, *La revanche de Dieu, chrétiens juifs et musulmans à la conquête du monde*, Seuil 1991

Gilles Kepel, *Fitna, guerre au cœur de l'islam*, Gallimard 2004

Jean Lacouture, *Nasser,* éditions du Seuil, 1971

Jean Lacouture, Gérard D. Khoury, Ghassan Tuéni. *A century for nothing, the Middle East from the Ottoman Empire to the American Empire.* Albin Michel, 2002

Annie Laurent and Antoine Basbous. *A prey for two beasts. Lebanon between the Lion of Judah and the Lion of Syria*. Beirut Ad. Daira editions, 1987

Henry Laurens. *The great game. Arab East and international rivalries*. Armand Colin, 1991

Henry Laurens. *Orientales,* vol. I, II & III. CNRS editions 2004.

Henri Laurens. *The Arab East, Arabism and Islamism*. Armand Collin, 2004

Henry Laurens. *L'Orient arabe à l'heure américaine, De la guerre du Golfe à la guerre d'Irak.* Hachette literature 2008

Henry Laurens, *The Palestine Question - Volume 4, The Olive Branch and the Fighter's Gun,* Fayard 2011.

Bernard Lewis. *Que c'est-il passé, L'Islam, l'Occident et la modernité.* Gallimard 2002.

Ziad Maged, *Syria, the orphan revolution*, Actes Sud. 2014

Georges Malbrunot, *Des pierres aux fusils*, *Les secrets de l'Intifada*, Flammarion, 2002

Sabrina Mervin, *The Shiite Worlds and Iran*, Karthala, Ifpo 2007

Benny Morri s, *Victimes, histoire revisitée du conflit arabo-sioniste*, Éd. Complexes, 2003

Nicolas Nasr. *Syrian bankruptcy in Lebanon, (1975-1981)*. Dar el Amal. Beirut, 1982

Marie-Thérèse Oliver-Saidi. *Le Liban et la Syrie au miroir français,* L'Harmattan 2010

Pierre Razoux, *The Iran-Iraq war, first Gulf war*, Perrin 2013

Pierre Razoux, *Tsahal, history of the Israeli army*. Perrin 2008

Nadine Picaudou: *La Décennie qui ébranla le Moyen - Orient, 1914-1923,* Brussels, Éd. Complexe 1992

Nadine Picaudou. *La déchirure libanaise*, Éd. Complexes 1989

Jonathan Randal, *Osama*. Albin Michel, 2004

Charles Rizk. *Les Arabes ou l'histoire à contresens.* Albin Michel, 1992

Pierre Rondot. *Les Chrétiens d'Orient,* Peyronnet editions, 1955

Jean Paul Roux, *History of Iran and Iranians*, Fayard 2006

Olivier Roy, *L'islam mondialisé*, Seuil 2002

Olivier Roy, *The Crescent and Chaos*, Hachette, 2011

Edouard Saab. *Syria or the revolution in the resentment.* Julliard, 1968

Simon Sabag Montefiore, *Jerusalem*, Calmann- Levy, 2011

Shlomo Sand, *How the Jewish people were invented*, Fayard 2008

Michel Seurat. *L'État de barbarie*. Édition du Seuil, 1989

Antoine Sfeir, *L'islam contre l'islam, l'interminable guerre des chiites et des sunnites*, Le Livre de Poche, 2013

Gilbert Sinoué, *The Egyptian Eagle*, *Nasser*, Taillandier. 2015

Ibrahim Tabet. *History of Turkey from Altai to Europe.* Éditions de l'Archipel, 2007

Ibrahim Tabet. *France in Lebanon and the Near East*, Éditions de la Revue phénicienne, 2011

Ibrahim Tabet, *Le monothéisme, le pouvoir et la guerre*, l'Harmattan, 2015

Ghassan Tueni. *A war for others.* J.C. Lattès, 1985

Thierry Zarcone, *Modern Turkey and Islam*, Flammarion 2004

Printed by Books on Demand GmbH, Norderstedt / Germany